The Midwestern
Ascendancy in
American Writing

Midwestern History and Culture

GENERAL EDITORS
James H. Madison and Thomas J. Schlereth

RONALD WEBER

The Midwestern Ascendancy in American Writing

INDIANA UNIVERSITY PRESS
Bloomington and Indianapolis

Library of Congress Cataloging-in-Publication Data

Weber, Ronald, date
    The midwestern ascendancy in American writing / Ronald Weber.
        p.   cm. — (Midwestern history and culture)
    Includes bibliographical references and index.
    ISBN 0-253-36366-7
    1. American literature—Middle West—History and criticism.
    2. Middle West—Intellectual life. 3. Middle West in literature.
    I. Title. II. Series.
    PS273.W4   1992
    810.9'977—dc20   91-46602

1 2 3 4 5   96 95 94 93 92

In memory of
Harley George Weber and Anne McCauley Weber

It had not kept its promise, so it was still the promised land.
—Glenway Wescott

CONTENTS

ACKNOWLEDGMENTS   ix

ONE. Warm Center, Ragged Edge   1
TWO. Rude Despair   25
THREE. The Voice of Want   49
FOUR. Beacon across the Prairies   69
FIVE. The Sweetness of Twisted Apples   91
SIX. Home Pasture   118
SEVEN. Bewildered Empire   146
EIGHT. The Savor of the Soil   174
NINE. We Are All Middle Westerners   196
Postscript   222

NOTES   227
INDEX   246

Acknowledgments

This book had its beginning, I realize now, in an undergraduate course in American literature at Notre Dame taught by John T. Frederick. At the time I knew nothing of Frederick's earlier teaching careers at the University of Iowa and Northwestern nor of his role as founder and editor of the *Midland* nor that he himself was a writer of fiction. What I did know was that his dark suits, wire-rimmed glasses, and courtly manner brought to mind another age—and that from him I was hearing for the first time about the literature of my own region of the country. I learned that Hamlin Garland had once lived a few miles from my Iowa home and had actually used the state's farms and small towns as material for stories. Willa Cather and O. E. Rölvaag and Sinclair Lewis came from neighboring states but had also turned the Midwest into fiction. Heretofore American literature had mostly meant to me the literature of New England—Dickinson's chariot, Thoreau's pond, Frost's road not taken. As for popular writing, my taste ran to the Western sagas of Zane Grey. That the ordinary landscape of my day-to-day world could yield something that might be called Midwestern literature, and that this work could be as engrossing as *Giants in the Earth* or as strangely moving as *Winesburg, Ohio*, came as pure revelation.

Years later my debt to Frederick took another direction. I came across a small volume called *The Midwest: Myth or Reality?* that had grown out of a symposium at Notre Dame in 1960. The essays addressed the question in the title from various contemporary angles—Russel B. Nye, for example, on Midwestern politics, John T. Flanagan on Midwestern literature. In a brief summing up at the end of the book, Frederick said the essays indicated that the word "myth" could be removed from the title. The Midwest was indeed a reality, one that was viable and meaningful. But he added a significant qualification: The Midwest might be real but its reality remained largely unknown. The region was still waiting for its interpreters—its social scientists and historians, its writers and painters and poets.

It continues to wait and probably always will. Regionalism in all its many manifestations remains one of the most elusive threads in the complex texture of America. But Frederick's remark caused me to begin an on-again, off-again process of thinking about one particular aspect of the Midwest, its literary history, and especially its history during its great period of national importance. In this book I have drawn together some of these thoughts. Underpinning everything I say is the work of many scholars, all of whom I have tried to properly acknowledge in the notes. An important general resource for anyone interested in Midwestern writing is the Society for the Study of Midwestern Literature, and I have drawn on its publications in numerous ways. I am especially beholden to those who took the time to read and comment on the work in manuscript or to listen and guide: Elizabeth Christman, James Dougherty, William Krier, Thomas Stritch, Thomas Werge. To Thomas J. Schlereth I have an earlier debt: He first suggested a book of this sort and gently urged it on me. Pat Weber helped once again with the many details of publication. Lastly, I note with thanks a research grant for work on the book from the Institute for Scholarship in the Liberal Arts of the College of Arts and Letters at Notre Dame.

The Midwestern
Ascendancy in
American Writing

ONE

Warm Center,
Ragged Edge

I see now that this has been a story of the
West, after all . . .

—*The Great Gatsby*

1

In her direct, common-sense manner Flannery O'Connor declared that "the best American fiction has always been regional," thereby cutting through reams of debate about the place and value of regionalism as a way of thinking not only about fiction but about American writing in general. The remark was offered in defense of writing grounded in her native South, so she added a capsule history of regionalism that emphasized the current stature of Southern literature, circa 1960:

> The ascendancy passed roughly from New England to the Midwest to the South; it has passed to and stayed longest wherever there has been a shared past, a sense of alikeness, and the possibility of reading a small history in a universal light.[1]

Every region of the country has known its share of bad regional writing—writing that trades on the quaint and the provincial, narrowing the imagination to the merely local. *Mere* regionalism—a kind of writing in which "regional" means "minor." But in the admirable sense O'Connor had in mind, regionalism has meant that the writer's roots are identifiably *somewhere*; the materials of the writer's art arise from a deep sense of a specific history, a specific locality. The implications of the work, however, remain unconfined; they flow out in the direction of the universal light O'Connor mentioned. Her fellow Southerner, Allen Tate, agreed. No literature, he said, "can be mature without the regional consciousness," and he clarified the point at which regional writing leaves off, joining the larger community of serious endeavor. By the genuine regionalist, Southern variety, Tate meant

> the writer who takes the South as he knows it today or can find out about it in the past, and who sees it as a region with some special characteristics, but otherwise offering as an imaginative subject the plight of human beings as it has been and will doubtless continue to be, here and in other parts of the world.[2]

John T. Frederick, a notable advocate of regional writing in the Midwest, made the same point in the same sensible manner:

> A good regional writer is a good writer who uses regional materials. His regionalism is an incident and a condition, not a purpose or motive. It means simply that he uses the literary substance which he knows best, the life of his own neighborhood, of his own city or state—the material about which he is most likely to be able to write with meaning. His work has literary importance only in so far as it meets the standards of good writing at all times and in all places.[3]

The present book looks back at the major achievements of Midwestern literature during the period of its ascendancy, to use O'Connor's term, that began well after the Civil War and came to a close with the early work of Hart Crane, F. Scott Fitzgerald, Ernest Hemingway, and the young writers of the 1920s. As such, it tries to recreate a chapter in American literary history, one fixed between the fading of the New England tradition and the emergence of the Southern literary renaissance between the two world wars—the Midwestern moment in American writing. During the period imaginative writing by Midwesterners and about the Midwest dominated, or very nearly so, American letters—the work of Edward Eggleston, Hamlin Garland, James Whitcomb Riley, Booth Tarkington, Theodore Dreiser, Henry B. Fuller, Floyd Dell, Edgar Lee Masters, Vachel Lindsay, Carl Sandburg, Zona Gale, Sherwood Anderson, Ring Lardner, Willa Cather, Sinclair Lewis, Ruth Suckow, O. E. Rölvaag, Carl Van Vechten, Glenway Wescott. Writers suddenly found interest—in the words of Saul Bellow, a latter-day successor of the Chicago phase of Midwestern writing—"in the seemingly blank heart of the interminable Midwest." They discovered that the

> ordinary lives of Midwesterners were only waiting for the transforming touch of art, that what we knew best was filled with the highest meaning, that here too the raw materials of literature were present, that this common life, our life, our very common selves, astonishingly enough, contained important meanings, that we belonged to that same human species which had supplied Sophocles with his Oedipus, Shakespeare with his Lear. Our surroundings had seemed so common, plain, barbarous, barren that it was difficult to believe this.[4]

For a time the most penetrating interpretations of American life emerged from the country's rural center and its magnetic city, the ungainly gathering of industrial villages called Chicago that—Bellow again—seemed to have "tumbled out of the void, from a huge blue heaven beside a huge blue lake."[5] The varied concerns of the work—the loss of a natural pastoral life, village mediocrity, escape to the city in search of the fullness of life, rural returns touched with feelings of nostalgia, guilt, and superiority—possessed a special urgency, seeming to reveal for the nation as a whole some central truths about American life. For a time Midwestern literature virtually *was* American literature.

This said, two large qualifications must be noted. First of all, the Midwestern day in the literary sun was of relatively brief duration. Although a small group of local-color realists caused a ripple of critical attention well before the turn of the century and the Indiana romancers dominated popular writing in the period immediately afterward, it was not until Edgar Lee Masters and Sherwood Anderson and especially Willa Cather and Sinclair Lewis and a rediscovered Theodore Dreiser drew widespread attention in the second and third decades of the twentieth century that Midwestern writing occupied the center of American literature. With Lewis's Nobel Prize at the beginning of the new decade in 1930, the first American so honored, the Midwestern ascendancy was at its zenith in popular acclaim; at the same time it was at its end as a major regional movement within American writing. Already Southern writing had begun its brilliant period with the appearance, in the year before, of *The Sound and the Fury* and *Look Homeward, Angel*. And a new generation of young Midwesterners led by Crane and Fitzgerald and especially by Hemingway had taken what was left of Midwestern regionalism and thrust it into the territory of literary modernism in which questions of localism were simply beside the point. "They had leaped at one bound," Alfred Kazin said of the young writers' embrace of the new, "from the Midwestern world of their childhood into the world of Caporetto, of Dada, of Picasso and Gertrude Stein, and their detachment from the native traditions now became their own first tradition."[6]

Secondly, if the Midwestern ascendancy was not particularly long lasting neither did it run particularly deep. It produced only a few works of unquestioned quality—works important for aesthetic reasons rather than social or historical reasons. Viewed in its entirety, the Midwestern ascendancy hardly matched the intellectual and imaginative reach of the New England renaissance of the first half of the nineteenth century nor of the Southern renaissance between the wars in the twentieth, in large part (questions of individual talent aside) because it never possessed in anything like the same measure the historical and cultural consciousness that deeply informed those other literary moments. In Dreiser, Anderson, Cather, and Lewis the Midwestern ascendancy produced major figures, yet it did not produce novelists of the towering stature of Henry James or William Faulkner, short story writers the equal of Nathaniel Hawthorne or Flannery O'Connor, poets of the rank of Emerson and Whitman or John Crowe Ransom and Robert Penn Warren. There is no Midwestern *Moby-Dick* nor *Absalom, Absalom!*, no *Walden* nor "Ode to the Confederate Dead." Nor are there the subtle regional analysts following in the wake of imaginative writers—no Perry Miller or F. O. Matthiessen, no gathering of critical thinkers the match of the Nashville Agrarians or ambitious cultural journalists the equal of W. J. Cash.

This broad view of the quality of Midwestern writing is, of course, arguable; at the very least it begs for refinement. But it is not my purpose to compare the work of the Midwestern ascendancy with that which emerged at other times from other regions. It seems important, nonetheless, to note at the beginning that in terms of "imaginative vitality"—a phrase used by Matthiessen in discussing the quality of the literature of New England in the age of Emerson and Whitman[7]—the body of work produced during the Midwestern ascendancy was surely important but only in a few instances of the very first importance. Looking back upon it from the vantage point of the present, as a regional movement it seems to exist in imaginative vitality where O'Connor placed it historically—in a middle range between the lofty peaks of New England and Southern literary achievement. If that is the correct location of the Midwestern ascendancy in American writing as a whole, it is not—as I have already implied—an inconsequential position. Far from it. For without the best work from out of the Midwest it is impossible—as Mark Schorer said of the major novels of Sinclair Lewis but a remark that applies equally to the work of Dreiser, Anderson, Cather, and the early Crane, Fitzgerald, and Hemingway—to imagine modern American literature. It formed the leading edge in the freeing of American writing from the grip of the genteel, bringing us for the first time face to face with contemporary life. It provided fresh visions of style and form on the route to modernism's preoccupation with literary manner. Even still it forms the foreground of our imaginative understanding of the national experience.

As much as one might wish to introduce the name of Mark Twain of Missouri into the roll call of Midwestern writers and to fix upon *The Adventures of Huckleberry Finn* as the great Midwestern novel, thereby claiming in a stroke the literary heights from New England and the South, it is evident that Twain and his great novel belong elsewhere. In the whole of his work there are, to be sure, memorable accounts of country and river life in what is technically the Midwest; Dawson's Landing in *The Tragedy of Pudd'nhead Wilson*, to take a single example, looks forward to the village revelations of *Spoon River Anthology* and *Winesburg, Ohio*. Nonetheless, the sense of place that emerges from Twain's work is distinctly more Southern and Western than Midwestern, his links to Faulkner and—as Kenneth S. Lynn has effectively shown—to the modes of Southwestern humor far more apparent than to Midwestern writers and Midwestern literary traditions. Allen Tate's classification of *Huckleberry Finn* as the "first modern novel by a Southerner"[8] is surely the correct one both in its understanding of the novel and of the imaginative world of its author. When Twain describes the river cities north of St. Louis in *Life on the Mississippi* his tone is that of a detached outsider who, with only slightly suppressed irony, notes the presence of "active, energetic, intelligent, prosperous, practical people." These Midwesterners, he pointedly notes, are people who "don't dream, they work." Everything about life in the northern reaches of the Mississippi Valley is so brisk, handsome, and well ordered that Twain is compelled to repeated passages of "homage":

> This is an independent race who think for themselves, and who are competent to do it, because they are educated and enlightened; they read, they keep abreast of the best and newest thought, they fortify every weak place in their land with a school, a college, a library, and a newspaper; and they live under law. Solicitude for the future of a race like this is not in order.[9]

Neither, one might add, is literary treatment in order for such a tableau of perfection. For Twain the energetic landscape of the Midwest provided only material for reporting. For his greatest imaginative work he turned back upon a very different regional world, one both more joyous and more complex and one freely given over to dream.

William Dean Howells, Twain's Midwestern contemporary, presents a different case. He spent his early boyhood in the southern Ohio town of Hamilton, a town that like Hannibal, Missouri, shared both Midwestern and Southern qualities, but unlike Twain he rapidly abandoned his past as material for fiction as well as in actuality. A campaign biography of Lincoln, written after Howells lost his newspaper job with the *Ohio State Journal* in Columbus, gained him the position of American consul in Venice. When he returned to the country after the Civil War, it was not to Ohio that he came but to New York for a short period of free-lance literary journalism before he ventured to Boston in 1866 as the assistant editor of the *Atlantic*, beginning his long and honored career as a literary arbiter. Although he would employ Midwestern characters in his novels and eventually return to the region as setting for fiction (in *New Leaf Mills*, for example, and *The Leatherwood God*) as well as in autobiography, he came to embody as a writer what seems now the Indian Summer of the New England tradition. Howells once called Twain, his cherished friend and fellow transplanted Easterner, the most desouthernized Southerner he had known. If the description applies to Twain, it applies equally to Howells and his Midwestern heritage. Twain and Howells deeply affected American writing by bringing fresh Western influences to bear on it, but neither of these towering figures can be fit comfortably into a tradition of Midwestern writing. Nourished by the region, neither was contained by it. To exclude them from a portrait of the ascendancy is, finally, only to acknowledge the obvious: the Midwest—every region—turns fuzzy on its borders, merging along with its writers into the claims of other regions, other traditions.

2

In an essay called "A Southern Mode of the Imagination," Tate once noted that if the literate New Englander was, in the language of Emerson's "The American Scholar," man thinking, the Southern gentleman was man talking.

When the rhetorical style eventually gave way to dialectic—that is, when the modern concern with internal conflict was wedded to inherited external story forms—the way was prepared for Faulkner and the dramatic rise of Southern writing. I mention Tate's argument in simplified form because of the lack of similar efforts within Midwestern culture to define a regional mode of imagination.[10] Indeed, the very notion of a distinct Midwestern imagination is at odds with a common view of the region as capable of being defined only in terms of what is most familiar and essential about America itself. Max Lerner has noted, in a comment characteristic of those directed to the Midwest, that almost everyone writing about the region has automatically taken the position "that any light cast upon it would somehow light up the whole of the American character."[11]

Why this should be so is matter for debate. Settlement and development in the region, it has been suggested, coincided almost exactly with the great transformation of capitalist enterprise in America, with the result that since the Midwest had little or no prior noncapitalist existence it came to reflect in particularly pure ways the values of the country's dominant middle-class business civilization.[12] Through this process, or simply because its rich land and raw materials and abundant energy and transportation so effectively fed the new commercial energies, the Midwest and the middle class became virtually interchangeable terms. Perhaps the most obvious and telling answer has to do merely with geographical location—the Midwest as the heartland of the country, removed from the Atlantic and Pacific edges that presumably tilt the nation toward Europe, toward Asia, toward whatever is foreign and exotic and ultimately at odds with what is genuinely American in American life. Following the Civil War there was a flurry of interest in moving the capital from Washington to St. Louis, a location both geographically and symbolically more at the nation's center. Still today the notion of the nation's heartland as the repository of bedrock American life—"the real body of America," as Sherwood Anderson called it[13]—remains with us. It is the place where "old normalcy floats heavy on the humid air," says the narrator of Richard Ford's novel *The Sportswriter* (1986).[14] In Jonathan Raban's *Old Glory: An American Voyage*, a British writer's 1981 account of a journey by small powerboat through the Mississippi Valley on its great river, the author is instructed by an informant in the Iowa town of Muscatine that he should not condescend to the Midwest but recognize it as the country's sensible center:

> "Look," he said. "Back East, you've got the old top-heavy bureaucracy. Then on the West Coast you've got all the excess of America. We're the calm, thoughtful center. We can moderate between the extremes. We can see both sides of the argument. If you take us out of the United States, you drain all the basic common sense out of the country."[15]

Reviewing the book in a bastion of the mid-Atlantic literary establishment, the *New York Review of Books*, Diane Johnson took note of just such a sense of the Midwest as basic America. Within Raban's account, she remarked, the reader discovered that

> America has a calm center, itself hearkening back and confirming itself, restoring its buildings, researching its history, defending its eccentricities against the frontier mentality of the West, the sissy affectations of the East, a rich storehouse of cultural certitudes trying to ignore the shifting values and faddish self-doubts of coastal America.[16]

If Midwestern life is thought of simply as American life, or at least American life in its most authentic state, it is to be expected that the region's analysts— Frederick Jackson Turner is the major and nearly only example—would tend to spread their claims over the nation as a whole. The Midwest might provide the starting point, the raw material, but inevitably discussions of the region become discussions of America and social and cultural life in general. In examining the Midwest, Glenway Wescott once said, it is always a mistake to over-particularize, for "what seems local is national, what seems national is universal, what seems Middle Western is in the commonest way human."[17] Herein is a central issue in considering Midwestern literary history. As O'Connor noted, regional writing thrives on the sense of alikeness and common ground—or as Tate put it, on a writer's sense of coming from a place with special characteristics. The Midwestern imagination, on the other hand, has tended to stress not special qualities but common ones—the very qualities possessed, or that properly ought to be, by Americans as a whole. If it is true that the best American writing has come from provincial and self-contained centers of life, then the Midwest has always been at a serious disadvantage. Typically it has been barren of rich local traditions, given over instead to a tendency to absorb the cultural life of other and older sections of the country—to see itself, once again, not so much as a distinctive American region but as America itself.

As a further complication, the region has presented to its writers a physical and cultural landscape that defies easy imaginative grasp. Among the twelve central states usually understood to comprise the region—a vast sweep of land extending from the Old Northwest of the Ohio Valley and the Great Lakes to the Upper Mississippi Valley to the dry western plains of the Dakotas, Nebraska, and Kansas—there is wide variation in climate, terrain, ethnic and racial makeup, and the organization of life. Farms and small towns and medium-sized cities coexist with centers of agribusiness and high technology and rust-belt heavy industry.[18] The result is that there have always been various Midwests, and within them varieties of Midwestern experience—a region so diverse as to suggest to some that the Midwest is not a region at all in any meaningful sense but merely, in one of the names once applied to it, a Great Valley of flattened space between the Alleghenies and the Rockies. The nameless narrator of William Gass's story "In the Heart of the Heart of the Country" lives snugly enough in a nameless small Indiana town yet perceives the Midwest as only a bewildering "dissonance of parts and people" and possessed of an "outlook never really urban, never rural either."[19] Certainly there was never within the region's broad reaches the unifying experience of the common yoke of colonial existence or the common misery of lost war, nor has there been much history of any sort.

The story of the Midwest is one of rural settlement and urban development undertaken with breathtaking speed. A scant thirty years after first settlement following the Revolution, Ohio, Indiana, Michigan, Illinois, and Missouri were comfortably part of the Union; forty years later, at the end of the 1870s, settlement was virtually complete; and before the century's close Chicago could celebrate its eminence as a center of economic power and high culture with the World's Columbian Exposition. From the frontier West the region was swiftly reduced to the Middle West, and then, further adulterating its westward standing, to the settled and progressive Midwest—or, reversing the angle of vision, the settled and progressive Mideast. From a region that had once been a destination it became a crossroads, inevitably experiencing the uncertain identity implied in the term.

Richard Gray began a recent book about the literature of the South—dauntlessly joining the seemingly endless procession of literary studies of that region—with the proper question for all regional works. "*Is* there such a thing as the South," he asked, "a coherent region and an identifiable culture that can be sharply differentiated from the rest of the United States?" His answer is that there probably is not—that, after the probings of modern historians and social scientists, the most that can be said is that the region offers some slight variations on the national norm. If this is the truth about the South, or by extension the truth about such other seemingly distinct regions as New England or the Southwest or the Mountain West, it is the overwhelming truth about the Midwest. If there is no South there surely is no Midwest. But Gray goes on to make a further and obviously necessary point for anyone undertaking a regional study: if the South of *fact* has receded in the wake of scholarly attention, the South of *idea* has remained perennially vigorous—and it is with the idea of the region, or with what he also terms the "Southern argument," that literature has been primarily concerned.[20]

The same point can be turned to the Midwest. Considered from the standpoint of fact, the Midwest presents some notable difficulties for regional analysis, as I have tried to briefly suggest. But the region is clearly more than the assembled facts about it. It is also a concept—a complex and perhaps ultimately mysterious tissue made up of experience and dream, history and myth—that has long existed and continues to exist. And it is primarily out of *this* Midwest that the literature of its ascendancy arose. This does not mean that the plain facts of Midwestern life had no bearing on its literature during its great period. A good deal of the work, especially that of the fledgling realists at the end of the nineteenth century, came directly out of a perceived conflict between the Midwest of idea—or the Midwest of argument—and encounters with its actual life. It is simply to suggest that despite what has been said (and no doubt more that might be) about Midwestern diversity and a thin history and a general lack of special characteristics that distinguish it from America as a whole, an intellectual and imaginative conception of something called the Midwest managed to emerge and survive in the nation's heartland and within the country as a whole.

It was here, in a territory of thought and feeling more than history, that the region's literary ascendancy had its deepest roots. It was in the idea of the Midwest that the sense of alikeness, the sense of special characteristics, was realized to a sufficient extent to stimulate a literary renaissance. It was here that for a time writers from out of the Midwest, in varying degrees self-consciously aware of themselves as coming from the country's rural and small-town center and flocking to its great city and beyond, found their material and their voice. "It was a time," as Sherwood Anderson would remark with appropriate vagueness, "of something flowering in Chicago and the middle west"[21]—a time when writers, as Nick Carraway would say in *The Great Gatsby* about his memory of returning to the Midwest from school at Christmas, were "unutterably aware of our identity with this country for one strange hour."[22] Ford Madox Ford recalled that when he was editing the *Transatlantic Review* in Paris in the early 1920s eighty percent of the manuscripts in English that he received came from the Midwest (though, to be sure, Ford's shaky sense of the region meant "west of Altoona"), and forty percent of them "were of such a level of excellence that one might just as well close one's eyes and take one at random as try to choose between them."[23] H. L. Mencken, then at the height of his power as a critic and commentator, could declare in 1920 that "with two exceptions, there is not a single American novelist of the younger generation—that is, a serious novelist, a novelist deserving a civilized reader's notice—who has not sprung from the Middle Empire that has Chicago for its capital."[24]

The period of alikeness was, once again, neither long lasting nor did it cut deep in literary quality, but it produced important imaginative writing that conveyed the tone and feel—the argument—of distinctive regional experience. Its central achievements—*The Hoosier School-Master, Main-Travelled Roads, Sister Carrie, Chicago Poems, Spoon River Anthology, Winesburg, Ohio, O Pioneers!, My Ántonia, Main Street, Giants in the Earth, The Grandmothers*—were clearly Midwestern books while at the same time obviously more than that. In 1932 Ruth Suckow—a figure of lesser note but in her time one of the most self-conscious of Midwestern writers—would look back at just such a litany of works and happily declare in the pages of the *English Journal* that there was no longer need to "convince anyone that there *can* be a middle western literature" since it was so evident "that there *is* a middle western literature."[25] The emphases betray the uncertainty that always clings to expressions of the Midwest as a special regional entity with a special literature or special anything else. Yet Suckow was right. Out of the Midwest had come a sufficient regional identity, a sense of a common ground of imagination, to give rise to a literature of distinctive stamp. In its literature the Midwest clearly existed, as it would exist nowhere else with quite the same clarity and coherence.

3

The Midwest's moment of literary ascendancy was the product of a gradual (if anything about the region's swift development can be called gradual) evolutionary process.[26] The West of high plains and mountains encouraged popular fiction from the beginning, but the agricultural West of woods and prairie proved stubborn literary material. The tiller of the soil, performing dull and laborious duties and restricted to the confines of the family, lacked the freedom and glamor that attached to the frontiersman and cowboy. Frank Norris, speculating in 1902 on an appropriate Western literature (by which he meant a literature for the trans-Mississippi West), thought a distinctive literature could only be built around the region's one truly heroic figure: "the man of deeds, the man of action, the adventurer, the pioneer." Such a figure seemed the stuff of a great national epic, though unfortunately one that had been dissipated in the unreal mists of Cooper's Leatherstocking stories and the dime-novel potboilers. It seemed certain to Norris, at any event, that a significant Western literature would not arise from the lives of "the prosaic farming folk of Iowa" or from "uneventful, unperturbed life" in any of its forms but from the romance of Western adventurers.[27] As an additional impediment to literary importance, the farmer bore with him the stigma of low social standing. While cultural spokesmen piously celebrated him as a virtuous yeoman and ideal citizen, his actual rank in society scraped bottom, leaving him less than a fit subject for novelistic traditions built around genteel heroes and heroines. Theocratic New Englanders added to the problem by troubling over the coarseness of the farmer and his location at the edge of authority. The prevalent social theory of the stages of society that saw history moving from the primitive to the agricultural to a final phase of refinement and sophistication placed a further limit on the farmer's literary appeal. Even when early Midwestern writers were occasionally moved to an immediate response to the experience of agricultural settlement, they found themselves uncertain about its appropriateness as literary material of interest to educated readers in the most advanced stage of society.

The initial literature of the region emerging from exploration and first settlement has been amply traced by such scholars as Ralph L. Rusk, Dorothy A. Dondore, and John T. Flanagan, an assembly of practical work in the form of travel accounts, guide books, histories, memoirs, sermons, and orations. Initial work in an imaginative vein was usually in the form of poetry and from the hand of newspaper editors, clergymen, lawyers, and occasional professional poets. An early anthology, William D. Gallagher's *The Poetical Literature of the West*, published in Cincinnati in 1841, printed the work of thirty-eight writers. A more ambitious enterprise was William T. Coggeshall's *The Poets and Poetry of the West*, published in Columbus, Ohio, in 1860 and running to nearly 700 pages. It collected the work of 152 poets from throughout the Midwest (among them a youthful William Dean Howells)—a representative selection, the preface declared, of "the respectable poetical literature of the great Central Valley of the United States."[28] What both anthologies disclose is that local verse had only fleeting connection with a distinctive sense of regional life; much of it might as easily have emerged from the English Midlands as the American Midwest, owing more to the English poets than to any native feeling for setting or character. When writers did turn to the local the result was often a conventional celebration of rural perfection, as for example in John Finley's hymn "To Indiana":

> Blest Indiana! in thy soil
> Are found the sure rewards of toil,
> Where harvest, purity and worth
> May make a paradise on earth.[29]

Not until the 1870s and especially the 1880s and early 1890s did farmers and rural figures in general begin to emerge from the obscurity of literary convention, class views, and social theory. Although their condition might be darkly portrayed, they were nonetheless seen as worthy of literary attention. An important factor in the shift was the local-color movement arising after the Civil War with its emphasis on the accurate rendering of locale, followed by the brief flowering of naturalism and realism in American writing—the effort to render things as they actually appear and in the language of common speech, to resist the heightened and to recreate the day to day. It has often been pointed out that in its raw beginnings realism offered a substitute for craftsmanship in that it asked only that the writer present his subject faithfully; all else—style, form, technique in general—was secondary. For Midwestern writers coming from cramped or nonexistent literary backgrounds, the fragile new doctrine of truth-telling held special appeal since it turned private experience into literary capital; they had only to write about the farms and small towns that they knew.[30] It was hardly surprising that the first significant group of Midwestern writers—Edward Eggleston, Joseph Kirkland, E. W. Howe, Hamlin Garland—enlisted, however tentatively, under realism's banner, nor surprising that popular success in each case was limited to a single book. Personal experience exploited, there was little else to fall back upon.

Commentators on Midwestern *belles-lettres* have usually ordered the work into three periods: pioneering efforts, largely centering around Cincinnati, that began as early as the 1820s; a fragile experiment with realism carried to its furthest extent by Garland in the early 1890s; and, after more than a decade of virtual silence in serious writing, a great awakening that began in the second decade of the new century.[31] The story of the Midwestern ascendancy properly opens with the middle period and ends with the triumph of the third. In recounting this story I make no effort to provide anything resembling a comprehensive account. I concentrate instead on what I take to be the best examples of Midwestern writing—an examination, in a phrase of Warner Berthoff, "of good work done."[32] By this I mean imaginative work of enduring stature, slight in some cases and certain in others, in American writing as a whole—work with clear Midwestern grounding (that is, written by Midwesterners and significantly about the Midwest; the work of Midwestern writers set elsewhere is another story) yet some national standing, work that has its ultimate center in the effort to respond to the human condition as it has been experienced at all times and in all places. These are not exact measuring tools and there are certain to be omissions—writers that ought to have been mentioned, books that should have been discussed, literary areas (drama, to take a glaring example) that should have been examined. Although the entire range of Midwestern writing during its period of ascendancy is not represented in these pages, I try to take into account most of what is best.

As F. O. Matthiessen pointed out in *American Renaissance*, there are various ways in which a book of this sort might be undertaken. One might try to detail *how* the Midwestern ascendancy came into being through the compiling of a descriptive literary history. Or one might emphasize *why* it came when it did through an examination of social, cultural, and economic factors. Or finally one might give primary attention to *what* its books were as works of art, to a study of form and content, meaning and implication. I have tried to remain on this last course, emphasizing an examination of individual writers and their most important works while arranging the study according to the emergence of Midwestern writing over time. In this opening section, however, I want to continue to develop a few more general thoughts about the overall nature of Midwestern writing, thoughts as open to question as such generalities are bound to be. Discussions of Midwestern writing have suffered, so it seems to me, from a lack of large organizing views of the sort that have provided a rich background—if only to refine or resist—for the extensive criticism of the literature of New England and the South. Sacvan Bercovitch has suggested that whereas earlier American literary history emerged from consensus—consensus both about the literary canon and the shape of our national history—a new literary history, alert to postmodern and pluralistic sensibilities, will emerge from dissensus. For Midwestern literary history, however, there has been little effort directed to consensus, let alone to the disassembling that follows. What I offer here is in the hope that better general perspectives on Midwestern literature may yet appear.

4

Lord Bryce in *The American Commonwealth*, attempting to give a sense of the uniformity of American life, found himself recalling the monotonous landscape of the Mississippi Valley that seemed to contain—as he put it with the exaggerated leveling sensibility often directed to things Midwestern[33]—"nothing deserving to be called a hill." He went on:

From the point where you leave the Alleghanies [*sic*] at Pittsburg [*sic*], until after crossing the Missouri, you approach the still untilled prairie West, a railway run of some thousand miles, there is a uniformity of landscape greater than could be found along any one hundred miles of railway run in Western Europe. Everywhere the same nearly flat country, over which you cannot see far, because you are little raised above it, the same fields and crops, the same rough wooden fences, the same thickets of the same bushes along the stream edges, with here and there a bit of old forest; the same solitary farmhouses and straggling wood-built villages.[34]

The literary landscape of the Midwest has not been similarly characterized by such uniformity or such sameness of effect. It does, however, seem characterized by a certain modesty or reserve in the figures it presents and the action it delineates. There are, to be sure, sweeping Midwestern novels with outsized characters and outlandish actions, and there surely is no lack of physical mayhem nor spiritual and psychological tumult. One thinks immediately of the grand scale of *Giants in the Earth* and *O Pioneers!*, of the warped lives given voice in *Spoon River Anthology* and *Winesburg, Ohio*. Still, Midwestern novels that might bear such dramatic, attention-grabbing titles as *The Sound and the Fury* or *The Violent Bear It Away*, or even *The Scarlet Letter* or *Miss Lonelyhearts*, do not (with, once again, the obvious exception of *Giants in the Earth*) come easily to mind. Midwestern books seem to more comfortably reside under restrained titles drawn from the names of places and characters—*Chicago Poems* and *Main Street* and *Iowa Interiors, Jennie Gerhardt* and *My Ántonia* and *Babbitt*. The Midwestern literary imagination has about it, at least in comparison with the South of Faulkner and O'Connor or the New England of Hawthorne and Melville or the Far West of Nathanael West, an essentially homely quality that shies away from the extremes of human experience. On the whole, it finds itself most at ease with stories of plain people in a plain environment living plain lives—a people not inclined to excesses of language or action, their dramas, even when filled with the rage or suppressed longing of Masters's epitaphs or Anderson's stories, enacted within limited emotional and spiritual ranges. In an article he once wrote about Anderson—the Midwestern writer who, together with Dreiser and Hemingway, came to exercise the most influence on American writing as a whole—Faulkner took note of the Ohioan's symbolic use of "a working horse" to represent the America he claimed as his literary territory, that (as Faulkner described it) "vast rich strong docile sweep of the Mississippi Valley." The qualities of the working horse, "sound and strong and valuable, but without recorded pedigree," seem to apply as well to the general nature of the Midwest's literature, valuable certainly but largely unspectacular, distinctly unFaulknerian.[35]

Such a broad and no doubt oversimplified view of the nature of Midwestern writing can perhaps be elaborated by returning for a moment to Howells. In the fall of 1899, at the peak of his reputation as the foremost American man of letters, he began a Midwestern speaking tour that took him to Michigan, Ohio, Illinois, Iowa, Nebraska, and Kansas—twenty-five appearances over a six-week period.[36] He was a poor public speaker who generally avoided the lecture platform, and the grinding schedule of railroad travel and social appearances only added to the discomfort of the trip; but the audiences that turned out to hear him were sizeable and his remarks were warmly praised in newspaper accounts. Howells had developed two lectures for the tour, but one proved the more successful and he began using it exclusively. In "Novel-Writing and Novel-Reading" he set out in lucid fashion his mature view of what he called the appropriate inward life and outward shape of fiction, a view meant to do nothing less than reverse the direction of American writing. He said that early in his career as a novelist he had learned that "what I must do in fiction if I were to do anything worth while, was to get into it from life the things that had not been got into fiction before." This meant discarding the "old superstition of a dramatic situation as the supreme representation of life" in favor of an account as faithful to lived experience as possible. In one of the lecture's most striking passages Howells declared that the true novelist

> will not rest till he has made his story as like life as he can, with the same mixed motives, the same voluntary and involuntary actions, the same unaccountable advances and perplexing pauses, the same moments of rapture, the same days and weeks of horrible dullness, the same conflict of higher and lower purposes, the same vices and virtues, inspirations and propensities. . . . he will try to give that general resemblance which can come only from the most devoted fidelity to particulars. As it is now, the representation of life in novels, even the most conscientious in its details, is warped and distorted by the novelist's anxiety to produce an image that is startling and impressive, as well as true. But if he can once conceive the notion of letting the reader's imagination care for these things; if he can convince himself that his own affair is to arrange a correct perspective in which all things shall appear in their very proportion and relation, he will have mastered the secret of repose which is the soul of beauty in all its forms.[37]

"Novel-Writing and Novel-Reading" was a summation of a theory of fiction Howells had developed in his own work and in a flood of reviews and literary articles in the *Atlantic, Century*, and *Harper's*. Earlier he had fastened on the term "effectism" to describe all that he wished to jettison in fiction—all the false manipulation of plot turns and suspenseful palpitations meant to evoke strong feeling in the reader. As against the fiction of effect, the novel of repose ought simply reveal the normal, inconclusive, frequently humdrum truth of everyday experience; it ought, by design, to be a middling sort of fiction meant to modestly illumine life's middle ranges. The Howellsian novel had, of course, no particular regional identification. It was intended as the American novel, an appropriate vehicle for exploring the flattening tendencies of democratic life. Yet the novel of anti-effectism, eschewing the startling and the impressive, seemed especially well suited to the physical and psychic character of the Midwest—a theory of fiction evolved by a Midwesterner and, or so it seemed to appear, with the unassuming nature of Midwestern experience in mind.

Hamlin Garland, an eager Midwestern protégé, drew directly on Howells's reduced sense of the novel in fashioning his own critical theory. The modern novel, he declared, was concerned with the "delineation of actual human life, not the fantastical visions of some social theorist or the fancies of some romancer's heated brain." He added that Howells would come to be seen "as a public benefactor for replacing morbid, unnatural and hysterical fiction with pure, wholesome and natural studies of real life."[38] Chicago-born Frank Norris would mock Howellsian realism (while Howells, with his usual generosity, would for the most part praise what he thought of as the young writer's Zola-like naturalism in *McTeague, The Octopus,* and *The Pit*) as the bloodless "drama of a broken teacup, the tragedy of a walk down the block, the excitement of an afternoon call, the adventure of an invitation to dinner."[39] Such later Midwestern writers as Anderson and Lewis would personally identify Howells with a repressive Victorian morality in fiction. Their variation on Howellsian realism would lean more toward the exposure of the hidden and the unpleasant than toward fidelity to the average. Yet Howells's sense of a novel devoid of effectism and devoted to what he called a poetry of the plainest fact helps clarify a main current in Midwestern writing running from Garland's sober portraits of farm life to Lewis's detailed cartoons of the middle-class town life, from Eggleston's tentative exploration of frontier manners to Cather's muted epics of pioneering. Appropriately, in his comment on the rise of Midwestern literature noted earlier, Saul Bellow would define the typical subject matter of the region in a series of homely terms: "ordinary lives," "this common life," "our very common selves." John Updike has pointed out that the Howells agenda for the novel has won the day in American writing as a whole to the extent of becoming *the* agenda: a continuing effort to portray the vast, natural, unaffected dullness (as Howells put it) of a national life essentially middling in nature.[40] In its early contributions to this effort, as in so many other respects, the Midwest offers itself as the most characteristic part of America—a middling region in a country whose literary genius has been given to the portrayal of middling life.

Yet if Midwestern writing of the ascendancy was given to mostly modest effects, within its unimposing main-street facade it often sheltered feelings of estrangement and resistance. In an article published in 1923 called "Indiana: Her Soil and Light," Dreiser, the first major writer to emerge from the Midwest (assuming one grants the exclusion of Twain and Howells), took note of the "poetic and folksy charm" that marked the work of so many writers of his native state, and he accounted for it by further noting the "agreeable and respectable and kindly social world" of their native experience.[41] He was thinking here of the best-selling effusions of such fellow Hoosiers as James Whitcomb Riley and Booth Tarkington as well as Gene Stratton-Porter, Charles Major, and George Barr McCutcheon, and though his mood in the article was mellow, he was also by implication locating himself within a different literary development, one that grew out of a more complex and edgy interaction with Midwestern experience.

Although the popular Indiana authors provide the chief exhibit, a strain of writing throughout the Midwest devoted to uncritical celebration of its down-home charms—to its fruitful fields and comfortable villages and sensible citizens—has long been evident. The work has invariably fallen from the heights of contemporary approval into the dustbin of popular culture or sunk from sight altogether, and properly so. The quality of easy and uncritical sentiment that Dreiser had in mind has nearly always informed what is weakest in Midwest writing (for that matter, any regional writing)—an addiction to local color, to the picturesque, for its own sake. This is the kind of parochial expression Ford Madox Ford had in mind when he remarked that "local literatures are as a rule a nuisance, the writers devoting to local distinctions of speech without interest and to local ill-manners that would be best forgotten, talents that might, in a wide scene, develop comprehension and catholicity."[42] Equally ephemeral has been an opposite strain—the literature of unrelieved lament usually directed to the limitations of farm and small-town life. Following in the wake of the extravagant popular success of Lewis's *Main Street* and *Babbitt*, and consequently confined largely to the latter part of the 1920s and the early 1930s, such work has been a less persistent feature of regional expression in the Midwest but one that, for a time, seemed to capture the very idea of the region's writing. John Riddell's deft 1929 parody in *Vanity Fair* of "The Gloomy Mid-West Story" (with its often-quoted conclusion: "She broke her arm at the elbow, just to hear it snap")[43] could assume an audience wholly familiar with a literature of rural futility.

What has endured, on the other hand, as the genuine literature of the Midwest has come from more penetrating and usually more ambivalent responses to the region. The same Dreiser who could cast a cool eye on popular Indiana writing could spread his own soft glow over his native state in his autobiographical works, viewing it—as he acknowledged in *A Hoosier Holiday*—through his "rose window of the west."[44] The point I wish to make, however, is that the best Midwestern writing has nearly always stood in opposition to popular responses to the region, and most frequently this has meant opposition to the Midwest of poetic and folksy charm. Dreiser himself came from an Indiana sharply removed from the kindly social world that nourished most of his Hoosier contemporaries; he knew intimately a Midwest of defeat. Other writers of significance have come from less hostile backgrounds or quite comfortable ones but they are all Dreiserians in the sense of experiencing some sense of removal from the conventional experience of the region, or from the conventional responses to that experience. Midwestern literature has found its greatest strength in resistance to the charming and the wistful, to an imagined world of serene images and untroubled lives. It has preferred instead a mode of truth-telling protest or of subtle rebellion that, taken to a far extreme, unsubtly proclaims with Glenway Wescott that "there is no Middle West" but only "a certain climate, a certain landscape; and beyond that, a state of mind of people born where they do not like to live."[45] I do not wish to make too much of a sense of estrangement or a current of resistance within Midwestern writing—resistance, once again, both to the Midwest of folk charm and to that of grim defeat. Yet it seems evident that for Midwestern literature a less easily held sense of the region's life, however that life is conceived, has been an enriching stimulus. If only briefly and often in the company of contrary urges to embrace and memorialize, attack and abandon, it has enabled writers to look upon the region with a fresh gaze and reveal it in ways that hold and expand in the mind.

5

Flannery O'Connor sought to capture an essential quality of Southern literature by citing a remark of Walker Percy (after he won a National Book Award) that the reason there were so many good Southern writers was "because we lost the War." Percy was not, O'Connor explained, talking about a lost war as subject matter for Southern writing; rather, he was saying that

> we have had our Fall. We have gone into the modern world with an inburnt knowledge of human limitations and with a sense of mystery which could not have developed in our first state of innocence—as it has not sufficiently developed in the rest of our country.[46]

Another general observation to be made about Midwestern literature is that its writers, at their bests, have also known or sensed a Fall. It is a Fall neither as elaborated nor as intensely felt as that known in the South; certainly it cannot be so firmly linked to specific historical events. It is a Fall, nevertheless, that has brought with it an awareness of lost innocence and of human limitation, in some hands a sense even of mystery.

What I have in mind is the Fall from pioneer perfection—an awareness of the failure to create or sustain within the Great Valley a rural Eden. It may be true that all regional expression is rooted in a vision of paradise lost as manifest in a compelling past set against a disappointing present.[47] The sense of decline from an earlier perfection has, at any event, provided a broad background for the particular dramas of Midwestern writing, lending to them an elegiac quality that is strong in some instances and faint in others. In an essay in 1923 about her native Nebraska, Willa Cather effectively captured just such a haunting sense of loss, as she had a decade earlier in her prairie epics.

> In Nebraska, as in so many other States, we must face the fact that the splendid story of the pioneers is finished, and that no new story worthy to take its place has yet begun. The generation that subdued the wild land and broke up the virgin prairie is passing, but it is still there, a group of rugged figures in the background which inspire respect, compel admiration. With these old men and women the attainment of material prosperity was a moral victory, because it was wrung from hard conditions, was the result of a struggle that tested character. They can look out over those broad stretches of fertility and say: "We made this, with our backs and hands." The sons, the generation now in middle life, were reared amid hardships, and it is perhaps natural that they should be very much interested in mate-

rial comforts, in buying whatever is expensive and ugly. Their fathers came into a wilderness and had to make everything, had to be as ingenious as shipwrecked sailors. The generation now in the driver's seat hates to make anything, wants to live and die in an automobile, scudding past those acres where the old men used to follow the long corn-rows up and down. They want to buy everything ready-made: clothes, food, education, music, pleasure. Will the third generation—the full-blooded, joyous one just coming over the hill—will it be fooled? Will it believe that to live easily is to live happily?[48]

In the novel *A Lost Lady* in the same year Cather set out a similar view through her sympathetic narrator, Niel Herbert. After the brash and ambitious Ivy Peters purchases the Forrester farm and drains the wild marsh, Niel reflects on the rapid decline from pioneer grace into the shallow commercial life of the second generation:

> The Old West had been settled by dreamers, great-hearted adventurers who were unpractical to the point of magnificence; a courteous brotherhood, strong in attack but weak in defence, who could conquer but could not hold. Now all the vast territory they had won was to be at the mercy of men like Ivy Peters, who had never dared anything, never risked anything. They would drink up the mirage, dispel the morning freshness, root out the great brooding spirit of freedom, the generous, easy life of the great land-holders. The space, the colour, the princely carelessness of the pioneer they would destroy and cut up into profitable bits, as the match factory splinters the primeval forest.[49]

The South lost a war, the Midwest a dream—a dream, as Nick Carraway of Minnesota says of the dream of Jay Gatsby of North Dakota, that had no doubt begun to vanish almost at the moment of its inception, lost "somewhere back in that vast obscurity beyond the city, where the dark fields of the republic rolled on under the night."[50] Such a loss may have unfortunate implications for the culture (as did, needless to say, the South's failure in war) while yet providing a fertile ground for literature. A regional culture perhaps always finds its most memorable stories and passionate voices in the moment of passage to a lesser phase;[51] certainly Midwestern writing seems to have been deepened and enriched in the awareness of loss. It is exactly when the splendid story of the pioneers is finished, as Cather put it, and no story of equal power is yet on the horizon that Midwestern writing comes most fully into its own, touched with a distant quality of regret even as it sought—as it so strenuously would in the latter part of the ascendancy—to free itself from all things Midwestern.

The particular nature of the agrarian dream in the Midwest has been examined by a number of scholars, chief among them Henry Nash Smith in *Virgin Land: The American West as Symbol and Myth*. Throughout the nineteenth century, as Smith has pointed out, two Wests existed—a Wild West of unfettered trappers and mountainmen, cowboys and Indians, and a domesticated West of the family farm with its sacred symbols of the plow and the fenced field. The agricultural West—continuously renewing itself, as Turner would declare at the end of the century, in the pure fields of experience just behind the expanding frontier—gave rise to a poetic vision of an ideal society in the nation's interior. The virgin land, plowed and set with crops, was transformed into an agricultural Eden, a mythical garden of the world, that seemed to define the central promise of American life—secluded, peaceful, fruitful, intimately tied to the goodness of nature and the life-giving round of the seasons, populated with a sturdy race of farmers living lives of freedom and virtue, simple yet supremely happy.[52]

The American origins of the garden myth can be traced back to Franklin, Crevecoeur, and Jefferson, and beyond such eighteenth-century thinkers to a European celebration of agriculture extending back from the French Physiocrats to the literary traditions of the pastoral in Greece and Rome. The emergence of agrarian thinking in the America of the Revolution was immeasurably strengthened by the opportunity to put ideology to the test: what in land-scarce Europe was only possibility could in land-rich America become reality. The opening of the vast agricultural land beyond the Alleghenies added further emotional weight to the agrarian vision. Here was the possibility of realizing on a scale previously beyond man's grasp the perfect rural landscape of family farms and contented communities. What was in origin a literary concept had been transformed into mass passion, and what was a vision of America as a whole took particular root in the fertile Midwest. In Herbert Quick's novel *Vandemark's Folly* (1922), "Cow" Vandemark, arriving in Iowa in the spring of 1855, characteristically feels the full force of the promise of regeneration with his first glimpse of the prairie:

> It was sublime! Bird, flower, grass, cloud, wind, and the immense expanse of sunny prairie, swelling up into undulations like a woman's breasts turgid with milk for a hungry race. I forgot myself and my position in the world, my loneliness . . . the problems of my life; my heart swelled, and my throat filled. I sat looking at it, with the tears trickling from my eyes, the uplift more than I could bear.[53]

Yet from the beginning the myth of a New World garden superimposed on the Midwest posed a central dilemma. It was an essentially static conception that was at odds with the changes wrought by another vision of American life, that embodied in the driving force of progress in its commercial and urban dress. Cities, a complex transportation network, and manufacturing soon appeared in the older sections of the Midwest, compromising a simple picture of rural bliss. Beyond this, farming itself as practiced in the Midwest inevitably altered the vision of a land of family farmers living amid self-sufficient plenty. Although it was assumed that the agricultural development of the region meant economic development and a rising level of affluence, involvement in commerce on a national or international scale was nonetheless seen as minimal. Abundance produced on the farm was for the farm. Yet rich land quickly erased such a restrained conception of farm economy, creating surpluses of grain and livestock and consequent participation in a market mechanism governed by bankers and merchants and afflicted with swings of price caused by faraway events. There was also the sticky matter of class structure. In theory the agrarian paradise lacked class distinctions; it was an egalitarian society constantly restored by the benign influence of nature. But in reality a familiar social structure was soon in place, dominated by economic power and religious and cultural traditions. Although such changes were swiftly enacted in the development of the agricultural Midwest, their complex relationship to the agrarian vision was seldom recognized by contemporary observers.

Indeed, it could not easily be. If the Midwestern garden was a tableau of perfection, change could play little or no part in it. Nor could ambiguity or qualification in any form. The experience of suffering, natural affliction, economic disaster—in theory, none had a foothold in the earthly paradise. When such evils did rear their heads, they could only be ascribed to sources located beyond the garden—in the East, in the Old World, somewhere. The lack of effective intellectual or emotional means within the garden itself for dealing with the murky or simply more complex aspects of human experience led inevitably to bewilderment and anger. Nonetheless, long after the Midwestern garden ceased in any real sense to resemble the garden of myth, the idea of an agricultural paradise in the heartland—simple, in harmony with nature, based on an economy of self-sufficiency, blessed by divine providence—continued to exercise a powerful hold on the imagination.

The question of the lack of correspondence between the vision of an agrarian utopia and actual experience needs more attention.[54] Historians believe that at the beginning of the nineteenth century, before the great push of settlement into the Great Valley, American agriculture outside the South was reasonably well represented by the image of the self-sufficient farmer living with his family on a modest-sized tract of land and with little involvement in the market economy. But in the period between 1815 and 1860 farming was swiftly transformed into a commercial venture; new transportation networks and an increased market caused by the rise of domestic manufacturing turned farming into a cash-crop endeavor and farmers into small entrepreneurs. The fertility of the prairies, the use of machinery on the flat terrain, and the employment of wage laborers on extensive holdings added to the thoroughgoing commercialization of agriculture. The shift was complete in Ohio by 1830, in Indiana, Illinois, and Michigan by the 1850s; what remained unfinished in the process was completed by the needs of the Civil War. Farming in the Midwest, James M. Cox has remarked, never involved growing crops so much as producing them.[55]

The rise of commercial farming was accompanied by increases in land values, and this in turn tempted the agrarian entrepreneur into trying his luck as a land speculator. The result was a farm population that frequently cashed in its profits and moved on to new locations, reenacting the process of settlement again and again. The passage by Congress in 1862 of the Homestead Act, with its vision of a permanent empire of family farmers established through the legal means of passing 160 acres of public-domain land into individual hands for a nominal fee, did little or nothing to halt the trend. As early as the 1830s a restless business-like spirit had seemed to Tocqueville the dominant character-istic of American farming.

> Almost all the farmers of the United States combine some trade with agriculture; most of them make agriculture itself a trade. It seldom happens that an American farmer settles for good upon the land which he occupies; especially in the districts of the Far West, he brings land into tillage in order to sell it again, and not to farm it: he builds a farmhouse on the speculation that, as the state of the country will soon be changed by the increase of population, a good price may be obtained for it.[56]

Here and there settled rural communities were formed with enduring attach-ments to the land, often communities with German or Scandinavian roots or those established by pietistic sects such as the Amish. John Mack Faragher, in a detailed study of the development of a small section of the Sangamon River area of rural Illinois along Sugar Creek, found considerable stability over time and an allegiance to social values. He concluded that the "individual, the cele-brated achievement of western American culture, was surely important; but it was the community along Sugar Creek which prevailed."[57] All the same, the broad agricultural Midwest under the sway of commercial farming and land speculation bore little resemblance to the simple paradise of the garden myth. On the whole the Midwest of fact was a varied and frequently unstable land-scape populated by bankers, store owners, middlemen of every sort, and farmers who struggled with machinery, mortgages, railroads, and the vagaries of soil, climate, and market conditions. The Midwestern countryside provided little if any shield against the swift and uprooting change of American life. Mark Twain remembered in *Life on the Mississippi* that when he had lived in Keokuk, Iowa, in 1857 there had been feverish real-estate speculation in which "everybody bought, everybody sold": "Anything in the semblance of a town lot, no matter how situated, was salable, and at a figure which would still have been high if the ground had been sodded with greenbacks."[58] When he came in the 1940s to write a book about the Sangamon for the Rivers of America series, Edgar Lee Masters would find the land of his late nineteenth-century youth virtually changed beyond recognition, and in his bewildered response effectively capture the sense of rural impermanence:

> But ah the landscape changes! Not merely by the disappearance of a barn or a house or a corncrib here and there, but by the vanishment of orchards, and strips of forest. . . . That country, billowing up and down, and once marked with houses and barns that I knew, was all strange.[59]

The shocks of natural disasters and economic depression in the western re-gions of the Midwest beginning in the 1870s led to the first glimmerings of awareness of a gap between what Henry Nash Smith calls "image and fact, the ideal and the actual, the hope and the consummation"[60] and culminated in the Populist revolt of the 1890s. In turn, the sobering experience of hard times had some bearing on the work of the early Midwestern realists; in one way or another and with varying levels of consciousness or conviction, they pointed out that the facts of the region did not match its fictions. Thereafter in Midwestern writing the garden myth, often particularized in a moment of rural perfection existing between the raw virgin land and its mechanized agribusiness future, provided writers with a similar measure of contemporary life, characters and events happily at one with perfection or, as more often the case, sadly removed from it. With the passing of the pioneering period a splendid story was over, lost somewhere back among the dark fields of the republic, and with its passing sounded the elegiac note that forms the often distant and faintly recognized background of much of Midwestern writing.

6

The reference to the language of Fitzgerald's novel suggests a final general consideration about the literature of the Midwestern ascendancy, one that again points to the ambivalence and complexity underlying its typical expression. Jay Gatsby's dream—a dream, Nick Carraway speculates, that had seemed to him so close to realization that it could not fail to be grasped—had no root in an idealization of nature, with its emphasis on regeneration of the body and spirit through contact with the soil, that was embodied in the garden myth. For Gatsby as for Sally Carrol Happer, the Southern belle who travels north to St. Paul to meet her fiancé's family in Fitzgerald's story "The Ice Palace," nature in the Midwest holds out no appeal. The solitary winter-bound farmhouses glimpsed from her Pullman car strike her as only ugly and bleak and "with each one she had an instant of chill compassion for the souls shut in there waiting for spring."[61] Although Gatsby came from farm people, in his imagination, Nick says, he never accepted them as his parents. From the beginning his imagination was drawn to a vision of material progress and sophisticated life that eventually took vivid and ideal form in the figure of Daisy Buchanan, and so his journey took him not into the heart of the country but to the blue lawns of Long Island. Nick himself, drawn eastward for schooling at Yale and then participation in the Great War, is equally responsive to the lure of civilization. Given what he has seen of the world, he tells us at the beginning of the story that the Midwest had come to seem to him the "ragged edge of the universe,"[62] and so he had left it behind—permanently, he had believed—for New York and a business life. In his removal from the region Nick seems typical. He is one who shares, in Glenway Wescott's remark about Midwesterners, a state of mind of people born where they do not like to live— one of those Midwesterners, in Gore Vidal's rephrasing, "with a dream of some other great good place."[63]

But leaving the Midwest is easier than ridding himself of its presence. Rather than take rooms in the city Nick settles on a bungalow in a commuting town because he had "just left a country of wide lawns and friendly trees" (3). At dinner during his first meeting with Tom and Daisy Buchanan and Jordan Baker it occurs to him that the languid Eastern evening is "sharply different from the West" with its more punctual, edgy style. Over a second glass of claret he confesses to Daisy that "you make me feel uncivilized" and wonders if they could not "talk about crops or something" (13). Even amid New York's towers Nick finds something "almost pastoral" in a warm summer afternoon (28). After Gatsby's murder, the East haunted for him now like a grotesque El Greco, Nick reverses his journey and returns home to a Midwest that now invites him as the "warm center of the world," a place of stability and moral attentiveness as against the "riotous excursions" of the discredited East (3, 2). From this vantage point of return he writes Gatsby's story, a labor of two years, yet there is no certainty he will remain. After the Great War he had also come back to the Midwest—and his move to the East had not been the permanent thing he had thought. Nick is, as he says of himself at one point, a "within and without" figure, "simultaneously enchanted and repelled by the inexhaustible variety of life" (36). In his attitude to the Midwest he swings back and forth, responsive both to the region as the comforting garden and to an opposed vision of civilization that propels him away in search of heightened life. It is precisely this interior division that makes Nick seem so deeply a creation of the region, leaving and returning in a back-and-forth, love-hate relationship, never fully rejecting, never fully accepting.

Henry Nash Smith has persuasively shown that the central difficulty in Turner's formulation of the frontier theory of American development was the historian's immersion in two opposed traditions. His view of the frontier grew directly out of the myth of the garden with its emphasis on rebirth and regeneration in a simple world of cultivated nature; at the same time, he was committed to the idea of civilization that held that societies progressed through stages and that the highest values were found in an urban environment. From one vantage point the Western farmer was seen as a blessed figure living in the agrarian utopia, from the other a coarse representative of an early stage of social and cultural development. The agricultural frontier was the source of American individualism and democracy, yet it was also a passing phase of national development. The dilemma Smith locates in Turner is precisely that (as he equally shows) within the American agrarian tradition in general and its especially intense formulation in the Midwest. Yet a problem calling for a solution from the standpoint of intellectual history—in the closing sentence of *Virgin Land* Smith refers to the need for a "new intellectual system"—seems a fruitful creative tension from the standpoint of literary history. Just as a legacy of defeat well served Southern writing, a central ambivalence within Midwestern life—a lingering feeling for an Edenic past as represented by the garden myth while in full pursuit of progress and the distant towers of refinement and culture—has enriched its literature in the sense of providing it with recurring situations of leave-taking and return as well as, and of more importance, an underlying complexity of conflicting and unresolved attitudes. The Midwest perceived as either the warm center of the world or the ragged edge of the universe has usually been a formula for imaginative work singing the folk charm of the region or dismissing it out of hand as beyond redemption. Held together in some degree of tension, on the other hand, the crosscurrents of Midwestern attitudes have now and then resulted in work of satisfying depth and implication.

Once again, at the end of *The Great Gatsby* Nick Carraway goes home to his and Fitzgerald's native St. Paul, evoked in one of the most familiar and nostalgic passages in the novel:

> That's my Middle West—not the wheat or the prairies or the lost Swede towns, but the thrilling returning trains of my youth, and the street lamps and sleigh bells in the frosty dark and the shadows of holly wreaths thrown by lighted windows on the snow. I am part of that, a little solemn with the feel of those long winters, a little complacent from growing up in the Carraway house in a city where dwellings are still called through decades by a family's name. (177)

Fitzgerald had had the experience of riding trains back to the Midwest from prep school and from Princeton, but his St. Paul was never the solid, timeless place he attributes to Nick. The Fitzgeralds moved repeatedly within the city, never establishing anything close to a home called by a family's name through the decades. When the Fitzgeralds moved to two addresses on prestigious Summit Avenue (at one of which Fitzgerald would write his first novel, *This Side of Paradise*) it was only to yet another rented house. Nick's return to the remembered Midwest of his youth may only be a quixotic gesture in the face of what his creator and perhaps Nick as well know to be true—that there is no warm center to the world, in the Midwest or elsewhere; that there is no place of fixed moral attention forever. Gatsby's dream of timeless perfection embodied in Daisy was already behind him, as Nick points out, overridden by history, and what is true of Gatsby's limitless vision rooted in the East must be equally true of Nick's simple and comforting version of the Midwest. It is another lost dream. Yet in the novel's final line Nick offers an ironic salute to the romantic temperament still alert to the American past and his own particular engagement with it in the act of journeying home. "So we beat on," he says, he now as Gatsby before him, "boats against the current, borne back ceaselessly into the past" (182). It is precisely out of such ambivalent responses to Midwestern experience, such complex displays of within and without feelings, that the region's most enduring literary expressions have emerged.

TWO

Rude Despair

> The main-travelled road in the West (as everywhere) is
> hot and dusty in summer, and desolate and drear with
> mud in fall and spring, and in winter the winds sweep
> the snow across it; but it does sometimes cross a rich
> meadow where the songs of the larks and bobolinks
> and blackbirds are tangled.
>
> —*Main-Travelled Roads*

1

In one of his innumerable volumes of recollection, Hamlin Garland recalled the meeting that turned him from his early ambition as a reform orator and lecturer on literary subjects to a writer of fiction. It was 1887 and he had just published a review in the *Boston Transcript* of a new Midwestern novel with the curious title of *Zury: The Meanest Man in Spring County*. The review was not a task he had tackled with enthusiasm. The author, a Chicago lawyer, was unknown to him and the setting, rural Illinois, struck him as ugly. But the book, surprisingly good, had drawn strong praise, Garland setting it down that Joseph Kirkland had written one of the first genuinely truthful accounts of what he called "American interior society."[1] After a note of appreciation for the review, Kirkland had followed with an invitation to Garland to visit when he passed through Chicago on a trip to Iowa and South Dakota. In due time the reviewer presented himself at the author's Rush Street home.

Kirkland explained that he was the son of Caroline Kirkland, the author of pioneering accounts of the Michigan frontier, and that he had lived much of his own life in downstate Illinois. *Zury* was based on personal acquaintance with Midwestern farm life. The talk then turned to predecessors among Western writers. Neither Howells nor Twain was mentioned; rather, Edward Eggleston was seen as the central figure, Kirkland agreeing with Garland that the Hoosier novelist had provided the first authentic literary accounts of the Midwest. It was Eggleston's work, Kirkland disclosed, that he had tried to better with *Zury*. Garland brought up E. W. Howe's *The Story of a Country Town* as another example of a new strain of Midwestern realism, but Kirkland dismissed the novel by the Kansas newspaper publisher as overly melodramatic. Garland then mentioned some articles he himself had written on farm life, later published as *Boy Life on the Prairie* (1899), but Kirkland responded that although articles were well and good Garland ought to try his hand at fiction; it was the best medium for conveying his knowledge of farm life. The older writer would not be put off by Garland's feeling that fiction was beyond him because of a professed inability to write dialogue. Fiction was something, Kirkland maintained, that Garland must come to as a writer.

The remark stayed with Garland throughout his western trip. "Can I move on into the short-story field?" he wondered. "Can I put the life of Wisconsin and Iowa into fiction as Eggleston has done for Indiana and as Kirkland is doing for Illinois?"[2] At his parents' South Dakota wheat farm he put himself to the test. He turned out a mild local-color story, based on an anecdote his mother had told him, called "Mrs. Ripley's Trip" and promptly sold it to *Harper's Weekly*. But another kind of story was simmering in him, one exposing what he now perceived as the inner truth of Midwestern life, and especially the grim features of farm existence as he saw them revealed in his mother's work-burdened and isolated world. In a letter to Howe he had previously pointed out the absence of genuinely penetrating literary accounts of the region:

> The West is not known as yet. All that vast, seething, transfiguring mass of men in the Mississippi valley, because they have not produced their own writers, are unknown. Travellers go through and write a few lines as observers. Here and there some one writes of material or semi-material things in prose. *None* have given the deep, unseen, true *life* of the people.[3]

Four years after his first story, and following continued editorial advice from the generous Kirkland about how to turn raw feelings into fiction, Garland published a slim volume of stories (two of them, in his view, novelettes) called *Main-Travelled Roads: Six Stories of the Mississippi Valley*. With the book he both joined and surpassed Eggleston, Kirkland, and Howe in the quartet of leading early interpreters of the region in a realistic vein. He had produced a work of deeply uneven quality, yet one that would endure as the most telling of his career and the central accomplishment of the first significant period of Midwestern writing. For the first time, as Garland himself had put it, the deep, unseen, true life of the region had found an effective voice.

2

Reading Edward Eggleston now, one hesitates before any conception of him as a literary innovator. The weaknesses of his seven novels with a Midwestern setting are all too apparent: his commitment to the love story tradition of sentimental fiction; the use of stock characters, stilted dialogue, and creaky plots;

an unwavering inclination to preach. Yet innovator of sorts he was. In American writing he holds a place at the forefront of the turn toward realism as well as at the beginning of the serious literary interpretation of the Midwest. In his first and most celebrated novel, *The Hoosier School-Master*, published in 1871, traces of the theory of stages of society, with its doctrine of frontier inferiority as seen from the perspective of civilization, still linger. A minor theme in the story is Bud Means's ambition to "git out of this low-lived Flat Crick way of livin'," a backwoods existence that tends to grind life down to a mean level. In the novel's preface Eggleston had alluded to a concern that readers from more "refined regions" even of the West might find offensive his treatment of the rough manners of what he termed "an exceptional phase of life."[4] Brother Sodom's fire-and-brimstone preaching is defended within the novel on the grounds that a "religion without fear could never have evangelized or civilized the West, which at one time bade fair to become a perdition as bad as any that Brother Sodom ever depicted" (203). Nonetheless, "Backwoods Life in Indiana"—as Eggleston indicated the novel's setting in the book's subtitle—is generally approached with genial good humor and a lack of moral or social disapproval. Frank Norris, in the context of a discussion of the Great American Novel (which he thought was bound to be sectional given the variety of American life), raised the example of Eggleston as one who "has gone deep into the life of the Middle West."[5] Even for a present-day analyst of the development of realism, Eggleston holds an honorable position as the author of "protorealist novels."[6]

"Want to be a school-master, do you?" demands a skeptical Jack Means in the novel's opening line, ushering the genteel hero, Ralph Hartsook, into the rough-and-tumble world of education in Flat Creek, Indiana. Though taken aback by the crusty school trustee's description of the hazards in store for him, Ralph is determined to succeed as a schoolmaster, and the early chapters follow his dogged efforts to keep order in a one-room school from which the "boys have driv off the last two, and licked the one afore them like blazes" (11). When he at length gains the upper hand through nerve, wit, and the aid of Bud Means, the school bully, Eggleston turns the novel to more familiar matters for readers of nineteenth-century popular fiction: on-again, off-again romance; mysterious night-time robberies for which the hero is wrongly accused; a lengthy courtroom scene; an ending in which good is rewarded and evil punished. Sympathetic characters are woven into the spare narrative (Shocky, Hannah, Bud Means) as well as appropriate villains (Pete Jones, Doctor Small), and over everything Eggleston casts a heavy spell of sentiment and religiosity. Both elements merge in Shocky, an outcast Dickensian figure who wavers between bleak doubt about divine providence ("I wonder if God forgets all about poor folks when their father dies and their mother gits into the poor-house") and ecstatic affirmation ("God ha'n't forgot us, mother; God ha'n't forgot us") (83, 169). In the epilogue the reader learns of Shocky's unlikely career as a professor, one W. J. Thomson, who spends his spare time "making outcasts feel that God has not forgot" (226).

Such as they were, the novel's ingredients were right for the time. *The Hoosier School-Master* sold 20,000 copies in its first year, was widely reprinted in local newspapers, and was immediately pirated by English publishers and brought out in a French translation with the imposing title *Le Maître d'École du Flat Creek*. In *Golden Multitudes*, a 1947 study of popular books in America, Frank Luther Mott estimated that the novel probably had sold a half-million copies to that point. The success of his first effort in full-length fiction overshadowed Eggleston's subsequent novels, including more substantial works such as *The Circuit Rider* (1874) and *Roxy* (1878), and his later distinguished career as a social historian. Eggleston's fate, shared with each of the early Midwestern realists, has been to be remembered primarily for a first book and for a place in literary history more than for his rudimentary art.

The novel appeared originally in installments in *Hearth and Home*, a family weekly magazine Eggleston was trying to revive in New York after careers in Minnesota and Illinois as a Methodist minister and a popular speaker on the Sunday-school circuit.[7] Up to this point in his life he had shown no interest in fiction; now he saw it as a means of breathing new life into the magazine. For material for his story he drew on memories of his Indiana boyhood in the Ohio River towns of Vevay, Madison, and New Albany, and especially on the experience of his brother, George Cary Eggleston (at the time an associate on the magazine and later his successor as editor), as a teacher in the backwoods community of Riker's Ridge. Originally, the plan was for a story in three installments, but with a sharp upswing in circulation after the first installment Eggleston pushed it to fourteen episodes and novel length. Extending the story meant going beyond his brother's experience and indulging in the familiar staples of melodrama; nonetheless, much of the work's immediate appeal came from the freshness of its regional setting and language. In a perceptive review in the *Atlantic*, Howells said Eggleston had drawn "a picture of manners hitherto strange to literature," adding that through the book "we are made acquainted with the rudeness and ugliness of the intermediate West, after the days of pioneering, and before the days of civilization."[8] The review, it so happened, was part of an effort on Howells's part, begun with his rise to the editorship of the *Atlantic* in the same year as the novel's publication, to bring more Western material into the pages of a magazine deeply identified with New England culture while yet holding on to its influential readers. When the question of reviewing Eggleston's book first came up, Howells was divided; given its subject matter, mention of the book was a considerable departure from the magazine's usual fare. Finally, stirred by Mark Twain's published recollections of the West as well as his own rekindled memories of Ohio, he went ahead, informing his readers that the book was important for anyone who seriously wished to understand the nation.

For the novel's appearance in book form, a limited edition of 2,000 copies published by Orange, Judd, and Company, the owners of *Hearth and Home*, Eggleston added a preface in which he pointed to a regional motive behind the work: a desire to break the literary monopoly of rural New England that had left the "back-country districts of the Western States" largely unrecorded. Only Alice Cary of Ohio, whose stories and sketches had appeared in the 1850s, had previously tried to write honestly about the rural West, but despite her contributions (which Eggleston qualified with a "perhaps"), the literary West remained the "unreal world" imagined in the adventure novels of Fenimore Cooper (5).[9] A preface written for an 1891 edition of the book took note of other influences. One was reading for review a translation of Hippolyte Taine's *Philosophy of Art in the Netherlands* with its emphasis on the use of common materials in pictorial art, a position easily carried over into local-color fiction. A more important influence was Eggleston's long-standing scientific interest in the language of the Indiana frontier as it had existed some forty years earlier. Eight years before his novel was published he had jotted down a list of dialect words and phrases that he called "Hoosierisms" ("heap of rain," "mighty purty," "all-firedest"), and in 1870 he corresponded with James Russell Lowell about the list. The enthusiastic response of the Harvard professor and author of the *Biglow Papers* gave legitimacy to the interest and seems a clear stepping stone on the way to *The Hoosier School-Master*, carrying over into the glimpses Eggleston gives of the folkways of rural life: coon hunts, spelling bees, revival meetings. Earlier literary uses of dialect had served to identify the low social status and regional standing of characters. With Eggleston, elements of that use remain, but more important is a fascination with Western speech and customs in themselves rather than as a measure of status or refinement—with simply describing, for example, a character carrying a "bucket of milk" and then pointing out within the text that the word "pail" was not used in Indiana (141). In the novel's original preface Eggleston had paid tribute to Lowell's "careful attention to dialects" and pointed out that although he himself had not provided a scholarly discussion of the "provincialism of the Indiana backwoods, I have been careful to preserve the true *usus loquendi* of each locution" (6).

Eggleston's feeling for Western folk speech and customs was genuine enough but fairly shallow, as least as it manifests itself in fiction. In his first novel it exists only on the periphery of a story centered on the refined schoolmaster, hardly distinguishable from any proper Easterner, and dominated by a mystery-story plot that Eggleston would continue to fall back upon in later novels. Early realism such as Eggleston's coexisted—in Bernard Duffey's apt phrase—in a twilight zone with the conventions of local-color fiction that inclined the writer to touch up reality, or nearly abandon it altogether, in the name of popular entertainment.[10] If Eggleston had one eye on actual experience, another was on the trappings of fiction drawn from books; the result was a work realistic in some of its detail yet sentimental and romantic in overall effect.

Eggleston's ambiguous literary example would be picked up in the two decades following *The Hoosier School-Master* in the mawkish local-color poetry of such figures as Will Carleton and James Whitcomb Riley and in the more sophisticated popular fiction of Gene Stratton-Porter and especially Booth Tarkington. In this sense Eggleston's contention in his 1891 preface that his novel was the "file-leader of the procession of American dialect novels" can be viewed with mixed feelings (6). But Eggleston's example led in another way as well—toward realistic interpretations of the rural Midwest increasingly free of the bias of social theory and class feeling. The most telling result of the latter line of development was a small body of agrarian protest writing arising from a far deeper commitment to Western materials than Eggleston's and far darker in its implication than anything he had imagined—the work of Kirkland, Howe, and finally Garland. It was this dual inheritance from Eggleston's initial interest in frontier speech and custom that Garland had in mind when he declared—in the setting of a New York testimonial dinner for Booth Tarkington during the First War—that "we must not forget that Edward Eggleston was the father of us all."[11]

3

In *Zury*, Kirkland carries on Eggleston's interest in the precise rendering of Western dialect, even appending to the novel a glossary of dialect terms. He also reveals Eggleston's delight in Western customs with lengthy accounts of farm activity on the Illinois prairie (the process, for example, of "niggering off" logs by building fires to separate them into lengths rather than the laborious process of chopping). And he exhibits many of Eggleston's weaknesses as a craftsman, including a taste for melodrama, a commitment to the notion of the novel as a love story, and the use of an intrusive narrative voice. Like *The Hoosier School-Master, Zury* is important as a cultural document, not as a work of art; yet it remains a far richer response to Midwestern material than Eggleston's book. It draws more deeply on personal experience, and in general it is a more substantial attempt at depicting—and, by implication at least, commenting upon—the experience of early settlement and development.

The story follows the career of Zury (short for Usury) Prouder from young manhood, when he comes to Illinois with his parents to take up prairie land granted his father for service in the War of 1812, through to middle age. Although sharp business practices carry his interests far beyond the farm, Zury stays on the original homestead and flourishes as a farmer. The initial paragraph announces the story's main theme—the triumph over the harsh forces of nature on the prairie through the determined exercise of will:

> Great are the toils and terrible the hardships that go to the building up of a frontier farm; inconceivable to those who have not done the task or watched its doing. In the prairies, Nature has stored, and preserved thus far through the ages, more life-materials than she ever before amassed in the same space. It is all for man, but only for such men as can take it by courage and hold it by endurance. Many assailants are slain, many give up and fly, but he who is sufficiently brave, and strong, and faithful, and fortunate, to maintain the fight to the end, has ample his reward.[12]

The novel's opening chapters vividly trace the fierce work of building up the 640 acres of virgin land. Faced with what seem insurmountable difficulties,

Zury redoubles his efforts, bringing to them a native inventiveness and almost superhuman energy. With the death of his parents he takes control of the farm and soon emerges as the most prosperous farmer and leading citizen in Spring County. He dominates local boards, is elected to the state legislature, and his business interests eventually extend to lead mining in western Illinois.

In a final chapter set in the 1850s, some thirty years after the first breaking of the prairie sod, Zury's prosperity is set out in glowing detail. The rough cabin has given way to a mansion filled with modern conveniences; attached to the house is a greenhouse which opens onto a flower garden and orchard; the surrounding fields reveal the most up-to-date agricultural methods. The thriving farm is also the abode of happiness and heightened life. Zury has a new wife (his third), Anne Sparrow McVey, and a lively young son; he is running for a seat in Congress; and—the final certification of success—a tour of Europe is in the offing. The farm and its abundant life clearly represent the achieved agrarian paradise. Nature's soil and man's labor, Kirkland says at the end, "have worked (like coral insects) to make a lovely island where was before a pathless waste" (509). Still, there are complicating factors which undermine any simple reading of the novel as a straightforward celebration of the garden myth.

Kirkland's book had a lengthy genesis compared to Eggleston's sudden turn to fiction and the rushed composition of *The Hoosier School-Master*. Like Eggleston, Kirkland came to fiction late in life; when he began writing *Zury* he was over fifty years old, with careers already behind him as a mine operator in down-state Illinois and a journalist and Chicago lawyer. There was nothing surprising, however, about his move to fiction. He had long intended to follow in the footsteps of his mother's accounts of family experiences in Michigan—in *A New Home—Who'll Follow?* (1839), *Forest Life* (1842), and *Western Clearings* (1845)[13]—but it was not until he was admitted to the bar in 1880 and his financial situation had eased that he felt himself ready to turn to writing in earnest. He had already developed a theory of qualified realism derived from Howells that he later expressed in a ten-word creed: "Let only truth be told, and not all the truth."[14] In 1883 he began putting theory to practice with a story drawn from the lives of Usual H. and John Meeker (Kirkland altering the surname Meeker to something more symbolically right for his central character), a father and son whose hard work, sharp business practices, and considerable fortune had inspired tall tales in the Illinois region Kirkland had known over a ten-year period. He drew as well on his early memories of the Michigan community where he had lived with his parents. When the novel appeared in 1887, reviewers recognized its feeling of authenticity. Howells, writing in *Harper's Monthly*, promptly praised Kirkland as an able recruit to realism who was "incapable of painting life other than he had found it."[15]

One notable thing Kirkland had found was that the farmer's exercise of will in beneficent nature was not a sufficient avenue to success. Howells correctly noted that Kirkland had drawn a literary portrait of a Western farmer whose aim was not self sufficiency or the simple joys of rural life but the accumulation of money. Although Kirkland gently satirizes the zealous pursuit of cash that gains his hero the reputation as the meanest man with a dollar in the county (he would pinch one, it is said, "till the eagle on it squealed"), it is clear that Zury correctly understands the nature of farm survival (65). Early in the account of Zury's struggle to maintain the farm, and just following the death of his sickly young sister, Kirkland sets out the bleak prospect before him:

> That evening was a sad one at the log hut. Half the section mortgaged and nothing to show for it but *this*. Not one cent in money, nothing to eat, drink, or wear, a growing crop that might be worth ten cents a bushel three months hence, and a little unsodded grave without even a fence around it. (50)

There is talk of going back East, but Zury hatches a plan to mortgage another quarter section and purchase hogs as a way of building a cash stake. He confides to his father the hard-eyed ambition that lies behind the plan:

> "Dad, I'm goin' t' own a mortgage 'fore I die; mind what I say."
> "Hope ye will, Zury. Yew'll have a holt of the right eend of the poker then; 'n' t' other feller he'll have a holt 'o the hot part, same's we've got naow."
> "You bet! An' it'll sizzle his hands, tew, afore I'll ever let up on him." (53)

Experience in the agrarian garden teaches Zury not that nature is sufficient but that "money was life; the absence of money was death," and so he seeks the power of cash with single-minded devotion (30). This leaves him, as Kirkland acknowledges, "a strong intellect pent into a narrow channel," an engaging but one-dimensional figure with neither friends nor interests, yet one who acts on the actual dynamics of farm life as against the messages of myth (65). In the agrarian setting Zury pursues a competing ideal—what Richard Hofstadter has called "the notion of opportunity, of career, of the self-made man." His career on the land vividly illustrates Hofstadter's argument that commercial farming in the Midwest hindered the development of a genuinely rural culture based on, as he puts it, "an emotional and craftsmanlike dedication to the soil, a traditional and pre-capitalist outlook, a tradition-directed rather than career-directed type of character, and a village community devoted to ancestral ways and habitually given to communal action."[16] Zury's dedication is to mortgages and notes more than to the soil, to individual endeavor more than to communal action. Kirkland provides any number of humorous glimpses of his ambition at work. In one, Zury recounts for his father his triumph over a local blacksmith:

> "I upped 'n' sold the smith a half an acre, 'n' took a mortgage on it, 'n' made him dew all aour repairin' b'way of interest on the mortgage, 'n' then foreclosed th' mortgage when it came dew, 'n' got th' land back, shop 'n' all. Business is business!" (77)

A prairie farm serves as his base of operations but Zury's methods are no different from those of any tough-minded urban or small-town entrepreneur.

Although in this sense the novel obviously qualifies the uneconomic vision of life at heart of the garden myth, it is doubtful that such broad implications were clearly formulated in Kirkland's mind. At the end of the novel it is said only that, as the myth would have it, nature's soil and man's labor have transformed the primitive homestead into a lush garden, the author bypassing the more significant role of notes and mortgages. Kirkland may have been equally unaware of the implications of his heroine's role in the story—a role that qualifies the garden myth in even more telling fashion.

From Lowell, Massachusetts, and an advanced thinker, Anne Sparrow comes to Illinois to teach in the county school. With her alien background she provides Kirkland with a spokesperson for many corrective views of rural life, among them a distinctly anti-romantic view of nature. She contrasts, for example, rural and urban poverty and ridicules the notion that it is better to live in the country than the city. In the East, she maintains, not even the poor-house folk would accept grim Western living conditions:

> . . . they would not have put up with it. And those naturalistic enthusiasts—how sublimely they talk about the charms of Nature! How sacred Nature's mysteries! How much more you adored her the nearer you got to her! How inalienable the rights of all her creatures, even the humblest and least attractive! Ugh! Did they know about bugs! Are malodorous parasites Nature's creatures with inalienable rights? Stuff! Mankind has been for twenty thousand years improving upon Nature, subduing her forces and killing her bugs—now the idea of going back! (109)

Yet Anne's place in the novel is even larger. She brings Eastern refinement and intellect to the primitive West, softening its rough edge, finally softening the roughest edge of all, Zury Prouder. It is true that Anne undergoes some change herself in that she comes to respect and depend upon the friendliness and openness she finds in Spring County, especially as these qualities are exhibited by Zury and by the Anstey family, Zury's poor but durable neighbors. John McVey, a character who shares Anne's Eastern background and civilized tastes, is portrayed as an ineffectual dreamer lacking Zury's strength of will; Anne eventually marries McVey in a desperate effort to provide her unborn child (by Zury, with whom, pathologically afraid of the dark, she spends a night during a prairie fire) with a father, yet she recognizes his weakness and feels little regret when he conveniently disappears on a trip to the distant West. Anne admires some of the human qualities she finds in the Midwest yet remains aware of what is narrow and unattractive about the region and refuses to fully accept life in Spring County for herself or her children. To finally win her in an improbable marriage, Zury must be transformed into Anne's vision of him—kindly, generous, a dialect-speaking country squire.

By novel's end Zury has emerged from poverty and narrow self interest to gentility and warm human feeling. The primary agent of transformation is not wholesome experience in the Midwestern garden but the demands of an Eastern figure of civilization whom Zury finally accepts, as Kirkland puts it, with "docility and devotion" (508). It is neither determined effort nor the accumulation of money that finally alters the Prouder farm into a lovely island but the refined presence of Anne Sparrow. Aunt Anstey would seem to be speaking for the author when she tells Anne in the novel's closing pages that she has been Zury's "chiefest heavenly marcy! He wuz a pootty poor speciment in them [early] days, 'n' would a be'n so yet ef it hadn't a be'n fer yew!" (519).

For present-day readers the strength of the novel is Kirkland's portrayal of Zury's single-minded drive to prosper on the farm—a part of the novel informed with earthy admiration for the character and a zest for rural life and speech. When Anne enters the story Kirkland's response to the actual conditions of Midwestern life gives way to book-inspired plot turns of romance. Yet Anne plays a significant role in the implications that can be drawn from the novel. Just as it is cash rather than beneficent nature or human will that forms the basis for Zury's success, it is Anne that inspires the change of character that renders him an idealized rural type. Kirkland had little to say about his intentions in *Zury* beyond the hope, expressed to Garland, of improving upon Eggleston; but taken as a whole, both the account of Zury's rise in the world and his inner change, the novel has the effect of calling into question most of the tenets of the garden myth. In *The McVeys: An Episode*, published the year after *Zury* and based on material cut from the novel before publication, Kirkland refers to the altered Zury as "possessed of a heart and soul fairly typical of the great and generous West in its ideal development."[17] If the passage is meant to affirm Zury's final identification with the garden myth in Kirkland's imagination, it sidesteps the fact that the means to that end, as Kirkland had amply recounted them, were hardly those set forth by the myth.

4

Rather than a realistic work in the line of *The Hoosier School-Master* and *Zury*, Kirkland maintained that Howe's *The Story of a Country Town*, published four years before his own book, "never had any existence outside of his [Howe's] tired brain."[18] What he apparently had in mind is the bookish melodrama that heavily burdens the novel—tolling church bells, a deserted wife maintaining a light in the window, a wandering sea captain united with a long-lost child, character names freighted with obvious meaning. There is another sense, however, in which Kirkland's comment points to what *is* authentic about the book, giving it a small but secure place in the early fitful development of realism coming out of the Midwest. The titles of Eggleston's and Kirkland's books emphasized characters; Howe's drew attention to an environment, a country town and surrounding farm district.[19] The most notable feature of the novel is the bleak effect, overwhelmingly sad and gloomy, of that rural world upon the jumble of characters. Kirkland may have sensed what we now know to be true: that the source of Howe's grim account was lodged deep within private experience.

Edgar Watson Howe grew up in Bethany, Missouri, the son of a farmer and later a newspaper editor who held ardent religious views of a fundamentalist sort. The father deserted the family when Howe was in his teens following a scandal involving his wife's widowed sister. Howe followed a career as a typesetter and printer in the Midwest, finally settling in Atchison, Kansas, where he edited and published a daily newspaper. After his retirement in 1910 he published for the next two decades *E. W. Howe's Monthly*, dispensing a popular cracker-barrel philosophy of rugged individualism and common sense. After moving to Atchison, Howe and his wife had lived apart, refusing to speak, and were soon divorced. Although Howe had suffered from his father's hard treatment of his children, his own children were subjected to the same angry ways. One of his sons later wrote a *Saturday Evening Post* article about him with the unsparing title "My Father Was the Most Wretchedly Unhappy Man I Ever Knew."

In a preface to a later edition of the novel, Howe said he wrote *The Story of a Country Town* at night and in a spirit of dissatisfaction after full days of newspaper work that left him constantly tired. When several publishers rejected the finished work, he printed it himself in an edition of 2,000 copies under the imprint Howe and Company. Howells and Twain, among others, received copies from Howe and responded with such enthusiasm that the book was republished in 1884 by the Boston house of James R. Osgood, starting it on its way to considerable success. Praise came from both Western and Eastern readers and centered on the book's originality in its portrayal of grim rural actuality. Within two years *The Story of a Country Town* had been reprinted twenty-five times; a half-century later *Publisher's Weekly* would estimate that a hundred editions had appeared from six different publishers.

Twain's letter to Howe after receiving the book was admiring (while humorously alert to the work's technical faults) but accurately predicted that "you may have caught the only fish there was in your pond." In Howe's subsequent novels—*The Mystery of the Locks* (1885), *A Moonlight Boy* (1886), *A Man Story* (1887)—realistic elements were overwhelmed by romance and problems of craft were magnified. It seems clear enough now that the strength of the first novel was founded on an exercise in self therapy, Howe trying to come to terms with his demons by writing about them. His harsh childhood, his relationship with his puritanical father, and a fierce strain of jealousy that twisted his feelings toward women all found a place in the novel. What seems authentic and oddly moving in the work is an autobiographical account of personal grievance—the workings of a "tired brain," as Kirkland had it—awkwardly interwoven with the conventions of melodrama. Even the geography of the novel is almost exactly drawn from Bethany, Missouri, and the surrounding area. But the novel's roots in Howe's private experience do not explain its importance for his contemporaries. For them, the heart of the book was the startling portrait of the agricultural West that Howells emphasized in a review—one that "does not flatter the West, nor paint its rough and rude traits as heroic," one in which "harshness and aridity" prevail.[20]

With the opening sentence Ned Westlock, the narrator, announces the high ambition that provides an ironic backdrop for the sense of disillusionment that pervades the story. "Ours was the prairie district, out West," he begins, "where we had gone to grow up with the country."[21] But as Ned describes it, the country district of Fairview is only a backwater in the wave of western migration, strangely bypassed for cheaper but less fertile land farther on. The occasional settler who remains is "too poor and tired to follow the others"; but whether he stays in Fairview or follows the current west he finds an equally forlorn world. Farther on are settlements "where he who was deepest in debt was the leading citizen, and where bankruptcy caught them all at last." In the Fairview district the inhabitants seem to feel no financial pressure, but Ned says that one of his earliest childhood impressions was "the fact that our people seemed to be miserable and discontented," and he wondered that "they did not load their effects on wagons again, and move away from a place which made all the men surly and rough, and the women pale and fretful" (2). The tone of the novel's opening is reinforced by Ned's description of his boyhood in Fairview—lonely, work-ridden, darkened by the fanatical morality of his father, the Reverend John Westlock.

The physical landscape is attractive enough—Ned describes Fairview as "very pretty country," and he says that everyone who came there was favorably impressed with the fertility of the soil (185). Nor, once again, is money a problem. Reverend Westlock is a prosperous farmer and most people in the district do well enough; in time, Ned says, the whole area experienced a "general prosperity" (57). But everyone is worn out by labor on the land. Lytle Biggs, a cynical rural politician who serves as a spokesman for Howe's own disillusioned views, says of farming that the notion that there is particular merit in contact with the land is a deliberate falsehood circulated by unscrupulous politicians not unlike himself. He tells Ned:

> "Getting up very early in the morning, and going about agricultural work all day in rough clothes, does not particularly tend to clear the conscience, but because politicians who occasionally have use for them have said these things, the farmers go on accepting them, stubbornly refusing to be undeceived, because it is unpleasant to acknowledge ignorance after you have once thought yourself very cunning." (240)

At the deepest level the blighted life of Fairview seems linked to spiritual failure. Everyone attends church services but there is little display of genuine religious conviction. "The business of serving the Lord was dispatched as soon as possible," Ned says, "to allow the people to return home and nurse their misery" (37). Reverend Westlock's dour morality yields him no pleasure—a religion of present misery in hope of future reward. When Ned looks back on his early life in Fairview, his dominant impression is of the "cold, changing shadow of the gray church." The rooms of the house in which he lived are imagined as "damp and moldy because the bright sun and the free air of heaven had deserted them as a curse" (11).

Western life is portrayed as no more appealing when the story shifts to Twin Mounds, the country town of the title where Reverend Westlock takes over a weekly newspaper while retaining his prairie farm. Narrow ambition rules the town—petty business affairs, heated biblical disputes, zeal for public office. When Reverend Westlock deserts his family for a woman who has sung in his church choir, the novel's focus turns to another compulsive character, Jo Erring, the narrator's uncle though only a few years older, who rises in the world through dint of energy and will to become a miller in the Fairview district only to be struck down by irrational jealousy. Jo murders Clinton Bragg (Reverend Westlock confessed to Ned that if he had not left Twin Mounds he himself would have murdered someone), an early suitor of his wife, Mateel, then takes his own life while awaiting trial. Mateel in turn suffers a mental breakdown and dies. In the novel's final chapter the reader learns that Mateel has been buried beside Jo in the Fairview churchyard and that Ned, now married to Agnes Deming, an old love, has inherited Jo's mill and land from his father and become an aristocratic figure. Howe reaches for some happy effects at the end, but the sense of gloom with which he began the novel lingers. Ned thinks about the graves of Jo and Mateel and again imagines the gray Fairview church where "the great bell is tolling a muffled requiem for their unfortunate history from the rickety tower" (413).

The stories of Reverend John Westlock and Jo Erring awkwardly divide the novel into two parts, and despite the emphasis on the town in the title most of the story's action takes place in the country district. Perhaps Howe's major technical weakness is an inability to dramatize crucial moments in the story, with the result that Reverend Westlock leaves a letter revealing his internal struggle and Jo Erring describes in lengthy talk his jealous torment. Yet these and other flaws detract little from what remains important about the book. In his review Howells saw that "it is not in the presentation of individuals, however, but rather in the realization of a whole order of things, that the strength of the book lies." That whole order of things apparent to Howe's contemporaries and still striking is the mood of failed promise clinging to at least the western region of the agricultural Midwest. Out of his sense of personal failure Howe was able to fashion an agrarian world marked by material success but strangely blighted in spirit—an "intolerably sad" Midwest, as Howells called it, that had "quenched the light of dreams in which [men] came out to possess the new land."[22]

5

Lytle Biggs informs Ned Westlock in *The Story of a Country Town* that in reality agricultural newspapers only pander to the ignorance of farmers, assuring them that whatever they do is right, bolstering their sense of themselves as happy yeomen. "Everybody except the farmers," he says about the papers, "knew what dreadful frauds they were" (239). Like Biggs's remark, Howe's novel has the effect of exposing the garden myth as fraudulent, and it is in this sense that it seems a forerunner of Garland's tales of agrarian disenchantment in *Main-Travelled Roads*. While Eggleston and Kirkland pursued an interest in folk language and custom into an elementary Midwestern realism, no such concern is apparent in Howe. His characters speak a conventional literary rhetoric without regional coloration and he shows little interest in the peculiarities of Western ways. In Garland there is more attention to capturing both the flavor of rural speech and the details of its characteristic life, but the striking connection that links his work with Howe more than with that of Eggleston or Kirkland is exactly the dark element in *Country Town* that Garland called a "singularly gloomy" quality, a "tone of weary and hopeless age."[23]

Yet if there is an evident carryover of feeling from Howe's novel to Garland's stories, the source of the feeling is quite different. The sadness that permeates Howe's novel has no clearly defined cause, though as much as anything it seems the product of a haunting sense of spiritual failure. For Garland the gloom that afflicts the agrarian garden is precisely located, or is meant to be, in an unjust economic system that dooms the farmer to a life of debt and unbroken toil. Howe's farmers succeed well enough, and Kirkland's Zury prospers; but Garland's farmers usually know only distress. At one level of intention his stories have the social purpose of bringing the plight of farmers to public light, thereby affecting the system. At a deeper level there is the realization that change is unlikely and that he can only uncover the hard truth about rural life buried beneath the rosy glow of the garden myth. In one of the stories a Garland-like character, briefly back in the Midwest, questions himself about the lives of farmers: "What could he do to make life better worth living?" And answers: "Nothing. They must live and die practically as he saw them to-night."[24] In each case the conviction behind Garland's vision, at once the product of his present personal experience and his awareness of the historic experience of the rural Midwest in the 1880s and early 1890s, gives to his work an edge of immediacy and group feeling lacking in the groping, backward-looking realism of his predecessors. At the same time Garland brought to his early stories a theoretical commitment to local-color realism of an impressionistic sort and a serious—if never serious enough—concern with craft. The result was work that, for the first time in Midwestern writing, retains some interest for literary as well as social and cultural reasons.

In his autobiographical volumes Garland told and retold the story of the unlikely transformation of a farm boy into a man of letters. Lured by a vision of ever richer land to the west, his father marched the family after the Civil War from Wisconsin to a succession of farms in Iowa, Minnesota, and South Dakota. Although Garland himself staked a claim on a homestead in the James River Valley of South Dakota, farm work held no appeal for him. Through a smattering of education he picked up a taste for reading (in *Hearth and Home* he devoured installments of *The Hoosier School-Master*) and a vague desire to become a teacher and orator. In 1884 he sold his claim and journeyed to Boston in search of something better. For a time he had only exchanged one kind of poverty for another, living in a cramped room, eating little, reading in the public library, until gradually he began scratching out a living as a reviewer, lecturer, and writer of articles. He also began the life-long practice of searching out literary figures that led to acquaintances with Howells and Whitman and, after his review of *Zury* in 1887, with Kirkland.

Kirkland's recommendation that he pursue fiction, together with his experience that summer as a transplanted Easterner returning home, turned Garland in a new direction. In fiction he would expose what he now perceived as the reality of farm life, cutting through the romantic idealization that obscured its true nature. "All the gilding of farm life melted away," he wrote about his new attitude.

> The hard and bitter realities came back upon me in a flood. Nature was as beautiful as ever. The soaring sky was filled with shining clouds, the tinkle of the bobolink's fairy bells rose from the meadow, a mystical sheen was on the odorous grass and waving grain, but no splendor of cloud, no grace of sunset could conceal the poverty of these people, on the contrary they brought out, with a more intolerable poignancy, the gracelessness of these homes, and the sordid quality of the mechanical daily routine of these lives.

His return to the West provided a flood of dreary impressions and his Eastern reading—Darwin and Spencer and especially the single-tax message of Henry George—handed him a framework for understanding. Nature was not to blame for the hopeless conditions of farm life. Man's laws were at fault.

> Instructed by my new philosophy I now perceived that these plowmen, these wives and daughters had been pushed out into these lonely ugly shacks by the force of landlordism behind. These plodding Swedes and Danes, these thrifty Germans, these hairy Russians had all fled from the feudalism of their native lands and were here because they had no share in the soil from which they sprung, and because in the settled communities of the eastern states, the speculative demand for land had hindered them from acquiring even a leasing right to the surface of the earth.[25]

A second trip to Dakota the following year only confirmed his bleak vision, especially as he saw again the ravaging effects of farm life upon his mother, who suffered a stroke during his visit. Guilt at having abandoned her as well as his own Western traditions was combined as a creative spur with a sense of superiority as an escaped Midwesterner and a sudden passion for truth telling. At the same time he was presented with an ideal outlet for his work in B. O. Flower's new reform magazine, *Arena*, where he was urged to expose Western conditions without the "slightest restraint."[26] It was at Flower's suggestion that he put together a collection of six stories, two of them previously unpublished, in *Main-Travelled Roads*, brought out by the Arena Publishing Company in 1891. In later editions more stories were added, finally bringing the volume to twelve stories in a final edition in 1930. The later work, projecting a more nostalgic view of the Midwest, altered the generally coherent attitude of the original volume and diminished its biting impact.

Although at age thirty-one Garland had, as he later recalled, "the Middle West almost entirely to myself" as subject matter,[27] he was soon edging away from full commitment to his material. Unlike the first novels of Eggleston, Kirkland, and Howe, his book sold little and stirred up a modest storm of resentment. Howells was perceptive and generous in *Harper's Weekly*, calling the book "heart-breaking in its rude despair,"[28] but critics and editorial writers in the West accused Garland of painting a falsely dark portrait of rural life. Claiming to be astonished by the reaction, Garland would shortly begin the process of separating himself from the radical embrace of the *Arena*, seeking literary approval by striking, as he put it, "a certain balance between Significance and Beauty."[29] But before that his outrage at farm conditions inspired a burst of activity in which he spun out a companion volume of stories, *Prairie Folks* (1892), and three tract works in support of rural economic grievances that had come together in the 1890s under the banner of the People's Party—*Jason Edwards* (1891), *A Member of the Third House* (1892), *A Spoil of Office* (1892). His critical statements of adherence to realism (or, as he called it, "veritism") and the new literary currents of the day, *Crumbling Idols*, followed in 1894 and the novel *Rose of Dutcher's Coolly* in 1895. With the latter work—an account, paralleling Garland's own career, of the adaptation of a young woman from Wisconsin to metropolitan life—he abandoned "significance" and with it the Midwest as imaginative ground, turning to a series of popular romances set in the Mountain West.

Varied explanations have been offered for Garland's hasty retreat from realism, and with it his failure to exploit the opportunity to become a major interpreter of the agrarian Midwest. He knew the region intimately, felt deeply about it, and had an important publishing outlet, yet his career as a writer of realistic fiction about rural life spanned no more than a half-dozen years. Part of the explanation was given by Garland himself—the ambition for literary approval and popular success that drew him away from the *Arena's* radicalism and into the genteel arms of Richard Watson Gilder, the editor of the prestigious *Century* magazine. The rural West provided Garland's subject but not his reading public and certainly not the company of the literary establishment to which he mightily aspired. In this view his early commitment to realism was more a matter of opportunism than conviction, the means urged by Kirkland and Howells for making his mark as a writer; when realism failed to gain him the literary place he wanted, he turned with unseemly speed to the popular romance. After the cool reception of *Rose of Dutcher's Coolly* he described himself as "saddened and depressed," feeling that "the Middle West should take a moderate degree of pride in me." He asked himself: "Am I not worthy of an occasional friendly word, a message of encouragement?"[30] With such an ingenuous revelation of self-pity the internal ground was prepared for abandoning serious agrarian fiction altogether.

Another view draws attention to Garland's lack of what one critic has called "intellectual stays"[31] together with a Midwestern background that gave little support to a committed life of art. The wispy culture of sporadic schooling, McGuffey Readers, and barnstorming lecturers encouraged a view of literature as embroidering life and reinforcing values. Furthermore, in the practical world of farm and town, literature was an avenue of upward mobility out of the Midwest and into fame and reward in the cultivated East.[32] To fully overcome his background simply took more artistic dedication and mental force than Garland possessed. What he abundantly possessed instead was humanitarian feeling and moral indignation—or what Henry James, in a patronizing but penetrating remark about a central quality Garland brought to his early stories, called "saturation" rather than talent. "There are moments," James noted, "when we are tempted to say that there is nothing like saturation—to pronounce it a safer thing than talent. I find myself rejoicing, for example, in Mr. Hamlin Garland, a case of saturation so precious as to have almost the value of genius."[33]

6

The drenching experience Garland channeled into fiction was, once again, made up of two main elements. On the one hand, there was the complex mixture of anger, guilt, and superiority stimulated by his various Midwestern returns from the East. On the other, there were the social theories gleaned from his reading and the objective conditions of natural disasters and economic decline that in the 1880s and early 1890s brought the boom times of land fever and rapid agricultural expansion in the western Midwest to a sudden halt. In "Under the Lion's Paw," perhaps his best-known story, Garland turned the latter aspect of his experience into one of his most effective narratives. Howells rightly called the story a "lesson in political economy"—a tightly-managed account embodying Henry George's thesis about the destructive social effects of absentee land ownership, a main grievance of the Populist audiences before whom Garland often read the story.[34] The Haskins family is pushed onto the dry plains of Kansas when they cannot afford better land to the east held by speculators. When their crops are destroyed by a grasshopper plague they back-trail across Iowa, meeting there the Councils, an agrarian couple of perfect virtue who help them settle on a rented farm. The owner, Butler, is a land speculator of seemingly decent stripe who at the end of the story reverts to form by setting a price on the farm double that originally mentioned. When Haskins protests that it is his labor and investment over a three-year period that have increased the farm's value, Butler points out that it is his farm. In a burst of anger Haskins nearly kills the speculator with a pitchfork, then accepts his hard terms before ordering him from the land.

With his eye held fast to the social argument of the story—the oppression of labor under the lion's paw of capital—Garland was able to exercise an unusual degree of control over his material. The visually precise opening paragraph is one of his best:

> It was the last of autumn and first day of winter coming together. All day long the ploughmen on their prairie farms had moved to and fro on their wide level fields through the falling snow, which melted as it fell, wetting them to the skin— all day, notwithstanding the frequent squalls of snow, the dripping, desolate clouds, and the muck of the furrows, black and tenacious as tar.[35]

The hard toil of Haskins and his wife in building up the farm is forcefully sketched: "Clothing dripping with sweat, arms aching, filled with briers, fingers raw and bleeding, backs broken with the weight of heavy bundles, Haskins and his man toiled on" (234). And the story's ending lacks the haze of uplifting sentiment that weakens many of Garland's conclusions. Butler beats a hasty retreat and Haskins, with no road of escape from the ceaseless work ahead, is left "seated dumbly on the sunny pile of sheaves, his head sunk into his hands" (240).

Although economic instruction is also a motive in "Up the Coule," the story draws more deeply on the crosscurrents of personal feeling evoked by Garland's Midwestern returns. For Howard McLane, a successful actor visiting his Wisconsin home, the rural landscape has the "majesty, breadth" of the garden myth from the vantage point of a Pullman coach (75). But the vision fades when he confronts farm life up close, replaced with a "sickening chill" in his soul at the sight of the forlorn farm and his brother, Grant, a worn and embittered farmer standing ankle-deep in muck (86). At a family gathering in his honor Howard senses the discontent of the farm people, their hunger for his experience of a larger world. The following morning at breakfast Grant's wife, Laura, pours out to him her loathing for farm life:

> "It's nothing but fret, fret and work the whole time, never going any place, never seeing anybody but a lot of neighbors just as big fools as you are. I spend my time fighting flies and washing dishes and churning. I'm sick of it all."

The solution is clear, the one Howard himself has taken. "I'd get away and I'd do something," Laura says. "I wouldn't care what, but I'd get away" (132–33).

Howard cannot suppress a sense of superiority at having made his own escape to the East and a life "so rich, so bright, so free" (141). With civilized disdain he notes that the farm house has neither books nor music; it is "a grim and horrible shed" with "nothing cosey [sic], nothing heart-warming" about it (136). At the same time he is also torn by guilt at having forsaken the farm and especially his mother. To redeem himself he decides to buy back the original homestead and install his mother in it before he returns to the East. In a final scene he confronts his brother with the offer of money, but Grant refuses. "Money can't give me a chance now," he says (145). Earlier in the story Howard had overheard Grant and his neighbors discussing farm conditions in economic terms. Speculators had pushed up the price of land and farmers were burdened with debt. Grant says the farmer is "like a fly in a pan of molasses. There ain't any escape for him. The more he tears around the more liable he is to rip his legs off." When someone asks what can be done, Grant says, "Nothin' " (127). The same hopeless response is voiced at the end of the story. Although lack of capital is exactly Grant's problem, the reason the old farm was lost, he responds to Howard with an all-encompassing confession of personal failure:

> "I mean life ain't worth very much to me. I'm too old to make a new start. I'm a dead failure. I've come to the conclusion that life's a failure for ninety-nine per cent of us. You can't help me now. It's too late." (145–46)

Garland's sense of the corrosive effects of farm life belie an economic solution to the story. Land speculation is clearly a blight in the Midwestern garden, but a more insidious evil is at work, drawing the farmer—if only at the level of suggestion—toward a different kind of violence than that proposed in "Under the Lion's Paw," the violence of self destruction. Perhaps because of his own depth of guilt, Garland refuses to allow the removal of Howard's guilt; just as the story offers no solution for Grant, there is no redemption for Howard. In a final stark paragraph the two brothers are left facing one another, hands clasped in understanding yet nothing changed between them.

In "A Branch-Road" Garland uses the same situation of contrast between a superior character who has escaped the farm and a defeated figure who has remained behind. Jealous misunderstanding separates two young lovers; when Will Hannan returns after an absence of seven years, prosperous from the cattle business in the Southwest, he finds Agnes Dingman a worn farm wife trapped in a marriage with a coarse husband. Like Howard McLane, Will is overwhelmed with guilt and asks Agnes's forgiveness for abandoning her. And like Grant McLane, Agnes responds that nothing can be done. But at this point Garland carries the story beyond "Up the Coule," and in so doing raises again another ideal vision in place of a failed garden myth. In the previous story the alternative vision is implicit in the figure of Howard, the Eastern actor; now it is directly set forth. "There's a chance for life yet," Will insists, and he conjures up for Agnes a future free of the farm and her husband (68). He will take her on a trip to the East or Europe, then to a life in Houston where she will have books and theater and concerts. As Agnes relents, he flings open the farmhouse door and pictures an old world of civilization superimposed on the discredited new world of nature:

> "See the sunlight out there shining on that field o' wheat? That's where I'll take you—out into the sunshine. You shall see it shining on the Bay of Naples. Come, get on your hat; don't take anything more'n you actually need. Leave the past behind you." (73)

The story ends with a gush of agrarian images ("the sun shone on the dazzling, rustling wheat, the fathomless sky, blue as a sea, bent above them"), but images now invigorated by escape to "the world that lay before them"—the superior world of refinement and success represented by Howard McLane and Will Hannan (74).

"Up the Coulé" and "A Branch-Road" are the most ambitious and compelling stories in *Main-Travelled Roads*, combining in complex fashion Garland's acute response to social conditions in the rural West with an awareness of superiority at having escaped to the refined East together with a nagging sense of guilt for having done so. Other stories, more in the vein of "Under the Lion's Paw," are given over to evoking the farmer's hard lot, thereby undermining glowing views of agrarian life. In these stories, however, Garland shows far less control over his fictional effects. In "Among the Corn-Rows" Seagraves, a young newspaper editor, is stirred by the beauty of the South Dakota prairie, but for Rob Rodemaker, who works a claim and must break the sod, the land is only a challenge. Rob is pleased enough with his life but he wants a wife to do the cooking and grace his lonely shanty. He travels to his native Wisconsin on a ten-day search for a bride and the story switches to Julia Peterson, grimly plowing in a sweltering cornfield. Garland again makes the point that the countryside holds beauty only for those with leisure; for those who must toil it is a place of bondage. When Rob proposes a marriage that will free her from work in the fields, Julia accepts, and the story trails off to a romantic ending, Garland only partly acknowledging the reality he has created—that Julia is exchanging the labor of her family's farm for the labor and loneliness of Rob's homestead. "She'd work, of course," he has her realize, "but it would be because she wanted to, and not because she was forced to." As Rob's wife she will be "a member of a new firm," and in her mind she is already blissfully "living that free life in a far-off, wonderful country" (182).

"The Return of a Private" is in the same mode of agrarian truth telling and exhibits Garland's same uncertain handling of his material. Private Smith comes home to a Wisconsin farm after the Civil War, sick and worn but uplifted by the beauty of the countryside and a loving family. The story is based on family accounts of the return of Garland's own father from the war, and in the evocation of an earlier time the Midwestern scene is treated with lyric affection. But when Garland lets himself dwell on present conditions the mood of the story turns dark. This is usually the case in his response to his material: viewed from a past perspective or a distant angle it stirs nostalgic feelings; viewed from present time or up close it stimulates anger.[36] The result is the ambivalence critics have repeatedly noted in Garland's portrayal of the Midwest as both compelling and tragic, lovely and grim. In "The Return of a Private" the dual angle of vision results in a rollercoaster of moods. Seen in a distant narrative light, Smith is exactly the yeoman of myth returned to the life-enhancing serenity of the family farm:

> Oh, that mystic hour! The pale man with big eyes standing there by the well, with his young wife by his side. The vast moon swinging above the eastern peaks; the cattle winding down the pasture slopes with jangling bells; the crickets singing;

the stars blooming out sweet and far and serene; the katydids rhythmically calling; the little turkeys crying querulously, as they settled to roost in the poplar-tree near the open gate. (215)

From this perspective Smith is an "epic figure" of the imagination, "a magnificent type" (214, 216). Yet what awaits him, when Garland draws close and outlines his present situation, is a litany of trouble: his farm is mortgaged, a renter has run away with his machinery, his children need clothing, he himself is sick and emaciated. In the final paragraph (removed from later editions of the book) Garland leaps ahead to glimpse a future that only underscores the bitter reality of the present: "He is a gray-haired man of sixty now, and on the brown hair of his wife the white is also showing. They are fighting a hopeless battle, and must fight till God gives them furlough" (216).

Garland was drawing on his warm feeling for the rural past in "Mrs. Ripley's Trip," a slight and nostalgic tale based on a family anecdote that he placed last in the volume. After years of scrimping and saving, an elderly woman is able to journey back from Iowa to visit her family in New York state. Her determination to make the trip, leaving her husband behind, is merely the occasion for local-color humor, but in other stories Garland used the theme of a woman's struggle for emancipation as a vehicle for showing the hollowness of the myth of rural perfection. Laura McLane in "Up the Coule" tells Howard she "was a fool for ever marrying" and sadly recalls a time when she was a teacher and "free to come and go" and with money of her own (134). Agnes abandons her marriage in "A Branch-Road," responding to a vision of travel and leisured city life, and Julia in "Among the Corn-Rows" is swayed by the prospect Rob holds out of marriage that will allow a "free life" (182). An especially effective use of the theme is found in "A Day's Pleasure," a story added to a later edition of the collection. Delia Markham, a farm wife, accompanies her husband on a rare visit to the country town, but once her few purchases are made she wanders the streets, weary and disconsolate. Mrs. Hall, an elegant lawyer's wife, takes pity on her and invites her to tea, and in the home the farm wife experiences an interlude of refinement and beauty—an interlude, Garland makes clear, of civilized life:

> She was shown all the pictures and books. Mrs. Hall seemed to read her visitor's mind. She kept as far from the farm and her guest's affairs as possible, and at last she opened the piano and sang to her—not slow-moving hymns, but catchy love-songs full of sentiment, and then played some simple melodies, knowing that Mrs. Markham's eyes were studying her hands, her rings, and the flash of her fingers on the keys—seeing more than she heard—and through it all Mrs. Hall conveyed the impression that she, too, was having a good time.

The story ends with Delia Markham and her husband returning to the prairie farm, the lonely conditions of her life unchanged but the day "made beautiful by human sympathy"—sympathy located within the story in a momentary escape made possible by the benevolence of a cultivated town woman.[37]

Garland could as easily, however, discover such sympathy exactly where the garden myth had it, in the breasts of hearty rural figures. This is apparent in the kindly attentions of the Councils to the destitute Haskins family in "Under the Lion's Paw"; in "God's Ravens," published in 1894 and included in later editions of *Main-Travelled Roads*, it becomes the central message of the story. Robert Bloom, a Chicago newspaperman, moves with his family to a Wisconsin town, hoping to recover his health in an idyllic rural setting. At first, things go badly; the weather is wet and cold and the country people seem dim and indifferent. Bloom grows bitter. He tells his wife: "Talk about the health of village life! it destroys body and soul. It debilitates me. It will warp us both down to the level of these people." But when he sinks deeply into sickness the villagers appear in a different light, nursing him back to health, unstinting in their devotion. "Oh, Robert, they're so good!" his wife tells him. "They feed us like God's ravens." Even nature does a turnabout, transformed into the lush garden Bloom had originally imagined:

> On every side the golden June sunshine fell, filling the valley from purple brim to purple brim. Down over the hill to the west the light poured, tangled and glowing in the plum and cherry trees, leaving the glistening grass spraying through the elms and flinging streamers of pink across the shaven green slopes where the cattle fed.[38]

7

"God's Ravens" is an imaginative projection of Garland's removal in 1893 of his parents from South Dakota to a home in West Salem, Wisconsin, the village near where he was born, and of his own frequent returns to what he christened the "Garland Homestead." Purchase of the home was an effort to recapture the idealized past of a Wisconsin childhood while putting behind the harsh experience of prairie farming. For his pioneering father, Garland recognized, the village home "meant a surrender of his faith in the Golden West, a tacit admission that all his explorations of the open lands with whatsoever they had meant of opportunity, had ended in a sense of failure on a barren soil."[39] The sentimental story arose from Garland's nostalgic recollection of an earlier and settled rural existence, a time that served, both in his fiction and in actuality, as an antidote to the hard facts of the present. In was only when he was able to imaginatively confront that present that Garland was able to set down fresh and powerful portraits of Midwestern life. From that perspective came the procession of country figures who, as Howells expressed it, "feel that something is wrong, and they know that the wrong is not theirs."[40] From the remembered past came the sentimentalizing tendency and uncritical acceptance of the garden myth.

Donald Pizer has suggested that once Garland returned his family to Wisconsin his guilt at having abandoned them was removed, and with it a powerful stimulus to his early stories of agrarian disenchantment was lost. What remained was only a sense of superiority to the rural Midwest, an attitude that inevitably limited his involvement with the region and his serious treatment of it as a writer. Garland's later view of the Midwest emphasized its lack of scenic beauty compared with the Mountain West and its lack of refinement compared with the East and Europe. The latter attitude is apparent in "Up the Coule" and "A Branch-Road," but in these stories it coexists in tension with his sense of having failed both his parents and the region. Together, the opposed responses were a source of creative power; "revulsion alone," as Pizer remarks, caused Garland only to "flee the West as subject matter and as theme."[41]

It is only in his first book that Garland was able to hold with some steadiness to the mixture of personal guilt and superiority, together with an acute awareness of rural conditions and an intellectual framework for understanding those conditions, that provided his real literary capital. He was able as well to knit the stories together into a coherent whole that bears some resemblance to a novel. He does this through the metaphor of the Western road used in the title of the collection and underscored in the dedication, in the preface, and in epigraphs to each of the stories. Within the stories themselves his characters are usually on the move as well, and usually engaged in a journey of return: Howard McLane and Will Hannan back to the Midwest, Private Smith back to his farm, the Haskins backtrailing across Iowa, Rob Rodemaker journeying from South Dakota to Wisconsin for a wife, Mrs. Ripley on a return visit to New York state. Coupled with the metaphor of the road and the use of the journey theme is the recurring theme of escape. Some of Garland's characters have already freed themselves from rural bondage, others struggle for freedom if only that of a passing sort. For still others there is no possibility of escape but only — as Garland put it in the book's dedication to his parents — the continuing "pilgrimage on the main-travelled road of life."

After Garland had turned his attention to romances of the Mountain West, Howells offered a gentle suggestion that he reconsider his earlier material and purpose:

> One day, I hope you will revert to the temper of your first work, and give us a picture of the wild life you know so well on the lines of *Main-Travelled Roads*. You have in you greater things than you have done, and you owe the world which has welcomed you the best you have in you. "Be true to the dream of thy youth" — the dream of an absolute and inspiring "veritism;" the world is yours.[42]

Garland's inability to act on the advice marks out the boundary of his importance as an imaginative writer. Only in the backward-looking form of autobiography, his once heated feelings now well layered with nostalgia, was he able to turn back to Midwestern material with *A Son of the Middle Border* in 1917, beginning a series of works of reminiscence. Garland seems now a tragicomic figure who found his true subject early yet chose to pursue the siren song of popular success—a minor writer finally and a case study of a national literary inclination for failure through success. Nonetheless, he left behind a volume of stories that have about them still the ring of authentic and outraged feeling, imperfect stories usually flawed by haste and a wavering vision yet sketching a moving portrait of rural failure.

Reading Garland now, one wishes he were better—a better craftsman and one more dedicated to the complexity of his own experience. Yet his strengths remain clear and valuable. One can still feel the anguish, expressed through Howard McLane in "Up the Coule," over the "infinite tragedy" of farm lives "which the world loves to call 'peaceful and pastoral' " (130). The story stands out as the finest work of early Midwestern realism—powerful and convincing in overall effect and with a startling rightness to some of its scenes. There is, for example, the first barn-yard meeting of the brother who has escaped with the one who has remained behind:

> They stood and looked at each other. Howard's cuffs, collar, and shirt, alien in their elegance, showed through the dusk, and a glint of light shot out from the jewel of his necktie, as the light from the house caught it at the right angle. As they gazed in silence at each other, Howard divined something of the hard, bitter feeling that came into Grant's heart, as he stood there, ragged, ankle-deep in muck, his sleeves rolled up, a shapeless old straw hat on his head. (87)

And there is the family gathering in Howard's honor at which an old man plays a fiddle, everyone growing silent under the melancholy sway of the music and the musician losing himself in his tunes:

> He played on slowly, softly, wailing Scotch tunes and mournful Irish love songs. He seemed to find in the songs of these people, and especially in a wild, sweet, low-keyed negro song, some expression for his indefinable inner melancholy.
> He played on, forgetful of everybody, his long beard sweeping the violin, his toil-worn hands marvelously obedient to his will.
> At last he stopped, looked up with a faint, deprecating smile, and said with a sigh:
> "Well, folkses, time to go home." (129)

In Midwestern writing before Garland there is simply nothing so good.

THREE

The Voice of Want

How was it that, in so little a while, the narrow life of
the country had fallen from her as a garment, and the
city, with all its mystery, taken its place?

—*Sister Carrie*

1

Early in 1899, Booth Tarkington, six years out of Princeton, received a letter
from Hamlin Garland that began: "Mr. McClure has given me your manuscript,
The Gentleman from Indiana, to read. You are a novelist."[1] Shortly thereafter
a book contract was forthcoming from the publishing house of Doubleday and
McClure, launching the young Indianapolis writer on one of the most prolonged, lucrative, and honored Midwestern literary careers. What presumably
caught Garland's eye as a reader for the publishing house were the faint regional
trappings of Tarkington's novel, qualities he had earlier discovered in the dialect
verses of another Indiana writer, James Whitcomb Riley. In Boston in 1886
Garland had come upon Riley's first book, *"The Old Swimmin'-Hole," and
'Leven More Poems, by Benj. F. Johnson, of Boone*, the poems originally printed
in an Indianapolis newspaper and supposedly from the hand of an Indiana
farmer. As he later recalled, Garland was struck by the originality of the work
in that the poems were written from the standpoint of a farmer and treated
plain rural subjects ordinarily ignored. He found himself deeply touched by such
sentimental verse as "Watermelon Time" and "When the Frost Is on the Punkin." Thereafter, Riley became what Garland called "a beloved figure in my
literary world" and the subject of lectures he was delivering in Boston. As Garland saw it, the poet's genius was located in a capacity to "transmute a flat and
commonplace landscape" into poetry that embodied "the humor, the self-cen-
tered philosophy, and the homely neighborliness of the mid-West."[2]

Beyond noting his always uncertain grip on a clear-eyed response to his own
rural material (and usually enthusiastic feeling for fellow writers), it is hard to
square the author of *Main-Travelled Roads* with such enthusiasm for two leading
figures of the group of Indiana writers who dominated popular American writ-

ing at the turn of the century. In championing Tarkington and Riley, however, Garland was at least implicitly making some distinction between the thin veneer of local-color realism that attached to their work and the full-blown romanticism of their Hoosier colleagues. "Something in the level lands of Indiana appeared to foster a fanciful fiction," Garland remarked about such historical concoctions as George Barr McCutcheon's *Graustark* (1901), Charles Major's *When Knighthood Was in Flower* (1898), and Maurice Thompson's *Alice of Old Vincennes* (1900), and he explained their immense success as a "natural reaction" to the dreary actuality of a rural world of "dusty roads and weedy fence corners."[3]

He might have added that the rise of the Indiana writers—"an amazing outbreak of sentimental imagining," as he aptly described it[4]—was also a reaction to that dreary rural world as it had been portrayed in the fiction of the agrarian realists, his own in particular. Reviewers had taken him to task for the boring monotony of his farm portraits, informing him that "the novelty of the region which he is introducing to literature is not sufficient of itself to maintain one's interest."[5] Garland had not failed to receive the message, nor had the writers who now set their work in the long-settled, more picturesque, and presumably more imaginatively appealing Midwest of rural Indiana—or more often in the never-never worlds of costume romance. The period of natural and financial hard times out of which Garland's stories had arisen, never as severe in Indiana and other older eastern reaches of the Midwest, had also passed, giving way in the later part of the 1890s to general economic prosperity. Farmers had entered upon a period of good times that would carry through to the end of the First World War—the golden age of Midwestern agriculture.[6]

Yet in another sense the Indiana writers were not reacting against the dreary aspects of country life as portrayed by the agrarian realists nor responding to the happy spirit of economic good times so much as maintaining a long-standing literary impulse to gild life by looking at the more smiling aspects of the region or, as was more often the case, looking beyond it altogether. For Midwesterners raised on the literary samplings of McGuffey Readers and an idealization of the village culture of New England, literature and the arts in general served to transport one to worlds elsewhere. If under the sway of Howellsian realism literature was thought to hold a mirror to nature, it was the uplifting and the distant that ought to be reflected, not the sordid and the familiar. In 1880, Lew Wallace of Crawfordsville, Indiana, had transported readers to the beginnings of Christianity in *Ben-Hur;* nearly two decades later, in 1896, Charles M. Sheldon, a Topeka, Kansas, minister, carried them in *In His Steps* to a contemporary Midwestern town whose inhabitants try to literally follow Christ's precepts. Both works were examples (as was the transformation of Chicago's Jackson Park into the neoclassical White City of the Columbian Exposition) of a style of imagination that sought uplift in the genial or the distant rather than on dusty roads or in weedy fence corners, and both were among the lofty best-sellers of the time. Against such a background the line of fledgling agrarian realism running from Eggleston through Kirkland and Howe and culminating in Garland seems only a momentary aberration in an otherwise continuous tradition of literary escapism in which Midwestern writers, as Garland noted, "bored by their surroundings . . . took flight into lands so remote that the flat prairies and flimsy towns of their daily walk were forgotten."[7]

2

Howells arrived in Indianapolis in November of 1899 on his Midwestern lecture tour and was properly lionized as one of the leading literary figures of the time. His guide on the day of his lecture was Tarkington, *The Gentleman from Indiana* just published. The following day a call was paid on Riley, who had been too ill to attend the lecture, in his Lockerbie Street home. Howells's talk, "Novel-Writing and Novel-Reading," was courteously received according to press accounts, yet in the Indianapolis of Tarkington and Riley his now familiar call for a literature of commonplace realism was strikingly at odds with the vigorous growth of romantic idealism in Midwestern writing and American writing in general. Lew Wallace's neighbor in Crawfordsville, Maurice Thompson, whose early sketches in *Hoosier Mosaics* (1875) had been fairly faithful to Indiana life, had become a leader in the anti-Howellsian movement. At a Hartford Theological Seminary lecture in 1893 he had asked his audience if they had

> observed how, as a man becomes a realist, he grows fond of being narrow and of playing with small specialties? Have you thought out the secret force which controls the movement of his so-called realism, and always keeps its votaries sneering at heroic life, while they revel in another sort of life, which fitly to characterize here would be improper? I can tell you what that force is. It is unbelief in ideal standards of human aspiration, and it is impatient scorn of that higher mode of thought which has given the world all the greatest creations of imaginative genius.[8]

Although Howells carried on, he was well aware of the change in the literary climate as the century came to an end. When a young follower in the campaign for realism, Stephen Crane, put before him in a newspaper interview the thought that "last winter . . . it seemed that realism was about to capture things, but then recently I have thought that I saw coming a sort of counter wave, a flood of the other—a reaction in fact," Howells responded gloomily: "What you say is true. I have seen it coming. . . . I suppose we shall have to wait."[9] As it turned out, there was nothing to wait for among the popular Indiana writers who were busily catering to a national literary taste for dream rather than reality.

Howells claimed to find promise in Tarkington's novel, and he praised Riley as "the poet of our common life."[10] Of the popular Indiana writers, the two alone survive with some claim on our attention today, though more for their usefulness in illustrating the removed vision at the heart of even the best (in Garland's estimation) Indiana writing of the period than for lasting literary qualities. Both were part of Crane's "flood of the other" rather than the re-emergent literary realism Howells awaited. When the lightning rod of that development arrived in the unlikely person of Theodore Dreiser, he would come, with fine irony, from Indiana, though from an underworld of poverty far removed from the comfortable towns of the historical novelists or the equally comfortable literary Indianapolis of Tarkington and Riley. And neither Howells nor Garland, let alone his fellow Indiana writers, would immediately recognize his startling presence among them.

In *Crumbling Idols* Garland complained that Western poets persisted in "writing blank-verse tragedies of the Middle Ages"; they were "poets of books, not of life."[11] Riley seemed an exception, one of the handful of writers Garland included in his critical manifesto among the adherents of the new regionalism—a poet, as he would say later, of the farm. Today, Riley's work seems as distant and bookish as that of the poets Garland scorned, its thin concern with Midwestern life overwhelmed by greeting-card sentimentality. The dominant characteristic of Riley's verse is not enthusiasm for rural ways so much as a vague and essentially literary nostalgia for "The Airly Days" and "The Good, Old-Fashioned People" of central Indiana as he had known them during a mid-century childhood in the village of Greenfield. His recreation of that lost Eden presumably touched a responsive chord in readers who wished to remember their own pasts in similar sunset terms, and they lavished honors upon him, turning him in his late years into an Indiana and national institution, the beloved poet.

Riley frequently wrote about children and was thought of as a children's poet. Indeed, he was a major presence in the general vogue of celebrations of the innocent young in post-Civil War American writing. His poems, Mark Twain gushed, made "my mouth water for an Elder Time, and a big toe with a rag around it."[12] Riley's psychological perspective, however, was always that of an adult looking back upon a vanished world and finding it glowing with memories of happiness and well being. The present world is seldom harsh or unfriendly by contrast but it lacks, for the adult imagination, the rich inner meaning of the past. Yet if Riley's poems were meant for adults, they were heavily tinged with the child's conventions of make-believe elevated to an adult level. He once wrote about "Dreaming again, in anticipation, / The same old dreams of our boyhood days / That never came true." The sense of dreaming about what never quite was suggests that Riley's bond with his readers was not simply nostalgia for rural life but a yearning for an imagined past, a world not so much recalled as invented. The Chicago novelist James T. Farrell would capture the phantasmagoric quality of Riley's work when he remarked that the poet sought to retreat to an "unreal little dream village" at a time when Midwesterners and Americans in general were in fact energetically moving in an opposite direction, toward an urban and industrial life.[13]

"A Country Pathway," a poem first printed in 1877, six years before his initial book appeared, suggests Riley's typical manner. The mature poet (Riley speaking here in his literary voice rather than in the vernacular style of a farmer or country poet) idly follows a country path running off a main road. It lures him "mile on mile / Out of the public highway," but as he continues on his thoughts become more alluring than the reality of the pathway. A "bright memory" of youth awakens in him and now he seems to be wandering through "pasture wealth" and "buttercups and flags." In a place of "puritanic quiet" his journey reaches its climax; the vague melancholy with which he began the walk is lifted and he has a vision of a pioneer homestead:

> And lo! through mists that may not be dispelled,
>   I see an old farm homestead, as in dreams,
> Where, like a gem in costly setting held,
>   The old log cabin gleams.

The poet knows full well that the old farm exists only in those "mists that may not be dispelled." Nonetheless, he pleads in the final two stanzas to be led on through the "smiling world" of the valley to the cabin door, here to be greeted by the household as "the prodigal / That wanders home to-day."[14] All of Riley's rural verse comes out of a similar backward progression of mind, a momentary return in an essentially dream-like or child-like state to a bucolic world of farm and village lit with a rosy glow yet impossibly removed from the actual "public highway" of modern life. Riley's genius was not so much his capacity, as Garland had thought, to transmute a commonplace landscape into poetry but to render in unshadowed popular verse an agrarian dream precisely as a dream— to conjure up "the days 'at's past and gone" and, at least in the poet's misty evocation of them, never were.

The Gentleman from Indiana, its roots firmly in the conventions of the sentimental novel of a local-color variety, is only slightly more in touch with the actualities of rural life. The story follows the triumphs of John Harkless, an educated young Easterner who buys sight unseen a failing country newspaper in Plattville, Indiana, and uses it as a crusading vehicle of civic improvement. Eventually, he routs a group of violent hooligans outside the town known as the White-Caps (for the white sheets they wear), wins the beautiful Helen Sherwood, and becomes a nominee for Congress. What Tarkington apparently means to celebrate is honest rural virtue as embodied in his Indiana gentleman, an idea possibly inspired by disparaging views of the Midwest he had encountered during his school days at Phillips Exeter and Princeton.[15] But the book makes a quite different case since the gentleman's virtues are not the product of Indiana but of his genteel Eastern origins and Ivy League education. Indiana, as seen from Harkless's Pullman car in the novel's opening paragraph, is a monotonous "sad expanse" and its inhabitants "incurious, patient, slow, looking up from the fields apathetically as the Limited flies by." He chooses to cast his lot with this unpromising setting, thereby asserting the theoretical superiority of small-town Midwestern simplicity to Eastern sophistication; all is properly redeemed in the end, and in the novel's final line Harkless can exclaim the wonders of the "beautiful people" he now finds about him.[16] Yet it remains that it is the virtuous striving of an Eastern import that has brought the rural district to flower, not its intrinsic merits.

3

In later years Tarkington thought of *The Gentleman from Indiana* as an inferior early work, locating his more important fiction, properly so, in the modestly realistic middle period of his career that produced ambitious family chronicles of social change in the urban Midwest: *The Magnificent Ambersons* (1918), *Alice Adams* (1921), *The Midlander* (1924). His true setting was never the countryside or the small town but a city similar to his native Indianapolis—an urban environment of medium size experiencing a melancholy Gilded Age decline from aristocratic old-family order to industrial complexity. At the turn of the century, however, Tarkington's sense of urban life in such a Midwestern milieu was as narrowly restricted as his sense of the country.

In a 1902 article in *Harper's Monthly*, broadly titled "The Middle West" despite a concentration on the city (Tarkington mentions Omaha, Minneapolis, Columbus, Cincinnati, and Indianapolis), he argued that the urban round of life in the country's center manifests the same refinements as in the East while remaining free of that region's stuffiness and narrow social restriction. Tarkington drew his illustrations from the world of dinners and dances, clubs and the theater, holding that Midwesterners in such settings are "easy-going" and possessed of "energy without rush, and gayety without extravagance." They entertain without lavishness, and "while nearly all are comfortable and well-to-do, none are 'barons'; only a few are rich, and these few live like their neighbors, not displaying their advantage." In this world of democratic merit it is not surprising to hear the voices of women in men's clubs, nor surprising to find people at home during the summer months, lounging on their own pleasant porches rather than vacationing at distant resorts. For these stay-at-homes there is always within easy reach a country club, the institution that drew Tarkington's warmest tribute in his celebration of Midwestern city life.

> The country club gives the gayest and happiest and laziest part of town's life, from the first of May until November. It is on a high bluff among tall forest trees, where there is always a breeze and always some coolness. Here there are to be found, nearly always, out-of-town men who serve as an excuse for a dinner, and out-of-town girls for whom dances are arranged; and here, on the terrace or on the river-bank below, or in quiet corners of the long veranda when the music of the Saturday evening hop is going inside, the youth of the city usually propose.[17]

V. L. Parrington's estimate of Tarkington was that he was a skillful writer but one whose art was destroyed by love of popularity—"a perennial sophomore, purveyor of comfortable literature to middle-class America."[18] Dreiser's dismissal was equally blunt and more sweeping: "He does not know reality, does not know life, work, the average human being, or sex."[19] Hemingway simply had it that "he had the wrong dope, that fellow."[20] Certainly Tarkington had no first-hand knowledge of the small-town world of Midwestern poverty that was Dreiser's Indiana in the 1870s and 1880s. Dreiser recalled staring as a child through the iron fences at the homes of the industrial barons of Terre Haute, glimpsing something of Tarkington's privileged world of porches and country clubs, but that was as close as he ever got. Nor did he have any place in the dreamy country world of Riley's rhymes. In New York in 1897 he would write for his song-writer brother, Paul Dresser, a verse for what would become Paul's most popular hit, "On the Banks of the Wabash":

> Round my Indiana home there waves a cornfield,
> In the distance loom the woodlands clear and cool.
> Often times my thoughts revert to scenes of childhood,
> Where I first received my lessons, nature's school.
> But one thing there is missing from the picture,
> Without her face it seems so incomplete.
> I long to see my mother in the doorway,
> As she stood there years ago, her boy to greet.

But bucolic lines that might have come from Riley's sentimental pen were simply the work of a hack journalist who had, by this time in his career, mastered the trick of tossing off something on nearly any subject.[21]

In the 1923 article referred to in the opening chapter, "Indiana: Her Soil and Light," Dreiser treated the popular writers of the state, Riley and Tarkington in particular, with genial good will. But he took note in their work of "a kind of wistfulness" that grew out of their experience of an agreeable and respectable social world, a world possessed of a poetic charm. Running through their Indiana was a mood which, as he put it, "those who are most intimate with it are pleased to denominate 'homey' or 'folksy'—a general geniality and sociability."[22] When it was turned to the material at hand rather than the far vistas of historical romance, popular Midwestern writing, and Indiana writing in particular, grew out of just such kindly experience and in turn portrayed a fictional landscape that wistfully evoked that experience. In his portrait of Indiana life in *The Hoosiers* (1900), Meredith Nicholson had defined the state as an "enlightened commonwealth" and its typical literary creation a figure who is "kindly, generous, humorous, and essentially domestic."[23] It was exactly a capacity to evoke such genial qualities of life that turned Gene Stratton-Porter into one of the most successful of American writers in the first quarter of the new century with her portrayals of adolescent Hoosier life in *Freckles* (1904) and *A Girl of the Limberlost* (1909). For his part, Dreiser could not have followed in such a tradition of neighborly, warm-hearted, backward-looking fiction had he wished. It was a tradition based on the shared experience of comfortable life in a genteel and secluded American heartland basking in the afterglow of the garden myth—the world on the other side of the iron fences.

Dreiser's Midwest was a succession of Indiana towns—Terre Haute, Sullivan,

Evansville, Warsaw—and a continuing melodrama of hard times and social shame that he would later describe as "one unbroken stretch of privation and misery."[24] There was never enough money for a large and emotionally extravagant family of ten children born over fifteen years to a pious German father and an American-born mother of Moravian background. And there was always the feeling of social inferiority—of existing beyond the pale of decorous society. In Warsaw, where Dreiser attended high school, his sister, Sylvia, became pregnant by a wealthy young sport in the town, and after the birth the baby joined the family as a relative, an explanation that deceived no one. Subject to wisecracks about his sister, Dreiser became a moody, solitary figure, the ultimate outsider, finding pleasure only in school. A sympathetic teacher offered encouragement, and later, in one of the many odd twists in an improbable life, she offered to pay all the boy's expenses for a year at Indiana University.

Dreiser's life as a college man in Bloomington was moderately successful: he passed his courses, joined a literary society, found some friends. But when he returned after the year to his clamorous family, now assembled in Chicago, college was quickly put behind. The city and its attractions held him; twice before the family had made brief forays into Chicago to change its fortunes only to retreat back to Indiana, and he felt himself on familiar ground, free of small-town social censure and in a place that pandered to dreams of success. He found a job of sorts in a real estate office, but it was his mother's sudden death in November of 1890 that separated him for good from his Indiana past. Sarah Dreiser had given the family what little stability and cohesion it had; now the storms of rivalries flared openly and the family members began to separate. A temporary job with a Chicago newspaper's Christmas charity campaign introduced Dreiser to the glamorous world of newspapering and fired him with ambition to become a big-city reporter, his press card envisioned as entrance to the worlds of the rich and famous. For the first time in his life he had a goal and he pursued it doggedly. By the summer of 1892, almost twenty-one years of age, he was a cub reporter for the *Chicago Globe*, beginning a writing career that would lead, with many ups and downs, to his final stature as the first major novelist from out of the Midwest.

These were the beginning glory days for a style of Chicago journalism with a literary edge. Eugene Field was writing his "Sharps and Flats" column in the *Daily News*, and Finley Peter Dunne, after years of reporting, would soon create in Mr. Dooley a spokesman for witty political comment. A recently arrived Indiana writer, George Ade, would use his column, "Stories of the Streets and the Town," to capture in charming vernacular the comings and goings of rural types in the bewildering city. The example of Dunne and Ade would in turn influence Ring Lardner, a young sports writer from Niles, Michigan, by way of the South Bend, Indiana, *Times*, who would become the most important humorist to emerge from the Midwest. Lardner would distinguish himself in Chicago journalism as a baseball writer and with the "In the Wake of the News" column in the *Tribune* before venturing East and into sudden critical acclaim as a fiction writer. Dreiser's cub reporting for the *Globe* was at the opposite end of the journalism spectrum. He proved to have little talent for ordinary fact gathering; with personal writing and especially Sunday-supplement features he did better, drenching his work in colorful details drawn from the city's lower depths. In the *Globe* he also published his first work of fiction, a revealing tale of a young writer from a background of poverty and sorrow who yearns for success.

After six months in Chicago, Dreiser was off on a newspaper odyssey that would take him to St. Louis, Pittsburgh, and finally to one of the most prestigious papers of the day, the *New York World*. Big-city daily journalism had rescued him from an impoverished and mute past; it had opened his mind and given him the rough beginnings of a literary voice. But with the *World* he touched a limit. He was on space-rate work, as were most reporters on the paper, and could barely eke out a living; when he did turn up a good story, it was handed over to a staff reporter to write. The New York journalism world seemed overpopulated with reporters who had been successful elsewhere but who had reached the boundary of their careers and were now drifting downhill. Sensing he was about to be fired, Dreiser quit the newspaper and joined the armies of itinerant poor on the city's mean streets. Before he again found his way up from poverty, this time through magazine editing and freelance writing, he was on intimate terms with cold and hunger, the night smells of flophouses, the hopelessness of failure.

In the summer of 1899, married now and doing well enough as a magazine writer, Dreiser went off to Maumee, Ohio, for a leisurely stay with an old friend from his newspaper days, Arthur Henry. Henry was writing a novel and urged Dreiser to do the same. The following September in New York, just turned twenty-eight, he began by writing the title *Sister Carrie* at the top of yellow copy paper, opening up with the name a flood of personal memories that would provide the rough outline of the story. His older sister, Emma, had moved to Chicago after numerous romantic affairs in Indiana, there to become entangled with an older married man, one L. A. Hopkins, a clerk for a chain of saloons. When Hopkins's wife discovered the affair, he absconded with money from his employer's safe and he and Emma fled to Montreal; from there, after returning most of the money, they went to New York to make a fresh start. During his days on the *World* Dreiser had lived with his sister and Hopkins, the latter then out of work and out of luck in the new city and beginning a spiral of decline, and he would devise a scheme in which Emma finally separated herself from her lover. But if Dreiser leaned heavily on Emma's story, one that read like a typical newspaper melodrama of the day, in the process of writing he altered and deepened it considerably, most notably in transforming real-life characters of simple dimension into the far richer figures of Carrie Meeber and George Hurstwood.

The novel was written rapidly, Dreiser submitting the manuscript as he went along to his wife and Arthur Henry for correction of his hasty and often convoluted prose and for serious editorial revision, especially of the work's final two chapters. The familiar story of the book's publication is one of bright prospects followed by nearly total disaster. After the conservative house of Harper and Brothers rejected it, Dreiser had the good fortune to have the novel read at Doubleday, Page by Frank Norris, whose recent novel in a naturalistic vein, *McTeague*, had caused a stir. Norris responded quickly and enthusiastically, later writing Dreiser that "it was the best novel I had read in M.S. since I had been reading for the firm, and that it pleased me as well as any novel I have read in *any* form, published or otherwise."[25] At a subsequent meeting in the offices of the publishing house no contract was signed but an agreement was reached with Dreiser about publication, a central fact when it transpired that Frank Doubleday, the senior partner in the firm, was opposed to the work. When Dreiser remained insistent, Doubleday carried through on the unwritten obligation to publish, and the work appeared on November 8, 1900 but accompanied by almost no promotion. Norris sent out 127 copies to literary figures and reviewers, with mostly favorable notices following, yet the book virtually vanished without a trace, selling only 456 copies in its first two years of life.

4

For the opening of *Sister Carrie*, Carrie Meeber's train ride from the Wisconsin village of Columbia City to sprawling Chicago, Dreiser drew on memories of his own excursions from the Indiana towns of his youth and later from his journalistic travels to the central city of the Midwestern imagination. In 1887 he had come to the city penniless, alone, and looking for work, an experience that provided him with many of Carrie's initial impressions of her new home, both its magnetic appeal and "amid all the maze, uproar and novelty" its "cold reality."[26] In 1893 on a train from St. Louis to Chicago for the World's Fair, Dreiser the journalist—a snappy dresser now in the manner of his jaunty salesman, Charles Drouet—had caught the eye of a young school teacher who would later become his wife. In 1898 he had arrived in Chicago as a successful magazine writer, triumphantly carrying letters of introduction to Marshall Field and Philip Armour, moving now with some assurance in the world of Hurstwood and his monied betters. Midwestern experience, his own coupled with what he knew of Emma's, provided both a first step into the novel, a way of beginning it, as well as scores of realistic details and an overall design. More importantly, it provided an attitude, a sense of the fragmented nature of existence and its random possibilities together with an opposed feeling of fixed destiny, that gave the novel its strikingly original inner life.

Dreiser's Midwest had been a landscape of constant instability, the family breaking up in one town under the weight of debt and social censure and reforming in another, with Chicago as the ultimate escape, the place of longing and changed fortune. It was a region that had encouraged no dreams of a Jeffersonian life on the land, no happy recollections of small-town existence within the snug fastness of the country, no accounts of urbane city routines. In the introductory section of *My Ántonia* a train ride across Iowa rekindles for the author and the book's narrator, Jim Burden, sun-lit memories of a country childhood:

> We were talking about what it is like to spend one's childhood in little towns like these, buried in wheat and corn, under stimulating extremes of climate: burning summers when the world lies green and billowy beneath a brilliant sky, when one is fairly stifled in vegetation, in the color and smell of strong weeds and heavy harvests; blustery winters with little snow, when the whole country is stripped bare and gray as sheet-iron. We agreed that no one who had not grown up in a little prairie town could know anything about it. It was a kind of freemasonry, we said.[27]

For Dreiser no such freemasonry of rural memory existed, nor did he harbor within himself Nick Carraway's recollection of the "thrilling returning trains of my youth" carrying him back to a Midwest of unchanging moral order.[28] There had been no experience of an enlightened commonwealth where the prevailing note was tranquillity. Small-town Indiana as Dreiser knew it was a world to be abandoned with scarcely a backward glance on the road to Chicago and then New York, the road to a future of possibility in place of a past of defeat. In the opening paragraph of the novel Carrie's ties to her girlhood home are "irretrievably broken" in the very moment that she leaves for Chicago (3). Even amid the sweaty labor of the shoe factory in which she goes to work, Dreiser allows her only fleeting thoughts of "Columbia City and the better side of her home life" (38–39). As they did the young Dreiser, the quickened rhythms of the city overwhelm Carrie and compel her forward, her yearning gaze fixed on an urban kaleidoscope of faces and styles and distant luxuries, never turned back upon memories of a compelling past.

Dreiser's background profoundly separated him not only from the comfortable Indiana writers of his day but from the agrarian realists who had preceded him (and, as well, from the more sophisticated realists who would rediscover him a decade and a half after *Sister Carrie*). As a consequence, he was largely free of the established literary and intellectual currents of the time, forced to rely on his own makeshift experience.[29] In its general outline, it is true, the story in *Sister Carrie* falls within the popular genre of the cautionary novel in which a young girl leaves home and makes her way through the hazards of urban life, there to be saved in the end by an appropriate marriage.[30] Dreiser draws directly on the moralizing function of such tales when he remarks in the third paragraph that such a young thing either "falls into saving hands and becomes better, or she rapidly assumes the cosmopolitan standard of virtue and becomes worse" (3). But the essential cultural grounding of the form is missing in Dreiser's hands in that his heroine does not carry with her the baggage of a village-formed morality that will be tested by the city but remain intact, nor is she an innocent victim of her would-be seducers. In the opening scene Carrie does not rebuff the attentions of Drouet but, the "instincts of self-protection and coquetry" at odds within her, encourages them to the point of giving him her new address before leaving the train (5). Dreiser may even have known E. P. Roe's *Barriers Burned Away* (1872), one of the great best-sellers of its time, a novel in which the former clergyman sends Dennis Fleet, his innocent hero, from a Wisconsin farm to Chicago after his father's death and just before the great fire.[31] Dennis finds success in the city but Roe's point is that chance plays no part in his rise. Success is simply the working out of God's benevolent design, a view that finds no echo in Dreiser's account of Carrie's fickle existence.

It is equally true that Dreiser had discovered Herbert Spencer during his newspaper days in Pittsburgh, and that the popular philosopher's chill universe of fate-tossed atoms deeply colored the novel. Dreiser frequently withdraws from the action for Spencerian asides of numbing abstraction, the source of his well-earned reputation as a turgid stylist (whereas in action passages he is capable of journalistic clarity and economy). Yet such passages are explanations after the facts of experience more than expressions of a full-blown naturalism dominating characters and action. Dreiser clearly brought to the novel ideas as well as literary conventions, but neither replaced the dominating influence on the work of his own fractured experience. It was all a Midwestern upbringing had equipped him with, and all he attributes to Carrie—a naive wonderment before the flow of events, constantly encountering life, as she feels in the moment of her entry into Chicago, as "a lone figure in a tossing, thoughtless sea" (11).

The new urban world had appeared in fiction by Howells and Crane and Norris and in Midwestern writing by Garland in *Rose of Dutcher's Coolly*, but never before had it been rendered with such density and so stripped of the grip of the past. Larzer Ziff has noted that when Carrie loses her virginity to Drouet, Dreiser casually asks what it is she has lost but asks with no apparent sense of the traditional value placed upon it. He does not mean to defy conventional morality with the story; he simply recounts what he knows to be the case. Henry F. May has similarly observed that what shocked Dreiser's contemporary readers was not what he said about American society but what he so casually showed. With *Sister Carrie* an old world and with it a good deal of old fiction is replaced by a flow of experience rendered fresh by separation from earlier attitudes. In one sense the publication date, 1900, could hardly have been more fitting, for with the book and the new century a sharply different kind of fictional response to American life was at hand. Yet in another sense the date was entirely wrong, for it would not be until the second decade of the new century that the novel would find an audience, and not until then that Dreiser would begin to have followers in a new and vastly deepened vein of Midwestern realism. After *Sister Carrie* was successfully republished in 1907, Dreiser said in a newspaper interview that his aim as a writer was "to tell about life as it is . . . the facts as they exist, the game as it is played!"[32] It was the unadorned truth-telling quality of the novel that a subsequent generation would claim as its own. It was the quality that Edgar Lee Masters had in mind when, in 1939, he told Dreiser that with the novel he had "cleaned up the country and set the pace for the truth and freed the young, and enlightened the old where they could be enlightened."[33]

5

After his moment of moralizing at the beginning of the novel about the fate of young girls removed from home, Dreiser goes on to paint a gaudy picture of the city itself as the real seducer:

> The city has its cunning wiles, no less than the infinitely smaller and more human tempter. There are large forces which allure with all the soulfulness of expression possible in the most cultivated human. The gleam of a thousand lights is often as effective as the persuasive light in a wooing and fascinating eye. Half the undoing of the unsophisticated and natural mind is accomplished by forces wholly super-human. A blare of sound, a roar of life, a vast array of human hives, appeal to the astonished senses in equivocal terms. Without a counsellor at hand to whisper cautious interpretations, what falsehoods may not these things breathe into the unguarded ear! Unrecognised for what they are, their beauty, like music, too often relaxes, then weakens, then perverts the simpler human perceptions. (3–4)

Carrie's natural place is the city, and she is seduced by its roar of life as surely as she is by Drouet and Hurstwood. Indeed, Carrie's Chicago lovers and the New York idealist, Robert Ames, *are* the city—"virtual accessories after the urban fact," Ellen Moers remarks[34]—in their embodiment of its glittering allure and shifting opportunities. In the city Carrie is free of small-town inquisitions, free to pursue—a dreamy pragmatist—her yearnings for something better. She does not suffer the triple fate of Dreiser's borrowing from the cautionary novel in the passage noted above (relaxation, weakening, perversion) but climbs an urban ladder[35] of success provided by Drouet, Hurstwood, and Ames, impelled by her one overriding impulse: "She would have a better time than she had ever had before—she would be happy" (27). Dreiser does not decry Carrie's ambition, and irony was never part of his literary equipment; her ambition was exactly his own. He can only document the unfolding of her fate, following with his odd combination of compassion and detachment the "blind strivings of the human heart" wherever they lead (455).

They lead first of all to "the lights, the crowd, the amusement" of the "great, pleasing metropolis" of Chicago (27). In Chicago, Carrie moves rapidly from her sister's working-class flat on Van Buren Street and a grinding job to a life of comfort as Drouet's mistress. For the flashy drummer, a genial sensualist, there is only a single response to the ease of seduction: "Oh, how delicious is my conquest." Carrie's response is only slightly more complex: "Ah, what is it I have lost?" Dreiser reports that she asks the question with "mournful misgivings," and he adds that there are moments of conscience when she accuses herself of failure (85). But in Carrie's deliberations with herself self-interest always wins out, and rapidly so. It is a final answer to all her questioning.

> There was always an answer, always the December days threatened. She was alone; she was desireful; she was fearful of the whistling wind. The voice of want made answer for her. (87)

Yet the answer has no permanence attached to it. She immediately begins to see her deliverer in a different light, aware of his limitations, aware even that she is more clever than he. When the polished front man of Fitzgerald and Moy's Adams Street saloon presents himself she believes she has discovered another and more glamorous Chicago type—the man of money and affairs, of ease and comfort and high position. Hurstwood's appeal is swift and inevitable, Dreiser explaining it on the uncomplicated grounds that the life of the city had awakened in Carrie an ambition for a more exalted existence.

As it appears in the sections of the novel involving Drouet and Hurstwood, Chicago is a place of wealth and cultivated taste yet also a crude developing metropolis only recently fashioned out of rural terrain. When Hurstwood seeks an anonymous setting to declare his love, he takes Carrie on a horse and buggy ride along a west side boulevard that is "little more than a country road" running through an "open grassy prairie" (116). Dreiser often describes the aspiring city in the inflated manner of a tour guide—or through Drouet's favorite response to its monuments of new wealth: "Fine, isn't it?" For Carrie the throbbing pace of the city is often bewildering; she was not one, Dreiser says, for whom change is agreeable. Yet her overriding response is enthusiasm, the city always adding to her sense of the possibilities of life, rendering her a willing victim of its "hypnotic influence," its "spectacle of warm-blooded humanity" (78, 73). What the city extracts in return for pleasure is money, and Carrie quickly realizes the iron laws of its significance. It is only when Drouet hands her "two soft, green, handsome ten-dollar bills" that the beckoning life of the city, its restaurants and theaters and fine clothes, comes within her grasp and she begins her ascent (58).

Chicago is the place of possibility, and the youthful Carrie is one of its rightful citizens. When the story shifts to New York, Hurstwood claims more attention. The pace of the story is altered as well. In Chicago events unfold slowly, keyed to the changing seasons of a year following Carrie's arrival in the city in midsummer and to the unraveling of a plot that involves Carrie's shift of allegiance from Drouet to Hurstwood, her discovery of Hurstwood's marriage, Mrs. Hurstwood's discovery of Carrie, the theft from the saloon safe, and finally the flight to Montreal and the marriage of Carrie and Hurstwood. In Chicago there is also pretense as well as possibility. Drouet pretends he will marry Carrie, Hurstwood pretends he is not married, Carrie overwhelms both her lovers with her play acting in Augustin Daly's melodrama of mistaken identity, *Under the Gaslight*. By contrast, the New York section of the novel has little plot development; there is a sense of solidity and inevitability, of fate working itself out in a setting that seems timeless and established. Dreiser makes clear the greater weight and wealth of New York, the intimidating sense of something already finished there, of a sea "already full of whales" (267). Here Hurstwood confronts his limits, as Dreiser had himself during his newspaper days on the *World*, and here he begins his slide into anonymity and suicide.

As the train bearing Carrie and Hurstwood eastward passes through Indiana, putting "Chicago farther and farther behind," Carrie feels with foreboding that she is being "borne a long distance off—that the engine was making an almost through run to some distant city" (249). She is in fact moving from a world still possessed of human qualities to one of cool impersonality.[36] Yet in the new environment it is Hurstwood who suffers, unable to reestablish the comfortable position of the insider he had known in Chicago, overwhelmed instead by a sense of New York as

> a city with a wall about it. Men were posted at the gates. You could not get in. Those inside did not care to come out to see who you were. They were so merry inside there that all those outside were forgotten, and he was on the outside. (300)

In New York, "Hurstwood of Chicago," as Dreiser calls him, sinks into the brooding and self-pity that Dreiser himself had known in the city. Once the thinly sustained facade of his Chicago life crumbles in the new environment there are no inner qualities of character for Hurstwood to draw upon. Carrie, on the other hand, after an initial period of dislike, is exhilarated by the city (311). "Its clear atmosphere," Dreiser says, "more populous thoroughfares, and peculiar indifference struck her forcibly" (275). Through the ministrations of Mrs. Vance, a sophisticated urbanite, she is introduced to the theater and the city's fashions and to Ames, the intellectual engineer from Indianapolis, who eclipses in her mind her faltering husband. Randolph Bourne noted that few American novelists could have resisted the temptation, once Ames enters the story, to improve Carrie's character under his elevating influence. But Dreiser treats the relationship as just another stage in what Bourne called the "vegetative sureness"[37] with which Carrie rises in the world; he allows Ames to pass into oblivion, left behind as Drouet and Hurstwood before. Unimproved, Carrie resumes her acting career, and with a princely salary of $150 a week she is able to move to a grand apartment in the Waldorf, surrounded now by admirers. When Hurstwood reads of her success in the newspaper, he thinks: "Ah, she was in the walled city now! Its splendid gates had opened, admitting her from a cold, dreary outside" (405). Yet Carrie's success bears with it loneliness and vague longing, turning her back upon the searching, future-yearning core of her being—the Carrie still waiting, as Dreiser says at the end, "for that halcyon day when she should be led forth among dreams become real" (455). The successful and unsatisfied Carrie is paired off in the book's last chapter with Hurstwood's failure and resignation, reduced in the final stage of his decay to a fifteen-cent room in a Bowery flophouse, there to switch on the gas and utter his final declaration of futility: "What's the use?" (453).

For many readers Hurstwood is the novel's most compelling figure. There is a hard clarity to his story, that of the gradual exposure of an underlying apathy and hollowness of character; and there is about his quiet and methodical end a quality of stolid dignity. While Carrie is clearly the figure at the center of Dreiser's imagination, she is nonetheless a more oblique creation. She understandably wishes to escape the drab poverty of her background and find ease and happiness, yet she seems moved by narrow self-interest softened only by fleeting moments of concern for others. Still, Dreiser insists that she is a figure of emotional greatness, and in part he seems to conceive of her as driven by a self-protective artistic temperament, fixed only upon her own survival and that of her art. But in the largest sense Carrie is perhaps best understood simply as the young Dreiser himself—a confused and ill-prepared figure from the country carried forward on the perplexing currents of a life both controlled and governed by chance and seeking to achieve at whatever cost the vague promptings of inner fulfillment. She memorably takes her place at the beginning of a procession of Midwestern refugees from the flattened hinterland to the mysterious city, there not to mourn a green utopia left behind but lured ever onward—as Dreiser says at the very beginning of his story—by "wild dreams of some vague, far-off supremacy" (4).

6

The year *Sister Carrie* was published Dreiser's father died in Rochester, New York, where he had been living with his daughter, Mame, and her husband, a fact of no small irony since Mame's affair with an older man back in Terre Haute, resulting in an illegitimate and stillborn child, had been a source of deep disgrace for John Paul Dreiser. His father's death turned Theodore Dreiser back upon his Indiana past once again, stimulating a second story involving another of his stained sisters and his pious Old World father with the working title *The Transgressor*. Jennie Gerhardt's story was deeply personal in that Dreiser dredged up youthful memories of poverty and social inferiority set against the teasing nearness of comfort and success; at the same time the story bore resemblance to the pattern he had established in his first novel. Like Carrie, Jennie is a young woman of beauty who falls into the hands of men of higher station, drifting off from Columbus, Ohio, where she and her mother work as cleaning women in a hotel, to Cleveland and eventually Chicago. But unlike Carrie, Jennie does not rise steadily in the world, leaving her lovers behind; and she possesses quite different qualities of character. She is a generous, yielding, sacrificial figure who in the end loses those she loves and is meant to gain final stature as a tragic heroine.[38]

Relying on the experiences of his sister, Dreiser wrote the opening chapters of the new novel as rapidly as he had those of *Sister Carrie*. After four months of effort he had finished forty chapters. On the basis of this early work he received advances totaling $750 from J. F. Taylor Company and the novel was scheduled for publication; but in late 1902 or early 1903 work was stopped. Dreiser was simply unable to finish the book, in part due to problems with depression and a variety of physical ailments; seven years would elapse, during which he returned to magazine editing, before he again picked up the manuscript and brought it to completion. After a considerable amount of editing and revision *Jennie Gerhardt* was finally published by Harper and Brothers in 1911.

Once again Dreiser clothed his story in the dress of a traditional cautionary tale. Eighteen-year-old Jennie is seduced by a hotel guest, Senator Brander, a man of fifty, and bears a child after Brander dies of a heart attack. Expelled from home by her father, she takes up domestic employment in Cleveland where she falls in with Lester Kane, the handsome son of a wealthy Cincinnati manufacturer and, like Dreiser, a lapsed Catholic who has adapted himself to a chill new world of moral relativism. It is here that Dreiser begins to shift the story from a conventional tale to an original and in many ways powerful narrative. Lester's desire for Jennie is direct and uncomplicated: he wishes her to bend to his will, her helplessness dominated by his brute power. For her part Jennie finally submits to Lester out of a combination of frank attraction to the luxury he provides and an altruistic wish to help her destitute family.

With Lester, Jennie suffers a second fall. When they move together to Chicago their relationship becomes known to Lester's family; yet in the face of social censure a tranquil household is eventually established in Hyde Park that includes Lester and Jennie as well as her illegitimate daughter, Vesta, and her old father. But finally Lester must choose between Jennie and family disapproval that brings with it the loss of his fortune. After a long period of indecision he at last leaves Jennie and eventually marries Letty, a wealthy widow of his own station; yet he cannot escape the awareness that he has wronged Jennie by not marrying her. On his deathbed, again united with Jennie, Lester expresses his deep sadness, Jennie her unceasing love. When Lester tells her she is "the only woman I ever did love truly," Jennie feels total happiness in "this confession of spiritual if not material union," certain that now she can live and die at peace.[39] However, in a final scene with a train leaving the railway station in Chicago and bearing Lester's body back to Cincinnati for burial, Jennie is left only with grief and a sense of abandonment. Lester is dead and her father and Vesta are dead; her family is reduced to two orphan children she has adopted out of a sense of compassion. Dreiser writes of her, viewing the scene apart from Lester's relatives, that she heard nothing

of the chatter and bustle around her. Before her was stretching a vista of lonely years down which she was steadily gazing. Now what? She was not so old yet. There were those two orphan children to raise. They would marry and leave after a while, and then what? Days and days in endless reiteration, and then—? (822)

In his early study of Dreiser, F. O. Matthiessen noted about *Jennie Gerhardt* that "the whole book gives the sense of being solidly planted in the Middle West."[40] This is true not in Dreiser's thin use of Midwestern locales—Columbus, Cleveland, Chicago—but in the book's grounding in the memory of his Indiana past. The opening scene, in which Jennie and her mother seek a hotel cleaning job, is one Dreiser deeply understood. He says of mother and daughter that "poverty was driving them"; in the mother's eyes there exists "a shadow of distress as only those who have looked sympathetically into the countenances of the distraught and helpless poor know anything about" (459). Although Jennie's story is an imaginative recasting of Mame's life, her character is drawn from what Dreiser remembered fondly about his mother—a character, as he says of Jennie at the novel's end, "born to yield, not seek" (821). In her ever-accepting nature Jennie differs dramatically from the restless and self-absorbed Carrie, and from Dreiser himself. Yet there is in the two novels the same hunger, rooted in the limitations of Dreiser's own Midwestern background, to participate, as he writes of Jennie, in the "panoply of power [that] had been paraded before her since childhood" (821). And there is the same sense of the mysterious workings of life, the constant drift that eludes understanding. When Lester visits Jennie after the sudden death of Vesta due to typhoid, hoping to provide her with comfort and advice, he expresses the fundamental Dreiserian position that "all of us are more or less pawns. We're moved about like chessmen by circumstances over which we have no control" (797). The less learned and self-conscious Jennie repeats Lester's view in her own terms yet instinctively softens it, turning it into a question that yields at least private comfort:

> Was it all blind chance, or was there some guiding intelligence—a God? Almost in spite of herself she felt there must be something—a higher power which produced all the beautiful things—the flowers, the stars, the trees, the grass. Nature was so beautiful! If at times life seemed cruel, yet this beauty still persisted. (801)

Despite the tragic quality of its ending with Jennie sensing the void that looms ahead, her yielding and enduring nature gives the novel a far milder tone than *Sister Carrie*, and in so doing it adds a more rounded view to Dreiser's fictional use of his Midwestern experience. The novel is far from the towering achievement Mencken thought when he proclaimed it "the best American novel I have ever read, with the lonesome but Himalayan exception of 'Huckleberry Finn'."[41] (In *This Side of Paradise*, the glamorous first novel that Scott Fitzgerald later characterized as a romance and a reading list, the bookish Amory Blaine takes note of his discovery "through a critic named Mencken of several excellent American novels," among them *Jennie Gerhardt*).[42] There is too little complication within Jennie's character, and neither she nor Lester possess the same strange claim on the reader's interest as Carrie and Hurstwood. Still, Jennie remains one of Dreiser's major creations and her story an effective refashioning of the Midwestern material that had sent Carrie before her on Dreiser's own journey out of the country and into the city. "Here, as in almost all of Mr. Dreiser's pages," Randolph Bourne (who thought the novel too much an attempt to do *Sister Carrie* again) remarked, "one can follow the pattern of life, sincere, wistful and unredeemed."[43] With Jennie's story following upon the successful reissue of *Sister Carrie* Dreiser had suddenly emerged as a major figure in the redirection of American literature.

7

T. K. Whipple, a perceptive contemporary critic of early twentieth-century American writing (and one who will be mentioned again in these pages), put his finger on Dreiser's curious place in Midwestern writing when he noted that "there are phases of Midwestern life which Dreiser does not touch, but those he treats he treats with authority."[44] What is remarkable about Dreiser, seen in a regionalist light, is indeed the absence from his fiction of much of the familiar Midwestern literary landscape. There is in his imaginative work no suggestion of a garden myth to affirm or deny, no stories of rural returns punctuated with ambivalent feelings, no current of resistance to a Midwest of folk charm or grim futility. *That* Midwest simply holds no place in his imagination; it is not rejected so much as it simply does not exist. Only in the form of autobiography in *Newspaper Days* (1931) and in the travel book *A Hoosier Holiday* (1916), based on a nostalgic auto trip to Indiana in his forty-fourth year (a celebrated author now but in his home state virtually unknown in comparison with Gene Stratton-Porter and other best-selling Indiana writers), did he return to his small-town Midwestern roots, mixing warm accounts of an idyllic landscape with resistance to rural provincialism. Placed in the company of Garland and Anderson and Cather, to say nothing of the company of Riley and Tarkington and the popular Indiana romancers, Dreiser hardly seems a Midwestern writer at all. His Midwest—the aspect of its life, as Whipple remarked, that he did treat in fiction and treat with authority—is the new urban environment populated both with refugees from the countryside and native urban figures, all of them animated by lust for life's elementary pleasures.

Dreiser was the first to render that brave new world with massive detail, to fully capture its strange mixture of exhilaration and tragedy, and to do so without a backdrop of the farm and small-town past. It was an achievement so original that in the years immediately following the initial publication of *Sister Carrie* he had neither literary successors nor a reading public. When both began to catch up with him in the second decade of the century he would seem to have illumined the way into a new urban America that for a moment had meant Chicago but was finally contained only by New York. As he recalled it in one of his autobiographical volumes, his first view of Chicago in 1887 had given him a sense of ecstasy and possibility hitherto unknown:

A veritable miracle of pleasing sensations and fascinating scenes. The spirit of Chicago flowed into me and made me ecstatic. Its personality was different from anything I had ever known; it was a compound of hope and joy in existence, intense hope and intense joy.[45]

This is exactly the response to the city he would eventually attribute to Carrie: "Chicago dawning, she saw the city offering more of loveliness than she had ever known, and instinctively, by force of her moods alone, clung to it" (454). But Chicago could hold neither Carrie nor her creator. It was in New York that Dreiser would find city life at what he called its keenest and most pathetic. In New York there was "none of that eager clattering snap so characteristic of many of our Western cities, which, while it arrests at first, eventually palls" but rather the languid "feeling of gross and blissful and parading self-indulgence . . . as if self-indulgence whispered to you that here was its true home." In his frank acknowledgment of the nature of that true home to which Americans were rapidly gravitating he could not have been more removed from the literary worlds of his Indiana contemporaries—from Riley's country pathways and Tarkington's country clubs and the Hoosier romancers' faraway lands. The urban-directed "voice of want," his and Carrie's, is, however, the one we now recognize as the authentic voice coming out of the Midwest and America as a whole as the century turned. In the city, as Dreiser proclaimed about his fictional world and the creative force behind it, "were huge dreams and lusts and vanities being gratified hourly. I wanted to know the worst and best of it."[46]

FOUR

Beacon across
the Prairies

Yes, it was an amusing thought, that Port Royal had
been built for such purposes—for growing up in. Port
Royal was not for everything, of course. It had sufficed
nobly. It had given him much. And now—

—*Moon-Calf*

1

Floyd Dell declared in 1912 that "the poetry of Chicago has been adequately rendered so far, by only one writer, and in only one book"—*Sister Carrie*. The judgment was offered in a series of articles about Chicago fiction, Dell holding that only Dreiser had captured the qualities of aspiration, of a liberating individualism, that marked the city as deeply as its hustling business spirit. His novel was "the most real, the most sincere, the most moving" of all Chicago novels. In it, Dell went on, Dreiser

> has not looked to see the badness of the city, nor its goodness; he has looked to see its beauty and its ugliness, and he has seen a beauty even in its ugliness. And in doing that he has given us, there is little doubt, the Chicago of the whole Middle West—a beacon across the prairies, a place of splendor and joy and triumph, the place toward which the young faces turn and the end of the road along which the young feet yearn to tread.[1]

Dell was writing from the vantage point of the start of the city's literary renaissance, those few years surrounding the Great War when it was at the center of what was advanced and liberating in American writing, and from the rediscovery of Dreiser's novel following its fresh publication in 1907 by the new firm of B. W. Dodge and Company. *Sister Carrie* stands at the beginning of that invigorating period, an inspiration to Dell and other writers drawn to the city from Midwestern farms and towns. In his Nobel Prize speech in 1930 Sinclair

Lewis said that the novel had come "to housebound and airless America like a great free Western wind, and to our stuffy domesticity gave us the first fresh air since Mark Twain and Whitman."[2] But in its original publication *Sister Carrie* was also the culmination of an earlier period of Chicago writing—the first halting attempts to find literary material in the commercial colossus beside the lake.

Henry F. May has pointed out—as, in effect, had Dreiser in his novel—that Chicago had little in common with the rural and town culture of the Midwest. What was appealing about it was precisely that it was different—the place where the Midwest encountered the cultivated East and the exciting, unsettling influences of Europe.[3] When Garland's Rose Dutcher determines to escape rural Wisconsin in search of the wider world, it is Chicago that leaps first to mind. Dell's fictional *alter ego* in *Moon-Calf*, Felix Fay, equally set on abandoning Iowa for the life of art, recalls in his bittersweet moment of leaving a map he had seen on a railway station wall:

> He saw again in his mind's eye, as he tramped the road, a picture of the map on the wall of the railway station—the map with a picture of iron roads from all over the Middle West centering in the dark blotch in the corner. . . .
> And then the hurt came again—the hurt of lost beauty, of unforgotten, unforgettable love. Felix quickened his steps. Another mile. And water. And forgetting.
> But his tramping steps went to the rhythm of a word that said itself over and over in his mind:
> "Chicago! Chicago!"[4]

When such young people actually arrived in the magnetic city they found a throbbing business world with bewildering extremes of wealth and poverty—the Chicago of Norris's *The Pit* (1903) and Upton Sinclair's *The Jungle* (1905). At the same time they found a city transformed between the leveling fire of 1871 and the World's Fair of 1893 into a cultural center of orchestras and museums, libraries and literary magazines.

Hamlin Garland's move to Chicago in the World's Fair year marked the entry of Chicago into the Midwest's literary imagination. Nearly a decade earlier, in search of the remnants of New England culture, he had left South Dakota for Boston; now his always sensitive literary antennae told him that Chicago was about to emerge as the new center of American writing and publishing. In the same year two Harvard undergraduates from Chicago founded the local publishing house of Stone and Kimball, putting out a variety of European and American literary works as well as an influential little magazine, the *Chap-Book*. For Garland they published a second edition of *Main-Travelled Roads*, the stories of *Prairie Songs*, and the essays of *Crumbling Idols* in which he preached his gospel of local-color realism and promoted Chicago's new eminence as a literary center—the three works all handsomely bound in an emblematic Midwestern green with a single cornstalk on the spine and three stalks of ripe corn on the cover. Garland now saw himself, an established author, as a major figure in the city's rising fortunes, a Midwestern native certain to be appreciated by its "splendidly American" population drawn from the heartland states.[5]

But when his Chicago novel, *Rose of Dutcher's Coolly*, largely written in the city and at his parents' new home in Wisconsin and published in 1895, drew a mixed reception, Garland began to withdraw his commitment just as he had earlier drawn back from his rural material. The *Dial*, one of the city's old-line review journals, found the style of the novel "slovenly" and objected to Garland's "repulsive lack of reticence" about sexual matters.[6] The *Bookman*, on the other hand, had praise for the work as "honest and strong and racy of the soil."[7] Garland, concentrating on the negative response, felt himself unfairly put upon by his fellow Midwesterners. "I resented this condemnation," he later wrote. " 'Am I not making in my small way the same sort of historical record of the west that Whittier and Holmes secured for New England?' I asked my friends."[8] He began making trips to the Mountain West, gathering material for the popular romances soon to roll from his pen, and there were lengthy stays in New York and trips to Europe. He would come to think of Chicago, as he confided to his diary after a visit to the city in 1923, as

> so appallingly bleak and drab that I want to get away from it. I feel its intellectual half-way house atmosphere. Its judgments are by men who have only advanced from Omaha or Sioux City or at best from some college and who are so sure of their opinions. I sense also the rude, crude taste of people who support such judgments.[9]

In 1916, when Garland abandoned Chicago for New York as the unquestioned center of literary activity, his hopes for Chicago had finally come true. The place had been right, his timing wrong. The fledgling Chicago literature of the 1890s culminating in *Sister Carrie* was followed by a fallow period, the reemergent genteel literary culture of the nineteenth century holding sway into the first decade of the new century, just as the moment of agrarian realism culminating in *Main-Travelled Road* had faded into the mellow idealism of the Indiana writers. When the Chicago renaissance made its belated appearance Garland was a pillar of an established literary order to be swept aside in the name of rebellion and liberation, Dreiser a prophet of the new age.

2

The Chicago stories Garland and Dell would construct would mirror, as had Dreiser's story of Carrie, their own experience—seekers from the hinterland lured by the city's offer of altered life. Another Chicago story came from within—an account of life among the cliff-dwellers from the hand of writers already within the urban gates. The story the outlanders told, containing obligatory scenes of railway arrival, was usually one of adaptation and triumph in the city.

For the established Chicago writers the primary subject was the clash between the strident new business culture and the values of settled and cultivated ways.

Born in Chicago and a member of a prosperous business family, Henry B. Fuller could trace his roots back to colonial New England.[10] After the death of his father in 1885 he took over the family's affairs, largely in real estate, and in 1890 he published his first novel, *The Chevalier of Pensieri-Vani*, a fictionalized travel book drawn from a Grand Tour and deep affection for things Italian. The work drew favorable attention from the Boston Brahmins of the day, including Howells, and was followed by a similar work of distant and idealized fiction, *The Chatelaine of La Trinité*. Then in 1893 Fuller sharply changed course, producing the first of two novels that broke new ground in the realistic treatment of urban material.

The Cliff-Dwellers was meant to capitalize on the attention the World's Fair brought to the city, its literature included. Fuller said the novel's theme was whether a young man should marry for attraction or for family connections, but this side of the work is obscured amid the portrayal of the city and its powerful business elite. In the offices of the Clifton, an eighteen-story skyscraper in which much of the novel's early action takes place and which provides its title, George Ogden, a newcomer from New England who comes to work for the Underground National Bank, is educated in the amoral world of the profit motive in which human behavior and business behavior seem irreparably severed. Among the business types he encounters is a brash booster, a spokesman for a society in which it appears to Ogden that the "bare scaffoldings of materialism felt themselves quite independent of the graces and draperies of culture," who instructs him in Chicago's centrality in the Midwestern imagination:

> "How much do you suppose people in Iowa and Kansas and Minnesota think about Down East? Not a great deal. It's Chicago they're looking to. This town looms up before them and shuts out Boston and New York and the whole seaboard from the sight and the thoughts of the West and the Northwest and the New Northwest and the Far West and all the other Wests yet to be invented. They read our papers, they come here to buy and to enjoy themselves."[11]

In the second part of the novel, Ogden having made his marriage choice, Fuller turns to the city's social whirl of conspicuous consumption in which Jessie Ogden leads the way and George is meant to pay the bills. The marriage is a disaster in that Jessie reveals none of the solid virtues of her Old Chicago family but instead is preoccupied with the "procession" of smart society. In the end Ogden marries again after Jessie's death, this time for attraction rather than for family, and settles into a life of simplicity and virtue that provides Fuller with a happy resolution of the tale.

Fuller continued his examination of business and society in Chicago in *With the Procession*, published two years later. Jane Marshall, the daughter of a wealthy but old-fashioned and principled Chicago clan, struggles to bring the family out of its entrenched ways and into the glittering procession of society. The founding father, David Marshall, is persuaded to move to a new mansion on the fashionable south side and to undertake attention-getting philanthropy; the social development of the Marshalls is paralleled in the story by modernization of their wholesale grocery business. The strain of change of both sorts is too much and David Marshall dies just after moving into the unfinished home, suggesting the inability of the old mercantile order to adapt to what Fuller calls the careless ways of the new order. In the end both the family and the business are fragmented—the inevitable result, the novel seems to say, of life in a city to which (in the words of one of the characters) "all its citizens have come for the one common, avowed object of making money. There you have its genesis, its growth, its end, and object."[12]

After *With the Procession* Fuller abruptly turned away from a fiction of contemporary realism and from Chicago as subject matter. In part, the explanation had to do with his flagging hope that with the "upward movement"[13] in the city following the World's Fair would come rapid improvement in cultural and social life. Even Garland, whose enthusiasm for Chicago's literary position always outstripped Fuller's, acknowledged that "as the glow of the Exposition faded . . . the city fell back into something like its former drabness of business enterprise, with little to offer the artist."[14] Both as a man and an artist Fuller also possessed a natural inclination to withdraw from enduring commitments. When Garland had congratulated him on *The Cliff-Dwellers* and his apparent allegiance to Howellsian realism, Fuller replied that he had "no fixed literary creed; on the other hand I experience now and then a disposition not to use the same model too many times running."[15] That disposition was clearly evident in the satires and dramatic sketches he turned to after his Chicago period and in his next novel, *The Last Refuge* (1900), another fictionalized travel book, this time set in Sicily.

Fuller was one of the first American writers to confront the new business-driven city as experienced by characters of high status. Among many other things about urban life he well understood, as would Dreiser in *Sister Carrie*, was the role of money as the final measure of all things in such an environment. He was also a fairly accomplished novelist in a technical sense, one of his critics even holding that he was "the most conscious stylist of late nineteenth-century American letters, next only to Henry James."[16] His limitation as a writer was his inability to fully give himself to his material for the long haul, leaving him finally on the fringe of literary importance, his lasting strength a brief but unblinking and immensely knowledgeable appraisal of affluent Chicago during the period of its first emergence into the national consciousness.

The Chicago novels of Robert Herrick belong to the same period and arise from a similar sensitivity to the clash of urban cultures. Herrick, however, treated the city from a significantly different angle—not from Fuller's position as an old resident within the gates but as a Harvard man in exile in John D.

Rockefeller's new university on the south side. Herrick joined the faculty of the University of Chicago to organize the program in rhetoric and composition in the World's Fair year, becoming, together with the poet William Vaughn Moody, one of the first of a new academic breed, the writer-professor. He would draw on the city in four realistic novels published between 1898 and 1905, all of them finding it dull, vulgar, obsessed with money, and hopelessly removed from his standard of all value—what he once termed "the Puritan yet broadminded ideal of Cambridge life."[17] Nonetheless, Herrick recognized the momentous shift in American life from the country to the city and with it a consequent shift in literary perspective, and recognized as well that no city at the turn of the century better typified the new urban spirit than Chicago. In its crude, hell-bent passage into the twentieth century it was the central American city.

From the University arising on the edge of the Midway Plaisance Herrick had a closeup view of the fair's tawdry end—the jerry-built structures meant to house visitors suddenly abandoned, thousands thrown out of work, the city as a whole plunged into a national depression that had only been postponed in Chicago by the financial windfall generated by the fair. When fire swept through all but one of the fair's deserted pavilions, the charred ruins seemed a fitting commentary on the city's dashed hopes, the dark city of daily struggle replacing the fleeting grandeur of the White City in Jackson Park. Although he was essentially a novelist of ideas and ethical questions, Herrick exhibited more willingness than Fuller to embrace social issues in his fiction and provide glimpses of the city's mean streets and working-class life.

Herrick first made use of a Chicago background in *The Gospel of Freedom* (1898), but it was in *The Web of Life*, published in the same year as *Sister Carrie*, that he dealt with his adopted environment most directly. Although the city still appalled him, he was aware of the particular literary stimulation it provided. "My strength is lost," he remarked, "as soon as I lift my foot from the prairie. Whatever I do will be done *there*."[18] In the novel Herrick effectively integrates the Chicago setting and the period—the social upheaval that followed the fair's close—with an unconventional love story. Every reference to the shuttered area of the fair revels in grim description:

> . . . Sommers turned his horse into the disfigured Midway, where the wreck of the Fair began. He came out, finally, on a broad stretch of sandy field, south of the desolate ruins of the Fair itself. The horse picked his way daintily among the debris of staff and wood that lay scattered about for acres. A wagon road led across this waste land toward the crumbling Spanish convent. In this place there was a fine sense of repose, of vast quiet. Everything was dead; the soft spring air gave no life. Even in the geniality of the April day, with the brilliant, theatrical waters of the lake in the distance, the scene was gaunt, savage.[19]

Herrick's powerful account of the fair's human aftermath is equally sunk in gloom:

The poor had come lean and hungry out of the terrible winter that followed the
World's Fair. In that beautiful enterprise the prodigal city had put forth her utmost
strength, and, having shown the world the supreme flower of her energy, had
collapsed. There was gloom, not only in La Salle Street where people failed, but
throughout the city, where the engine of play had exhausted the forces of all. The
city's huge garment was too large for it; miles of empty stores, hotels, flat-build-
ings, showed its shrunken state. Tens of thousands of human beings, lured to the
festive city by abnormal wages, had been left stranded, without food or a right to
shelter in its tenant-less buildings.[20]

As the story opens, the city's sullen atmosphere and the threat of labor violence are mirrored in the vague discontent of Howard Sommers, the hero, with
his career as a surgeon and his friendship with the upperclass Hitchcock family.
He falls in love with Alves Preston, the forlorn wife of an ailing and violent
patient, and begins a small rebellion against the life of privilege. The rebellion
turns serious when he leaves his position in a private clinic and takes Alves as
his mistress after the death of her husband (and following the great fair fire and
during the outbreak of the Pullman strike). After idyllic months spent together
in Wisconsin, Alves comes to believe she is hindering his career and takes her
own life. With her death Sommers recognizes that his period of revolt is over
and that he will return—in the novel's title—to the ordinary web of human
activity. Yet his rebellion has not been without point for he reenters life with a
new feeling for his fellowmen and a desire to adjust himself to them. In due
course he marries Louise Hitchcock, a daughter of privilege who has come to
accept some of his social views, and he regains his professional status by taking
over a modest practice in Chicago—his new life of compromised values in tune,
with Herrick's blessing, with a more moderate and sensible social climate that
has arisen in the country.

While *The Web of Life* was well received elsewhere, confirming cherished
views of the city as crassly opportunistic, in Chicago it drew outraged protest,
setting off a long-standing feud between the local press and the professor. Fuller
responded to the public attack with a private letter to Herrick that offered an
explanation for his own retreat from Chicago fiction: "Why should we goad
Chicago too cruelly?—the poor place is 'too dead easy.' It is like a hippopota-
mus howling under hatpins; it makes the wretched beast seem so undignified!"
Herrick nonetheless continued to prick the beast. In his 1905 novel *The Memoirs of an American Citizen* he treated the same period of social and economic
turmoil in a meat-packer's recollection of his rough-and-tumble rise through
Chicago business to the United States Senate. Later, he would explain that,
given his literary attitude and the forceful presence of the city, he had no choice
but to continue on:

I had taken my literary creed of realism seriously and felt morally bound to represent by words what my mind saw when it looked forth upon Chicago,—its
streets, its buildings, its dirt, its noise, its slovenly incompleteness, its rather crude
social life.[21]

3

Herrick's portrait of the city remains convincing in its detail, yet the odor of Cambridge *hauteur* that attaches to it is equally apparent. As Floyd Dell saw in a perceptive comment on Herrick in his series of articles on Chicago fiction, Herrick condemns the city as it is and has no faith in its future, seeing it only "as a muddy pathway down to hell, trampled and bloody in a monstrous and useless conflict."[22] The typical Midwestern outlander's response to Chicago was, once again, quite different—that of deep attraction to its offer of expanded life. Like Dreiser's Carrie, Rose Dutcher is inevitably drawn to Chicago from rural Wisconsin and in the city finds love and success, but beyond this surface similarity Garland's earlier story is wholly different. Carrie Meeber, a "half-equipped little knight" for whom knowledge is a "sealed book," is propelled forward on tossed seas by a dim desire for happiness, and in this she bears some resemblance, as was noted before, to the sentimental heroine of popular nineteenth-century fiction.[23] Rose's journey, on the other hand, is one of intellectual and artistic growth, the story of the development of the New Woman of the 1890s that Garland had found portrayed in Ibsen's dramas. In a chapter on Ibsen in *Crumbling Idols* such women were defined as healthy, vigorous, active agents who "re-act upon men, they rise above men at times in the perception of justice, of absolute ethics; they are out in the world, the men's world."[24]

The novel clearly has its autobiographical elements. It follows the intellectual awakening that carried Garland himself on an outward journey from his native Wisconsin and draws upon the feelings of guilt and euphoria engendered in him by his escape. Rather than Boston as destination, Rose travels only as far as Chicago, the new mecca of cultural transformation. And rather than treat his own growth directly, as Dell would in two novels of coming of age in the Midwest, Garland creates in Rose another of his sympathetic women characters, returning to the emotional center of much of his fiction but now casting upon a woman the story of urban emancipation just as in earlier tales he had cast upon her that of rural defeat. Yet like Garland himself and unlike Dreiser's Carrie, Rose cannot easily turn her back upon the rural past. Memories of family and place cling to her, complicating her feelings, coexisting with the compelling need for self development.

Rose's early life on the Dutcher farm is described as the "pagan-free" existence of a mythical Midwestern childhood. It is the joyous, physical, outdoor life of a motherless natural creature, casually exposed to what Garland calls the "dramatic and furious episodes of the barn-yard," oblivious to any sex distinction that limits her freedom and only lightly guided by an adoring father.[25] The first epiphany in her life comes when a circus performer strikes her as pure beauty, stimulating a sexual awakening that leads, in a desire to be worthy of him, to the flaring of ambition. Improbably, she determines to become a great scholar and launches upon a furious reading campaign, leading to a second awakening that takes place when she leaves the farm for the University of Wisconsin. On the train to Madison a chance meeting with a woman lawyer saves her from the advances of a conductor, the woman then advising Rose that denial—in the sense of postponing marriage until at least age thirty—is a necessary requirement for a woman's entry into professional life.

During her university days Rose's beauty matures as her intellectual horizons widen, yet she sternly resists the trap of marriage. A suitor who wants to sweep her off to a village life is informed that

> "All I want is to be let alone. I'm going to Chicago. I want to see the world. I can't be shut up in a little town like Lodi. I want to see people—thousands of people. I want to see what the world is like. I may go to Europe before I get done with it. I'm going to study art. I'm going to be great. I can't marry any one now." (147)

Marriage, however, is easier to escape than her father's devotion. When she returns to the valley farm after graduation she finds he has built a new house, assuming she will return to country life. There is strong appeal in such a sheltered existence. But the feeling stays with her that real life, and with it real love, are to be found only in the city, Garland here repeating through Rose the sense of redirection of Midwestern life that he had forcefully expressed in such stories as "A Branch-Road," "Up the Coule," and "A Day's Pleasure." For Rose the lure of civilization is more compelling than nature's appeal.

> This was the age of cities. The world's thought went on in the great cities. The life in these valleys was mere stagnant water, the great stream of life swept by far out and down there, where men and women met in millions. To live here was to be a cow, a tadpole! Grass grew here, yes—but she could not live on grass. The birds sang here, yes—but there were Patti and Duse and Bernhardt out there in the world.
>
> Here you could arise at five o'clock to cook breakfast and wash dishes, and get dinner, and sweep and mend, and get supper, and so on and on till you rotted, like a post stuck in the mud. Her soul would wither in a such a life. She was already slipping back into shiftlessness, into minute untidiness—into actual slovenliness. There was no stimulus in these surroundings, she told herself; everything was against her higher self. (172–73)

Rose at last must act on the need to leave the farm despite the pain caused her father, her guilt only modestly redeemed—as was Garland's own after abandoning his parents on a prairie farm—with plans for future visits.

On the train someone says, "See that cloud? . . . that's Chicago," and with the smoke on the horizon Rose is introduced to the city, the place of her full flowering (181). As was Carrie, she is assaulted at first by the sight of "dirt and murk, and all unloveliness," but again like Carrie she quickly discovers the other city of grand mansions and beautiful people and determines to claim a place among them (181–82). A letter of introduction to another professional woman, a doctor named Isabel Herrick, provides a first foothold in this world.

Rose, recognized as a diamond in the rough, is brought into the company of the right people, among them Warren Mason, a journalist, intellectual, and would-be novelist. When she reads some of her poetry at a dinner party (following a bucolic whistling demonstration) Mason finds the verse derivative but recognizes powerful inner qualities in Rose.

The courtship that follows occupies the rest of the novel. Rose remains passionate about her destiny; after a concert she feels, as she had in the presence of the circus performer, a sense of her special future, one that Garland repeatedly defines in terms of her removal from the somnolent rural past:

> In that one instant the life of the little coule, the lonely, gentle old father, and the days of her youth—all her past—were pushed into immeasurable distance. The pulling of weeds in the corn, the driving of cattle to pasture were as the doings of ants in a dirt-heap.
>
> A vast pity for herself sprang up in her brain. She wanted to do some gigantic thing which should enrich the human race. She felt the power to do this, too. (271–72)

Mason hardly seems the fit object of Rose's grand passion. He is a worn, older, pipe-smoking figure, critical and disillusioned, given to talk rather than action, among other things dry disquisitions on the "marriage question" and the need of both parties to retain freedom. Yet she considers him "a man of the great intellectual world . . . a man of national reputation living quietly under an assumed name," and it is with Mason that she falls in love (382). In its final quarter the novel trails off into a sentimental romance leading to a modern marriage in which Rose's portion will be criticism for her poetry, Mason's the healing of his cynicism.

The unlikely joining seems to have arisen out of Garland's wish to suggest some union of country and city for a younger generation arising in the Midwest. He wished to suggest, in other words, something of what he understood as his own situation, the country boy come triumphantly to the city and attentive to the best qualities of both. Rose is formed in the country and carries with her its simplicity and vigor while yearning for the varied and civilized life of the city. When Mason visits the Wisconsin farm after a proposal of marriage via letter and sees Rose in her native setting, the uncompromising city man appears to grow younger and is forced to admit that the landscape is "lovely—perfectly pastoral. Worthy a poem" (400). When Rose recites a poem in the pastoral setting Mason blesses her journey of development by confirming that she has found her true voice as an artist. Yet when it is time to leave for Chicago he returns to his vision of the city as the true human center, informing Rose that

> " . . . down there life is. Infinite novelty, ceaseless change. As you love the country, so I love the city. It is a greater pleasure to me to meet men than trees, and concerts more than winds in the pines. Artist souls, poets, people who do and think, are there, and so I must go." (402)

Rose affirms both Mason's view and his character in the novel's final line—"I realize it all, and I choose it"—yet she will bring to the city exactly what he lacks, an open, spontaneous, life-affirming vigor associated with the land (403).[26] Rose's father is part of an older rural generation left behind when she leaves for the city and marriage, pathetically weeping out of a sense of loss. It is a rural generation, Mason says, presumably voicing Garland's own sense of a fresh urban direction for his fiction begun with the novel, no longer worth portraying as "heroic sufferers, as the new school of fiction sets 'em forth" (391). Garland's main-travelled road now leads not back to the blighted country and denunciations of agrarian injustice but to Chicago, seen as the ideal meeting point of rural energy and urban refinement.

Most of the negative criticism of *Rose* was directed to the novel's sexual candor. As noted earlier, Garland stressed the fact that a farm upbringing brought with it sexual knowledge, and he drew attention to a young girl's developing sexuality, matters ordinarily kept under the literary rug. Rather than weakening her in the future, Rose's early sexual awareness is shown as part of a natural and positive moral outlook, and in the end she enters into marriage with an upright figure in the person of Mason. Although Garland was willing to treat a woman's sexuality in the story, daring enough in his time, he kept within the boundaries of Victorian morality by limiting his portrayal to the development of healthy adult attitudes. Donald Pizer has pointed out the revealing difference in the train-bound seduction scenes in *Sister Carrie* and *Rose*.[27] Drouet's desire for Carrie is not condemned by Dreiser—and Carrie does not flee his attentions. Garland's trainman, on the other hand, eyes Rose with the "glare of a sex-maniac," drawing forth the author's indignation and causing Rose to cling to her seat in terror (90). And while Rose is rescued in the end by a fellow passenger, for Carrie there is neither rescue nor its need. What in Dreiser is simply the depiction of amoral human behavior, in Garland is a shameless violation of moral propriety. He wishes to acknowledge Rose's sexual nature and her position as a New Woman while holding to the comforting responses of approved moral conduct.

In addition to the sexual theme in the novel, Garland appeared to break new ground in his treatment of marriage, but here as well he worked within circumscribed limits. Repeatedly in his stories he had shown the farm woman's workworn and subservient life. Rose, on the other hand, is bent on staying free of male domination, whether her father's love or the marriage offers of suitors. Nonetheless, she allows her poetry to be judged by Mason, and it is just as she finds her voice as a poet that she agrees to enter into marriage. Mason insists on her freedom ("I want you as comrade and lover, not as subject or servant, or unwilling wife"), and Rose chooses marriage with full deliberation (380). Yet with marriage the question of her growth as a woman and an artist seems at least partly set aside in favor of conventional expectations. With Mason's final declaration of love, Garland declares that "the whole world reshaped itself" for Rose and with a sense of inevitability she "set her face toward wifehood and fame with such a man as companion, friend and lover" (401, 402).

Garland clearly means to suggest that the mature Rose will now maintain her art within marriage, fulfilling a prophecy of one of her Wisconsin mentors: "To most women marriage is the end of ambition, to you it may be an incentive. If you are big enough, you will succeed in spite of being wife and mother" (151–52). Still, marriage, even one on Mason's terms of principled freedom, strikes the reader as a conventional and even sentimental fate for one with Rose's passion for a special destiny.

As with his stories, one wishes that Garland had possessed more artistic conviction and more steadfastness in the face of criticism. With *Rose of Dutcher's Coolly* he opened up new themes and a vision of urban life enriched by rural vigor that might have led to real advance in his work. Nonetheless, despite its limitations the novel is his best. It retains some of the freshness and idealism of the 1890s, and it remains historically important both as an early feminist novel and for announcing a major theme in Midwestern writing, the escape of the talented young from the provinces in search of the self. Rose would be recreated in Felix Fay and George Willard and Nick Adams, and in Carol Kennicott she would experience reversal, the ambitious city girl sent to the town, there to struggle with the marriage question refashioned anew.

The novel is also important for its hopeful portrait of Chicago as the new literary center of the country—an embodiment in fiction of what Garland had put forth as argument in *Crumbling Idols*. The novel hesitates, however, before the next step, that of full embrace of the city as literary material. Rose's early poetry is imitative, as Mason sees and as Rose herself comes to recognize, because it "stood upon the graves" of the great figures of Europe and New England. It is weakened because she had "considered literature as something necessarily afar off, in England or France, in Boston and Cambridge." While Chicago is the place for her escape, that it also "might be the subject of literature had not occurred to her" (220). Mason advises her to do what he himself has not done as a writer—to turn her attention to the swirling urban scene about her, to "deal with the city and its life":

> "See these lovers walking before and behind us. He may be a clerk in a bank; she the banker's daughter. That man Harvey, in whose box you sit tonight, was a farmer's boy, and his wife the daughter of a Methodist preacher in a cross-roads town. How did they get where they are, rich, influential, kindly, polished in manner? What an epic!" (275–76)

But in fact Rose finds her authentic subject when she returns for the summer to her native region. In Wisconsin, Garland says, "rhymes grew in her mind upon subjects hitherto untouched by her literary perceptions," the familiar objects of country life. She feels now the "splendid peace which comes when the artist finds at last that art which is verily his," and it is when she recites one of her country-inspired verses that Mason finally pronounces her a true poet (374–75).

Chicago as it is glimpsed in the novel is a place of mills and money only beginning to establish itself in the arts. When one character inveighs against its "lack of art atmosphere," Isabel Herrick insists that "all the hard conditions of Chicago are changing. All that was true a few years ago is not true now. The materialism you war against, no longer dominates us. We are giving a little time to art and literature" (295, 296). Although Rose, unlike Carrie, finds in Chicago a circle of friends attentive to art and ideas, Garland makes clear that the city as a flourishing center of culture is a matter of hope more than reality. Materialism still holds sway. Yet it is through Rose that he voiced his own earnest vision, one swiftly to be abandoned, of the "city's developing thought"—a time when "Paris and the Rocky Mountains met here with Chicago and the most modern types of men and women" (297).

4

Garland had put Chicago and the Midwest firmly behind him as subject matter when Dell arrived in the city in the autumn of 1908. In his two best novels, however, Dell would return to the theme Garland had announced in *Rose*—that of a Midwestern artistic and intellectual awakening that leads inevitably to Chicago, the city now in the full flush of its renaissance. What is surprising in retrospect is that so much time elapses between Dell's removal to Chicago and his classic accounts of Midwestern exodus in *Moon-Calf* in 1920 and *The Briary-Bush* the year following. When the books appeared Dell himself had long since departed Chicago for New York's Greenwich Village and an editing job on the *Masses*, and by 1920 Midwestern writing had already reached a high-water mark with the publication in the year of Sherwood Anderson's *Poor White*, Sinclair Lewis's *Main Street*, and Scott Fitzgerald's *This Side of Paradise* together with Dell's first novel. Part of the explanation for the delay is that *Moon-Calf* was a number of years in the writing and went through several revisions before Dell found a narrative style—thanks to the experience of psychoanalysis, he maintained in his autobiography—that finally made possible the use of personal material.

Dell came to Chicago with hope of continuing a newspaper career that had begun in Davenport, Iowa, a metropolitan center of 100,000 where he had moved with his family in 1903 after boyhood years in the small Illinois towns of Barry and Quincy.[28] Books and ideas already had a hold on him, and in Davenport he had found a lively intellectual life that included a socialist party local and such aspiring literary figures as Susan Glaspell and George Cram Cook. In those days Dell fancied himself both a self-taught intellectual and a poet, one happily lost in a dream world that insulated him from humdrum reality. He managed to secure a foothold in reality, and launch upon his life's work as an editor and writer, when he became a cub reporter on a Davenport newspaper. He wrote at the same time for a socialist publication and his poems began finding their way into print, including some in national publications, gaining him a local reputation as a boy-poet who also happened to be a socialist and a reporter. When at length he lost his newspaper job he finally made his move, age twenty-one, to Chicago, the obvious next step on the journey of the gifted young out of the provinces.

Unlike Carrie Meeber and Rose Dutcher, Dell entered the city expecting the worst. He tried to suppress his poetic side—the inner life that he would designate as his fictional hero's "moon-calf" nature—and put forward his worldly self, anticipating harsh and indifferent treatment. As it turned out, he need not have bothered. Chicago's literary and artistic renaissance, just underway, was made to order for Dell and Dell for it; the boy-poet with advanced ideas and bohemian tastes swiftly became one of its central ornaments. At the same time he advanced with unlikely speed in the practical world of Chicago journalism. He soon had a reporter's job on the *Evening Post*, a conservative paper with a small circulation directed to the business and professional elite and with a tradition of some intellectual interest. The literary editor, a learned young Irishman named Francis Hackett, had used his relative freedom from editorial policy to develop a thoughtful page of liberal social interests; in 1908 he was ready to expand to a separate weekly supplement. Dell was asked to become his assistant on the *Friday Literary Review*, a job in which he was soon turning out reviews on all manner of books. After eleven months on the job he became the associate editor of the eight-page tabloid, and in 1912 he replaced Hackett as the editor.

With the *Review* Dell was at the hub of Chicago's literary life. He championed in its pages the new voices of liberation such as Ezra Pound and fresh figures from the hinterland such as Vachel Lindsay. At the same time he was living out the new freedom with his wife, Margery Currey, a schoolteacher and sometime journalist whom Dell had married in 1909. First in a north side apartment in Rogers Park and later in the artists' colony along 57th Street on the south side in left-over structures from the World's Fair converted to inexpensive studios, the Dells set the standard for advanced, unconventional behavior. By his own account, 1912, the year of his ascent to the editorship, was the single most astonishing year of the Chicago renaissance. Maurice Browne opened the Little Theater on the fourth floor of the Fine Arts Building on Michigan Boulevard with plays of Yeats, Strindberg, and Schnitzler. Harriet Monroe founded *Poetry: A Magazine of Verse*, with Dell one of the poets asked for contributions. From abroad came the Irish Players with productions of Synge and Lady Gregory. And there was the *Review* itself, in its short life rapidly become what Sherwood Anderson called "the leading literary mouthpiece of the middle west."[29] At age twenty-five Dell was its major voice, repeatedly attacking the genteel tradition's ideas of beauty and sentiment and calling for a new literature of vital realism. What realism meant for him was simply the direct and honest response to experience. Convention should be set aside in literature and all areas of life, and consequently the modern artistic endeavor—as Dell put it in a comment on Shaw—was bound to reveal a "fundamental quarrel" with traditional society.[30] In an editorial called "Literature and Life" in which he argued the case for the new literature, he noted that "the poets have always preached the gospel of disorder. The novelists from Fielding to Galsworthy have spoken in behalf of the man at odds with society."[31] A Chicago novel that admirably fit the *Review's* prescription for new writing was Norris's *The Pit*, the story of Curtis Jadwin's attempt to corner the world's wheat market in the whirlpool of commodity trading on LaSalle Street. But it was the author of *Sister Carrie* more than any other who manifest what Dell and his tabloid had in mind—an author wholly unbound by convention, capable when turned to the subject of Chicago of embracing both its terror and its beauty.

Dell's Chicago days ended as abruptly as his rise to a position of cultural leadership had begun. While in New York in 1913 to report on new autumn books for the *Review*, he learned that the *Post's* owner, irritated by Dell's review of a book by Jack London, had vented his frustration by firing several departmental editors. When the paper's managing editor resigned, Dell followed suit. His subsequent move to New York signaled a transition to a larger stage, as it would for other Chicago figures who would undertake the same migration. He had established himself at the center of Midwestern intellectual life, now it was time to carry the standard of liberation elsewhere. There was no bitterness in the move; Dell had simply used up Chicago and needed fresh stimulus. In *Homecoming*, an autobiography that carries his life through his thirty-fifth year, he offered a graceful farewell to the city that had served him so well:

> I had been happy in Chicago; never would it seem to me a grey and ugly city. I loved the lake, Michigan Boulevard with its open vista and its gleaming lights, the Parks, even the preposterous loop district with its sudden architectural leap into the sky; I had seen beauty there, enough to fill my heart; there had been days and nights of talk and laughter; the years had passed in a golden glow of friendship; and it was a city haunted everywhere by the memories of love, its pain and its glory. It had been a generous city to a young man. I would always be grateful for what it had given me.[32]

His first two novels, Dell remarked in his autobiography, were the "imaginative interpretation of memories" more than imaginative fictions.[33] In *Moon-Calf* and *The Briary-Bush* he followed the story of his intellectual and artistic odyssey from the obscurity of Illinois and Iowa towns to Chicago prominence, making only occasional departures from his recollections. But if the adventures of Felix Fay were his own, his hero's character was nonetheless shaped to a thesis. By his own account, Dell underplayed Felix's social side and emphasized a shy and sensitive nature, in so doing creating in Felix the familiar figure of the dreamy Midwestern artist in embryo.

Moon-Calf, the better of the two accounts, takes Felix from the fictional towns of Maple and Vickley to Port Royal, the Davenport of Dell's own provincial days. In Maple the schoolboy who spends all his time in the library scribbles on his tablet his future goal: "Felix Fay, the Great Novelist, was born here, May 10, 1886."[34] By the time he begins high school in Vickley he is a confirmed intellectual, finding in books "endless, unrolling vistas of new and fascinating ideas" (109). The Mississippi River city of Port Royal eventually provides the urban setting in which Felix can fully spread his wings as an artist and thinker. There he binds his poems into small booklets with ink-designed covers, quite content with the "solace of magic words" until a socialist comrade informs him that his verses about life are a consolation for not actually living it (163).

Involvement with the socialist local and later a reporting job on the *Port Royal News* turn Felix toward ordinary realities, underscoring the central clash in the novel between the claims of an inner world of ideals and artistic detachment and an outer world of action and commitment. Likewise, there is tension in Felix's attraction to radical stances as against an opposed need for the conventional and settled. The latter is illustrated in his romance with Joyce Tennant. When the young woman adopts his ideas of freedom, allowing her to dally with him while keeping a commitment to another suitor, Felix is troubled by his success. "His conscience irked him," Dell points out, and adds that for Felix the unconventional affair with Joyce now lacked "the glamour it shone with in theory" (351).

The affair with Joyce is paired off with Felix's friendship with a young writer, Tom Alden, a figure based on Dell's friend George Cram Cook. After he loses his newspaper job Felix goes to live with Tom on a farm, the two of them writing novels, the prose form suggesting a greater balance in Felix's life now between the dreamy poet and the practical journalist. When Joyce decides on a conventional marriage with her suitor, the prospect of Chicago enters the story even though Felix has landed a job on a second local newspaper. Joyce tells him in tones of reproach that as a writer he has absorbed all he can from Port Royal. Having taken in the experience that she and Tom and the town have to offer, his self-interest dictates that he move on.

> "You are a writer, you want experience. Here am I—and you take me!—You want to learn how to write novels. There's Tom—and you take him.—And when you're through with us, you move on. You need Chicago—and you'll take that. Oh, I know from the things you've said lately—it's neither me nor Tom, now; it's Chicago." (391)

Moon-Calf drew favorable critical reaction and sold well, going through eleven printings that totaled 38,500 copies. Heywood Broun in the *New York Tribune* even ranked it ahead of Lewis's huge best-seller among the novels of 1920: "Drop whatever you are doing and read Floyd Dell's Moon-Calf. Yes, Main Street can wait. . . . We'll say it's some novel." Chicago reviewers were equally laudatory. In the *Tribune* Fanny Butcher declared that "*Moon-Calf*, by Floyd Dell, is the most important first novel by an American that has come from the presses this fall," and in the *Daily News* Harry Hansen said the book sounded "the clearest and most promising note struck in American literature in our day and generation." Dreiser even weighed in with high praise in a letter to Dell, telling him the book was both "an intimate and faithful picture of middle west American life" and a "delightful piece of writing as well."[35] Readers now find less to admire. The novel is, as Dreiser suggested, written in a clean-lined manner that holds up reasonably well, but the structure is wholly episodic, loosely arranged only around the three locales of Felix's life, and the Joyce-Felix affair in the dominant Port Royal section is overly drawn out. The book is of more interest than Scott Fitzgerald thought when he dismissed it at the time of publication as a bogus masterpiece "without glamor, without ideas, with nothing except a timorously uninteresting report of a shoddy and uninteresting life."[36] Yet it remains true that Felix commands interest largely as a type, the developing artist-intellectual uncertain about himself and his values, and the book about him seems finally another minor Midwestern classic, important chiefly for historical reasons.

That history lodges it among the revolt-from-the-village books that Carl Van Doren identified in a celebrated 1921 article in the *Nation*—a series of works lifting the veil of innocence and serenity from small-town America. Van Doren located the beginnings of what he called the "newest style in American fiction" with Edgar Lee Masters's *Spoon River Anthology*, and among its successors included work by Anderson, Lewis, Zona Gale, and Dell. Yet Van Doren acknowledged that Dell's novel was far removed from Masters's strident village protest; it was a work that grew not out of anger but from what Van Doren termed a "revolutionary detachment from village standards." Dell was not trying to settle old scores by showing the intellectual and spiritual poverty of provincial life; instead, he wrote as if war against the village had been settled or was no longer worth troubling over. Although Felix blunders and suffers through the course of the novel, he grows steadily, largely free from any repression. The result for Van Doren was a beautiful novel that gave way neither to blind hatred of small-town life or local-color sentimentality, a work that was "everywhere stiffened with intelligence."[37]

Van Doren was clearly right in noting what was different about *Moon-Calf*, and Dell himself remarked in his autobiography that it was "ridiculously untrue" to consider his book an exposé of the Midwest.[38] What satire exists in the book is aimed, with softened edges, at Felix rather than at his background—at his moon-calf nature, his susceptibility to radical ideas, the division within him between the ideal and the practical. Dell's attitude toward Felix's Midwestern upbringing was signaled in his dedication of the book to B. Marie Gage, his second wife and a native of Minnesota, with the words that his tale recorded the "grim yet generous hospitality" of the region "to the fantastic beauty of young American life." Port Royal especially, a city of some size and complexity, offers Felix abundant room for development, and although the smaller communities of the story provide less stimulus, Dell treats them as pleasant enough stages in Felix's growth. When Felix is about to leave Port Royal he salutes the city in terms that recall Dell's own valedictory remarks about Chicago:

> He had been happy in Port Royal: it had given him love, and painful wisdom, and the joy of struggle. He would like to write a poem about it. The town had been built for him, though they who built it had not known. It had been built for young men and girls to be happy in, to adventure in, and to think strange and free and perilous thoughts. (394)

It is true, as the intellectual Rabbi Nathan informs Felix, that Port Royal may not be a typical Midwestern city in that it has a dual heritage of idealistic and bookish New Englanders and German immigrants who "brought with them a taste for music, discussion and good beer" (254). Nonetheless, it *is* a Midwestern city, and neither Felix nor Dell makes a strenuous effort to isolate it from the rest of the region. Felix moves on, as had his creator before him, because it is his nature to gravitate to the major centers of artistic and intellectual life. The provincial past of villages and a small city is not so much rejected as closed off, once-useful stepping stones on an out-bound journey of fulfillment. "It had sufficed nobly," Felix muses about Port Royal as he leaves it. "It had given him much. And now—" (394).

In *The Briary-Bush* Dell recounted the next stage of Felix's odyssey, again drawing deeply on his own life but with less adherence to fact. And he used again the episodic form of his first novel with large divisions directed to the places in which he had lived, this time within Chicago. The novel is, as Bernard Duffey notes, the central fictional account of the artist-intellectual in Chicago at the beginning of its cultural boom. It also remains of interest as the continuing story of Felix's development. Yet the freshness of the earlier novel is missing; the course of Felix's development is more certain, his practical side gaining the upper hand, his future settled. When he marries Rose-Ann Prentiss, a girl he had met during his first days in the city, the novel is given over to the question of freedom versus domesticity within marriage, with Dell coming down finally on the side of the latter. After many marriage trials the novel ends with Felix and Rose-Ann making plans for a house and family, convention triumphant. Felix has a last moment of regret for his old "dream of freedom" but concludes now that it was "a dream only—and worthy only the farewell tribute of a faint and shadowy regret."[39]

With the novel Dell seemed to be turning his back on Felix's ideal of an unfettered life, and also on a young generation that had thrilled to *Moon-Calf* as a study in provincial revolt. The metaphor of the briary-bush was meant to draw attention to the ordinary concerns and feelings of life that include involvement with others. When Felix and Rose-Ann try to escape commitment in the name of freedom, their marriage falters; when they accept it, the marriage is renewed. Dell's obvious point in the further adventures of Felix Fay is that happiness requires that he rein in his intellectual ideals in favor of the practical and conventional side of his character, a life turned now toward people more than ideas. What begins in *Moon-Calf* as a portrait of the developing artist-thinker ends in *The Briary-Bush* as a marriage study commending ordinary domestic arrangements.

Clearly the two novels must be placed together to see Dell's full view of Felix, one in which the division in his character is finally resolved in favor of Dell's own eventual turn away from bohemian excess in favor of the settled and the everyday. In his autobiography Dell remarked that the course Felix traveled in a few years in Chicago—an inner journey from "being a poetic infant" to accepting "adult responsibilities"—was one that he had taken himself ten years later. "It was," he added, "what one wishes one's life had been like," and, significantly, he ended his autobiography with the fact of his becoming a father for the first time at age thirty-five.[40] For good reason fervent admirers of the first novel felt betrayed by the second, and the critical response generally ranked it as the lesser work.

Then as now, the best part of *The Briary-Bush* is the portrait Dell draws of Felix's swift rise in Chicago during the beginning years of its intellectual ferment. On the train from Port Royal he expects the worst about the city and prepares himself for the survival of the fittest, the letters of introduction he carries with him seemingly as ineffectual as a paper sword. He has burned his novel before leaving on the assumption that the grim city will allow no time for writing. The reality turns out quite different: he meets helpful people, finds pleasant lodgings in Community House, and even the city streets strike him as beautiful. After landing a reporting job on the *Chronicle* he soon finds himself the assistant drama editor and in the thick of new artistic ferment. He is able now to marry Rose-Ann and settle in a studio-salon near Jackson Park in a temporary building left over from the World's Fair. Here he tries to write a popular play, drawing the wrath of Rose-Ann who adopts his idealistic posturing just as he tries to abandon it. Felix's rapid rise in Chicago journalism and in artistic circles continues when he becomes the newspaper's head drama critic and has a play produced by the Artists' Theatre. In the end, his broken marriage put back together, he tells Rose-Ann that "Chicago was too damned nice to me." It had not provided the resistance he needed; it had not confronted him with a world in which "ideas counted for something—where people put you in jail if you disagreed with them" (418). The way is thus prepared, though nothing is said directly in the novel, for Felix to move to New York, here to pit himself against a larger and more intractable world.

5

In what Dell saw as the pivotal year in Chicago's artistic life, 1912, Dreiser returned to the city. *Jennie Gerhardt* was behind him as well as *The Financier*, the first volume of his Frank Cowperwood trilogy based on the career in Philadelphia, Chicago, and London of the business tycoon Charles Yerkes. Now he was doing research at the Newberry Library for the second volume and conducting interviews about Yerkes's manipulation of the gas and traction business in Chicago during the years Dreiser himself had struggled to gain a foothold in the city. Chicago had changed since that raw time and so had Dreiser. The shy and ineffectual dreamer now represented the advanced edge of what was fresh and provocative in literature. During his two-month stay in the city there were meetings with Garland and Fuller, writers identified with the past; a more admiring audience was awaiting him in such figures of the city's renaissance as Masters, Anderson, Maurice Browne, and Dell. On the front page of the *Friday Literary Review* Dell had already warmly praised *Jennie Gerhardt*, finding the tale of seduction set in part in the city's fashionable Hyde Park section even superior to *Sister Carrie*. The Chicago critic's warm reception of the novel did nothing, however, to deter Dreiser's enthusiasm for a young woman Dell was also interested in—only one of several women he found time to pursue along with his library research.

Dreiser wrote the novel in New York following his return from Chicago, taking longer than usual because of abundant material and then a severe cutting of the holograph and the typescript to meet the publisher's wish for a more compact volume than *The Financier*. When the work was set in print, Harper's abruptly decided not to publish, presumably because the account of Yerkes's adventures struck too realistic a chord. To Dreiser it seemed a repeat of his difficulty with *Sister Carrie* until another publisher, the John Lane Company, came to the rescue and the novel appeared without fuss in the spring of 1914.

The Titan closely followed the Chicago experience of Yerkes in the middle 1880s. Frank Cowperwood, a powerful and attractive figure with the personal motto "I satisfy myself," is drawn to the city from the East rather than the Midwest, and drawn for its business possibilities rather than the cultural magnetism that had captured Rose Dutcher and Felix Fay.[41] To the details of Yerkes's Chicago period Dreiser grafted some of his own Chicago adventures from 1912–13, especially that of the older man able to gather the affection of beautiful girls from younger rivals. Other aspects of Dreiser's life found their way into his conception of Cowperwood, from the sense of initial arrival in Chicago as an outsider and confrontation with an established society to the feeling of being trapped in a marriage to a woman he no longer loved (as Dreiser now felt himself to be) to Cowperwood's Dreiserian "appetite for the wonders of life."[42] Cowperwood's several sexual escapades occupy much of the narrative, especially affairs with Rita, Stephanie, and the seventeen-year-old Berenice, these alternating in the narrative with repeated accounts of his business dealings. Cowperwood's attraction to women is frankly sensual but in Berenice he at last finds a pure, Platonic form of beauty that he realizes has long been his goal—an unconvincing discovery given his attachment to sexual variety but one meant to cast him in a modestly heroic mode as a figure responsive to an ideal. The aspect of the novel that holds more interest than Cowperwood's pursuit of love is his pursuit of power, though here again Dreiser attaches to him ennobling qualities meant to give to his eventual downfall an element of tragedy.

His first sight of Chicago on the train coming from the East enlivens Cowperwood with a sense of business possibilities. A branch of the Chicago River, "filthy, arrogant, self-sufficient," is deeply inspiring: "Here was life; he saw it at a flash. Here was a seething city in the making" (3, 4). He glimpses as well in that first moment the form of urban enterprise that will preoccupy him: "Even more than stock-brokerage, even more than banking, even more than stock-organization he loved the thought of street-cars and the vast manipulative life it suggested" (5). From this point Cowperwood launches into a series of deals culminating in his control of public transportation in the city, his hard methods undiluted by ethical considerations yet comparatively more attractive than the hypocritical moralizing of his opponents. His frank dishonesty has at least the benevolent effect of improving the quality of public life, Cowperwood gaining riches while the public enjoys better transportation.

Cowperwood fails in the end to force the Chicago city council to grant lengthy extensions to his street railway franchises when the public outcry following revelations of his business practices pushes the politicians into an unfamiliar position of civic virtue. For Dreiser this conclusion is not to be understood as the triumph of good over evil. The book has about it, as Mencken said of *Jennie Gerhardt*, "no more moral than a string quartet or the first book of Euclid."[43] What it does have, as Mencken also saw about the earlier novel, is a view of life. In a brief epilogue called "In Retrospect," Dreiser declares in his most inflated prose that a "balance is invariably struck" between the ambition of men like Cowperwood and the need of the nameless masses, keeping the one from wholly winning out over the other—the strong becoming too strong, the weak too weak. Cowperwood's heroism exists in his challenging the "equation" in a burst of individual striving, his tragedy—or, as Dreiser says, his pathos—in the discovery "that even giants are but pygmies, and that an ultimate balance must be struck" (551). Yet the balance exists only for the time being since change always rumbles beneath the surface, continually giving rise to elemental forces of nature like Cowperwood.

The Titan has none of *Sister Carrie's* strange fascination. The life of Chicago is thinly treated, and no character comes to life with the immediacy of Hurstwood or Drouet. Cowperwood's aggrieved and embittered wife, Aileen, makes some claim on the reader's interest, but the central figure of Cowperwood himself is more interesting in Dreiser's overall conception of him than in the actual rendering of his middle years in Chicago. The strongest case for the novel is a historical argument first set out by Mencken, Dreiser's most astute and enthusiastic critic, in an admiring review in *Smart Set*. Mencken held that in the novel Dreiser had "thrown overboard all the usual baggage of the novelist" in the sense that he had rejected the prevailing fictional formulas of the day, especially those catering to the desire of the sentimental for "heart interest" or "sympathy." Carrie Meeber and Jennie Gerhardt might possibly be understood as the soft heroines of popular fiction, but no one could make the same mistake about Frank Cowperwood, a figure wholly without appeal to the emotions. "He is no hero at all," Mencken declared, "but merely an extraordinary gamester— sharp, merciless, tricky, insatiable."

As a fictional figure Cowperwood is not so lacking in conventional touches as Mencken maintained, especially as seen in his pursuit of ideal beauty in the person of Berenice. But Mencken was right in that with *The Titan* Dreiser moved even farther beyond the "wallowed rut of fiction" than he had with *Sister Carrie*.[44] He began the period of Chicago's entry into the literary lime- light with a story deeply lodged in his own early experience—the amoral waif tossed to success by large forces. Then at the turning point into the full day of the city's renaissance he created out of his own growing sense of strength a figure of power, one even less morally bound than Carrie yet brought down by the "equation" balancing life's forces. Whatever its shortcomings as effective fiction, *The Titan* was a forceful and original novel in conception, one befitting Dreiser's status in the second decade of the century as a guide from out of the past who was showing the way into the literary future. Two years after the novel appeared one of his Midwestern successors, Sherwood Anderson, would celebrate in the *Little Review* the plodding "path" Dreiser had worn through the bleak wilderness of American letters. Thanks to his example other writers could now walk with the qualities he lacked—with "grace, lightness of touch, dreams of beauty bursting through the husks of life."[45]

FIVE

The Sweetness of
Twisted Apples

> George Willard, he felt, belonged to the town,
> typified the town, represented in his person the
> spirit of the town. Elmer Cowley could not have
> believed that George Willard had also his days of
> unhappiness, that vague hungers and secret
> unnamable desires visited also his mind.
>
> —*Winesburg, Ohio*

1

Mencken was thinking of Dreiser's work when he wrote in 1915 that Chicago ("epitome of the United States, of the New World, of youth")[1] was the only American city of the past quarter-century, San Francisco excepted, to inspire a first-rate novel. Over the next decade other writers drawn to Chicago from the Midwest would enrich the city's literary reputation, inspired by Dreiser's example and the city's vigorous cultural life, yet Chicago itself would only infrequently appear in their best work. The one certain masterpiece of the period, Sherwood Anderson's *Winesburg, Ohio*, would return for characters and setting to the rejected provincial past, like Floyd Dell's *Moon-Calf* setting its hero toward the beacon on the prairie only in the moment of farewell.

Much of the work coming out of Chicago in the period and capturing national attention was in the form of poetry rather than fiction. Anderson remarked later that "all over the middle western country, for a time, there was an upflowing of interest in verse."[2] Dell claimed that with the founding of *Poetry* so many poets found their way to the city that he had to clear one from his desk at the *Evening Post* each morning to begin work. Little of the verse, much of it given over to Chicago's breathless spirit of liberation, remains of interest. The single major work that has endured on the fringes of literary life, Edgar Lee Masters's *Spoon River Anthology,* looked back, like *Winesburg, Ohio*, to the abandoned countryside for its material and to a discredited garden myth for its spirit. It was a revolt-from-the-village work that genuinely revolted, one that portrayed—as Carl Van Doren noted—the Midwestern village as lacking "even the outward comeliness which the village of tradition should possess."[3]

With *Poetry's* appearance in 1912, Chicago suddenly vaulted from the literary capital of the Midwest to an international center of modern verse. The journal drew support from the well-heeled and well-placed of the city—Henry Blake Fuller was a member of its first advisory committee—and its pages were open to a host of now-forgotten local poets as well as the downstate Illinois triad of Masters, Sandburg, and Lindsay. Yet from the start *Poetry* was located in Chicago, not bounded by it. In the first number Harriet Monroe—a poet herself whose Chicago career, at age fifty-two, reached back to the earlier generation of Garland, Fuller, and Herrick—announced her editorial intent to "print the best English verse which is being written today, regardless of where, by whom, or under what theory of art it is written."[4] The aim was given substance by the energetic efforts of Ezra Pound, the magazine's European talent scout, which brought in contributions in addition to his own from William Butler Yeats, T. S. Eliot, and Robert Frost. Early issues also carried work by D. H. Lawrence, James Joyce, Wallace Stevens, and William Carlos Williams. Set against the efforts of such luminaries of modernism, the "jing-jing-jingled" rhythms (as he himself characterized them) of Lindsay's "General William Booth Enters into Heaven" and the sloganeering of Sandburg's "Chicago"— both among the journal's prize works—now seem at best quaint. Yet in their time they were at the forefront of what was fresh and vital in the new writing, and by virtue of their appearance in *Poetry's* pages they were removed from provincial measure and placed within the stream of the best of modern writing.

Two years after *Poetry's* appearance Margaret Anderson launched the *Little Review*, another landmark in Chicago's rise to an international literary stage. Acquainted with Dell in his *Friday Literary Review* days as well as Dreiser and Anderson, she brought to the enterprise unbridled enthusiasm for the liberating in all its forms. Potential contributors were briskly informed that the conditions of acceptance were that

> you must know English prose; you must write it as though you are talking instead of writing; you must say quite frankly and in detail the things you would not be allowed to say in the prostituted, subsidized, or uninteresting magazines; and you must be true.[5]

The journal's first number included contributions from Dell and Lindsay and a "New Note" by Sherwood Anderson which captured the journal's passion for the fresh in a plea for "the reinjection of truth and honesty into the craft" of writing. The "new note," Anderson went on, is

> an appeal from the standards set up by money-making magazine and book publishers in Europe and America to the older, sweeter standards of the craft itself; it

is the voice of the new man, come into a new world, proclaiming his right to speak out of the body and soul of youth, rather than through the bodies and souls of the master craftsmen who are gone.[6]

In an editorial after the first year of publication Margaret Anderson described her aim as nothing less than the creation of "some attitude which so far is absolutely alien to the American tradition."[7] It was a vision certain to fall short even in Chicago of the renaissance, and by 1917 she was off to New York with the journal and subsequently to Paris where she would find lasting fame by printing portions of *Ulysses* and some early Hemingway. In its Chicago days the *Little Review* favored criticism and carried only a small amount of imaginative work, and that mostly poetry. The journal's most useful function was to serve as a cheerleader for the city's literary enthusiasm, in so doing helping give some shape to its free-wheeling adventure into the new.

2

When Harriet Monroe, searching for potential contributors for *Poetry* among magazines in the Chicago public library, came across a Vachel Lindsay poem called "The Proud Farmer," she at once solicited work for the journal. In January 1913 the magazine carried the thunderous "General William Booth Enters into Heaven," the first of several Lindsay poems to appear in its pages. The association of the troubadour from Springfield with the Chicago renaissance had, however, earlier roots. In 1909 Dell had favorably reviewed a privately-printed collection of his work, *The Tramp's Excuse*, finding the unknown author, with considerable accuracy, as "something of an artist; after a fashion, a socialist; more certainly, a religious mystic; and for present purposes it must be added that he is indubitably a poet!"[8] Then in 1910 Lindsay produced in Springfield and at his own expense a single issue of *The Village Magazine*, a hand-decorated and handsomely produced vehicle for his poems. Among them was "The Illinois Village," a celebration of prairie towns as an antidote to soulless urban life:

> O you who lose the art of hope,
> Whose temples seem to shrine a lie,
> Whose sidewalks are but stones of fear,
> Who weep that Liberty must die,
> Turn to the little prairie towns,
> Your higher hope shall yet begin.
> On every side awaits you there
> Some gate where glory enters in.[9]

The magazine also carried four editorials proclaiming the need for a new localism. When the editorials caught the eye of Garland, Lindsay was invited to

Chicago to address the Cliff Dwellers, a club Garland had helped found, and to speak to students at the Art Institute, where he himself had once studied. Later, when Garland passed through Springfield, he met with Lindsay's parents, majestically advising them from his position as overseer of Midwestern writing that "Your son is a genius. Be patient with him a little longer."[10]

Lindsay was hardly in need of Chicago's blessing to secure his break with regional convention nor to affirm his course as a writer. A free spirit preaching the gospel of beauty and with a visionary religious sensibility linked to a Campbellite heritage, he had spent three years at Hiram College in Ohio followed by long tramps around the country as a vagabond poet, peddling his verse for bread and then retreating to a room in his parents' comfortable Springfield home, there to bombard editors with his work. "General Booth" first took shape during an excursion in California. General William Booth, the blind commander-in-chief of the Salvation Army, had recently died in London at age eighty-three, catching Lindsay's imagination and filling him with the sense of the heroic old leader embodying his own mission of tramping and preaching. The poem, written in a burst of intensity, was refined down to fifty-six lines, and with its appearance in *Poetry* Lindsay felt his life instantly altered. After a decade of obscurity he came in his thirty-third year into the possession of fame—and a fixed poetic reputation that he never escaped.

Lindsay had submitted two versions of the poem, one with directions that it be sung to the tune of the battle hymn "The Blood of the Lamb" with accompaniment by bass drums, banjo, flutes, and tambourines. Harriet Monroe chose this version, though with some trepidation about its appropriateness for her new journal; later, she would consider the poem among the journal's greatest triumphs. The poem conveyed the Blakean religious fervor of Lindsay's long apprenticeship with its vision of Booth leading a motley assembly of the world's poor to union with "King Jesus":

> Hallelujah! It was queer to see
> Bull-necked convicts with that land make free.
> Loons with trumpets blowed a blare, blare, blare
> On, on upward through the golden air!
> (Are you washed in the blood of the Lamb?)[11]

More intriguing to readers, and increasingly to Lindsay himself, were the poem's hard-edged sound effects, its word play of rattling banjos and tambourines. In "The Kallyope Yell" he would fasten on the fairgrounds calliope as a symbol of the strident, blaring quality of American life and celebrate its sound with thumping repetition:

> I am the Kallyope, Kallyope, Kallyope!
> Hoot toot, hoot toot, hoot toot, hoot toot,
> Willy willy willy wah HOO!
> Sizz, fizz. . . .[12]

His most celebrated exercise in submerging substance into effect would come shortly thereafter with "The Congo," a poem inspired by the evangelistic zeal of African missionaries but remembered for its drumming refrains of "Boomlay, boomlay, boomlay, BOOM" and "Mumbo-jumbo will hoo-doo you."[13]

At a Lincoln's Day banquet in Springfield in 1914 Lindsay gave a rousing recital of "The Congo," a performance repeated a month later in Chicago at a dinner arranged by Harriet Monroe for the visiting Yeats. Thereafter the writing of poetry took second place to public performance, the unknown poet tramping the country replaced by the popular entertainer on the lecture circuit. Until his death by suicide in 1931 Lindsay remained a public poet, audiences expecting and receiving renditions of his familiar poems during one-man shows that the poet dubbed the Higher Vaudeville. Meanwhile his collections of new work languished. In an introduction to his *Collected Poems* in 1923 Lindsay acknowledged that he had found failure in success "for having written a few rhymed orations," and he quoted Keats on the sweetness of unheard melodies to suggest another side of his work, a poetry of romantic and religious idealism.[14] Although some critics have tried to find in Lindsay a true artist and visionary thinker, his reputation remains locked in the boisterous work that began with his association with *Poetry*—an eccentric and subrational folk poetry that emerged from what he termed his "travelling, oratorical life"[15] and that for the most part was removed from Midwestern experience and rural and village celebrations that had marked some of his earlier verse. When his *Collected Poems* appeared, T. K. Whipple remarked that of all living American poets Lindsay's reputation rested upon the smallest achievement in terms of bulk—some half-dozen poems linked to his Higher Vaudeville that included, in addition to those already mentioned, "Abraham Lincoln Walks at Midnight," "Bryan, Bryan, Bryan, Bryan," and "The Chinese Nightingale." "The rest of his *Collected Poems*," Whipple noted, "are best forgotten—are necessarily forgotten by his admirers."[16] It is a judgment that still holds.

3

Poetry played a similar role in launching Carl Sandburg's career after years of obscurity. As with Dreiser before him and Anderson later, nothing in Sandburg's background suggested a literary future. A Swedish working-class background and early years in Galesburg, Illinois, bent him toward menial jobs and later itinerant farm labor and railroad work throughout the Midwest. A year's tuition to Lombard College in Galesburg after service in the Spanish-American War began a literary apprenticeship with a leaning toward poetry along Whitmanesque lines. By 1907 he had made the obligatory shift to Chicago for the literary young with work as an associate editor of *The Lyceumite*, a magazine of the Lyceum and Chautauqua movement, and subsequently on a theatrical publication. There was an interlude in 1910–12 when he was in Milwaukee as private secretary of the city's Socialist mayor, a time during which his own political convictions were formed, before he returned to Chicago to begin a long newspaper career, primarily with the *Chicago Daily News.*

In the fall of 1913 Sandburg dropped off at *Poetry's* office on Cass Street (now Wabash Avenue) a sheaf of poems about Chicago. Some of his earlier work had been rejected by the magazine but now he was warmly embraced. An editor recalled that she was "not prepared for the sweep and vitality of the Chicago Poems which he brought into the office the first day I met him. They quite took us off our feet and it was with much pride that we introduced this new star in the firmament."[17] The March 1914 issue led off with Sandburg's "Chicago" with its now familiar cataloguing of the city's big-shouldered attributes:

> Hog Butcher for the World,
> Tool Maker, Stacker of Wheat,
> Player with Railroads and the Nation's Freight Handler;
> Stormy, husky, brawling,
> City of the Big Shoulders. . . .

Two years later Sandburg collected his work under the title *Chicago Poems,* bringing forth from Harriet Monroe praise for "verse of massive gait whether you call it poetry or not" and from Amy Lowell a declaration in the *New York Times* that it was "one of the most original books this age produced."[18]

Sandburg's verse did indeed seem different—direct, simple, a free-verse prose-poetry of blunt language and common feeling. And the subjects of the best poems were equally different—the glimpsed lives of the city's working-class poor. The stentorious public poet of democratic affirmation who would appear in later years, especially in his book of the thirties, *The People, Yes,* is only dimly seen; for the most part emotion is reigned in, narrowed by a reportorial confinement to details of place and situation. In "Muckers," for example, men simply watch ditch diggers "Stabbing the sides of the ditch / Where clay gleams yellow," the poem concluding that while some decry the job, others covet it. In "Subway" "worn wayfaring men / With the hunched and humble shoulders / Throw their laughter into toil"; in "Mill-Doors" factory workers are "old before you are young"; in "Working Girls" young women tramp off in the morning to stores and factories with "little brick-shaped lunches" under their arms. "Mamie," one of the collection's most effective poems, is a narrative report of a small-town Indiana girl who dreams of "romance and big things" in far-off Chicago "where all the trains ran," then switches to her actual city life where she now wonders if the trains run to even larger places where there is

> romance
> and big things
> and real dreams
> that never go smash.[19]

Dreiser found the "fine, hard, able paganism" of *Chicago Poems* delightful,[20] no doubt glimpsing in the work an extension of the unflinching urban portrait he himself had drawn in his Chicago fictions. Sandburg followed the book, however, with *Cornhuskers* in 1918, a collection of verse that drew on rural memories rather than Chicago days and that was deeply tinged with exactly what was so notably lacking in Dreiser—nostalgic feeling for Midwestern rural life. "I was born on the prairie and the milk of its wheat," Sandburg began "Prairie," the best-known of the poems, and went on to develop an explicit city-country contrast that vigorously asserted the enduring nature of the "prairie arms," the "prairie heart":

> I am here when the cities are gone.
> I am here before the cities come.
> I nourished the lonely men on horses.
> I will keep the laughing men who ride iron.
> I am dust of men.

But consistency of feeling or attitude was never a feature of Sandburg's work, and the poem seemed to end on a quite different note, one that now evoked the prairie world in an elegiac light—as "a bucket of ashes"—and to put stress on a future of "new cities and new people":

> I speak of new cities and new people.
> I tell you the past is a bucket of ashes.
> I tell you yesterday is a wind gone down,
>   a sun dropped in the west.
> I tell you there is nothing in the world
>   only an ocean of tomorrows,
>   a sky of tomorrows.[21]

Although he remained one of the star discoveries of *Poetry* and a name to conjure with in Chicago long after its other literary lights had drifted away, after 1919 Sandburg's creative energies turned more toward the six-volume life of Lincoln that would become the centerpiece of his long career. He continued to produce a body of poetry notable for exactly what is lacking in Lindsay, its bulk, but with *Chicago Poems* and *Cornhuskers* his most striking and original work was behind him.

4

Masters, the third of the downstate Illinois poets and the oldest, was not a *Poetry* discovery, to Harriet Monroe's lasting regret. He was considerably influenced by the magazine's free verse, however, especially as it was manifest in Sandburg's work, and after the appearance of the Spoon River poems he became one of its inner circle. Oddly, *Spoon River Anthology* appeared in book form before *Chicago Poems*, and Masters, abruptly a center of attention in his middle forties, would contribute a dust-jacket blurb for the work that helped alter the course of his own career.

Born in Kansas, Masters grew up in central Illinois, first in Petersburg and then Lewistown, the latter located near the Spoon River. He followed his father into law after a year at Knox College in Galesburg where he studied Greek and his reading of such free thinkers as Spencer and Huxley gained him the nickname "the Atheist." Boredom with village ways soon prompted a move to Chicago where he eventually entered into a legal practice with Clarence Darrow, already a celebrated defender of liberal causes. A first volume of poetry appeared two years before *Sister Carrie*; a second volume followed in 1910, both works characterized by a romantic spirit and little attention to the immediate facts of Masters's life. During the same period he published in Chicago a number of plays drawing on more contemporary material and alternating in mood from realism to melodrama. The poems brought Masters no attention and his plays were never produced.

When Dreiser came to Chicago for research on *The Titan*, he quickly called on the lawyer-poet. The two had begun correspondence following a letter by Masters praising *Sister Carrie*, the book coming to his attention after its republication; now Masters supplied Dreiser with leads about Charles Yerkes's Chicago career and set up interviews with some of Yerkes's contemporaries. Shortly thereafter Masters met Sandburg in Chicago, the poet reminding him of a Swedish cobbler he had known in Lewistown; when Sandburg brought him a sheaf of his early poetry the work struck Masters as "poetry in substance and prose in form."[22] Harriet Monroe's magazine was now appearing but Masters gave it little attention. He associated it with an earlier generation of Chicago writers, including Fuller and Garland, and with what he thought of as the city's habitual amateur spirit. His interest picked up when he read Sandburg's "Chicago," but when he came to write his autobiography in 1936 he would make a point of distancing himself from the work by noting Sandburg's limited sense of the city as a place of "packing plants, and criminals, and dirty alleys."[23]

Masters located the immediate origin of *Spoon River Anthology* in a visit of his mother to Chicago in 1914 and long talks about Lewistown and the town's characters that rekindled a buried interest in the past. After he put his mother on a return train he immediately wrote the opening poem, "The Hill," and two or three of what would become the book's epitaphs. At the same time the idea came to him of making a book in which, as he later recalled, he would "put side by side the stories of two characters interlocked by fate, thus giving both misunderstood souls a chance to be justly weighed."[24] Masters's plan for a dialectical work arising from joined figures gave way to mostly individual portraits, the poems turned out rapidly in bursts of almost trance-like creativity on weekends and spare moments drawn from his legal practice. In a letter during the midst of composition he informed Dreiser that he was writing "the Spoon River stuff into which I am pouring divers philosophies—taking the emptied tomato cans of the rural dead to fill with the waters of the macrocosm."[25] One of the work's first readers was Sandburg, who offered praise and at the same time brought Masters more of his own poetry—work that now struck Masters as either touched with a "rough tenderness" or simply "shocking, forthright with a sudden turn of rude realism." Through Sandburg's eyes the lawyer-poet began to see a Chicago he had barely noticed, the grimy working-class city yet also a city populated by artists and men and women living together in as much freedom as in Paris. The year 1914 struck him as altogether "miraculous," a joyously rich and creative period that—he added with the advantage of hindsight—was to be swept away by the Great War.[26]

In that year the Spoon River poems began appearing in *Reedy's Mirror,* a St. Louis literary and political magazine that billed itself as "The Mid-West Weekly." The editor, William Marion Reedy, an iconoclastic libertine and an avid supporter of the new literature, had been an early champion of *Sister Carrie*, writing in the *Mirror* that "its veritism out-Howells Mr. Howells and out-Garlands Mr. Hamlin Garland."[27] He and Masters were old acquaintances (the "Literary Boss of the Middle West," Masters affectionately called the editor)[28] and Reedy had published some of the Chicago lawyer's early work, though he had also urged him toward more direct use of his own experience. The first Spoon River installments in the *Mirror* were signed with the name of Webster Ford, the pseudonym meant to separate the careers of poet and lawyer. Only late in the weekly appearances of the poems in the magazine did Masters's own name appear, and this at Reedy's insistence that literary fame would not dash his legal career. Eight and a half months after it had begun, the series ended in the *Mirror* with an epitaph for "Webster Ford," its concluding lines urging upon the young, in the ebullient language of the Chicago renaissance, "hearts heroic" and lives as "fearless singers and livers."[29]

In addition to first publishing the Spoon River poems Reedy likely exerted a good deal of influence on their creation. In her autobiography Harriet Monroe maintained that because Reedy had refused his "classic tales in verse and begged him to get up to date in style and subject," Masters had launched into new work "as a kind of challenge to the free-versifiers whose voices in *Poetry* were beginning to excite the critics."[30] She added that the poems originally might have been intended as parody, a possibility that gains strength from Reedy's recollection that when the poems were accepted for publication Masters was "surprised, half suspecting I was guying him"—and from the fact that Masters, once the poems began appearing in the *Mirror*, sought to change the overall title to one he considered more properly literary, "Pleasant Plains Anthology."[31] Reedy, to his credit, held out for the original title.

Together with the influence of Reedy and the example of the free verse of Sandburg and the imagist poets appearing in *Poetry*, the Spoon River poems were affected by Masters's reading of *The Greek Anthology*, a collection of ironic epigrams and epitaphs spoken by the dead and written by anonymous ancient Greeks, the work brought to his attention by Reedy in 1909. And over everything there was the looming example of Dreiser. In Dreiser's work Masters discovered an open-eyed examination of the contemporary scene, including its buried sexual dimension, together with an ironic sense of destiny's shaping effects. Although in person he found Dreiser limited in literary knowledge, the novelist's work seemed possessed of "vast understanding . . . of people, of cities, of the game of life."[32] After their meeting in Chicago, Dreiser and Masters made a trip together to central Illinois that perhaps played into Masters's interest in the literary uses of the region. When *Spoon River Anthology* appeared, one of its epitaphs, "Theodore the Poet" (probably sent on for Dreiser to read before its original publication in the *Mirror*), spoke of a writer whose vision "watched for men and women / Hiding in burrows of fate amid great cities, / Looking for the souls of them to come out"—the very act Masters would perform for the anonymous inhabitants of an imagined Midwestern village (41).

Following book publication by Macmillan in 1915 (with a second edition with new poems the following year) *Spoon River Anthology* swiftly became that rare thing, a popularly successful work of poetry. Critical reaction was equally positive, though Masters was taken to task here and there for the unpoetic form of his free verse, his sexual directness, and the unrepresentative nature of his village figures. Floyd Dell was surprisingly reserved. He was not sure that Masters's free verse added up to real poetry, and he felt that what he called the poet's "high ironic attitude" had caused him to slight the goodness of American life. He saluted, however, "a strange impressiveness, akin to greatness" in the work that caused one to respect it if not like it.[33] Ezra Pound's enthusiasm was uncontained: "At last! At last America has discovered a poet."[34] But in a second article about Masters, Pound was more cautious and perceptive. He now found the poems "rather too numerous" and the method tending to the mechanical. When Masters published two new volumes of poetry in 1916, *Songs and Satires* and *The Great Valley*, both returning to the ethereal mode of his earlier work, Pound concluded that he had simply "gone off into gas."[35]

Harriet Monroe was equally struck by Masters's lack of understanding, given the nature of his subsequent work, of what he had wrought in the Spoon River poems. When he brought her proofs of *Songs and Satires* she was astonished that he had gone back to the manner of what she called his "ineffectual early period." Although she protested that a new book should contain only recent poems of his best quality, capitalizing on his sudden and hard-won success, he made only minor changes in the volume. Over the years books flowed regularly from his pen, each—in Harriet Monroe's view—"containing many candidates for the wastebasket diluting a few profoundly beautiful poems,"[36] and Masters's reputation trickled away. By 1920 his miraculous Chicago period was over. He abandoned his law practice and moved to artist's digs in the Hotel Chelsea in New York, a full-time writer. Among many subsequent works of poetry and fiction was *The New Spoon River* in 1924, a second volume of graveyard verse from the now suburbanized village. A decade later, in 1935, came a biography of Lindsay.

Harriet Monroe's conclusion that Masters was "the worst self-critic I have ever known"[37] is borne out not only by his later career and lack of development of the vein of poetry originally struck in *Spoon River Anthology* but by the celebrated volume itself. The assembled cast of village types, "all, all . . . sleeping on the hill," is more inclusive than necessary, with the result that there is unavoidable repetition (1). And Masters added at the book's end "The Spoonaid," a mock-epic that works over the same ground as the epitaphs, with that followed by the "Epilogue," a rambling and seemingly pointless verse drama.[38] An addition to the 1916 volume, the latter was perhaps meant to lend to the book a more elevated and literary tone. But what holds up best about *Spoon River* are simply Masters's admirably compressed (as if, the poet May Swenson remarked, "the dead disdained to babble")[39] glimpses of a Midwestern village world of lives unfulfilled and misunderstood, a shade world of plain truths sharply removed from the happy village of traditional belief and popular literature.

In the book there are more success stories rising from the grave than is usually remembered, many of them recalling a glowing pioneer past of Jeffersonian self-sufficiency and sturdy endurance. In "Lucinda Matlock" and "Davis Matlock"—portraits drawn from the lives of Masters's grandparents—the subjects heroically "bear the burden of life" and find in the grave "sweet repose." Those who moan in death are said to be a younger generation of "Degenerate sons and daughters," those for whom "Life is too strong" (229). "John Wasson," once a soldier in the Revolution, made his way to Spoon River with his wife, there to cut buffalo grass, fell the forests, build schools and bridges, creating a satisfying life from nothing (212). "Rutherford McDowell," a photographer, records in the faces of the descendants of the noble pioneers a litany of loss:

> With so much of the old strength gone,
> And the old faith gone,
> And the old mastery of life gone,
> And the old courage gone,
> Which labors and loves and suffers and sings
> Under the sun! (227)

Yet the affirmations and unabashed appeals to sentiment that appear with increasing frequency in the latter pages of the work are overwhelmed by more forceful revelations of twisted lives and tortured eternities, figures for whom the unflinching truth of their story is a final gesture. They speak of hypocrisy and repression, loneliness and blighted unions, misfortune and misadventure— of lives gone wrong, truths unacknowledged. From the town banker, "Thomas Rhodes," there is the smug assertion of the conservative wisdom of lives "self-contained, compact, harmonized, / Even to the end" (109). But most of the Spoon River dead cry out with the anguish of the town poetess, "Minerva Jones," one who "thirsted so for love!" and "hungered so for life!" (22). "Doc Hill" sacrificed his days to the town because "My wife hated me, my son went to the dogs" (32). "Emily Sparks," an old maid school teacher with a "virgin heart," dreams of an idealized schoolboy burned free of dross until there is "Nothing but light!" (18). "Margaret Fuller Slack," her writing career dashed by the birth of eight children, bitterly concludes that "Sex is the curse of life!" (48).

When Sherwood Anderson read Masters's book he assumed, with some reason, that it was "founded on hatred. A burning arose in him [Masters] and galvanized his lackadaisical talent into something sharp and real. Then the fire went away and left the man empty."[40] That may well be an accurate capsule account of the unexpected emergence of *Spoon River Anthology* in Masters's work and its equally sudden disappearance as a model for his future verse: a fire quickly stirred and quickly dampened. The frustrated cry of the artist who has fled to Rome, "Archibald Higbie"—a figure "weighted down with western soil" and unable to expunge the town from his soul—may point to long-suppressed and not wholly conscious anger within Masters himself:

> I loathed you, Spoon River. I tried to rise above
> you,
> I was ashamed of you. I despised you
> As the place of my nativity.
> And there in Rome, among the artists,
> Speaking Italian, speaking French,
> I seemed to myself at times to be free
> Of every trace of my origin. (194)

Surely much of the original appeal of the collection stemmed from just such harsh village debunking. The epitaphs stripped away what lingered of the myth of idyllic life in the Midwestern garden, in so doing bringing to a bitter conclusion a development begun in the work of the agrarian realists and seen most notably in Howe's *The Story of a Country Town*. *Spoon River Anthology* brought Howe's bleak vision, and especially his sense of spiritual dislocation, to a popular audience in a popular form. It was an exposé, as Bernard Duffey remarked, in a time now ripe for exposés—a time when Chicago had become the center of the Midwest and farms and small towns were understood as provincial backwaters and escape was the only salvation. For one moment the Illinois towns of his past concentrated Masters's attention, providing him with a firm imaginative hold on reality and freeing him from the more conscious and vaporous literary designs that dominated his poetry early and late. Usually his work arose from what he thought poetry ought to be; with *Spoon River* he allowed himself to speak directly out of his own experience, allowed his sense of the truth of that experience, the bitterness as well as the sentiment, to rise freely to the surface. In light of his career as a whole the epitaphs seem almost accidental. "His name was up," as Sherwood Anderson remarked about the appeal of his single successful book, "but not as he had wanted it to be."[41]

For present readers the epitaphs no longer possess the quality of urgently fresh revelation that they had for Masters's contemporaries. Spoon River and Winesburg, Gopher Prairie and Maple Valley, have long since become familiar country towns of the literary landscape. Still, Masters's verse remains the most enduring poetic achievement to emerge from the Chicago period of Midwestern writing, compressed portraits of common life rendered in common speech, largely free of the elevating tendencies of romance and ideal vision, expressions of flat truth. About them still is a ring of the real.

5

While Lindsay, Sandburg, and Masters were all deeply affected by Chicago's revolt against social restraint and literary custom, Sherwood Anderson seems a pure creation of its heady swirl. He was eagerly embraced by the inner circle of the renaissance, in time becoming one of its foremost figures of rebellion, the man from the provinces who in mid-life abandons business for art. In Chicago he published his first awkward apprentice novels, accounts of men who wend their way to the city. And in a Chicago boarding house close by the offices of *Poetry* and the *Little Review* he wrote the lyric stories that evoked his barren small-town background and marked his final removal from it. On the departing train for Chicago, however, Anderson's fictional self, George Willard, sees not only that "the town of Winesburg had disappeared" but recognizes that he possesses now "a background on which to paint the dreams of his manhood."[42] In Chicago of the renaissance Anderson both shed the constricting skin of his past and began the invention of a new life and with it a new literature, one that he understood was composed of vigorous purpose and Whitman-like affirmation. In this work he both portrayed his barren past and sought, in the telling phrase of Brom Weber, to "fructify his wasteland."[43] He believed, as he told Van Wyck Brooks in a letter, that he had within himself a "soil for the raising of a crop if the stones can be taken away."[44]

Out of his stone-filled personal history he created in *Winesburg, Ohio* a work of lasting power, becoming together with Dreiser a major force from out of the Midwest in the final separation of American writing from the grip of Victorian restriction. His search for the crop of affirmation met with far less success. It resulted in work frequently weakened by sentiment, exhortation, and muddled thought, causing stinging defection by earlier disciples and a long slide in critical esteem. Beyond the haunting stories of *Winesburg, Ohio* and some of his later story collections, what has endured best about Anderson's work is a prose manner that Faulkner termed a "primer-like style":[45] simple and colloquial to excess yet, at its finest, evoking an odd inner poetry, a prose manner of romantic realism that has found continuing life in American fiction. Scott Fitzgerald believed Anderson almost wholly lacking in ideas but praised his writing ("God, he can write!") and described his style as "about as simple as an engine room full of dynamos."[46] Hart Crane, a younger refugee from Ohio, thought the stories could be read over and over again without the distraction of " 'situations' and 'plots' spilling out into one's lap"; what endured about them was a "lyricism, deliberate and light, as a curl of milkweed seeds drawn toward the sun."[47] If the final test of a writer's lasting worth is his capacity to affect the work of subsequent generations, then Anderson remains one of the most enduring of Midwestern writers.

A few months after *Spoon River Anthology* was published Anderson was lent a copy by one of the young boarders at what amounted to an artists' colony that had been created at 735 Cass Street.[48] An older figure rapidly nearing middle age, Anderson was separated from his family and living alone in the boarding house among what he called the Little Children of the Arts, trying to make his way as a writer while keeping a foot in the world of business as a copywriter with the Taylor-Critchfield advertising agency. He stayed up all night reading the poems and was impressed by them, though in later comments he steered clear of any suggestion of powerful influence by Masters's book of the sort that Carl Van Doren set down when he called *Winesburg, Ohio* "the *Anthology* 'transposed'."[49] Hart Crane, reviewing the book in a literary journal, thought the relationship of Masters and Anderson more one of "discoverer" to "settler." The older writer had struck a spark that was a "mighty seedling of dynamite, cold and intense," but in Anderson's book there was a development in the direction of a "finer reticence" and a more "sustained inner illumination and bloom."[50] What seems evident, at any event, is that Masters's book influenced Anderson in the sense of giving him the idea, or at the least reinforcing his own, of a connected series of stories of the buried lives of Midwestern villagers.

Sometime in the fall of 1915, before he had read Masters, Anderson had written a sketch he called "The Book of the Grotesque" that he thought might provide a title for his collection. "Grotesque" was nearly an in-word at the time—Arthur Davison Ficke, for example, a poet late of Davenport, Iowa, had just published ten short verses in the first issue of the *Little Review* under the title "Ten Grotesques." As Anderson used the word the reference, according to his own interpretation, was to single "truths" that people had allowed to define their existence, tragically limiting their embrace of life's uncertainty and development, its open-ended nature. Himself in flight at age thirty-nine from such life-denying truths as "businessman," he appeared in the sketch as an old writer—a George Willard, reversing *Winesburg's* ending, dreaming at the end of a career rather than the start—who writes a book about the long procession of grotesque figures passing through his mind. The book is never published yet it hardly matters; the old writer has saved himself by the "young thing inside him" from possession of single truths—exactly the salvation Anderson hoped for himself in the unfolding life of art (5).

The sketch was followed by "Hands," the story of Wing Biddlebaum, a recluse living on the edge of town who speaks only to George Willard, the reporter for the *Winesburg Eagle*. While he speaks his hands flail the air like the "beating of the wings of an imprisoned bird," a distinguishing feature and the source of local fame as a strawberry picker, yet a feature that "made more grotesque an already grotesque and elusive individuality" (9, 10). Out of his strange kinship with the reporter comes a need to instruct the young man. Wing passionately tells him that the wish to be comfortably part of the town prevents him from following his own dreams. Wing himself is lost inside a mental picture, one in which George Willard and other young men flock to his kindly attention in the agrarian garden.

> In the picture men lived again in a kind of pastoral golden age. Across a green open country came clean-limbed young men, some afoot, some mounted upon horses. In crowds the young men came to gather about the feet of an old man who sat beneath a tree in a tiny garden and who talked to them. (11)

Inspired by the vision, Wing for once forgets his hands, which "stole forth and lay upon George Willard's shoulders," caressing the reporter (12). When he realizes what he has done he abruptly breaks off the conversation and hurries away, leaving George Willard perplexed and fearful. Anderson then supplies the background. As a school teacher in Pennsylvania named Adolph Myers, Wing had caressed his young charges out of an excess of gentle love, bringing accusations of homosexuality and cruel banishment from the town. Uncertain about what has happened to him but feeling his hands must be at fault, he had changed his name to one seen on a box at a freight station and had tried to hide himself in a life of anonymity in Winesburg. Anderson ends the story by returning to the lonely figure in his house outside the town, preparing for bed. When he sees bread crumbs on his floor Wing, bird-like, picks them up and puts them in his mouth, his expressive fingers moving rapidly like "the devotee going swiftly through decade after decade of his rosary" (17).

The story is obviously a protest against the single truth of sexual labeling, and beyond that an expression of affection for rejected figures like Wing living on the fringe of society, figures confused by their own lives, lurching into passionate expression one moment, then turning away from themselves in fear. Anderson's narrative reflects the confusion in that it doesn't build in controlled fashion to a climax; rather, it casually weaves together past and present without regard for scenic progression, casually interrupting itself for explanations and asides. At one point the reader is informed that Wing's life, "sympathetically set forth," is really a "job for a poet" (10). The story and those that followed it are in fact expressions of a poetic sensibility, tales more than stories (reflected in the subtitle Anderson would give to the collection, "A Group of Tales of Ohio Small Town Life"), yet fully realized and strangely affecting in their human feeling and gentle visionary manner.

"Hands" was Anderson's breakthrough. With the tale he found a style and an attitude toward his past, one that mingled rejection with compassion, an attitude far removed from the simple hatred he ascribed to Masters. He later recalled that after finishing the story he told himself: "It is solid. . . . It is like a rock. It is there. It is put down. . . . See, at last I have done it."[51] He had, he added, at long last found his true vocation. The story had been written in one burst of energy though subsequently revised. Now other stories quickly followed in which he drew on Ohio memories as well as present experience in the Chicago rooming house, many written in one sitting in the evenings or during his working days at the Taylor-Critchfield agency. They would not be collected into *Winesburg, Ohio* until 1919, but individual tales began appearing in print over the winter of 1915–16. Floyd Dell took "The Book of the Grotesque," "Hands," and "The Strength of God" for the *Masses*. Of more importance to Anderson, certifying his arrival as a serious writer, was the interest in his work by *Seven Arts*, a new publication appearing in New York in the fall of 1916 with Waldo Frank and Paul Rosenfeld among its editors and Van Wyck Brooks and Robert Frost on its advisory board. Over a ten-month period *Seven Arts* would publish four of his tales, introducing Anderson to a New York literary world of greater breadth and sophistication than he had known in Chicago.

The appearance of the collected tales in book form, the title changed from *The Book of the Grotesque* on the advice of the publisher, was greeted with modest sales but strong reviews. Although there were inevitable comparisons with Masters, Anderson usually prevailed. "Here is the goal that *The Spoon River Anthology* aimed at," Mencken proclaimed, "and missed by half a mile." Burton Rascoe, the literary editor of the *Chicago Tribune*, thought that while Masters was "bitter, reproachful, and removed," in Anderson there was "fraternal pity and a homely tender feeling of participation in human destiny."[52] Anderson himself, deeply pleased by the critical response, was filled with creative energy. He was nearly finished with the novel *Poor White* that would appear the following year, and new tales had been accepted by *Smart Set* and the *Dial*; rather than repeating himself, he wanted to press on to new experimental work in substance and manner. He was also, in his forty-third year, ready to abandon Chicago. The city had been the end of a long road of development that had led to a changed existence and the greatest single work of his writing career, but it had served its purpose. The tangles of his personal life, the chains of advertising work, and need for fresh literary inspiration all pushed him onward. During its few years in the literary limelight Chicago was a way station in the flight of writers out of the Midwest, rarely the goal itself. Anderson drew on the city more deeply than most during its brilliant moment, and was more deeply altered by its siren song of liberation, but by 1922 he too would leave it permanently behind.

6

It was fortune rather than art that had first drawn Anderson to Chicago. The year was 1896 and he was nineteen. His mother had died the previous year and there was no compelling reason to remain in Clyde, Ohio, with his garrulous father, a ne'er-do-well figure given to popular entertaining and the telling of tales, an embarrassment to his son. In *Winesburg, Ohio* Irwin Anderson would make an appearance as the father of George Willard, a figure who has failed at everything yet "when he was out of sight of the New Willard House and had no fear of coming upon his wife, he swaggered and began to dramatize himself as one of the chief men of the town" (31). As a boy Anderson had been nick-named "Jobby" for his eagerness to earn money with odd jobs. Chicago now beckoned him not for its upward movement or as the literary city of Garland, Fuller, and Herrick but as a place for real money.

After two years as nothing better than a warehouse laborer in the city he volunteered for the Spanish-American War, arriving in Cuba four months after the war ended. When he returned from service he enrolled at Wittenberg Acad-emy in Springfield, Ohio, where he lived in a boardinghouse along with a brother who was an artist with a local magazine and with men involved in advertising and newspaper work. Out of the association came the offer of a job as an advertising solicitor in Chicago; when Anderson promptly accepted, ed-ucation was put behind him for good. Within months of his return to Chicago he was a copywriter as well as solicitor and working out of an office in the Loop, a success at last in his identity as "Jobby". Physically attractive, outgoing, persuasive, Anderson took with gusto to the ad man's world of promotion. Soon he was also turning out sketches and articles on all manner of subjects for *Agricultural Advertising*, a monthly journal put out by his advertising agency, his first rough efforts at trying to discover himself through writing. By 1904 he was sufficiently established to marry Cornelia Lane, the educated daughter of a Toledo wholesaler, and to think about moving on.

From 1906 to 1912 he was back in Ohio, living out a stage of his life that in retrospect would take on mythic dimension, the businessman struggling to give birth to the artist. For a brief time he was president of a mail-order firm in Cleveland that he had previously done business with in his advertising work, then he moved on to Elyria as head of a roofing and painting firm, building up the business over a five-year period and rising to membership in the town's commercial elite. Although his business was in a shaky financial state, in Elyria and in his early thirties he enjoyed the success that had originally propelled him from Clyde—the kind of comfortable front-porch, country-club, middle-class Midwestern life that Tarkington had hailed in the pages of *Harper's Monthly*. It was exactly the kind of life that he now began to resist. He had been writing for years but his work, the time stolen from his business and an increasingly stifling domestic life, turned personal and therapeutic, an effort to strip away the falsehoods of his current existence and find the truth about himself and life. Drafts of two novels emerged, *Windy McPherson's Son* and *Marching Men*, together with a stream of disparate notes and reflections, all intended to free himself from the clever American go-getter he felt he had become.

On a day in November 1912 he left his office in Elyria and four days later turned up in Cleveland, dazed and dirty and with little memory of his wander-ing. He was hospitalized for mental collapse but recovered quickly and soon returned to Elyria and his family.[53] In the myth that he later wove around his defection from a past existence, Anderson simplified the story to one of conscious choice of art over business, skipping over financial and family pressures, exhaustion brought on by long stints of night-time writing, and the heavy drinking that played into his collapse. It was true, however, that from this point on his life was irrevocably set in a new direction. In Elyria he severed his business connections and in February made his third journey to Chicago, returning to his old advertising job with Taylor-Critchfield. His family would join him in a few months and there was the continuing need to make a living, but he was determined now on a new life as a writer.

In his altered state Anderson was ripe for admission to the counterculture that had sprung up around Floyd Dell and Margery Currey and the *Friday Literary Review*. Through his brother, Karl, now an established painter, Anderson met Dell and was introduced into the bohemian colony along 57th Street. Though still an advertising man and, nearing his thirty-seventh year, considerably older than most of the colonists, Anderson quickly became one of their number. They exuded exactly what he sought, freedom from convention and the serious pursuit of art. He in turn seemed to embody what they envisioned as the essence of rebellion, a proletarian writer who had arisen from the people and now rejected the corruptions of a commercial culture in the name of higher truths. Among the colonists Anderson also found an appreciative audience for his readings from the manuscripts he had brought with him from Elyria. As his literary standing grew among them his appearance changed, his dress taking on artistic flair, his hair lengthened and left disheveled. He became the Anderson, both dashing and soulful, that Alfred Stieglitz would capture in a well-known portrait in 1923.

When Dell, whom Anderson would later call his "literary father,"[54] read the manuscript of *Windy McPherson's Son*, he was so enthralled that he wrote in the *Friday Literary Review* that he had seen "an unfinished novel by a yet unpublished writer which if finished as begun will overtop the work of any living American writer."[55] In the fall of 1913 Dell was off to New York and the editorship of the *Masses*, taking Anderson's manuscript with him, convinced he could find a publisher. After several unsuccessful efforts he finally found a taker in the John Lane Company, the publisher of two of Dreiser's novels. When the work appeared in 1916, with its dedication to "the living men and women of my own Middle Western home town," Anderson was already at work on the Winesburg stories. In retrospect the novel seemed to him immature in that it was affected by his reading of other writers and not yet turned to his new sense of the life about him.[56] It did, nonetheless, reflect elements of that life that Anderson was trying to shed. Sam McPherson comes to Chicago from an Iowa village after early chapters in which Anderson recreated aspects of his own early years in Ohio. He is intent, as "Jobby" Anderson once had been, on making his way; but wealth and power gained, satisfaction refuses to follow. He leaves the city for the life of a vagabond worker among the ordinary folk. When satisfaction remains as distant as before, he returns with three neglected children to his childless wife, reviving an earlier notion that fulfillment might be gained through nurture. Despite an impulse to again flee, he admonishes himself that he must yield to other lives, other needs. The ending of the story is bleak, holding out little chance that Sam will find contentment in an embrace of domestic duty. Anderson revised the ending in a subsequent edition, but the bleakness held. Sam's sense of home and family is still that of "a shut-in place in which he was to live what was left of his life"[57]—Anderson's own dark response to the stifling quality of his life before his escape to Chicago.

By the time the novel was published Anderson was divorced from his wife and had married Tennessee Mitchell, a sculptress who had once had a tempestuous affair with Edgar Lee Masters and a charter member of the 57th Street group. Praise for the first novel came from important quarters, including the *Nation*, the *New Republic*, and Dell's *Masses*. In *Seven Arts* Waldo Frank drew favorable comparisons to Dreiser and Twain, lauding Anderson at middle age as a great writer emerging on the American literary scene. *Marching Men*, Anderson's second published novel, was quite different. It was a social novel in which a Chicago lawyer and charismatic leader, Beaut McGregor (whom Anderson would later describe as a combination of Abraham Lincoln and the labor leader John L. Lewis), despises the disheveled working masses yet develops what Anderson calls the "vague and shadowy" idea of organizing them into marching companies in which they will somehow "march fear and disorder and purposelessness away."[58] Blind faith in the discipline of marching had its roots in Anderson's brief military career in the Spanish-American War, but the appeal of order was also located in the disintegrating quality of his life in Elyria as businessman, husband, and father. One of the strengths of an otherwise confused and ill-organized novel was an unsentimental portrayal of Chicago working-class existence as oppressively slovenly:

> A people calling itself great and living in a city also called great go to their houses a mere disorderly mass of humans cheaply equipped. Everything is cheap. When the people get home to their houses they sit on cheap chairs before cheap tables and eat cheap food. They have given their lives for cheap things. (100–101)

Against this "vast gulf of disorder" in urban life Anderson raised a mystical image of natural grandeur in the corn fields stretching beyond Chicago. The corn fields have no functional relationship to the story beyond the fact that they are not "disorderly" and as a result convey a "lesson of the corn" that has "never been told to the young men who come out of the corn fields to live in the city" (156).

Marching Men was coldly received and Anderson expected the same treatment for the odd work that followed. He later said that in the novel he had tried to create an epic poem of movement; in *Mid-American Chants* he turned directly to verse—forty-nine loose prose-poems celebrating a distantly-glimpsed rural world beyond the city. Perhaps inspired by Sandburg's burst of rural nostalgia in *Cornhuskers*, Anderson chanted the alternative if vague glories of a natural life, offering himself as a Midwestern singer for a region—as he said in the book's foreword—that was hungry for song amid the "grinding roar" of a

new urban and industrial life. In their solemnity before corn and their un-
guarded simplicity ("My head arises above the cornfields. / I stand up among
the new corn")[59] the songs were ripe for the ridicule that greeted the appearance
of a sampling of them in *Seven Arts* and *Poetry*. Collected in book form in
1918, they received scant critical attention. Yet for Anderson it hardly seemed
to matter; though still an advertising man, he had emerged from the discredited
past into his new life of exuberant freedom as a man and vast expectation as a
writer. He saw the poems, as he noted in a letter, as a "break" in his writing
life and as a "new conception" and acceptance of his Midwestern experience.[60]
After the failure of his second novel and the book of verse he turned his attention to collecting the Ohio tales that had emerged from an earlier and more
complex phase of his Midwestern experience. Francis Hackett, who had reviewed *Windy McPherson's Son* favorably in the *New Republic*, found a New
York publisher in B. W. Huebsch, a small firm with a large reputation for
having introduced James Joyce and D. H. Lawrence to American readers. In
May 1919 it added to its luster with the publication of *Winesburg, Ohio*.

7

Anderson frequently distinguished himself from his fellow Ohioan Howells,
whose work he found flat and circumspect. Rather than the tidy realism of the
commonplace, he sought a literary approach that was loosely ordered and more
subjective and poetic—a romantic realism in which experience is distilled and
transformed by imagination into a dreamlike state resembling surrealism. He
had little interest in structure or plot or in the development of character over
time. His strength, as Malcolm Cowley pointed out, was in the creation of
moments of revelation without sequel—"the flash of lightning that revealed a
life without changing it."[61] He reversed the pattern of Enoch Robinson's life in
"Loneliness," the tale of an Ohio painter who goes to New York and there,
after marriage, sees himself "in the role of producing citizen of the world" and
so gives up his search for "the essence of things and played with realities" (171).
Anderson's realism was directed to inward essences rather than outward realities; appropriately, he dedicated the Winesburg tales to his mother "whose
keen observations on the life about her first awoke in me the hunger to see
beneath the surface of lives." As a result his fictional world lacks solidity. Neither his settings nor his characters are provided with sensual, sharply defined
exterior qualities that hold in the imagination, nor does he offer fully rendered
dramatic scenes. His gaze always directs the reader inward to fragile psychological and spiritual states that he tried to capture in a manner influenced by
Gertrude Stein's language experiments in *Tender Buttons* with prose rhythms
derived from self-conscious simplicity and calculated repetition. It was reading
Stein, Anderson believed, that had first helped him glimpse an alternative to
Howellsian realism, thus freeing the poet within him and enabling him to view

writing not as the transcription of external experience but the recreation of internal realms.

The town that emerges from the tales is clearly a Midwestern village located in a long-settled agricultural region. It is a pleasant enough place—in "Drink" a "thriving town" where residential streets are "clothed in soft green leaves" and behind the houses men are seen "puttering about in vegetable gardens" (256, 263). The countryside beyond is equally attractive—in "The Untold Lie" a softened pastoral landscape in which "the low hills were washed with color and even the little clusters of bushes in the corners of the fences were alive with beauty" (250). In "Adventure" the spring landscape glows with bucolic perfection:

> . . . when the rains have passed and before the long hot days of summer have come, the country about Winesburg is delightful. The town lies in the midst of open fields, but beyond the fields are pleasant patches of woodlands. In the wooded places are many little cloistered nooks, quiet places where lovers go to sit on Sunday afternoons. Through the trees they look out across the fields and see farmers at work about the barns or people driving up and down the roads. In the town bells ring and occasionally a train passes, looking like a toy thing in the distance. (129)

Yet town and country remain only thinly glimpsed. They possess little social reality or ongoing life, existing more as a series of still photographs offering minimal background for the tales. In "Sophistication," for example, Anderson suddenly shifts from a scene at the fair ground to a rapid, generalized sketch of the town before just as suddenly returning to the fair grounds:

> In Winesburg the crowded day had run itself out into the long night of the late fall. Farm horses jogged away along lonely country roads pulling their portion of weary people. Clerks began to bring samples of goods in off the sidewalks and lock the doors of stores. In the Opera House a crowd had gathered to see a show and further down Main Street the fiddlers, their instruments tuned, sweated and worked to keep the feet of youth flying over a dance floor. (296–97)

Likewise, neither town nor country have much bearing on the lives of Anderson's characters. In "Queer" Elmer Cowley accuses "public opinion" and the "judgment of Winesburg" for labeling his family as strange, and other characters in other stories are equally pigeonholed by the town (234). Still, they do not seem actively repressed by environment so much as victimized by their own fettered natures—their seizure, in Anderson's explanation, by life-denying single truths. For the most part they remain detached from the particular circumstances of time and place as well as from other lives, turned inward upon their own aching loneliness and unfulfilled longing.

Alice Hindman in "Adventure" remains true to Ned Currie who has long ago left the town to make his fortune. At night she arranges a blanket into a human form on the bed and caresses it like a lover. One evening, overwhelmed by passion and loneliness, she ventures into the street and runs naked through the rain. When she sees a man stumbling home she calls out to him to wait, then discovers him to be old and nearly deaf; in shame she crawls through the grass to the house. In bed in her nightdress she tries to soberly face the fact "that many people must live and die alone, even in Winesburg" (134). In "The Strength of God" a minister, Curtis Hartman, contends with the desire to spy on Kate Swift in her bedroom from the bell tower where he prepares his sermons. He wishes only "to do the work of God quietly and earnestly," yet he is wracked with temptation to "look again at the figure lying white and quiet in the bed" (175). When one winter night he sees Kate Swift unclothed on her bed, weeping and beating the pillow with her fists, her slim figure appears to him like the boy in Christ's presence portrayed on a leaded window of the church. He flees to the office of the *Winesburg Eagle* and breathlessly informs George Willard that God has manifest himself in the body of a naked woman. His trial is over; he believes himself possessed now of the strength of God. Wash Williams in "Respectability," the ugliest man in town, hates women. They are all "bitches" (136). When at length he tells his story to George Willard the reporter imagines Wash transformed into a "comely young man with black hair and black shining eyes." "Something almost beautiful" comes into his voice as he tells his "story of hate" (140). As a young husband in Columbus he had discovered the wife he deeply loved had three lovers who came to the house while he worked. After he sent her home to her mother in Dayton, the mother summoned him to visit, and there in the parlor, with Wash anxious to forgive, his wife was presented to him naked. The mother is now dead, he bitterly tells George Willard, and his opportunity to kill her gone.

One by one the citizens of Winesburg step from anonymity to reveal their stories, often in disjointed bursts of disclosure to the young reporter, then in embarrassment and disorder turn back into their hidden worlds. Until the final story, when he leaves Winesburg for the city, George Willard remains passive and confused in the face of such disclosure, contending with his own uncertain identity and nervous sexuality, removed himself from the parade of grotesques only in that his life still stretches before him. He embodies Anderson's own diffuse sense of the suffocating inner world of the town and, at the same time, his sympathetic attraction to its deformed inhabitants. In his final act of separation from the town he also bears with him Anderson's desire to create through his writing an alternative life.

In "An Awakening" George Willard leaves behind the ordinary existence of the town as represented by Ransom Surbeck's pool room and talk about women and in the bracing night air he suddenly feels the power of a new life. He instructs himself about a future in which he must get in touch with something "orderly and big":

> "In every little thing there must be order, in the place where men work, in their clothes, in their thoughts. I myself must be orderly. I must learn that law. I must

get myself into touch with something orderly and big that swings through the night like a star. In my little way I must begin to learn something, to give and swing and work with life, with the law." (219)

His mother, a worn and reclusive figure in the shabby New Willard House hotel run by his swaggering father, is equally alert to the needs of her son's future. She finds a "secret something" in him that she had allowed to be killed within herself (30). When he tells her in "Mother" that he must eventually leave the town, she angrily assumes that the move is only intended to make his fortune in business, the reverse of her hopes for him.

> The woman in the chair waited and trembled. An impulse came to her. "I suppose you had better wake up," she said. "You think that? You will go to the city and make money, eh? It will be better for you, you think, to be a business man, to be brisk and smart and alive?" She waited and trembled. (36)

Kate Swift in "The Teacher" identifies the boy's special qualities with a future as a writer: "In something he had written as a school boy she thought she had recognized the spark of genius and wanted to blow on the spark." As a writer, she instructs him, he must "not become a mere peddler of words. The thing to learn is to know what people are thinking about, not what they say" (192). Her eagerness to guide her former pupil is transferred into "the passionate desire to be loved by a man"; yet after she allows herself one evening in the newspaper office to fall into George Willard's arms, she immediately flees from him (194). It was the sight of her subsequent confusion and frustration, weeping and beating her fists into the pillow in her bedroom, that had caused Reverend Curtis Hartman to proclaim her an instrument of God.

With his mother's death in the strange and powerful tale "Death," George Willard, at age eighteen, arrives at his maturity and the beginning of the future predicted for him. He decides that a life that is orderly and big requires that he set aside his existence as "the Ohio village boy" in favor of the prospect of a newspaper job in the city (286). In "Sophistication" he seeks out Helen White, the banker's daughter who is home from college for the annual country fair and with whom he has long been half in love. He wants to tell her of the "new impulses that had come to him," to make her "feel the change he believed had taken place in his nature" (287). In the grip of the sadness that also accompanies his new sophistication, the voices and sounds of the town now get on his nerves. Wesley Moyer's boasting of horsemanship at the livery barn, ordinarily a matter of intense interest, leaves him only angry. With Helen White he walks out to the fair ground on the night after the fair has closed. "There is something memorable," Anderson notes, about a closed fair ground on the edge of a Midwestern town—a haunted quality in a setting so suddenly drained of overflowing life. The scene gives rise to one of the most striking passages in the Winesburg stories:

On all sides are ghosts, not of the dead, but of living people. Here, during the day just passed, have come the people pouring in from the town and the country around. Farmers with their wives and children and all the people from the hundreds of little frame houses have gathered within these board walls. Young girls have laughed and men with beards have talked of the affairs of their lives. The place has been filled to overflowing with life. It has itched and squirmed with life and now it is night and the life has all gone away. The silence is almost terrifying. One conceals oneself standing silently beside the trunk of a tree and what there is of a reflective tendency in his nature is intensified. One shudders at the thought of the meaninglessness of life while at the same instant, and if the people of the town are his people, one loves life so intensely that tears come into the eyes. (295)

George Willard's vocation has dimly formed within him. He and Helen White embrace and kiss, but although "he wanted to love and to be loved by her . . . he did not want at the moment to be confused by her womanhood." Instead, he begins to "think of the people in the town where he had always lived with something like reverence"—the people, those who both repel and attract him, who will provide his material in what will become a life of art (296).

His leavetaking from Helen and the town on an April morning in the following story, "Departure," is reported in matter-of-fact terms. He takes a solitary walk in the country, then on Main Street the clerks sweeping the sidewalks ask him how it feels to be going away. At the train station people wish him good luck; his father tells him to keep a sharp eye out in the city. His thoughts, Anderson says, are not "big or dramatic" but of "little things": Turk Smollet wheeling boards through the street; Butch Wheeler lighting the town's lamps with a torch; Helen White putting a stamp on an envelope in the post office (302, 303). Such is the ordinary material, once again, in which the future writer, in his "growing passion for dreams," will find his subjects. He leans back in his train seat "with the recollection of little things occupying his mind" and closes his eyes. When he opens them again Winesburg has vanished. His old life has been transformed into the "background on which to paint the dreams of his manhood" (303).

8

Winesburg's table of contents—the twenty-four stories set down under the title "The Tales and The Persons"—adds the central character's name to the title of each tale: each tale "concerning" a character. Yet finally the names blur; the book becomes a single suppressed cry of thwarted life. At the same time Anderson's reverence for his characters remains evident. In the precisely apt metaphor offered in "Paper Pills," the people of the town are "twisted little apples that grow in the orchards of Winesburg": gnarled apples that the pickers have rejected yet apples nonetheless delicious in the sweetness gathered in little round places on the sides (19). "Only the few," Anderson remarks, "know the sweetness of the twisted apples." Yet however appealing the rejected figures of

Winesburg, those who can follow Anderson's own path and that of George Willard leave the town behind. The good apples picked from the trees are "put in barrels and shipped to the cities where they will be eaten in apartments that are filled with books, magazines, furniture, and people" (20). As George Willard leaves on the train and Winesburg slips away from him a rural world of Ohio small-town life is abandoned in a general rush to the city. In their concentrated focus on inner states Anderson's tales still seem vividly modern, yet they also have about them the quality of period pieces emitting the sweet sadness of a rural Midwestern world that in 1919 had already—in the phrase Scott Fitzgerald would soon use—become part of the vast obscurity beyond the city.

Before the Winesburg tales were published in book form Anderson had turned once again to the material of his past in his work on *Poor White*, the third of the seven novels he would eventually publish. His treatment now of life in a version of Winesburg called Bidwell lacks the ambivalent feelings at the heart of the tales. In a straightforward manner he celebrates a Midwest of rural perfection that he believed had existed before the turn of the century and the coming of the corrupting influences of industrialism—an agrarian garden of craftsmanship and honest labor in which thought and poetry had a natural existence. With *Mid-American Chants* Anderson had become increasingly aware of himself as a Midwestern writer in possession of themes drawn from regional experience. After *Poor White* appeared he told Paul Rosenfeld in a letter that his early New York advocates—a bookish group that included Brooks, Frank, and Rosenfeld himself—had "always a little misunderstood something in me." He had been raised in a different atmosphere—"among workers, farmers, etc., here in the Middle West" and in his "inner consciousness" had "conceived of what we roughly speak of as the Middle West, and what I have so often called Mid-America, as an empire with its capital in Chicago." However narrow in scope, herein was his natural material. He wanted to make a Midwest of "these little, ugly factory towns, these big, sprawling cities into something":

> I wish it would not sound to[o] silly to say I pour a dream over it, consciously, intentionally, for a purpose. I want to write beautifully, create beautifully, not outside but in this thing in which I am born, in this place where, in the midst of ugly towns, cities, Fords, moving pictures, I have always lived, must always live.

It was a vast undertaking, he acknowledged, for Midwesterners are "a little ashamed of trying for beauty"; they are emotionally flattened. He himself was a victim of "Mid-America as a walled-in place." Yet his task as a writer was to see "the houses cleaned, the doorsteps washed, the walls broken away"—a transformation beyond the reach of his lifetime yet his agenda as a Midwestern writer.[62]

The story of Hugh McVey in *Poor White* extends the accounts of Sam McPherson and Beaut McGregor. A young man twisted in his youth—this time in the direction of a mechanical spirit that results in the invention of farm machinery that subverts the rough independence of rural life—Hugh discovers at length the buried poet within himself. Once, he had thought the transformation of Ohio into industrial villages "invariably good," but finally he desires only the play of natural "light and color" over the towns.[63] The novel ends, in a scene that returns to the ending of *Windy McPherson's Son* and points once again to the highly personal nature of Anderson's art, with McVey entering his house under the command of his stolid and pregnant wife. It is a domestic conclusion that in *Poor White* seems essentially positive despite the sexual unease of the marriage and the fact that McVey is now afflicted with the "disease of thinking" that is making him "useless for the work of his age."[64]

Though Anderson had difficulty fusing the various parts of *Poor White*, especially the story of Clara Butterworth, McVey's wife, with that of McVey himself, the novel remains by far his best. The opening section describing McVey's early life in a Mississippi River town in Missouri, obviously inspired by Anderson's devotion to Mark Twain, is strongly handled, as is Anderson's feeling for the imagined integration of life in a pre-industrial Midwest. Nonetheless, Anderson's real strength was never for the novel but the short tale of compressed, underlying lyricism. After *Winesburg, Ohio* and *Poor White* his best work would appear in his story collections: *The Triumph of the Egg* (1921), *Horses and Men* (1923), *Death in the Woods and Other Stories* (1933). And it was here—in his typical avoidance of the conventions of plot and climax, in an inclination for the grotesque and the anti-heroic, in the flat poetry of his language—that he would exert his greatest influence on subsequent generations of writers.

In the period immediately after the publication of *Poor White* Anderson's reputation within the literary community was at its height. In the fall of 1921 the *Dial* had awarded him a $2,000 prize for service to American letters, an award bestowed in later years on Eliot, Williams, and Pound. In 1922 he was finally able to resign his Chicago advertising job and begin a period of roaming about the country that corresponded with a new sense of development in his work. As he now saw it, his early novels had been imitative realistic efforts; then beginning with *Mid-American Chants* he had launched upon the vein of Midwestern work turned up in *Winesburg, Ohio*, *Poor White*, and *The Triumph of the Egg*. Now, in his newest phase, he sought nothing less than to embrace the vast sweep of modernity in America. He felt himself committed to the novel form as a requirement for success, yet with the novels of contemporary life that began to appear—*Many Marriages* in 1923 and especially *Dark Laughter* in 1925—his career abruptly dipped from its high point into a downward spiral from which it never recovered.

Hemingway, befriended by Anderson during the older writer's final days in Chicago, repaid him with sophomoric but effective parody in 1926 in *The Torrents of Spring*. Inspired by the appearance of *Dark Laughter*—ironically, Anderson's most popular novel—Hemingway wickedly caught the chopped-up sentences of Anderson's prose manner, the disdain for plot, and the open feeling for his characters that could seem naive and effusive. The parody was heartless but deserved; *Dark Laughter* was a poor novel by any measure, and with it what was left of Anderson's stature crumbled in the estimation of the literary community. In a letter Scott Fitzgerald had declared that Anderson was *"one of the very best and finest writers in the English language today,"* but his verdict on *Dark Laughter* was that the book was simply *"lousy."*[65]

New work kept appearing at a steady pace, including volumes of direct autobiography in *A Story Teller's Story* (1924) and *Tar: A Midwest Childhood* (1926), and Anderson would continue to recreate his life, moving from residence in New Orleans to rural Virginia, editing country newspapers and becoming a political journalist, marrying four times in all. But after the middle 1920s his career as a significant American writer, belatedly begun, was suddenly over. Once himself at the cutting edge of the avant-garde, he was seen by younger and more daring writers, many of them like Hemingway and Fitzgerald and Hart Crane from out of the Midwest, as a literary pioneer gone stale. Faulkner, who had been close to Anderson during his New Orleans period, had ridiculed him in 1926 in an introduction to *Sherwood Anderson and Other Famous Creoles*, a small book privately printed and subscribed in New Orleans. In 1953 he looked back at Anderson's career in an *Atlantic* article with a hard eye yet a more balanced sense of appreciation for both the warm and vulnerable man and the writer. He believed that Anderson's true material as a writer had always been limited, with the result that he was "only a one- or two-book man." Style had eventually replaced substance in his work, a style that had been created with laborious effort out of "almost a fetish of simplicity"—yet a style, finally, that was

> just style: an end instead of a means: so that he presently came to believe that, provided he kept the style pure and intact and unchanged and inviolate, what the style contained would have to be first rate: it couldn't help but be first rate, and therefore himself too.

Still, when Faulkner recalled what he took to be Anderson's best work—*Winesburg, Ohio* together with some of the tales in *The Triumph of the Egg* and *Horses and Men*—the writer survived his dismissal. Indeed, he seemed in retrospect "a giant in an earth populated to a great—too great—extent by pygmies, even if he did make but the two or perhaps three gestures commensurate with giant-hood."[66]

SIX

Home Pasture

For the first time, perhaps, since that land emerged
from the waters of geologic ages, a human face was
set toward it with love and yearning.

—*O Pioneers!*

1

"A Robin's Egg Renaissance" that fell from the nest too soon was Sherwood
Anderson's description of Chicago's few years of literary and cultural leadership, and he wondered in retrospect if he and others should have remained in
the city. "Had we stayed in the home nest, in Chicago, when it all began for so
many of us, the Robin's Egg might have hatched."[1] But almost no one did stay.
New York, the nation's great cultural sponge, eventually absorbed the renaissance as it had all literary movements that had sprung up in the provinces. The
railroads drawing the energetic and the accomplished out of the interior ultimately led there.

One by one most of the Midwestern writers who had known Chicago days
made their way to the city or to the East, there to settle permanently or to
establish a temporary base: Garland, Dreiser, Fuller, Herrick, Dell, Lindsay,
Sandburg, Masters, Anderson, Lardner and such Chicago literary journalists
and men of letters as Ben Hecht, Harry Hansen, and Burton Rascoe. By at least
1926, Bernard Duffey estimates, the chief figures of the renaissance had all
departed, with no young writers having arisen to take their places. The excite-
ment had passed, as Saul Bellow would remark, and Chicago began to "export
exiles," in so doing leaving the city "to the boorish, aggressively, militantly dull
middle-class."[2] Greenwich Village had replaced 57th Street, with a transplanted
Floyd Dell as one of its leading cultural arbiters and bohemian stylists. Other
literary and artistic colonies offered isolation and splendid scenery—Taos and
Santa Fe in the Southwest, Carmel and Monterey in the Far West—but none
matched the Village's frayed urban charm and its location at the center of
publishing and the swirl of the nation's cultural life. Yet when America as a
whole became too parochial for its writers even the Village would give way to

the free life and favorable exchange rate of the Left Bank. "There was never a day so gay for the Arts," Ford Madox Ford would begin his autobiography, "as any twenty-four hours of the early 'twenties in Paris."³

Willa Cather, the most accomplished writer to emerge from the Midwest in the period, bypassed the Chicago renaissance entirely. In 1895, during a final semester at the University of Nebraska, she made her first visit to Chicago for a week of performances by the New York Metropolitan Opera, the beginning of an abiding passion for opera. Over the course of her life she would pass through the city many times and would use it as partial setting for two of her novels, *The Song of the Lark* and *Lucy Gayheart*. It is during a Chicago Symphony performance of *The New World Symphony* that Thea Kronborg, off from Moonstone, Colorado, to Chicago to study music, is awakened to her vocation as an artist. In the fall of 1899, a journalist now located in Pittsburgh, Cather was urged by a friend to move to Chicago and establish herself as the city's leading woman journalist. Although the idea had strong appeal to her, nothing came of it.⁴

When Cather finally left Pittsburgh in 1906 it was for New York and an editing job with *McClure's* magazine. By the time Dell ascended to the editorship of the *Friday Literary Review* in Chicago she had shed magazine work for the full-time pursuit of fiction. When the first of her two celebrated Nebraska novels, *O Pioneers!*, appeared in 1913 at the height of the Chicago renaissance—with one of the most enthusiastic reviews coming from Dell at the end of his Chicago period—she had already taken up residence in Greenwich Village. From her apartments on Washington Place and then on Bank Street she eventually came to know some of the writers who had drifted away from Chicago, Dreiser and Dell and Anderson among them, yet she was close to none of them and had no interest in identifying herself, as Anderson so strenuously did, as a Midwestern writer. Of the bohemian life of the Village she was always an observer rather than a participant, and when the appeal of the new expatriate life in Paris became a flood tide in the 1920s she was an established middle-aged novelist turned back upon a taste for the past.

If Cather's career as a Midwestern writer did not follow traditional lines leading from the provinces to Chicago and then beyond, neither did her work fit into a familiar pattern. She struck a fresh note in serious writing in response to the region, one of deep and lyric affection that arose from a romantic imagination that invested ordinary lives and homely incidents with heroic stature. At the same time her romanticism was mingled with realistic awareness of the limitations of Midwestern life and especially the desires luring the talented and ambitious, herself among them, beyond the narrow existence of farms and small towns. If her Nebraska novels celebrated an achieved pastoral life located in the pioneering past or what remained of it, they also subtly measured such a life against present realities. Still, it was a myth-making more than a truth-telling impulse that gave rise to her best-known Midwestern fiction, a desire to form works of art more than report actualities. Rather than the realism of the commonplace of Howells, a writer she continually disparaged, she espoused the

Henry James credo that "art *makes* life, makes interest, makes importance."[5] Dell sensed something of the fundamentally aesthetic aim of her work, so rare in Midwestern writing, in his review of *O Pioneers!* The novel seemed to him "the most vital, subtle and artistic piece of the year's fiction"—a work clearly "touched with genius." Although the story Cather told was hardly extraordinary ("Everyone knows a dozen like it") and dealt with none of the "large ideas which, rightly enough, agitate this generation," the reader was compelled onward. He was attracted by the qualities of a calm and attractive narrative voice, and beyond that an attractive authorial spirit, that caused him to place himself completely in her hands and to feel a "kind of nobleness" in which life "loses the taint of commonplace and becomes invested with dignity."[6]

2

Cather's earliest attempts at portraying Midwestern life were in a very different vein. *Main-Travelled Roads* appeared the year after she left Red Cloud, Nebraska, for the state university at Lincoln and began writing short fiction, and her first stories seem especially indebted to Garland's accounts of the inner and outer toll of country life. In critical comments at the time, however, Cather aggressively distanced herself from what she considered Garland's lack of romance and style. She speculated about a new play called *Nebraska* that had appeared in 1895 that it would likely deal with " 'barren, wind swept prairies; fields of stunted corn, whose parched leaves rattle like skeletons in the burning south wind,' all that sort of rot which Mr. Hamlin Garland and his school have seen fit to write about our peaceable and rather inoffensive country."[7] On another occasion she contrasted a poetic tale that had appeared in *Cosmopolitan* with Garland's habitual lack of "imagination and style": "No man ever tried his hand at fiction and persisted in the vain attempt who so utterly lacked these essential things as Mr. Garland. Art is temperament and Hamlin Garland has no more temperament than a prairie dog."[8] Cather later repudiated her earliest stories as false, distinguishing between (with an orchard metaphor that recalls Anderson's) sound apples meant for market and bad ones best left forgotten on the ground. Questions of quality aside, certainly the first stories were notably at odds with her later treatments of her Nebraska experience.

That experience began in 1883 when her family moved to the dry wind-swept high prairie of Nebraska from the sheltered and well-established world of the Shenandoah Valley of Virginia. An uncle and an aunt first made the trek west, followed by a grandfather and grandmother, all lured on by promotional literature that emphasized the fertility of the land and ignored the presence of speculators and the lack of trees and water. Expensive land in Iowa had pushed Cather's aunt and uncle farther west to Nebraska where they purchased railroad land in the south-central part of the state near the town of Red Cloud and also staked a homestead claim. Cather's grandparents soon settled nearby, both families at first living in sod dugouts.

When Cather, age nine, arrived with her family she found a raw pioneer community on a vast, barren plain subject to sharp swings of weather. There were some 7,000 people in the county, with Red Cloud as the county seat, and a good deal of prairie sod was as yet unbroken by the plow. After they arrived in the town by railroad the family was taken by wagons into the country to the grandparents' home, crossing a tableland area known locally as the Divide since it lay between the Republican and Little Blue rivers. The journey made a lasting impression on Cather's imagination. Gone were the trees and mountains of Virginia; only open range land with scant fencing and roads that were faint trails through high grass occupied the eye. She felt overwhelmed and nearly extinguished by the great sweep of the land, feelings she would later project into Jim Burden's first sight of the Nebraska prairie in *My Ántonia*:

> I had the feeling that the world was left behind, that we had got over the edge of it, and were outside man's jurisdiction. I had never before looked up at the sky when there was not a familiar mountain ridge against it. But this was the complete dome of heaven, all there was of it. I did not believe that my dead father and mother were watching me from up there; they would still be looking for me at the sheep-fold down by the creek, or along the white road that led to the mountain pastures. I had left even their spirits behind me. The wagon jolted on, carrying me I knew not whither. I don't think I was homesick. If we never arrived anywhere, it did not matter. Between that earth and that sky I felt erased, blotted out. I did not say my prayers that night: here, I felt, what would be would be.[9]

In the year and a half she lived on her grandparents' farm Cather quickly adapted to her new life, finding freedom in the open landscape and fascination in the lives of neighboring immigrant families of Swedes, Norwegians, Bohemians, Germans, Russians, and French Canadians. In Nebraska's early years the foreign-born population greatly outnumbered the American-born, and for Cather the lives and languages of these people brought variety and vitality to the dreary sameness of the plains. Yet if her early stories are accurate reflections, her first memories of Nebraska life were of an unrelieved existence in a desolate landscape, a life of monotonous routine and for the immigrant families of often desperate struggle.

When her father moved to town to open a real estate and insurance office, Cather's life on the Divide ended. In 1884 Red Cloud was an expanding rail-road and farm town of 1,200 and compared to the country a place of bustling life. Here Cather began her formal schooling, and here she began the extensive reading, as well as the extracurricular study of Latin and Greek, that marked her adolescent years. The local opera house was a particular attraction, offering performances of touring companies and a setting for amateur theatricals. In Red Cloud a personality also began to assert itself, one that relished noncon-formity and was fully aware of special gifts. She cropped her hair short, adopted male dress, and affected the name William Cather, Jr.—resistance presumably to the expected behavior of a young girl and a prelude to what she thought of as the male career of a medical doctor.

The next stage of her development, the beginning of the process that would remove her from Nebraska in reality only to return in memory, began in 1890 when she left Red Cloud for the frontier capital city of Lincoln and university days. In all, she spent five years in Lincoln, the first in a Latin preparatory school to satisfy entrance requirements. Her interest in medicine soon gave way to the humanities. A class essay on Thomas Carlyle that appeared in both a local newspaper and a campus literary publication after submission by her English professor turned her in the direction of writing. In 1892 a short story, "Peter," appeared in a Boston magazine called *The Mahogany Tree* after submission by another professor. After five years of Nebraska homesteading, an immigrant figure, Peter Sadelack, has been reduced to an old man who drinks too much and has lost contact with his family. Homesick for his native Bohemia, hating the country and farming, pushed out of his place in the household by a domineering son, he finds consolation only in his violin. Memories of a life of concerts and theater in Europe contrast with the harsh world of the farm. When he grows too feeble to play the violin, he steals off to the barn and kills himself with a shotgun. The story's stark closing only reinforces a mood of despair: "In the morning Antone found him stiff, frozen fast in a pool of blood. They could not straighten him out enough to fit a coffin, so they buried him in a pine box."[10] In *My Ántonia* in 1918 the tale would reappear, worked into the account of the death of Ántonia's father. In "Lou, the Prophet," a second somber story appearing in the college literary magazine, a prairie farmer succumbs to religious madness. After seven years of homesteading Lou cannot get ahead; when he loses his cattle after a bad year the girl he hoped to marry chooses a more successful farmer. The great calamity of his life is the threatened loss of his corn crop, bringing with it the prospect of financial ruin. In his anxiety his mind gives way to inflamed religious visions; before the authorities arrive to lock him up as a threatening lunatic he disappears into the country.

Cather's first appearance in a prominent national magazine, "On the Divide," published in the *Overland Monthly* in 1896, recounts the bleak days of Canute Canuteson, a giant Norwegian who lives alone in a cabin and tries to scratch a living from the soil. After ten years he has little to show for his effort. The landscape viewed from his window suggests a version of hell rather than the paradise of the agrarian garden:

> He knew by heart every individual clump of bunch grass in the miles of red shaggy prairie that stretched before his cabin. He knew it in all the deceitful loveliness of its early summer, in all the bitter barrenness of its autumn. He had seen it smitten by all the plagues of Egypt. He had seen it parched by drought, and sogged by rain, beaten by hail, and swept by fire, and in the grasshopper years he had seen it eaten as bare and clean as bones that the vultures had left. After the great fires he had seen it stretch for miles and miles, black and smoking as the floor of hell.[11]

His life in nature turns Canute in upon himself, there to live in a world of florid fantasy in which he carves figures of toiling men and dancing devils.[12] As more settlers appear in the district Canute finds some social life, and the action of the story shifts to his relationship with the Yensen family. Canute drinks with the father, listens to the garrulous talk of the mother, falls in love with the daughter. When Lena rejects him as a husband, he carries her off to his cabin and forces a preacher to marry them. Then his nerve fails him and he spends his wedding night in the snow outside the cabin. When Lena, frightened and lonely, timidly invites him in, she opens the door to find him sobbing at her feet—the story's ending and a slight note of ironic affirmation.

One of Cather's biographers, James Woodress, has noted the contrast between such early stories of rural defeat and the pleasure the young writer apparently found in Nebraska life in the same period. Back in Red Cloud for summer vacations she took long rides across the prairie and enjoyed the spectacle of the harvest. In a letter back to Lincoln she once urged friends to visit a countryside that seemed a glorious garden, green and beautiful with corn.[13] All the same, the early stories, written in Lincoln and later in Red Cloud after her graduation, continued to portray grim pioneer farm existence in a world of uncooperative nature. The plight of immigrants who confronted the prairie while their memories of a different life were still fresh in mind had an especially strong hold on her imagination. "It is useless," she said directly in "On the Divide," "for men that have cut hemlocks among the mountains of Sweden for forty years to try to be happy in a country as flat and gray and as naked as the sea."[14] Her dark response to farm life also owed something to the natural catastrophes and economic depression of the early nineties that clouded the western regions of the Midwest for recent immigrants and established figures alike. In the panic year of 1893 Cather's father was among the many who suffered financial damage. A Midwestern contemporary later identified with the popular literature of the region's folk charm, William Allen White of Kansas, similarly began his writing career with stories of rural defeat. "A Story of the Highlands," appearing in his first book of stories in 1896, *The Real Issue*, depicts a farm wife who succumbs to madness and finally death during a prolonged drought on the arid plains of western Kansas. The grim descriptive language might well have come from the hand of the early Cather:

> The even line of the horizon is seldom marred. The silence of such a scene gnaws the glamour from the heart. Men become harsh and hard; women grow withered and sodden under its blighting power.[15]

3

Cather discovered journalism during her final two years at the University of Nebraska. A journalism course taught by the managing editor of the *Nebraska State Journal* led to a regular job with the Lincoln paper and a career that would eventually propel her eastward and into the status of one of the leading women journalists of the time. At the *Journal* she turned out a stream of columns, features, and reviews, becoming in the second term of her junior year the

paper's regular drama critic, a position in which she quickly developed a reputation extending beyond Nebraska for knowledgeable and acerbic comment.
"The best theatrical critics of the west are said to be connected with the Lincoln, Neb., press," a Des Moines newspaper had noted with her work in
mind.[16]

When the *Journal* after her graduation in 1895 offered her only a space-rate
job, she returned to Red Cloud while continuing as a contributor to the paper.
She wrote voluminously and her reputation as a journalist grew, but no regular
position came her way. As an alternative to journalism she unsuccessfully
sought a teaching appointment at the University. Her break came when she was
suddenly handed the job of assistant editor of a magazine being revived in
Pittsburgh under the name *Home Monthly*. The *Journal's* publisher was acquainted with one of the publishers of the new magazine and likely put in a
good word for his columnist and critic. However the job came about, Cather
accepted it eagerly and at age twenty-two put Nebraska behind her.

In addition to overseeing the usual editorial tasks of magazine publication
she wrote a good deal of *Home Monthly's* copy under several pseudonyms
while also sending back a weekly column to the *Journal* and working as a
part-time critic for the *Pittsburgh Leader*. Cather had little interest in the
magazine's mixture of what she called home and fireside stuff and at other
times simply trash, but it was a steady job at a princely salary compared to
what she had received in Lincoln. The city of Pittsburgh was also an attraction.
The hills and woods were a pleasant contrast to Nebraska and there was greater
access to music and theater as well as abundant social life. During her Pittsburgh days she received two marriage proposals but apparently made a decision
at this point in her life to remain single, seemingly convinced that married life
and her desire for a life of art would not mix.[17] Women writers especially, she
believed, found it difficult enough to fully commit themselves to their work.
"Married nightingales seldom sing," she wrote about an opera singer who had
left the stage for matrimony.[18]

During her second year in Pittsburgh, Cather left the *Home Monthly* for the
position of day telegraph editor with the *Pittsburgh Leader* while continuing
as a theater and music critic and doing some general reporting. She followed
the grind of daily journalism on the *Leader* until the spring of 1900; what came
next were several years of high school English teaching in Pittsburgh. Cather
may have been encouraged to switch careers by the acceptance of a story by a
major national magazine, *Cosmopolitan*. In "Eric Hermannson's Soul" she returned to Nebraska material for an ambitious and accomplished story about a
stalwart young Norwegian who comes to the Divide at eighteen to work in the
fields and play his fiddle at dances. When first seen in the story he is a primitive
force who slips away from prayer meetings to play his fiddle for Lena Hanson,
an enticing figure of freedom and experience "whose name was a reproach
through all the Divide country" and who would appear later in Cather's fiction
as the seductive Lena Lingard of *My Ántonia*. When his soul is won by a

fundamentalist preacher, Eric crushes his fiddle and turns into another of the sober and dull Norwegian exiles who "are dead many a year before they are put to rest in the little graveyard on the windy hill." Cather then introduces Margaret Elliot, an Eastern sophisticate visiting the Divide, whose beauty entices Eric into again playing the fiddle and attending a dance she gives before her return to the East. During the dance he reemerges as a young man of robust feeling; "the devil is loose again," an observer whispers when he sees him dancing.[19] In a final confrontation with the contemptuous preacher, Eric holds his new ground, in possession of his own soul once again.

In the story Cather develops for the first time an East-West conflict, and clearly locates her sympathies with the West. While talented and beautiful, Margaret Elliot is "critical, unsatisfied, tired of the world at twenty-four"; she belongs "to an ultra-refined civilization which tries to cheat nature with elegant sophistries." About the West and a "giant barbarian" like Eric Hermannson there is life-enhancing vigor; it is Eric's passion that awakens Margaret's buried feeling. At the same time it is Eastern culture and grace as represented by Margaret that lift Eric out of his religious lethargy and return him to himself. When after the dance the two climb a windmill to find cooler air, the Western sky is a dazzle of beauty. "How sweet the corn smells at night," Margaret says, and Eric replies, "Yes, like the flowers that grow in paradise, I think."[20] Although the two go their separate ways at the end, the story suggests that it is the momentary union of Western vigor and Eastern culture that unlocks a renewing passion in each of them and casts over the agrarian landscape an aura of perfection.

Cather's first book, *April Twilights*, was a collection of poems rather than stories, a slender and undistinguished volume published in 1903. Although she later claimed not to have taken herself seriously as a poet, during her Pittsburgh years she wrote verse regularly and sold some of it to national magazines. But the sudden shift in her fortunes that sent her from Pittsburgh to New York came about through her stories. Her name had come to the attention of S. S. McClure, the editor and publisher of *McClure's*, and he wrote her asking to see her work (not knowing that some had already been rejected by the magazine). After she sent him a bundle of stories, she was summoned to his New York office where McClure enthusiastically informed her that he would take some of the stories for the magazine and later publish a book of stories. It was the beginning of a long association with the dynamic editor and his magazine.

The stories that appeared in *The Troll Garden* in 1905, published by McClure, Phillips, and Co., concentrated on the world of art and artists. A story of this sort, "Paul's Case," would become one of Cather's best-known works. Only two of the stories used Western material. In "A Wagner Matinee" a woman musician from Boston has been exiled to the Nebraska plains for thirty years, becoming there one of Garland's work-worn farm wives. When she returns to Boston to collect a legacy and stay with a nephew, her pianist's fingers have become "bent and knotted" and she wears "ill-fitting false teeth, and her skin was as yellow as a Mongolian's from constant exposure to a pitiless wind." The nephew takes her to a concert and watches the details of refined life sink into her soul, repeating his own experience when he had come east from Nebraska "fresh from ploughing forever and forever between green aisles of corn, where, as in a treadmill, one might walk from daybreak to dusk without perceiving a shadow of change." At the end of the concert the aunt cries out that she does not want to leave, the nephew understanding that she resists returning to her bleak plains existence: " . . . the tall, unpainted house, with weather-curled boards; naked as a tower, the crook-backed ash seedlings where the dish-cloths hung to dry; the gaunt, moulting turkeys picking up refuse about the kitchen door."[21]

Its unadorned portrait of farm life had caused a furor back in Nebraska when the story first appeared in *Everybody's Magazine* in 1904. Cather had also drawn in the story on the pioneer experience of her aunt and uncle, causing added displeasure among family members. She defended herself on the grounds that she had not tried to set down an accurate portrait of any family members, that the story evoked pioneer times rather than the present, and that she had intended the story as praise for stalwart farm wives. Whatever the particular experience behind the tale, Cather was clearly drawing on a continuing sense of a Nebraska upbringing that, as she put it in a letter at the time, had only half-nourished her. She was content enough with the story's hard edge of prairie accusation to reprint it without change in *The Troll Garden* the year following its magazine publication, this despite Nebraska friends who only, as she put it, wanted her to "write propaganda for the commercial club."[22] When she came to prepare a collected edition of her work in the 1930s, however, her sense of her Midwestern past long since altered, she made changes in the story to fit it more comfortably among her major accounts of a Nebraska of memory.

The other Western story in the collection, "The Sculptor's Funeral," was an angry satire directed to the region's self-satisfied philistinism. When the body of a distinguished artist, Harvey Merrick, is returned to Sand City, Kansas, for burial, his old friends reduce his accomplishments to their own narrow-minded level. One of their comments is that Merrick's father made a mistake in sending his son to the East for school. "There was where he got his head full of trapesing to Paris and all such folly. What Harve needed, of all people, was a course in some first-class Kansas City business college."[23] The story ends with an embittered lawyer, a drinker who has failed to escape the town but understands the sculptor's larger vision, denouncing Sand City's values. One example of Merrick's sculpture is mentioned in the story, a bas-relief of his mother done after a visit to his home that depicts a

thin, faded old woman, sitting and sewing something pinned to her knee; while a full-lipped, full-blooded little urchin, his trousers held up by a single gallus, stood beside her, impatiently twitching her gown to call her attention to a butterfly he had caught.[24]

The work suggests a more sympathetic approach to Midwestern life on the part of Merrick, but it was one that Cather herself was not yet ready to adopt.

4

An internal dispute in 1906 left *McClure's* without Ida Tarbell, on whom much of the regular editorial work had fallen, and such important writers as Ray Stannard Baker and Lincoln Steffens. McClure had seen trouble coming and had already journeyed to Pittsburgh to secure the services of Cather. Before the end of her teaching year she was whisked off to New York and put to work on the staff of one of best general magazines of the day. Founded during the Panic of 1893, *McClure's* had not only survived but forged a solid reputation with an aggressive mixture of muckraking journalism, profiles and interviews devoted to the prominent, and fiction by well-established British and American writers. Suddenly Cather was at the pinnacle of metropolitan magazine journalism, an absorbing and demanding world that would occupy most of her attention for the next six years.

She threw herself into the new job, wanting to justify the faith placed in her by the volatile and charismatic McClure and to succeed in a traditional male career. She accomplished both. Within two years she was the magazine's managing editor and McClure considered her a brilliant and loyal employee, one of the few who could work with equanimity and for any length of time under his interventionist style of editorial direction. The price of success was that she virtually abandoned her writing career during her years on the magazine. Soon after she arrived in New York she wrote a friend that she wondered if she would ever write another line of anything that truly mattered.

During her first year of reading and editing manuscripts for the magazine McClure sent her to Boston with a manuscript he had bought on the life of the founder of Christian Science, Mary Baker Eddy, that was long on research and short on writing skill. McClure had already assigned a writer to checking the facts and rewriting the work; Cather was to pick up where this writer had left off. She moved to Boston and for several months devoted herself to the assignment that eventually resulted in a highly praised fourteen-part series in the magazine. For Cather, the story was uncongenial and grinding work, but it had the benefit of placing her for a time in New England. She found the rich historical and literary legacy of the region a far cry from Nebraska and deeply satisfying; in addition she made new and important friendships, among them the author Sarah Orne Jewett, the first notable woman writer Cather had come to know. When they had appeared in 1896, Cather had been captivated by the local-color stories in *The Country of the Pointed Firs;* later she considered the collection an enduring American classic. Although Jewett was considerably older when they met and their relationship lasted only sixteen months until the

Maine author's death at age sixty, she exercised a vital influence in moving Cather away from journalism into a full-time pursuit of literature.

In gentle but direct terms, Jewett told her young friend that her writing was hindered by magazine work. It could not easily be combined with a demanding activity that drained off energy and mental concentration. "Your vivid, exciting companionship in the office," she said in a letter in 1908, "must not be your audience, you must find your own quiet centre of life, and write from that to the world."[25] Jewett's advice and example began to turn Cather not only away from journalism but from the genteel Jamesian fiction that had been her model if not always her practice, directing her attention to what Jewett called her uncommon equipment. "You have," Jewett pointed out, "your Nebraska life,— a child's Virginia, and now an intimate knowledge of what we are pleased to call 'the Bohemia' of newspaper and magazine office life."[26] But Cather was not immediately ready to cut the ties with *McClure's* that gave her a lofty position, a good salary, and an exciting life in New York. It would not be until 1911, with McClure about to be removed from power in a financial reorganization, that she took a leave of absence that ended in her deciding to sever the connection with the magazine for good. As it had turned out, she had been a long time acting on a biting assessment of journalism and literature she had set down as early as 1895:

> Journalism is the vandalism of literature. It has brought to it endless harm and no real good. It has made an art a trade. The great American newspaper takes in intellect, promise, talent; it gives out only colloquial gossip. It is written by machines, set by machines, and read by machines. No man can write for any journal in this country without for the most part losing that precious thing called style.[27]

In 1911 she finished revisions on *Alexander's Bridge*, her first novel, and turned finally to full concentration on her Western material. The immediate fruit was a lengthy and romantic tale of stormy love in which she drew on the world of immigrant families on the Divide. In "The Bohemian Girl," published in *McClure's* in 1912, Nils Ericson returns to the Divide after years of seeking his fortune abroad and is reunited with his mother and brothers, all prosperous land owners. He meets again his old love, Clara Vavrika, the daughter of a tavern owner in the Bohemian community and now unhappily married to Nils's brother, Olaf, a self-satisfied politician interested only in maintaining his position. Love is rekindled and at length Nils sweeps Clara away from her dull life. In a postscript to the story in which a younger brother fails in an attempt to emulate Nils's leave-taking, it is learned that Nils and Clara have escaped abroad, there to live in comfort and happiness.

As the plot turns, neither of the main characters finds Nebraska life fulfilling. Satisfaction is gained elsewhere. But with the story Cather was drawing closer to a more sympathetic and richly textured handling of her Midwestern material and to finding her authentic fictional manner. As against the worn, emotionally-starved figure removed to Boston in "A Wagner Matinee," farm wives gathered for a barn-raising seem to Nils Ericson to possess the dignity of a Dutch painting:

> They all had a pleased, prosperous air, as if they were more than satisfied with themselves and with life. . . . he fell into amazement when he thought of the Herculean labors those fifteen pairs of hands had performed: of the cows they had milked, the butter they had made, the gardens they had planted, the children and grandchildren they had tended, the brooms they had worn out, the mountains of food they had cooked. It made him dizzy.[28]

In later years Cather described *Alexander's Bridge* as a shallow and conventional work in a Jamesian manner and the story that followed it as one of her first real fictions. Many of its elements would reappear in altered form in *O Pioneers!*: males who return to the high plains and an old love; a background cast of dull, materialistic brothers; a stalwart woman who successfully farms the home place. Immediately after "The Bohemian Girl" Cather set to work on another long story tentatively called "Alexandra" that would remain unfinished until its incorporation into the novel.

The year 1912 seemed to Cather a watershed point in her life, setting off her apprentice writing from her mature work, and for very different reasons than Dell marked the same year as the astonishing moment in Chicago's tumultuous literary emergence. She spent the spring of the year in Arizona visiting her brother and exploring the Southwest, the start of a long fascination with the region that seems to have had its source in a sense of separation from Eastern confinement and deep feelings of inner release as a woman and a writer.[29] In June and July she was back in Red Cloud for five weeks, seeing the Bohemian country again and observing the wheat harvest, her senses sharpened by her time in the Southwest and feeling a desire now to drench herself in her Nebraska memories. Favorable critical response to "The Bohemian Girl" reinforced her new attitude toward her past. Staying in Pittsburgh in the fall of the year while writing a Nebraska story of adulterous love called "The White Mulberry Tree," it suddenly came to her that the tale could be combined with "Alexandra" to create what she called a "two-part pastoral" and her second novel.[30] As an epigraph for the work she used a poem, "Prairie Spring," written after her return to Nebraska from the Southwest. In it the "flat land, / Rich and sombre and always silent" and "tired men" and the "eternal, unresponsive sky"—the dark physical and psychological landscape, in other words, of her early Midwestern fiction—are now set off against a bright vision of "Youth, / Flaming like the wild roses, / Singing like the larks over the plowed fields." The novel's title was taken from Whitman's hymn to westward migration, "Pioneers! O Pioneers!" and the book dedicated to Sarah Orne Jewett, the writer who had urged Cather to give herself to her native material.

5

The story opens "one January day, thirty years ago"—1883 from the date of publication—in the windswept town of Hanover, Nebraska, where Alexandra Bergson and her young brother, Emil, have come on errands with a neighbor, Carl Lindstrum.[31] With the return home the reader learns that Alexandra's Swedish father is dying after years of hard struggle with the wild land. To Alexandra and his sons, Lou and Oscar, he bequeaths a full section of unmortgaged land, charging them with maintaining it and with following the decisions of Alexandra, the oldest child. In the years that follow Alexandra dutifully manages the land and adds more, guided by a deep conviction that the future is bright and that she and her brothers will become rich farmers.

With the second part of the novel, sixteen years after the father's death, Alexandra has been proved correct. Lou and Oscar are married and have farms of their own while Alexandra, unmarried, remains on the home place, one of the richest farms on the Divide. The "shaggy coat of the prairie" has been plowed and tilled to a "vast checker-board, marked off in squares of wheat and corn" (174). Subdued and populated, the land is adorned with steel windmills and crisscrossed with telephone wires. Once a landscape of emptiness, it has been transformed into a garden-like world of enclosure with "order and fine arrangement manifest all over the great farm; in the fencing and hedging, in the windbreaks and sheds, in the symmetrical pasture ponds planted with scrub willows to give shade to the cattle in fly-time" (178). Alexandra is content with her achievement but lonely. Carl, the cherished friend from her childhood, has moved away and her brothers have sunk into dull, greedy lives. Her attention is turned upon Emil, now twenty-one, and a young friend, Marie, married to a darkly jealous Bohemian farmer, Frank Shabata. When Carl returns, a mature figure of thirty-five, her affection for her old friend is rekindled, but with Lou and Oscar's suspicions that he wants her property Carl goes off again in pursuit of his own fortune. In the novel's brief third part, "Winter Memories," Alexandra's stoic pastoral existence ("Her mind was a white book, with clear writing about weather and beasts and growing things") is contrasted with a recurring desire to be "lifted and carried by a strong being who took from her all her bodily weariness" (238, 239).

In the fourth section the developing passion between Emil and Marie results in tragedy. When Frank finds them lying together beneath a white mulberry tree in the orchard he fires three rifle shots, killing them both. Carl reappears in the story when the news reaches him, and with his help Alexandra comes to accept her failure to detect the love affair earlier. Carl tells her about Marie that "there are women who spread ruin around them through no fault of theirs, just by being too beautiful, too full of life and love. They can't help it. People come to them as people go to a warm fire in winter" (288). With the novel's end Carl and Alexandra are planning to marry—a winter marriage between friends— and Cather turns to an evocation of the land and Alexandra's primary relationship to it. "You belong to the land," Carl says to her, "as you have always said. Now more than ever" (289). As Alexandra takes his arm and they walk to the gate of her farm home, she leans heavily against him while confessing her lone-liness—the closest she will come, or allow herself to come, to realizing the fantasy of being removed from herself by a figure of superior strength—and Cather provides a lyric conclusion:

> They went into the house together, leaving the Divide behind them, under the evening star. Fortunate country, that is one day to receive hearts like Alexandra's into its bosom, to give them out again in the yellow wheat, in the rustling corn, in the shining eyes of youth! (290)

When the novel appeared Cather wrote in a presentation copy to a friend that "this was the first time I walked off on my own feet—everything before was half real and half an imitation of writers whom I admired. In this one I hit the home pasture and found that I was Yance Sorgeson and not Henry James."[32] The home pasture was the core of memory of her Nebraska youth stripped of harshness and the sense of deprivation that had once encrusted it, seen now from the vantage point of an Eastern life in which she was a secure professional writer entering middle age as a time of wonder and perfection. At the end of the novel's first section, "The Wild Land," Alexandra realizes that she possesses a "new consciousness of the country," a "new relation to it":

> She had never known before how much the country meant to her. The chirping of the insects down in the long grass had been like the sweetest music. She had felt as if her heart were hiding down there, somewhere, with the quail and the plover and all the little wild things that crooned or buzzed in the sun. (173)

Through Alexandra, Cather expressed her own new relationship to the land. It seemed to her now, as it did to Alexandra, "rich and strong and glorious," and in Alexandra she imagined a figure equal to its bounty and spirit. "For the first time, perhaps, since that land emerged from the waters of geologic ages," she said about her heroine, "a human face was set toward it with love and yearning" (170).

The reader sees little of the actual process of transforming the wild land into the Edenic garden. It is Alexandra's determination to succeed that Cather con-centrates on, not the details of her effort; time is encapsulated and through most of the story Alexandra and her brothers are already rich farmers beyond the reach of failure. It is the romance of the heroic pioneer period as experi-enced by a woman uniquely, almost mystically, attuned to the land that occu-pies Cather's attention. With the passing of this period, shadows appear—Carl's restless journeying, the carping materialism of Lou and Oscar, Alex-andra's loneliness, the unsettling intrusion of romantic love in the tragic affair of Emil and Marie. When she visits the cemetery after the deaths of the young lovers, the dead seem to Alexandra more real than the living. At the end of the novel life returns in the union of Alexandra and Carl amid nature's still-fresh bounty; for Carl, Alexandra replaces her black mourning clothes with a white dress that signals the shift in the story's tone. Finally, the novel celebrates a pastoral future that can be raised on the accomplishments of stalwart pioneers like Alexandra. Alexandra declares, "The land belongs to the future, Carl. . . . We come and go, but the land is always here," and the novel's closing line speaks as well of the "shining eyes of youth" that will inherit hearts like Alexandra's (289, 290). There remains, however, an elegiac quality to the ending, a sense of pastoral perfection located in the period of the land's transformation from wild prairie to sweet garden. Cather strongly evokes the future but it is the past remembered within Alexandra and Carl that provides the novel's concluding feeling. As they walk together toward the gate to the farm house and their future together, Alexandra first directs Carl's attention to the past ("How many times we have walked this path together, Carl"). Although she then speaks of what is ahead of them ("How many times we will walk it again!"), the concluding sentence returns to the backward view: "Does it seem to you like coming back to your own place?" (290).

Cather's own sense of coming back to her authentic material in a mature and more congenial mood freed her from her "half an imitation" of other writers in method as well as subject. The novel is authentically realistic in setting and detail, yet it is the great sweep of the story and Cather's lyric language that hold in the mind—the romantic Whitmanesque strain suggested in the book's title. In organization the book is appropriately loose and episodic, qualities that have caused some critics to view it as structurally flawed, especially the melding of the Emil-Marie story with that of Alexandra and the land.[33] Cather frankly acknowledged that she had composed a two-part pastoral and was untroubled by a form that seemed to her organic, meaning one dictated by a story that flowed freely from her new sense of her natural material. It was not plot that stirred Cather in her new manner but character, place, and emotion arising from a remembered past on the Divide that now held epic proportion in her imagination.

6

Cather took special pleasure in the favorable response of Western reviewers to *O Pioneers!* They found the novel, she informed a friend, "true to the country and the people."[34] Praise came in almost equal measure from Eastern publications; rather than losing an audience with her prairie material, as she feared might happen, she had added to a growing reputation. She was not ready, however, to wholly commit herself to Nebraska fiction. After ghost writing S. S. McClure's autobiography for serialization in the magazine, she turned for her next novel to her passion for opera and a story of an artist's growth. *The Song of the Lark* brought more glowing reviews, including Mencken's estimate that with the novel Cather had entered the small group of the most important

American writers. The following year she traveled west to mark her new stature with an honorary degree from the University of Nebraska, the first it had granted to a woman.

She was now well into the writing of a second Nebraska novel, one that would again find in farm life the material of a prairie epic. For the figure of Ántonia Shimerda she drew on the life of Annie Sadilek Pavelka, a Bohemian farm wife she had known since they were children together on the Divide and with whom she had kept in contact during return visits to Nebraska. It was a life that seemed to sum up for Cather all her long fascination with the immigrant experience; the structure of the novel would simply follow her memories of Annie from youthful arrival on the Divide through middle age. There would be no gripping drama in the story—nothing like the account of tragic love inserted into *O Pioneers!*—but rather an accumulation of life's ordinary incidents in a Howellsian manner. She would also depart from the earlier novel by telling the story through a narrator, an approach that seemed to her proper for a novel meant to evoke feeling rather than recount action. Since Jim Burden would be a lawyer rather than professional writer, he would seemingly write the story with no attention to literary craft; there would be only the casual and artless flow of memory. "I didn't arrange or rearrange," Jim would say in the book's introduction to his account of Ántonia. "I simply wrote down what of herself and myself and other people Ántonia's name recalls to me. I suppose it hasn't any form."[35]

Work on the novel went slowly due to periods of illness and the need to produce short stories for income. Much of the writing was done in Jaffrey, New Hampshire, a rural retreat Cather had discovered as a summer and fall escape from New York. Before the manuscript was finished she was already sending copy to the publisher and reading proof on the early sections. The book appeared in September 1918, illustrated with simple drawings by W. T. Benda and dedicated to two Nebraska friends. Once again, the critical reception was positive. Randolph Bourne, considered by Cather the best reviewer of the day, found the book totally authentic. The author, he noted, "knows her story and carries it along with the surest touch. It has all the artistic simplicity of material that has been patiently shaped until everything irrelevant has been scraped away."[36] Sales, however, were modest. Cather's royalties in the first year following publication were $1,300, in the second $400. After the novel she would leave her publisher, Houghton Mifflin, for the new and, she hoped, more enterprising firm of Alfred A. Knopf.

Cather's decision to employ a male narrator as her *alter ego* has provoked question from the novel's publication until now. Since she had used the device in her short fiction, there was nothing new about it; she pointed out as well that with McClure's autobiography just behind her she felt confident in using a male voice at book length. Whatever the explanation, the use of Jim Burden as narrator casts the novel, as against *O Pioneers!*, as a male romance of the prairie. Although Ántonia has a sturdy reality as a distinct and admirably independent female character, it remains that the reader's perception of her is funnelled through Jim's fervent feeling. As he insists in the introduction, she is *his* Ántonia. This fact, even when stripped of questions of gender consideration, adds a pleasing edge of complexity to the novel, making it Cather's most subtle and many-layered treatment of her Midwestern memories. Critics have frequently noted, and with considerable awe, the variety of interpretation inspired by a work that possesses such surface simplicity and a substance notably devoid of striking events.[37]

The Jim Burden of the book's introduction is a Nebraskan transplanted to New York, now the middle-aged legal counsel for a Western railway and unhappily married to a restless woman who is a patroness of the arts. He remains a romantic by nature, Cather's authorial voice informs us in the introduction, and despite his Eastern life is devoted to the West, "still able to lose himself in those big Western dreams" (712). During a long summer train ride together across the Midwest, Jim and the author remember the Bohemian girl who summed up for both of them "the country, the conditions, the whole adventure of our childhood"; the very mention of her name brings back the past, setting "a quiet drama going in one's brain" (712, 713). They agree to write down what they remember of Ántonia but Jim alone complies, arriving at the author's New York apartment one afternoon with his manuscript. "Read it as soon as you can," he says, "but don't let it influence your own story," to which the author pointedly adds that "my own story was never written" (714).

Jim's account follows, of course, Cather's own recollection of her Nebraska past—the early days in the country shared with Ántonia who lives on a nearby farm, the eventual move to the country town where Ántonia also comes to work as a hired girl, the years of separation from Ántonia in Lincoln and finally at Harvard as a student, the concluding reunion with Ántonia when both are in middle age. Likewise, the transformation Ántonia undergoes in Jim's imagination from a lively immigrant girl to a towering figure of Western myth ("She was a rich mine of life," he proclaims at the end, "like the founders of early races") is clearly shared by Cather (926). Yet it remains that Jim is established from the beginning of the novel as an unreliable narrator, subject to the enthusiasms rooted in a romantic temperament and a failed and childless marriage, sexually timid as a young man, not immune from a sense of class superiority to Ántonia, subjecting her to stern male judgment when he learns she has borne a child out of wedlock. At the same time that she embraces Jim's idealized sense of Ántonia and her pastoral world, Cather distances herself from him, allowing the reader an edge of awareness not permitted to Jim himself, deepening finally the elegiac quality that permeates the story he relates.

From his first glimpse of Ántonia as a wild young thing of fourteen until his final reunion with her as a worn farm wife, it is a vision of Ántonia that holds Jim's attention more than his response to a flesh-and-blood person. It is a vision first of elemental immigrant life, later of abiding pastoral fulfillment. "The idea of you," he eventually reveals to her, "is a part of my mind; you influence my likes and dislikes, all my tastes, hundreds of times when I don't realize it. You really are a part of me." Ántonia is properly confused by her role in Jim's life as an "idea" and feebly responds, "How can it be like that, when you know so

many people, and when I've disappointed you so?" (910). When Jim sees
Ántonia again after twenty years of separation, it is still a vision held in his
mind that dominates him. The reality is that Ántonia is now a "stalwart, brown
woman, flat-chested, her curly brown hair a little grizzled"; her altered appearance comes to Jim as a "shock." Yet as he looks at her "the changes grew less
apparent" and she once again becomes a stirring mental conception (914).
Jim's idea of Ántonia is not without substance. Set against the background of
an Edenic farm and surrounded by attractive children she seems indeed at the
novel's end the prairie heroine he envisions. Nonetheless, Jim's attention is directed to a moving idea more than a portrait of reality; he finds in Ántonia
what he wishes to find. Although now she is a "battered woman," she lends
herself in his imagination "to immemorial human attitudes which we recognize
by instinct as universal and true. I had not been mistaken" (926).

Jim may not be mistaken about Ántonia but his vision of her is heavily
weighted on the side of romantic myth—a vision, once again, Cather obviously
shares while alert, as Jim never seems to be, to the shadow of complexity. Jim
identifies his vision of Ántonia with an earlier time, a period of youth and
pioneer vitality. He announces the passage from Virgil that provides the book's
epigraph, *Optima dies . . . prima fugit*, and interprets it as "the best days are
the first to flee" (876). Yet he never seems to consciously feel, or to feel so
strongly, what the reader feels—the powerfully elegiac quality of a story that
is turned back upon a historical moment in which a figure like Ántonia could
flourish. Jim's own story—Cather's story; the reader's story—is one of leaving
the country for the city and career and the discontents (as Cather quietly but
clearly notes them in recounting Jim's life) of civilization. By clinging to
Ántonia's story of heroic survival, Jim keeps the juices of life flowing within
himself. Still, that story remains rooted in an existence unlikely to survive despite the emphasis at the end of the novel on Ántonia's happy brood of children
(in sharp contrast to the childless Alexandra, who can look forward only to her
brothers' children as heirs, or to Jim himself) who will carry something of her
rich life into the future.

A central and often-noted symbolic moment in the novel occurs near the end
of the second book when Jim joins the hired girls working in Black Hawk—
Ántonia, Tiny Soderball, Lena Lingard—for an outing in the country. At the
end of the day, watching the sun set, they are startled when a "great black
figure suddenly appeared on the face of the sun":

> We sprang to our feet, straining our eyes toward it. In a moment we realized what
> it was. On some upland farm, a plough had been left standing in the field. The
> sun was sinking just behind it. Magnified across the distance by the horizontal
> light, it stood out against the sun, was exactly contained within the circle of the
> disc; the handles, the tongue, the share—black against the molten red. There it
> was, heroic in size, a picture writing on the sun.

The plough magnified against the western sun seems a compelling image of an
agrarian paradise carved from prairie and plains—the dream that had drawn

the Shimerdas to Nebraska from the old world of Bohemia, Jim's grandparents from the new world of Virginia. It is a dream of heightened life in which the land is first conquered, then admitted by the triumphant farmer into a comfortable partnership in which it provides lasting aesthetic and spiritual blessing as well as material gain—precisely the dream that Alexandra Bergson turns into historical reality. Jim is deeply responsive to the dream as he remembers its embodiment in his early Nebraska experience and as he discovers its continued embodiment in the figure of the pioneer woman, Ántonia. Yet Cather makes clear that the plough's heroic stature against the western sun is fleeting, time-bound. Even as Jim and the hired girls whisper about it

> our vision disappeared; the ball dropped and dropped until the red tip went beneath the earth. The fields below us were dark, the sky was growing pale, and that forgotten plough had sunk back to its own littleness somewhere on the prairie. (865–66)

The passage seems calculated to indicate Cather's awareness of what another narrator, Fitzgerald's Nick Carraway, would call a "transitory enchanted moment." It is a moment of pioneer achievement soon lost or abandoned or from the very beginning more illusion than real possibility, the "heroic" plough reduced to its true or eventual "littleness." But what Cather knows or senses about the necessary qualification that must be placed upon the garden myth seems to elude Jim. His "burden" in the story is to bear the dream in its full, unreduced glory, devoid of a sense of separation between dream and reality—devoid, indeed, of any sense of complexity.[38] In the closing line of the novel Jim celebrates what has become his central possession in his version of Ántonia, the memory fixed forever in his mind of a "precious" past they shared together. It is a lovely memory of an enchanted time, and Jim's account of it has moved readers more powerfully and over a longer span than any other single novel of the Midwest. Yet it is a memory, as Jim adds, that is essentially "incommunicable" (937). Although he links the two terms that define his memory—precious and incommunicable—he gives no attention to the obvious tension between them. He never realizes what Cather so clearly implies through his narrative, that the time he celebrates, embodied so wondrously in Ántonia, is both lovely and lost.

7

Jim's own story, once again, and that of the other young country figures in his account—including, for a time, Ántonia herself—is one of flight from rural life. When he first arrives in Nebraska as a child, transplanted as Cather had been from Virginia, he is overwhelmed by the feeling of emptiness:

> There seemed to be nothing to see; no fences, no creeks or trees, no hills or fields. If there was a road, I could not make it out in the faint starlight. There was nothing

but land: not a country at all, but the material out of which countries are made. No, there was nothing but land. (718)

Yet in the garden of his grandparents' farm home his experience of the land is very different. Despite a fear of snakes, he feels a sense of shelter and deep peace in the garden; in the sunshine, surrounded by pumpkins, he is "entirely happy," feeling himself "dissolved into something complete and great" (724). That sense of participation in something larger than himself is maintained throughout the novel's long first book in which Jim comes to know the Bohemian family that has taken up the neighboring farm. Although Ántonia, four years older than Jim, becomes his exuberant companion of the countryside, her family's story as Jim recounts it is one of brutal work and frequent defeat. Ántonia's father commits suicide; her brother Ambrosch becomes a calloused farm laborer; Ántonia, hardened by country routine, becomes the subject of jokes by farm-hands. Jim's life on the comfortable farm of his grandparents is far different—a life in the country but not of it in the sense of total dependence on rural labor. When Jim reproaches her for acting like Ambrosch, Ántonia correctly tells him: "If I live here, like you, that is different. Things will be easy for you. But they will be hard for us" (802).

Jim's separation from Ántonia grows when he goes to the country school and later moves with his grandparents to the country town of Black Hawk. When Ántonia comes to town as a hired girl the relationship is resumed but the dif-ferences of circumstance remain. The immigrant country girls working in Black Hawk possess a special physical vitality that Cather richly evokes in the novel's second book; nonetheless, the town boys, Jim included, keep a proper distance since their "respect for respectability was stronger than any desire" (840). Jim recounts an explicit sexual dream in which the dark temptress, Lena Lingard, barefoot and wearing a short skirt, lies beside him in a harvest field. "Now they are all gone," Lena says to him, "and I can kiss you as much as I like." Jim notes that he "used to wish I could have this flattering dream about Ántonia, but I never did," nor is he able to act on his dream of Lena, less an idea to him than Ántonia but like Ántonia identified with the exciting yet removed world of immigrant experience (854). Even at the beginning of their relationship Jim distances himself from Ántonia's vitality, a vitality forever foreign to his sense of identity and proper destiny. Alone together after their first meeting, the two young people make a "nest in the long red grass" while Jim helps Ántonia with English words; in gratitude she tries to give him the silver ring she wears on her finger. "When she coaxed and insisted," Jim says, "I repulsed her quite sternly. I didn't want her ring, and I felt there was something reckless and extravagant about her wishing to give it away to a boy she had never seen before" (729).

The separation from Ántonia and country life is completed in the brief third book, set in Lincoln over the course of Jim's university days. When Lena comes to Lincoln during his sophomore year to begin a dressmaking business, excite-ment returns to his life; reminded again of the exuberant hired girls, he remarks that "if there were no girls like them in the world, there would be no poetry" (880). Although he finds himself half in love with Lena, when the opportunity comes to follow a favorite teacher to Harvard to finish his education he is quick to go. In the fourth book Jim returns to Black Hawk for summer vacation before beginning law school and learns that Ántonia, who had gone off to Denver to marry a flashy railway conductor named Larry Donovan, has returned home to the farm, pregnant and abandoned. She is now a devoted and proud mother but once more under the thumb of Ambrosch and subject to country routine.

When Jim visits her on the farm he speaks of his own plans for a law career in New York. Ántonia understands that "it means you are going away from us for good," and she reestablishes her own opposed identification with the rural landscape by telling him how miserable she would be in a city: "I'd die of lonesomeness. I like to be where I know every stack and tree, and where all the ground is friendly. I want to live and die here" (909–10). It is at this point that Jim announces his disembodied passion for Ántonia as an idea that evokes for him his rural past, and Ántonia responds in kind by declaring that she cannot wait to tell her daughter "about all the things we used to do." Although she is a young woman of twenty-four and Jim just twenty, it is their shared past that links them—a past abandoned by Jim in his movement away from the country yet now restored by Ántonia in her return to it. Ántonia tells him: "You'll always remember me when you think about old times, won't you? And I guess everybody thinks about old times, even the happiest people" (910).

As the two walk together across the fields at sundown, Jim—his idea of Ántonia intensified by her physical presence—is vividly alert to the landscape. He feels "the old pull of the earth, the solemn magic that comes out of those fields at nightfall. I wished I could be a little boy again, and that my way could end there" (910). In a sense his way does end "there," in the lingering glow of the night fields, in that perfection is forever identified in his mind with the few years of pioneer life he once shared with Ántonia. Although he has in fact put such a life behind him, as have such other country figures as Lena and Tiny, he will continue to "come back" to it, a vow Ántonia recognizes as directed more to memory and imagination than actual presence. He will always be present for her, she tells him in response, in the same sense that her dead father continues to hold a place in her mind (911).

When Jim does return, twenty years gone by, nothing essential has changed. Ántonia, happily married now to Anton Cuzak and surrounded by a large family of lively children, still retains "the fire of life" and is even more deeply identified with country existence (917). In an enclosed orchard on her farm described in terms of agrarian peace and plenty, she reaffirms her rural roots, telling Jim that on the farm she is never lonesome as she used to be in town. And she continues to exercise a powerful hold on Jim's imagination, her life summing up for him the rural perfection he himself has abandoned:

> She had only to stand in the orchard, to put her hand on a little crab tree and look up at the apples, to make you feel the goodness of planting and tending and harvesting at last. All the strong things of her heart came out in her body, that had been so tireless in serving generous emotions.

It was no wonder that her sons stood tall and straight. She was a rich mine of life, like the founders of early races. (926)

The fifth and final book of the novel simply celebrates that perfection. When Jim leaves the farm and returns to Black Hawk the glow of his reunion with Ántonia quickly fades. The town disappoints him; his old friends have either moved away or are dead, and he feels an odd sense of depression. Only when he walks out of town into the country do his spirits revive and he feels himself "at home again" (936). He comes upon a fragment of the road that once led from town to his grandparents' farm and the Shimerdas's, his mind occupied with the memory of his arrival in Nebraska as a child. On the edge of the forgotten road, watching the haystacks turn color in the evening light, he once again feels "the sense of coming home to myself." The road at the end of the story returns him to the road of arrival at the beginning, giving the novel a final cyclical form and suggesting Jim's journey in memory back to an ideal time—to "the precious, the incommunicable past" shared with Ántonia that the novel so richly celebrates (937). But the old road suggests as well the journey in fact that led him away from the country to a life in civilization and the experience of its vague discontents—the situation with which the novel begins in the introduction.

One of Cather's many accomplishments in the novel is her capacity to establish Ántonia as a thoroughly alive presence. From Jim's first meeting with her to the reunion at the end the reader feels her full-bodied vitality. At the same time she exists in the novel as an idea or an image of rural perfection that can only be maintained through memory. Jim last sees Ántonia waving her apron in goodbye, a simple detail of realistic action; at this point she vanishes from the story as a physical presence and remains only as an idea, the position she occupies in the introduction as the remembered Bohemian girl who "seemed to mean to us the country, the conditions, the whole adventure of our childhood" (712). Except as it can be made to exist in memory, that world is gone for Jim, as it is for the authorial voice of the introduction and generally for a culture that has left rural ways behind. What remains is the world, as we learn about it in the introduction, in which Jim actually lives—or the world of Tiny Soderball, as Jim recounts it in the novel's fourth book, in which there is "solid worldly success" but no elation and indeed an inner chill in which "the faculty of becoming interested is worn out" (895, 897). Cather's overriding triumph in the novel is a narrative complexity that allows her to portray a pastoral world with full romantic approval and continuing appeal while retaining a clear-eyed detachment that consigns that world to the dream vision of an irrecoverable past.

8

After *O Pioneers!* and *My Ántonia* Cather gave extended treatment to her home pasture material in one other novel, *One of Ours*, a work that ironically brought her both commercial success and serious critical disapproval. In the years following the First War Cather's sunlit memories of youth were assaulted by the failed hopes and riotous excess of the Jazz Age. Increasingly disenchanted with the foreground of American life in the 1920s, she began, like a world-weary Jim Burden, to dwell on an ever-more-distant past. She would later announce—a remark frequently pointed to by commentators on her work—that the "world broke in two in 1922 or thereabouts,"[39] and suggest that her subsequent work was written by a backward-looking author for similarly inclined readers. In that year of world separation she joined the Episcopal Church during a Christmas visit to Red Cloud, her seeming indifference to religious faith to this point in her life replaced with attraction to its ancient comforts.

Her first novel of the twenties, however, dealt on the surface with the world of the immediate present. *One of Ours* was thought of as Cather's war novel (with its epigraph, *"Bidding the eagles of the West fly on,"* seeming a heroic reference to the war though it was drawn from Vachel Lindsay's poem about Bryan and the rise of Western populism), and critics leaped upon her unconvincing treatment of besieged France and the experience of men in war. Yet most of the book—its first three lengthy sections—was given over to a slow-paced account of the development of her rural hero, Claude Wheeler, a Nebraska farm boy and unfulfilled idealist. Claude simply wants more than a Nebraska of prairie land and small towns and a farm family bent on material gain can provide. Unlike the immigrant figures of Alexandra and Ántonia, he remains unsatisfied in an agrarian environment. Although he finds beauty in nature and takes pleasure in the Wheeler farm built up by his "land hog" father, he yearns for a larger world, convinced that "there was something splendid about life, if he could but find it!"[40] As Cather views him, Claude is dreamy and naive yet wholly sympathetic and clearly superior to those around him in thought and awareness. Through him she offers her own vigorous satire directed to a post-pioneer Midwest that has lost its yearning and grown dull, petty, and materialistic.

Among other failings, Claude sees all about him the poor stewardship of the land. Rather than plant trees, for example, farmers ruthlessly cut them down because they are signs of the past:

> Claude felt sure that when he was a little boy and all the neighbours were poor, they and their houses and farms had more individuality. The farmers took time then to plant fine cottonwood groves on their places, and to set osage orange hedges along the borders of their fields. Now these trees were all being cut down and grubbed up. Just why, nobody knew; they impoverished the land . . . they made the snow drift . . . nobody had them any more. With prosperity came a kind of callousness; everybody wanted to destroy the old things they used to take pride in. The orchards, which had been nursed and tended so carefully twenty years ago, were now left to die of neglect. It was less trouble to run into town in an automobile and buy fruit than it was to raise it. (1023)

In the neglect of the land the country people also mirror their neglect of one another:

> The people themselves had changed. He could remember when all the farmers in this community were friendly toward each other; now they were continually having lawsuits. Their sons were either stingy and grasping, or extravagant and lazy, and they were always stirring up trouble. Evidently, it took more intelligence to spend money than to make it. (1023–24)

Coexisting with Cather's criticism of the agrarian garden in its modern dress are, however, warm descriptions of country life and farm routine, the most detailed in her Nebraska fiction. Claude swings from aversion to his surroundings to comfortable oneness with them. The latter sense is especially strong when it eventually comes about that he is leaving the country for good:

> As he walked on alone, Claude was thinking how this country that had once seemed little and dull to him, now seemed large and rich in variety. During the months in [army] camp he had been wholly absorbed in new work and new friendships, and now his own neighbourhood came to him with the freshness of things that have been forgotten for a long while,—came together before his eyes as a harmonious whole. He was going away, and he would carry the whole countryside in his mind, meaning more to him than it ever had before. (1139)

Following an ill-starred marriage and increasing loneliness, Claude finds in the war in Europe his chance for escape. He enlists, becomes an infantry second lieutenant, and is sent to France, joining the tide of crusaders for democracy in 1917. Here he finds what he has longed for under the guidance of David Gerhardt, a fellow officer and Eastern representative of civilization who introduces him to French culture and the wonders of the Old World. In their first major action both Claude and Gerhardt are killed, and Cather ends the novel with a brief return to the Wheeler farm and a message from the War Department about Claude's death. His letters continue to arrive at the farm in the days that follow, full of his belief in the war and his new-found world, and his mother concludes that "he died believing his own country better than it is, and France better than any country can ever be." Cather then adds, "And those were beautiful beliefs to die with," the line seeming to sum up her own sense of the best the Midwest and the nation had to offer at the turn into the general cynicism of the 1920s—a romantic yet admirable idealism rooted in an earlier and better time of pioneer aspiration (1296).

"We knew one world and knew what we felt about it," Cather would write to a friend just before the appearance of *One of Ours* in 1922, "now we find ourselves in quite another."[41] To her critics, that was precisely the problem with the novel: it treated the contemporary world yet in its mood it was backward looking; consequently, it failed to reflect the massive lost-generation disillusionment of the post-war era. Hemingway, among others, would take harsh notice (in a passage to be mentioned later) of Cather's removal from the realities of the time in her unreal treatment of the war. In the novels that followed she turned back not only to the old world she knew and remembered in such nostalgic works as *A Lost Lady* (1923) and *Lucy Gayheart* (1935) but to more distant pasts that increasingly held her imagination.

In *The Professor's House* (1925) she turned away from Nebraska memories entirely, creating in Godfrey St. Peter a professor at Hamilton University near the shores of Lake Michigan who has just completed a monumental prize-winning history, *Spanish Adventurers in North America*. One lengthy part of the story is devoted to Tom Outland, St. Peter's most gifted student, and the discovery and its aftermath of an ancient cliff city in New Mexico. The novel was the first full fruit of Cather's visits to the Southwest that had begun over a decade earlier, the stark landscape and the history of Spanish conquest of Indian culture now occupying her as had immigrant pioneer life on the Divide. In *My Ántonia* her new interest had been briefly transferred to Jim Burden during a picnic scene in which he tells the hired girls about a farmer's discovery of a metal stirrup and sword of Spanish make, suggesting that Coronado had journeyed as far north as Nebraska. Two years after *The Professor's House* she gave full rein to the lure of the Southwest—and to the interest in religion that accompanied her flight from the wasteland of the present—in *Death Comes for the Archbishop*, the historical novel that became the major critical and commercial success of her career.

After *Shadows on the Rock* (1931), another historical novel for which she turned to the far different setting of seventeenth-century Quebec, Cather made a last and memorable return to her Nebraska material. *Obscure Destinies*, published in 1932, collected three stories stimulated by memories of the Divide and Red Cloud. One of them, "Neighbour Rosicky," deeply recalled the Nebraska novels and would appear frequently in anthologies, joining "Paul's Case" and "The Sculptor's Funeral" among her best-known stories. For the portrait of the old Bohemian farmer Cather drew on Annie Pavelka's husband, and for Rosicky's devoted family she returned to Ántonia's fictional family seen a decade later. Anton Rosicky had been a city man, living in poverty in London and New York; in the West he is transformed into a landowner and an embodiment of the Jeffersonian vision of free and dignified rural life. The thought that his son, Rudolph, may leave farming for an Omaha factory stirs Rosicky's deepest fear: "To be a landless man was to be a wage-earner, a slave, all your life; to have nothing, to be nothing."[42] It seems to him that for all his sons "the worst they could do on the farm was better than the best they would be likely to do in the city" (60). Neither Rosicky nor his country-bred wife, Mary, have been eager to get ahead, preferring—as their friend Doctor Burleigh reflects in the story—to enjoy a comfortable, generous, and debt-free rural existence rather than put their life in the bank.

The story is simple in outline yet richly textured and deeply moving. In the opening scene Doctor Burleigh tells Rosicky that at age sixty-five he has a bad heart and must slow down. When Mary learns of the doctor's order the family pitches in to protect the old farmer from heavy labor. During a long winter of relative inactivity he recalls his hard years in the city, an unnatural existence in which "they built you in from the earth itself, cemented you away from any contact with the ground" (31). Worry about the future on the farm of Rudolph and his lonely American-born wife, Polly, provide what little tension there is in the story. Hoping to brighten their lives, Rosicky lends the young people his car for trips to town and the movies. One spring day he rakes Russian thistles in an alfalfa field that his sons are too busy to see to and suffers a heart attack. When he is found by Polly and helped into her house, there is a scene of communion between the two in which Polly tells him about the child she is expecting and comes to see the essential truth of the old farmer's character:

> She had a sudden feeling that nobody in the world, not her mother, not Rudolph, or anyone, really loved her as much as old Rosicky did. It perplexed her. She sat frowning and trying to puzzle it out. It was as if Rosicky had a special gift for loving people, something that was like an ear for music or an eye for colour. It was quiet, unobtrusive; it was merely there. (66)

Taken to his own home, Rosicky dies the next day and the story returns to Doctor Burleigh driving out to the farm some weeks later to visit the family. He pauses at the country cemetery where Rosicky is buried and is struck by the rightness of the place for the old farmer, surrounded by his own fields and with neighbors passing as they drive to town. The feeling of an urban cemetery ("cities of the forgotten" where the dead are "put away") is absent, replaced with an "undeathlike" sense of openness and freedom, the qualities that had originally drawn Rosicky to the West. In the story's final line Doctor Burleigh realizes that the farmer's life is now "complete and beautiful" (71). It is a conclusion that recalls the young Jim Burden feeling so entirely happy in his grandparents' garden that even death seems to lose its sting:

> Perhaps we feel like that when we die and become a part of something entire, whether it is sun and air, or goodness and knowledge. At any rate, that is happiness; to be dissolved into something complete and great. When it comes to one, it comes as naturally as sleep.[43]

The story is typical Cather in its lack of a dramatic plot and use of quiet incidents to build a strong sense of character and feeling. Behind the story are personal emotions stimulated by her father's death (like Rosicky of heart failure) in 1928, the year the story was written, and a return to Red Cloud for the funeral that once again enkindled feelings about her family and her Nebraska life. With the story Cather reached a final stage in the shift in thought that had brought her from her early harsh treatment of pioneer life through to the richly sympathetic portrayal she had begun with *O Pioneers!* and brought to her most complete statement in *My Ántonia*. There is about the story of a man possessed of a great heart rather than simply the bad heart the doctor diagnoses a direct, undisguised romantic sweetness that surpasses anything in the two novels.

Through an obscure immigrant farm family Cather is able to evoke an ideal time and place, a calm and heroic existence in the agrarian garden that remains unshadowed even in death. With Rosicky she carries to conclusion that serene vision with which O *Pioneers!* ends: "Fortunate country, that is one day to receive hearts like Alexandra's into its bosom, to give them out again in the yellow wheat, in the rustling corn, in the shining eyes of youth!"[44]

All the same, there is about "Neighbour Rosicky," as about all Cather's backward-looking work, the clear elegiac note. Mary, younger than Rosicky, will continue the manner of his life; his sons will remain on the land; Rosicky's spirit will endure. Yet there is a sense of lost perfection about Rosicky's passing that no amount of affirmation in the final cemetery scene can entirely lift. The Rosickys are not, as Doctor Burleigh reflects, industrious "pushers" like their neighbors. Unlike one particular neighbor, Tom Marshall, they do not possess "a big rich farm where there was plenty of stock and plenty of feed and a great deal of expensive farm machinery of the newest model" (15, 8). Their lives are lived against the grain of rural progress—against the grain of a progressive culture that has followed Jim Burden's road from out of the country into the city. It is not only the satisfaction of Rosicky's life that holds the reader's attention but its uniqueness—an immigrant life able, for a time, to hold out against the tides of material desire. Rosicky is exceptional, a throwback to an earlier and more innocent age; like the image of the plow against the setting sun in *My Ántonia*, he assumes larger-than-life proportion in the imagination. Cather does not add within the story the subsequent image of the plow's littleness, yet the Midwestern fall from rural perfection, already apparent in the material pursuits of Rosicky's neighbors, holds a place in the reader's response to the story, providing a frame of sober reality for a noble salute to a better time. Surprisingly, there is a sense in which this most seemingly gentle of Cather stories bears out what T. K. Whipple thought was her underlying theme, the superior individual's resistance to an inferior society, in the contrast between Rosicky and the surrounding community. In this Rosicky joins with Alexandra and Ántonia and Claude, figures who find comfort amid family and friends yet are set in opposition to a surrounding world of declining post-pioneer spirit in which only untarnished nature seems fully worthy of them. "No wonder," Whipple remarked, "Miss Cather's characters find more sustenance in the companionship of the prairies than of their neighbors; the prairies are better company."[45]

9

The Depression gripped Nebraska when *Obscure Destinies* was published and Cather was well aware of the plight of old friends on farms and in small towns. For the Pavelkas she paid taxes so they would not lose their farm, and she sent money and food to other families who were in dire straits. Hard times on the land, however, provided no stimulation for the imagination of a writer who felt she had cut her ties with contemporary life. Her trip to Red Cloud in the year before *Obscure Destinies* was published was her final return to Nebraska, and with the book the world of her home pasture was similarly closed off to her as fictional material. All her major work, in fact, was now behind her.

Looking back, one is struck by how much of that work has endured—as many as six permanent books beginning with *O Pioneers!* and *My Ántonia* and including *A Lost Lady, The Professor's House, Death Comes for the Archbishop*, and *Obscure Destinies*. The number is remarkable for a modern American writer, as Harold Bloom[46] and others have noticed, placing Cather in the company of Faulkner as a novelist of sustained accomplishment. For Midwestern writing, with its string of one-book triumphs, it is all the more remarkable. No one wrote as well about the region over a longer period. And no one produced a single work more aesthetically satisfying and culturally subtle than *My Ántonia*. In that work, as well as in *O Pioneers!* and in stories like "Neighbour Rosicky," Cather exemplified as well as anyone what has always been best about regional writing, work that distinctly arises from place yet remains uncontained by place. It was Midwestern work whose importance, almost for the first time, was not historical and social but emphatically literary.

SEVEN

Bewildered Empire

Would he not betray himself an alien cynic who
should otherwise portray Main Street, or distress the
citizens by speculating whether there may not be other
faiths?

—*Main Street*

1

Sinclair Lewis, usually generous in remarks about other writers, was especially
approving when it came to Willa Cather's fiction. In his Nobel Prize address
her work was described as that of a pure artist who had provided an authentic
interpretation of the "peasants of Nebraska."[1] When he considered the work
of fellow members of what he elsewhere called the "Middle Western group"—
an alliance based on nothing more than the fact of birth "within a couple of
thousand miles of one another"—he concluded that "not even Mr. Hamlin
Garland has given a more valid and beautiful expression than has Miss
Cather."[2] In praising Cather, Lewis showed unerring if ironic taste, for it is hard
to imagine a writer whose work was more opposed to his own in subject and
feeling. Cather's great subject was the past, Lewis's the immediate present. Her
tone was elegiac, his boisterously satirical. Her language was suffused with quiet
lyricism, his gaudy with slang and journalistic inflations. In *O Pioneers!* and
My Ántonia, Cather concentrated her attention on those aspects of her past
that she wished to celebrate, seemingly excluding all else. Lewis, in the scattered
use he made of his past, was less selective, with the result that his fiction lacked
Cather's inner coherence and consistency of mood.

T. K. Whipple, an early and still acute critic of Lewis, located the source of
the dominant characteristic of his fiction, the satire, in an abiding hostility to
an environment that had treated him with hostility. If Cather's early argument
with Nebraska faded from the surfaces of her fiction, Lewis's argument with
Minnesota remained raw—and remained a fundamental weakness, in Whipple's view, in that it formed a "defensive shield" around the writer against
which new and potentially enriching experience "rattles off like hail from a tin

roof." Yet if Lewis's past stimulated within him "cordial and malignant hatred,"[3] it also provided a set of values, or at least a set of attitudes, that he held to the end. Some of Cather's critics have maintained that she eventually triumphed over the Midwest in that her imagination settled on its heroic pioneering life and then passed beyond it altogether in her later work in pursuit of an austere and finely-balanced art. In this sense Lewis never graduated from the Midwest. Its main streets and bewildered lives continued to provide grist for his satire while at the same time offering the only objects of admiration he could ever uncover.

Even in their approach to the texture of fiction Cather and Lewis were at odds. Cather was a "cool, gray genius," as Lewis called her,[4] who favored an underfurnished fiction stripped as bare of detail and sensation as the stage of a Greek theater. Lewis, on the other hand, obsessively created in his novels the equivalent of Sears Roebuck catalogues. John Hersey, briefly in the late 1930s Lewis's secretary, has provided a vivid account of the research and development that lay behind the writer's novels of abundance:

> He left notebooks all around the house. . . . He said he needed to know everything about the characters and the setting of a story before he started writing. Maps of imaginary towns sketched in pencil, floor plans of houses, life histories, word portraits in the most painstaking detail, characterizing anecdotes, breeds of pets, dishes served at table, names of eccentric specimen shrubs that a particular character would be sure to have planted outside the house—there was an astonishing wealth of groundwork in those loose-leaf notebooks.[5]

There were, to be sure, points of connection in the experience of Cather and Lewis. Both grew up in the later years of the nineteenth century (Cather the elder by twelve years) in remote areas of the Midwest, Cather in a Nebraska shading into the arid plains, Lewis in a Minnesota on the edge of the north woods. As young writers both were influenced by Garland's stories of Midwestern life in *Main-Travelled Roads*, though unlike Cather, Lewis was fulsome in his praise of the older writer's early work; and both made a point of distancing themselves from Howellsian realism, Cather because of its flat, plodding quality, Lewis its gentility. Both knew intimately the life of prairie villages, aspects of Cather's portrait of Black Hawk in *My Ántonia* bearing some resemblance to Lewis's acid treatment in *Main Street*. An example is Cather's account, mentioned earlier, of the social stratification of the town that kept its young men at a distance from the compelling country girls working as domestic help—a passage worthy of Lewis's gleeful satire:

> The Black Hawk boys looked forward to marrying Black Hawk girls, and living in a brand-new little house with best chairs that must not be sat upon, and hand-painted china that must not be used. But sometimes a young fellow would look up from his ledger, or out through the grating of his father's bank, and let his eyes follow Lena Lingard, as she passed the window with her slow, undulating walk, or Tiny Soderball, tripping by in her short skirt and striped stockings.

The country girls were considered a menace to the social order. Their beauty shone out too boldly against a conventional background. But anxious mothers need have felt no alarm. They mistook the mettle of their sons. The respect for respectability was stronger than any desire in Black Hawk youth.[6]

Although both Cather and Lewis quickly left their small towns and the Midwest behind for journalism, the East, and frequent (in Lewis's case, nearly continuous) travel, there were repeated and nostalgic return journeys. For him, Lewis once said,

> forever, *ten miles* will not be a distance in the mathematical tables, but slightly more than the distance from Sauk Centre to Melrose. To me, forever, though I should live to be ninety, the direction *west* will have nothing in particular to do with California or the Rockies; it will be that direction which is to the left—toward Hoboken Hill—if you face the house of Dr. E. J. Lewis.[7]

Red Cloud was etched as deeply in Cather's experience, its village lives and landscape borne in the brain—as Lewis would come to say of George F. Babbitt—like "every street and disquiet and illusion" of Zenith.[8] Finally, after early struggle both writers found success with critics and the public alike, though Cather's success came later in life and hardly matched the bestsellerdom of Lewis's triumphant decade of the twenties that saw the appearance of *Main Street, Babbitt, Arrowsmith, Elmer Gantry*, and *Dodsworth* and was capped in 1930 by the Nobel Prize.

Still, it is the differences between the two that remain striking—differences most apparent, once again, in the nature of their art. In her major Nebraska fiction Cather pursues an essentially realistic method into an enlarged romantic world of prairie myth that, while deeply textured with complexity and ambivalence, is nostalgic and celebratory. Lewis's attitude toward his Midwestern material was far more uncertain and divided, with the result that his work swings between extremes of sardonic resistance to the region and sentimental idealization. Presented in the dress of massively detailed realism, his novels become—as critics from Constance Rourke to Mark Schorer have noted—equally "large," but the expansion is rooted in an inclination for the grotesque and the absurd.[9] Finally they are transformed into Dickens-like fables, or into what Frederick J. Hoffman has called a "half-real, half-fantasy world," a world "derived from the real but unreal in its actual effect."[10] In a review of Cather's *One of Ours* Lewis casually referred to the "somewhat fabulous Middle West" of Cather and Garland,"[11] but the true Midwest of fable, a region sketched in broad cartoon-like strokes, was Lewis's own special territory. Lewis was a collector of specimens, as T. K. Whipple aptly put it, a master of "that species of art to which belong glass flowers, imitation fruit, Mme. Tussaud's waxworks, and barnyard symphonies," a world displayed in "accurate and unbearable detail" yet finally a "counterfeit world" in relation to actuality.[12]

Lewis's divided response to the Midwest provides some explanation for the immense popularity of *Main Street* and *Babbitt*, the centerpieces of his career, as does the enlarged and fabulous nature of his work. One could sympathize with Carol Kennicott and George Babbitt or mock them, either way, and with either response the moral of Lewis's fables was so excessively rendered, so *there*, as to be inescapable. The books became cultural events; they seemed to portray a middle-class Midwest in a new and absorbing light, assaulting its provincialism if yet coming around at the end to acceptance of much that they ridiculed. To read Lewis's novels in their time was to be liberated from what was narrow and bound in American life, and so to venture upon the new shores of modern literature. But the very qualities that brought Lewis sudden success contributed to the equally sudden slide in his fortunes. What Sherwood Anderson called Lewis's "sharp journalistic nose for news of the outer surface of our lives"[13] simply did not wear well. What was once so fresh soon became overly familiar and tiresome. Beyond this, Lewis's satire came to seem unfocused, lacking an intellectual or moral basis—or too simplistic, lacking in shading and complexity. The prodigious research that Lewis brought to his novels and an ear marvelously tuned to the patterns of colloquial speech appeared only to mask an insensitivity to nuance and aesthetic arrangement. While Cather's novels rose over the years in critical estimate as subtle works of high art, Lewis's were dismissed as thin, time-bound, essentially journalistic. In an mock obituary written in 1941, ten years before his death, he predicted, correctly, that unlike such Midwestern writers as Dreiser and Hemingway he would have no literary descendants—"no 'school' of imitators whatever." As a qualifying note, however, he added that it was unclear whether this lack of influence indicated a "basic criticism of his pretensions to power and originality, or whether, like another contemporary, Miss Willa Cather, he was an inevitably lone and insulated figure" whom his critics lacked the perspective to adequately measure.[14]

2

In the summer of 1905 the twenty-year-old Lewis, just finished with his second year at Yale, first glimpsed a novel that would become *Main Street*. Through the long, dull season in Sauk Centre (after a previous summer of working on a cattleboat to Europe) he occupied himself by reading *Main-Travelled Roads*, among many other books consumed by a voracious reading habit, and with talks with Charles Dorion, a young lawyer recently come to town who possessed literary and radical interests. For the introduction to a special edition of *Main Street* in 1937, Lewis would remember that

> In 1905 . . . I began to write *Main Street*. But the title, then, was *The Village Virus*, and the chief character was not Carol Kennicott but Guy Pollock, the lawyer, whom I depicted as a learned, amiable, and ambitious young man . . . who started practice in a prairie village and spiritually starved. I must have written about

twenty thousand words of that script, but I remember nothing whatever about the details, and the script is as clean gone and vanished.[15]

Dorion clearly provided a model for Guy Pollock but there seems never to have been a 20,000-word script. There was only the glimmering of an idea rooted in developing dissatisfaction with Sauk Centre and carried along in the disease called the village virus.

Garland's somber accounts of rural life played an important role in the young writer's developing attitude toward the village. In his Nobel Prize speech Lewis would remember Garland as a "harsh and magnificent realist" before he was tamed by deference to Howells into a "genial and insignificant lecturer," and he would single out *Main-Travelled Roads* as well as *Rose of Dutcher's Coolly* as "valiant and revelatory works of realism."[16] (Just the year before his acceptance speech, in the novel *Dodsworth*, Lewis had portrayed the Howellsian influence in a mildly attractive light with reference to an older and milder era in the city of Zenith when it was "still in the halcyon William Dean Howells days; not yet had it become the duty of young people to be hard and brisk, and knowing about radios, jazz, and gin.")[17] Lewis may also have been acquainted with the novels of Kirkland and Howe, the agrarian realists who had preceded Garland in driving a wedge into the traditional praise of village life, and with Cather's early short fiction. But it was Garland's work that he chose to recall as an influence. In Garland's tales he discovered an environment similar to Sauk Centre, and discovered as well the possibility of writing about the townspeople as he felt about them rather than as the happy-village tradition suggested he portray them. In Garland he found, as he put it, "one man who believed that Midwestern peasants were sometimes bewildered and hungry and vile—and heroic. And, given this vision, I was released; I could write of life as living life."[18]

The release was slow to manifest itself. Fifteen years would elapse between the first stirrings of the novel and *Main Street's* electric arrival upon the literary scene. In the long interval Harry Sinclair Lewis would pursue an uneven literary apprenticeship in the course of a haphazard journey that freed him from Sauk Centre's limitations while repeatedly casting him back upon his sense of its virtues. His father was a stolid country doctor in the town of nearly 3,000 people in an attractive northern prairie area of lakes and wheat farms, the profession that also drew his invariably successful and much-admired older brother, Claude. Lewis himself, a harsh-faced red-head inept at games and outdoor pursuits, spent a solitary boyhood of reading and dreams of a more exotic environment. He began a habit of detailed diary jottings and there was some local journalism and efforts at verse, but his real beginnings as a writer came when he escaped his meager life in Sauk Centre for Yale after six months of preparatory school at Oberlin Academy in Ohio.

His life was no less solitary at Yale but a lively intelligence attracted the attention of his professors and contributions to undergraduate magazines brought literary recognition. Fiction writing began to claim his attention, yet at the same time that his literary aims were coming into focus his feelings about Yale's indifference to him as a radical thinker and budding artist were turning into hostility. At the beginning of his senior year he fled college life for a brief episode as a janitor and handyman at Helicon Hall, Upton Sinclair's communal experiment near Englewood, New Jersey, and then he was on to New York for a fling at free-lance writing. After a sense of duty brought a sudden return to Yale, following readmission by a special vote of the faculty, he finished his degree and was graduated in 1908, a year after his class.

His plans now were either for the academic life or journalism. What in fact followed were several years of itinerant wandering about the country during which newspaper success eluded him (leading to the conclusion, as he informed his father in a letter, that "I can't do newspaper work; am a less excellent newspaperman every year")[19] and outlets for his free-lance writing were few and far between. Nonetheless, hack journalism and popular fiction flowed from his pen together with copious observations of behavior kept in note form and a bulging file of plot outlines. When a surprising sale of a story to *Red Book* brought in seventy-five dollars he determined, erroneously, that he could live by his writing and set off to the new bohemian literary community in Carmel, California, there to perform some part-time secretarial work and devote himself to fiction. Among the communalists was Jack London, to whom Lewis was soon selling story plots for sums of five to fifteen dollars apiece.[20]

After Carmel came grubby editorial work in Washington, D.C., followed by more of the same in New York, where he would remain from the end of 1910 through 1915. Among his acquaintances now were such Midwestern writers recently removed from the Chicago renaissance as Susan Glaspell, George Cram Cook, and Floyd Dell, who had gathered together in Greenwich Village and spent summers in Provincetown. Like Cather, however, Lewis kept his distance from New York's heady literary and political life and its exciting new periodicals, among them the *Masses* and *Seven Arts*, just as he would have no connection with Chicago and the rise of *Poetry* and the *Little Review*. Mark Schorer notes about Lewis's curious detachment from the ferment of the time that he could not bring himself to read Marx or such fashionable figures as Nietzsche, Bergson, and Freud. The new music of Bartok and Schoenberg held no interest for him, nor did the Garnett translations of Dostoyevsky that were all the rage.

A plausible explanation is that Lewis simply lacked genuine radical sympathies. His resistance to American values came out of an older tradition of small-town outsiders and scoffers who delighted in pricking orthodoxy and exposing hypocrisy but were seldom themselves genuinely antireligious or immoral and generally espoused only mild forms of political and social deviation. The strain of what Henry F. May calls "Innocent Rebellion" in pre-World War I America suggests the boundaries of Lewis's revolt against convention. As a movement of liberation it was iconoclastic but hopeful, and although it attacked the standards of the dominant majority it shared a good deal with them. It was precisely for this reason, May notes, "because it was shocking and exciting but not repulsive or frightening, [that] the Innocent Rebellion succeeded in breaking down the barriers."[21] Lewis would eventually coin the term "Hobohemia" to convey all his mistrust of the free life whether lived on 57th Street or in Greenwich Village. In 1921, faced with an unhappy prospect of reviewing Cather's *One of Ours*, a book he wanted to applaud but found disappointing, he took a swipe in a letter to H. L. Mencken at writers, Cather included, who chose to live in the Village: "Funny what Greenwich Village does to all these birds. I see Sherwood Anderson is living there now. Send him back to Chicago or New Orleans or Prague or somewhere."[22] Through Carol Kennicott he would direct a barb at the Chicago renaissance, drawing on his experience in the city while working up background for his novel *The Job*. Carol, a Chicago resident during a year of library training, revels in the city's cultural possibilities but draws a firm line at bohemian excess:

> She almost gave up library work to become one of the young women who dance in cheese-cloth in the moonlight. She was taken to a certified Studio Party, with beer, cigarettes, bobbed hair, and a Russian Jewess who sang the Internationale. It cannot be reported that Carol had anything significant to say to the Bohemians. She was awkward with them, and felt ignorant, and she was shocked by the free manners which she had for years desired. But she heard and remembered discussions of Freud, Romain Rolland, syndicalism, the Confédération Générale du Travail, feminism vs. haremism, Chinese lyrics, nationalization of mines, Christian Science, and fishing in Ontario.
>
> She went home, and that was the beginning and end of her Bohemian life.[23]

Another explanation for Lewis's removal from the currents of liberation is simply that he was preoccupied with making his way in editorial circles and especially as a commercially successful writer. For the publishing house of Frederick A. Stokes Company, his employer in 1910–12, he dashed off to order a boy's book, *Hike and the Aeroplane*, under the name Tom Graham. At the same time he was at work with fierce diligence on what would be his first real novel, *Our Mr. Wrenn*, published in 1914, and then a second, *The Trail of the Hawk*, published the following year. Both books, written in time grasped from work and on commuting trains, were frank attempts at mass-market success. In *Our Mr. Wrenn*, a work influenced by Lewis's reading of H. G. Wells's *The History of Mr. Polly*, a little man breaks free of mouse-like existence only to turn back to the known and the secure. *The Trail of the Hawk* followed a small-town Minnesota boy's climb to fame as a dashing aviator through a career as a creative businessman and finally into romance and marriage, Lewis drawing for the latter part of the novel on aspects of his marriage in 1914 to Grace Livingstone Hegger, a staff member at *Vogue* magazine. Lewis liked to think, not unreasonably, that his Horatio Alger tale foretold the early career of Charles Lindbergh. The book also prompted him to look back to his debt to Garland, acknowledged in a warm letter to the older writer:

If I ever succeed in expressing anything of Minnesota and its neighbors, you will be largely responsible, I fancy; for it was in your books that the real romance of that land was first revealed to me. This is a responsibility which you may find it mighty heavy to bear if I learn to write as badly as most of the writers who have chronicled that fabulous land of Titans, the Great West. But it takes years to learn to write as badly as one can, and perhaps you will be spared the onus![24]

The two books sold little but received critical applause. There seemed something original about them, notably Lewis's capacity to combine the lifelike with a fanciful humor. In their interweaving of realism and romance they possessed for many reviewers a strong Dickensian quality. With a continuing eye to freeing himself from editorial work, Lewis turned to the lucrative mass-magazine market, and in the summer of 1915 he struck it big with the acceptance of a humorous story called "Nature, Inc." by the *Saturday Evening Post*, the most widely read American magazine of the day. Other stories for the magazine quickly followed, written to the formulas of popular taste and riddled with cliché, with fees reaching $1,000 a story. A professional writer at last and with a broad audience that he had not found with his novels, Lewis promptly cast off his present job with the publishing firm of George H. Doran Company and launched upon a life of wandering and writing that he would follow the rest of his days.

A story rejected by the *Post* and eventually published by *Smart Set* in 1916, "I'm a Stranger Here Myself," offers glimpses of the developing satirical bent of Lewis's mature work. A Midwestern couple from Northernapolis in the state of God's Country tour the South and the East, dutifully exploring the flora and fauna and the local industries but finding comfort only in places that remind them of home—places like New Chicago in Florida that are "wide-awake and nicely fixed up and full of Northern hustle." Lewis's gift for mimicry of the provincial middle class is evident in lengthy reproduction of the typical talk on the hotel porch among tourists who are "broad-gauged, conservative, liberal, wide-awake, homey, well-traveled folks." When the couple return finally to Northernapolis, Lewis provides an ironic twist. Eager to be on familiar ground where "we know every inch, and we won't have to ask questions and feel like outsiders," the sight of new buildings that have gone up in their absence leaves them feeling suddenly bewildered and lost, strangers themselves (with Lewis commenting that "this isn't a satire, but a rather tragic story").[25]

Along with pot-boiling stories came more novels. Of these, the most interesting was *The Job* in 1917. Una Golden's story, bearing echoes of that of Carrie Meeber, is a working girl's struggle to leave the small-town existence of Panama, Pennsylvania, behind and find both a foothold in the New York business world and sexual, or at least romantic, happiness. The book looks forward to the major fiction in the greater control Lewis exercises over style and structure—though the work remains overly long and the ending is sacrificed to sentimental expectation—and in some of its characterization. Eddie Schwirtz, a middle-aged salesman Una marries out of loneliness, is a boorish philistine steeped in the lingo of banality—a cruder version of George Babbitt. Into Una's true love, Walter Babson, a Kansas farm boy turned restless New York editor and (as he defines himself with self-directed satire) "typical intellectual climber," Lewis injects some of his own uncertain regional identity. At one point Walter explains to Una his reasons for wanting to return to the Midwest and make a fresh start by emphasizing the tug-of-war within him between convention and the modern instinct:

> "I suppose there's a million cases a year in New York of crazy young chaps making violent love to decent girls and withdrawing because they have some hidden decency themselves. I'm ashamed that I'm one of them—me, I'm as bad as a nice little Y.M.C.A. boy—I bow to conventions, too. Lordy! the fact that I'm so old-fashioned as even to talk about 'conventions' in this age of Shaw and d'Annunzio shows that I'm still a small-town, district-school radical! I'm really as mid-Victorian as you are, in knowledge. Only I'm modern by instinct, and the combination will always keep me half-baked, I suppose. . . . I'm a Middle Western farmer, and yet I regard myself about half the time as an Oxford man with a training in Paris."[26]

Free Air (1919), the last of Lewis's apprentice novels, is a breezy travelogue laced with romance and based on an automobile trip Lewis and his wife had taken from Minneapolis to Seattle. There is little of note about the book beyond a brief appearance of Gopher Prairie, described as a prairie town of 5,000 though the "commercial club asserts that it has at least a thousand more population and an infinitely better band than the ridiculously envious neighboring town of Joralemon."[27]

Lewis now directed his overflowing energy to *Main Street* while continuing with hack work for magazines. In comparison with his other novels, he knew he had a major work on his hands. His new publisher, Alfred Harcourt of Harcourt, Brace, was informed that the book was "a dignified and serious production, with reality & drama in it." Lewis specified that the dust-jacket cover should feature "a real Middlewestern Main Street" and must not be "humorous or cartoon-y."[28] The term "dignified" seemed to capture his sense of this new stage of his work, and he used it often, though Donald Brace of the publishing firm cautioned him that the book's cover ought to "look dignified and serious, but not too dignified and serious."[29] The writing was done during long, absorbed bouts in a small rented room in Washington, where the wandering Lewises had temporarily landed. By the end of February 1920 a first draft was finished, and by the end of July Harcourt, Brace had the completed manuscript. When the novel appeared in October, one of the great success stories in American publishing would begin to unfold.

3

In *Main Street*, as Mark Schorer noted, Lewis reversed the formula of *The Job*, this time sending a girl from the city to a village, and while the uncaring city finally yields success to Una Golden, the stubborn village resists to the end the entreaties of Carol Kennicott. As Lewis seems to have understood it, the key difference between the two young women is that while Una holds to a job as a means of modern identity, with domestic bliss following, Carol gives up a job for domestic life and is nearly swallowed up in the process. When we first glimpse her in the opening paragraphs, a student at Blodgett College, it is against a distant background of the flour mills and skyscrapers of Minneapolis and St. Paul. Although Minnesota born, she is a city girl; her early years were spent in Mankato, a town carefully distinguished from prairie villages as "white and green New England reborn," and her adolescence in Minneapolis (6). Nonetheless, she has no real place in either town or city. Alexandra Bergson and Ántonia Shimerda are intimately tied to the rural landscape of the pioneering past, yet neither does Carol have a link to those stalwart times. On the novel's first page Lewis makes clear that "the days of pioneering, of lassies in sunbonnets, and bears killed with axes in piney clearings, are deader now than Camelot" (1). What has come in their place is defined only by lack of definition, a world—as Guy Pollock eventually instructs Carol—that has "lost the smell of earth but not yet acquired the smell . . . of factory-smoke" (155). It is within the unformed and "bewildered empire called the American Middlewest," as Lewis begins the story, that a "credulous, plastic" girl must make her way (1).

A sociology class during her senior year at Blodgett pushes Carol in the direction of an ambition: she will transform a prairie village into a garden suburb. "Nobody has done anything with the ugly towns here in the Northwest," she instructs herself, "except hold revivals and build libraries to contain Elsie books. I'll make 'em put in a village green, and darling cottages, and a quaint Main Street!" (5). Instead, she goes off to Chicago for library training. Three years in the public library of St. Paul follow, but the job brings neither a sense of direction nor personal satisfaction. When Dr. Will Kennicott of Gopher Prairie appears in her life she is only too willing to exchange a job and the city for marriage and a small town, in so doing resisting the movement of the time from country to city. With Carol's entry into Gopher Prairie in chapter 3 Lewis inverts the familiar Midwestern railway scene. Unlike Carrie Meeber or Felix Fay or George Willard, "the moving mass of steel" bears Carol only from a Colorado honeymoon to the homely confines of the town, there to be turned back into the heart of the bewildered empire (20).

Lewis's narrative method in *Main Street*, developed first in *The Job*, is the scenic unit, often crisply condensed, propelling the story swiftly forward or leisurely expanding it through a barrage of detail. The latter approach is shown in its best light in the *tour de force* account—and the point at which the novel shifts into satire—of Carol's first walk, thirty-two minutes long, through the extent of the town. The period from the reader's first glimpse of Carol at Blodgett College through her marriage—roughly from 1906 to 1912—is treated in quick strokes; then Lewis settles in for the bulk of the story, bringing it through the next eight years, or up to the time of publication in 1920. Here he provides variation upon variation on the main theme of the rise and fall of Carol's rekindled hope of turning a Midwestern village into an oasis of beauty,

culture, and high-minded thought. Against this foreground story other responses to the town are set out: Kennicott's, the practical doctor with useful
work to perform who maintains that Gopher Prairie is decent and progressive
and as good a place as any, and Bea Sorenson's, a hired girl who arrives in the
town on the same day as Carol and finds it a center of urban life compared
with the farm. And Lewis provides character types who live against the grain,
or try to, of the town's smiling mediocrity: the introspective lawyer, Guy Pollock; the reform-minded school teacher, Vida Sherwin; the free-thinking work-
man, Miles Bjornstam; the budding aesthete, Erik Valborg.

There also are glimpses of an alternative landscape in the prairie land just
beyond the town, a lush and virile world as Lewis describes it, suggesting a life
both more highly charged and more threatening. Kennicott swiftly introduces
Carol to the town's preoccupation with hunting and fishing in the surrounding
paradise of woods and lakes—a feature of Lewis's own boyhood experience in
Sauk Centre. In the countryside Carol also has her first close look at a farmhouse, described in the same bleak detail as Garland's prairie shelters:

> The dooryard was of packed yellow clay, treeless, barren of grass, littered with
> rusty plowshares and wheels of discarded cultivators. Hardened trampled mud,
> like lava, filled the pig-pen. The doors of the house were grime-rubbed, the corners
> and eaves were rusted with rain, and the child who stared at them from the kitchen
> window was smeary-faced. (56)

The fields beyond the dreary farmhouse, on the other hand, possess the golden
quality of the garden myth, and on the return drive to town Lewis's account of
them nearly exhausts a palette of color:

> Mounds of straw, and wheat-stacks like bee-hives, stood out in startling rose and
> gold, and the green-tufted stubble glistened. As the vast girdle of crimson dark-
> ened, the fulfilled land became autumnal in deep reds and browns. The black road
> before the buggy turned to a faint lavender, and was blotted to uncertain grayness.

In her country excursion Carol finds, as Lewis pointedly adds, "the dignity and
greatness which had failed her in Main Street" (58).

When Carol accompanies Will on medical calls to prairie farms the sense of
dignity and greatness reappear, the satirical intent of the novel giving way to
heroic images and another parade of color:

> The sunset was merely a flush of rose on the dome of silver, with oak twigs and
> thin poplar branches against it, but a silo on the horizon changed from a red tank
> to a tower of violet misted over with gray. The purple road vanished, and without
> lights, in the darkness of a world destroyed, they swayed on—toward nothing.
> (189)

A night spent in a farmhouse in the face of an oncoming blizzard fills Carol
with a sense of elemental life and admiration for Will's rugged manhood and

brisk devotion to duty. Still, rural life provides only pleasing interludes; it is linked to the pioneer past, admirable and distantly attractive but effectively gone. At one point Carol reads up on the Minnesota pioneers, inspired by the passing fancy that the way to change Gopher Prairie is to recover that world—to "follow them on the backward path to the integrity of Lincoln, to the gaiety of settlers dancing in a saw-mill." Despite harsh struggle pioneer life was a "buoyant life"; the town must be turned back to the earlier simplicity and grace of such an existence (150–51). But when she actually encounters an elderly pioneer couple, the Champ Perrys, they reveal themselves as narrow and boring, and soon pioneer life fades in Carol's imagination to "but daguerreotypes in a black walnut cupboard" (153).

Cather's Ántonia can realistically take up country life after town and city experience, and Jim Burden can plausibly journey back to the country in memory. But for Carol, a city girl exiled in a small town, no such possibility exists. A solitary walk through the town on a thirty-below-zero day leads her into the countryside, where she is aware of an exhilarating strangeness and her own alien presence:

> The grove of oaks at the end of the street suggested Indians, hunting, snow-shoes, and she struggled past the earth-banked cottages to the open country, to a farm and a low hill corrugated with hard snow. In her loose nutria coat, seal toque, virginal cheeks unmarked by lines of village jealousies, she was as out of place on this dreary hillside as a scarlet tanager on an ice-floe. (112)

She hurries back to the town, "all the while protesting that she wanted a city's yellow glare of shop-windows and restaurants, or the primitive forest with hooded furs and a rifle, or a barnyard warm and steamy, noisy with hens and cattle." But her world is neither the civilized city nor the countryside in either its primitive or cultivated aspect; it is merely the village—"these yards choked with winter ash-piles, these roads of dirty snow and clotted frozen mud" (113). Gopher Prairie's outer dreariness is bad enough but its inner poverty is worse—its inclination to what Guy Pollock calls the village virus, that withering away of ambition on the part of those "who have had a glimpse of the world that thinks and laughs," submission finally to the comfortable average (156). The only hope of escape is to flee in the single direction realistically open to her, to the city. At length—thirty-six chapters into the novel—Carol takes her option, in so doing acting out at last the typical journey of her generation. Yet Carol, her young son, Hugh, in tow, is anything but certain of her intentions even at this late point. She variously tells Kennicott that she may be gone a year or a lifetime; that she is in search of "a greatness of life"; that she wants real work to do; that she means to spare him the spectacle of her discontent with Gopher Prairie (422). Only her destination is firm—Washington and the opportunities it provides for war-time work.

"The chart which plots Carol's progress is not easy to read," Lewis says about her Washington days, meaning that her response to freedom and city life is as uneven and uncertain as her efforts to tame Gopher Prairie (430). At times, Washington seems simply a mirror of the town, equally dull and petty; at other times, Carol feels genuine growth within herself, her life expanded by wider horizons. Thirteen months after her flight Kennicott reappears in the story and coaxes her into a vacation in the Deep South. When he returns to Gopher Prairie she debates her future for several more months, swinging between a softer vision of the town stimulated by renewed feelings for Kennicott and her old attitude of disdain. When she finally relents and goes back, her Washington rebellion nearly two years old, she is pregnant once again.

Carol's reinitiation into the town is rapidly sketched in a single chapter. Nothing about Gopher Prairie has changed but Carol has. At age thirty-three, a mother for the second time, she has accommodated herself to what she so long resisted; she sees herself now in historical perspective, simply one of the vast many who "aspire and go down in tragedy" in the "struggle against inertia" (450). In a final scene with Kennicott she bravely insists on the essential rightness of her rebellion:

> "I do not admit that Main Street is as beautiful as it should be! I do not admit that Gopher Prairie is greater or more generous than Europe! I do not admit that dish-washing is enough to satisfy all women! I may not have fought the good fight, but I have kept the faith."

Kennicott hears her out but pays no attention. His mind is happily filled with practical matters, with the weight of the ordinary that flattens life in Gopher Prairie. The novel's last hum-drum lines belong to him—and to the triumph of the village virus:

> "Sort of feels to me like it might snow tomorrow. Have to be thinking about putting up the storm-windows pretty soon. Say, did you notice whether the girl put that screw-driver back?" (451)

4

What Lewis attacks with satiric gusto in *Main Street* are the myriad failings of middle-class, middle-brow, middle-level existence in the Middle West—hypocrisy, materialism, righteousness, provincialism. What he holds out as stable and admirable is the other side of the coin, the virtues of the middle class as he had seen them in his father and his brother and as he projects them through Will Kennicott—common sense, optimism, kindness, devotion to duty. Although in far milder forms, the book's satire embraces the stolid figure of Kennicott as much as it does Harry Haydock or Dave Dyer or Ezra Stowbody; yet when Kennicott defends himself to Carol against the artistic pretensions of Erik Valborg by describing a country doctor's grinding routine, the satire drops away. Lewis is squarely in Doctor Will's corner:

"Do you realize what my job is? I go round twenty-four hours a day, in mud and blizzard, trying my damnedest to heal everybody, rich or poor. You—that're always spieling about how scientists ought to rule the world, instead of a bunch of spread-eagle politicians—can't you see that I'm all the science there is here? . . . . I bring babies into the world, and save lives, and make cranky husbands quit being mean to their wives. And then you go and moon over a Swede tailor because he can talk about how to put ruchings on a skirt! Hell of a thing for a man to fuss over!" (396)

When William Allen White sent him a letter praising the book, Lewis wondered to his publisher if it should not be passed on to the Pulitzer Prize committee. White had said: "With all my heart I thank you for Will Kennicott and Sam Clark; they are the Gold Dust Twins of common sense. I don't know where in literature you will find a better American, or more typical, than Dr. Will Kennicott."[30] Despite the satire he had directed to Kennicott, Lewis found nothing to object to in White's view of Kennicott as the novel's sensible center. Indeed, he pointed out to his publisher that the comment was especially useful for its publicity value because of White's position as an acknowledged spokesman for the Midwest.

Both praise and satire are equally apparent in Lewis's attitude toward Carol. He is heart and soul on the side of her aspirations for freedom and beauty, an escape from the ordinary and the commonplace—a life of greatness. Carol is meant to stand out against the flattened mass of the town, an admirable figure of restless striving and the sensitive heroine of the novel's subtitle, "The Story of Carol Kennicott." But Lewis equally reveals her superficiality, the lack of a sustained plan of action for reforming the town, the flighty romanticism at the core of her rebellion. Percy Bresnahan, a native son who has made good as president of the Velvet Motor Car Company of Boston, seems to speak for Lewis when he tells Carol she is "so prejudiced against Gopher Prairie that you overshoot the mark; you antagonize those who might be inclined to agree with you in some particulars but—Great guns, the town can't be all wrong!" (285). When Erik Valborg speaks of the Midwestern landscape with awe and a sense of possibility ("But look over there at those fields. Big! New! Don't it seem kind of a shame to leave this and go back to the East and Europe, and do what all those people have been doing so long?"), Carol momentarily agrees but then quickly reverts to the cliché terms of rebellion and tells him: "Go! Before it's too late, as it has been for—for some of us. Young man, go East and grow up with the revolution!" (343). When she tries to explain to Hugh on the Washington train the reason for her flight from Gopher Prairie, Lewis puts into Carol's mouth the full-blown nonsense (variously colored, once again) of self caricature: "We're going to find elephants with golden howdahs from which peep young maharanees with necklaces of rubies, and a dawn seal colored like the breast of a dove, and a white and green house filled with books and silver tea-sets" (424).[31] The novel's satire seeks out the highbrow striving of Carol as exactly it does Kennicott's lowbrow contentment. She remains to the end of the story the credulous and plastic girl met in the beginning, as bewildered herself as the bewildered empire of the middle-class Middle West.

In the broad pairing off within the novel of the claims of Carol and Will—the pairing off of rebellion and convention—Lewis was dramatizing his own wavering response to his experience. He was both Carol and Will; his Midwest was both Nick Carraway's ragged edge of the universe and his warm center of the world. From one point of view such ambivalence is the book's crucial flaw, from another it adds texture to a fairly thin, if numbingly fleshed out, story line of idealistic striving and eventual defeat. At the time of publication, differing responses to the book had the one certain effect of stimulating sales, as T. K. Whipple noted with the remark that Lewis "caters to all tastes because he shares all points of view." He added that "whatever one's likes and dislikes, whether boosters, malcontents, romantics, radicals, social leaders, villagers, bohemians, or conventional people, one can find aid and comfort in the work of Sinclair Lewis."[32]

A disagreement with Floyd Dell over Carol's position in the novel illustrates the differing responses the book stimulated. After the appearance of *Moon-Calf*, Lewis had sent Dell an appreciative letter, suggesting that he and Dell (and Zona Gale, whose *Miss Lulu Bett* also came out in 1920) shared an intent to expose the inadequacies of Midwestern life. But Dell's reading of *Main Street*, as he later explained in his autobiography, suggested that the novel was an exposé of Carol rather than of the Midwest, just as he had meant *Moon-Calf* as an exposé of Felix Fay's immaturity and naiveté rather than of his environment. When he learned that Lewis had meant to celebrate Carol's rebellion, and that he assumed Dell was in full sympathy with Felix's similar revolt, Dell set him straight:

> . . . not at all, I told him—I thought it would serve 'Felix Fay' and Carol Kennicott right if they had to marry one another and live on a desert island the rest of their lives. My book was doubtless tender to its hero, and said all that could be truly said in his behalf; but I knew better than to think of him as a model or ideal personage; he had a great deal to learn about life.[33]

Lewis's response was to insist again on the similarity of Felix and Carol, the two characters differing only in the fact that Felix, as a male, has greater freedom of movement than Carol and that his town of Port Royal is a lively city rather than Carol's remote village. "Give Carol," he added, "just one Felix Fay (who isn't silly & you know it!) & she would be contented enough to begin to create life about her." Dell's final remark on the matter was to return to his original view that Lewis was "too kind to your heroine and too cruel to the . . . Middle West."[34]

It was not Lewis's uncertain focus that struck Sherwood Anderson but his use of language. When *Main Street* appeared, Anderson wrote Lewis a fan letter, and Lewis responded with warm words for *Winesburg, Ohio*. But the spectacle of *Main Street's* huge success while *Poor White* languished was more than Anderson could stomach. "I suppose *Main Street*, for example," he was soon writing to Hart Crane, "has sold more in one week than *Poor White* altogether."[35] No doubt Anderson was also aware that in *Winesburg, Ohio* and *Main Street* he and Lewis shared common literary territory, the Midwestern hinterland, yet brought to their material radically opposed methods. Writing about Lewis in the *New Republic* in late 1922, Anderson zeroed in on one aspect of the difference—Lewis's "dull, unlighted prose" that lacked "lights and shades":

> The texture of the prose written by Mr. Lewis gives one but faint joy and one cannot escape the conviction that for some reason Lewis has himself found but little joy, either in life among us or in his own effort to channel his reactions to our life into prose.[36]

In portraying Lewis's limitation, Anderson was also trying to define his own prose manner. T. K. Whipple would come to think a general comparison with Anderson useful for portraying Lewis's flaws as a fiction writer—"superficiality," "meretricious writing," a preference for surfaces, as he would put it, as against Anderson's "hunger to delve into the lives of men and women."[37] While Anderson's doubts about Lewis eventually developed into a deep-seated grudge, Lewis for his part held to a generous enthusiasm for Anderson's work. In the Nobel Prize speech Anderson was singled out as a "great colleague" in the effort to wrest American writing from the grip of the genteel tradition.[38]

Other Midwestern voices offering praise and dissent were heard as well. Vachel Lindsay began a spirited campaign to make everyone in Springfield, Illinois, read *Main Street*, causing Lewis to inform his publisher that "doubtless much of Springfield regard their poet as quite mad, but doubtless also there's a few hundred people who regard him as inspired—as I most certainly do!"[39] (In *Babbitt*, a book of Lindsay's verse would appear in Verona Babbitt's room and is deemed by her father—a compliment given the source—"quite irregular poetry" [271].) Garland's initial response, on the other hand, was indignation, the book seeming to him a libel against descendants of the pioneers. Meredith Nicholson drew a distinction between Minnesota towns like Gopher Prairie, which he was willing to accept as crude and indifferent to beauty, and the happy and attractive villages of Indiana. Dreiser maintained silence about the new generation of his followers, as did Edgar Lee Masters despite Carl Van Doren's *Nation* article that put *Spoon River Anthology* at the forefront of the literature of village revolt. Fitzgerald, also beginning a meteoric rise in 1920, sent a fan letter from one Minnesota writer to another, but Hemingway (after reading *Main Street* together with his wife when it first appeared and, she recalled, studying it deeply) would later sneer that Lewis made his reputation by exploiting the "much-abused American Scene."[40] Hemingway's fictional *alter ego* Nick Adams would include among the writers important to him "old guys like Sherwood" and "older guys like Dreiser" but not Lewis.[41] In *Green Hills of Africa* in 1935 Lewis would be among the American writers specifically dismissed by Hemingway as unimportant.

At the time of publication any doubts about the book on the part of Midwestern writers were overwhelmed by waves of critical praise and commercial success. A notably ironic feature of its reception was that the news it brought of the barren underside of village life seemed so utterly fresh, as if nothing like it had come before. Yet for nearly a half-century since Eggleston's *The Hoosier School-Master* there had been a strain of criticism in Midwestern writing directed to rural and small-town ways, criticism that had reached a peak in the years just before *Main Street* with *Spoon River Anthology, Windy McPherson's Son,* and *Winesburg, Ohio.* The attention of the reading public had nonetheless remained fixed on the traditional and sentimental depictions of village life emanating from the popular Indiana writers, Riley and Tarkington, Meredith Nicholson and Gene Stratton-Porter, and from the Friendship Village stories of Zona Gale's untroubled Wisconsin that had appeared in the early years of the century and continued to reign as the American village of popular imagination. Lewis's dissenting view—less rigorous finally than that presented in Masters's epitaphs or even Anderson's stories but bolstered both by greater specification and greater generalization—came at the right time and in the right form. "It remained for a novel in the customary form," Carl Van Doren remarked, "to bring to hundreds of thousands the protest against the village" which earlier Midwestern books had only "brought to thousands."[42]

Since Carrie Meeber left Columbia City at the turn of the century Americans had been steadily leaving farms and small towns for the attractions of urban life. The First War both added to the flight to the city and called attention to those left behind, with the result that by 1920 an audience was amply prepared for a satire directed either to an abandoned past or one still providing the frustrating confines of life. At the same time, Lewis's book had the shock effect of ice water on an audience still captivated by the myth of the idyllic hinterland, an audience inclined to find Carol Kennicott frivolous while another found her sympathetic. In either case, receptive readers were there—and Lewis met them head-on with his slashing indictment. Through Carol he directly set out within the novel the nature of traditional literary treatments of small-town America:

> In reading popular stories and seeing plays . . . she had found only two traditions of the American small town. The first tradition, repeated in scores of magazines every month, is that the American village remains the one sure abode of friendship, honesty, and clean sweet marriageable girls. Therefore all men who succeed in painting in Paris or in finance in New York at last become weary of smart women, return to their native towns, assert that cities are vicious, marry their childhood sweethearts and, presumably, joyously abide in those towns until death.
>
> The other tradition is that the significant features of all villages are whiskers, iron dogs upon lawns, gold bricks, checkers, jars of gilded cat-tails, and shrewd comic old men who are known as "hicks" and who ejaculate "Waal I swan." (264)

And through Carol he commented directly on the opposed reality of village life—a life of "dullness made God":

> It is an unimaginatively standardized background, a sluggishness of speech and manners, a rigid ruling of the spirit by the desire to appear respectable. It is contentment . . . the contentment of the quiet dead, who are scornful of the living for their restless walking. It is negation canonized as the one positive virtue. It is the prohibition of happiness. It is slavery self-sought and self-defended. (265)

Readers snapped it up—to quarrel with Lewis, to delight in the satire, to merely find out what all the fuss was about. The public reception turned *Main Street's* appearance into a remarkable moment in American literary history, a serious novel become a national cultural event. Every aspect of the novel seemed touched with insistently *American* qualities, contributing all the more to its success. "No other American small town has been drawn with such exactness of detail in any other American novel," Carl Van Doren noted, and he added that the book spoke with an "American voice" about "American conditions."[43] For many readers American fiction was still overshadowed by the productions of the commanding British novelists: Compton MacKenzie, H. G. Wells, John Galsworthy, Arnold Bennett, Hugh Walpole. The territory of modernist writing seemed equally the preserve of foreign authors: E. M. Forster, Virginia Woolf, D. H. Lawrence, James Joyce. Lewis's novel was a vivid reminder for American readers of the presence of a national literature that spoke directly to the native scene and in the native language. The novel's American quality was equally part of its appeal to readers abroad, where eventually it would be translated into a dozen languages, if only to confirm a view of Americans as crude and provincial. A particularly enthusiastic response to the book, emphasizing its contribution of a new current of "wholesome" satire to American writing, came from Galsworthy, a delight both to Lewis and his publisher:

> . . . remarkable book indeed . . . it seems to me that so wholesome and faithful a satiric attitude of mind has been rather conspicuously absent from American thought and literature. I *think* your book may well start a national mood toward Main Streets and other *odd places* of national life . . . altogether a brilliant piece of work and characterization.[44]

5

Not surprisingly, Sauk Centre's first response to the mirror Lewis held up to it was indignation. The local newspaper kept several months of stony silence, and in the nearby town of Alexandria the book was banned from the public library. Within two years, however, the mood had shifted, with Lewis now viewed as an honored local son. Time changes all, and bad publicity can be interpreted as better than none at all; but one also suspects that Sauk Centre made the discovery that *Main Street* could be read in ways that provided comfort as well as provoked embarrassment. Certainly its author, in comments following publication, seemed to stress the affirmative aspects of his book. In an article in the *New York Evening Post* treating "The Pioneer Myth" in American imaginative work, he maintained that he wrote out of "a love of Main Street . . . a belief in Main Street's inherent power."[45] To Carl Van Doren, who had located *Main Street* within the tradition of village revolt in his *Nation* article, he protested that, first of all, he could not be said to have been influenced by Masters's attack in *Spoon River Anthology* since he had yet to read the book (though Masters, along with Dreiser and Anderson, is one of the Midwestern authors Lewis has Carol read in the novel). What little he had come to know about the epitaphs indicated that they were "quite detached pictures of personalities with no especial relation to any small town or any revolt against a small town." Secondly, he resisted Van Doren's suggestion that he hated "all dull people, that is, unintelligent people," by insisting that "I certainly do love all of the following people, none of whom could be classed as anything but 'dull' ": Bea, Champ and Mrs. Perry, Sam and Mrs. Clark, Will ("dull about certain things but not all") and Carol Kennicott, Guy Pollock, "and almost all of the farmer patients."[46]

In such comments Lewis was revealing anew the ambivalent attitude he brought to his Midwestern material—the division at the heart of *Main Street* and one that he was now in the process of duplicating in *Babbitt*. Before *Main Street* appeared he had begun to work up a new novel. It was a story, as he described it, devoted to an

> Average Business Man, a Tired Business Man, not in a Gopher Prairie but in a city of three or four hundred thousand people (equally Minneapolis or Seattle or Rochester or Atlanta) with its enormous industrial power, its Little Theater and Master of the Fox Hounds and lively country club, and its overwhelming, menacing hunt, its narrow-eyed (and damned capable) crushing of anything threatening its commercial oligarchy.[47]

While on a Midwestern lecture tour in the winter and spring of 1921, promoting contemporary American writing as well as *Main Street*, he pursued his detailed research for the new novel. The conception of the central character was already fixed in his mind—a figure, he informed Alfred Harcourt, "a little like Will Kennicott," though with a larger setting within which to operate, and "utterly unlike Carol" in that he lacks her highbrow yearning.[48] He also no doubt had in mind an outline of the plot he would put his character through—exactly the one he had used in *Main Street*: an awakening to a restrictive environment, struggle against it, flight, eventual return and compromise. The structure of the story, a single day in his character's life from alarm clock to alarm clock, was suggested by a passage in *Main Street* directed to Carol's interest in Vida Sherwin's life after her marriage to Raymie Wutherspoon: "The greatest mystery about a human being is not his reaction to sex or praise, but the manner in which he contrives to put in twenty-four hours a day."[49] The only thing that wasn't immediately certain was the character's name, which would also provide the book's title. Lewis went through *Pumphrey* and *Fitch* before settling on *Babbitt*. It was a commonplace name, he told Harcourt with spectacular prescience, but one people would remember, and he predicted that "two years from now we'll have them talking of Babbittry."[50]

The only competition in American letters for his portrait of the Average Business Man (also termed by Lewis the Tired Business Man and the Average Capable American) in a medium-sized city came from Tarkington in his treatments of Indianapolis. In a book such as *The Magnificent Ambersons*, however, Lewis thought that the Hoosier novelist "romanticizes away all bigness." Presumably, he meant that a sense of specific reality vanished in Tarkington's effort to associate his business figures with older American values, whereas he wished in *Babbitt* to "make Babbitt big in his real-ness."[51] When his lecture tour took him to Indianapolis, Lewis went out of his way to praise the native son; when his views, much to his distress, were distorted in the local press, he was quick to send an explanatory letter to Tarkington. It was not, as it turned out, the commercial culture of Tarkington's bustling home town that would provide the bulk of the research material on life in the Average American City of Zenith but that of Cincinnati, where Lewis took up a residence for over a month.

The actual writing went forward in a variety of cities, in America and abroad, as the itinerant Lewis and his wife savored the fruits of success while keeping to the vigorous promotion of *Main Street*. When the new novel appeared late in 1922 it was a soaring best seller and national cultural event all over again— and in large part for the same reason the earlier novel had been such a wonder: it was open to various and heated interpretations. Readers found it a portrait both true and distorted, comic and cynical, profoundly American and un-American. Like *Main Street* before it, *Babbitt*—though on a larger and, for most readers, more representative scale—brought middle-class American life into exact focus, allowing it to be seen, and consequently responded to it, for almost the first time. In the glare of Lewis's manner the novel's social and psychological landscape seemed exactly the American landscape or a traitorous assault on it, George F. Babbitt a classic and concrete example of Mencken's *boobus Americanus* or a cartoon figure stuffed with attitudes but lacking real life. The immediate result was that nearly everyone felt the need to read the book, including those immersed in Babbittry who rarely read anything.

In George F. Babbitt Lewis released something new into literary accounts of the businessman—not the predatory industrialist of Herrick's *The Memoirs of an American Citizen* or the robber baron of Dreiser's *The Titan* but the compromising middle-level entrepreneur who depends on the tricky winds of public relations. Babbitt's field of operation is not the vast and impersonal city but Zenith, a Gopher Prairie grown larger and wealthier, more sophisticated and diverse, yet for all that still a provincial backwater and subject to the same satire Lewis directed to small towns with their boosterism and pretensions to high civilization. When Chum Frink, the local poet, returns from a lecture tour of small towns, he luxuriates in the company of Zenith's advanced thinkers:

> "Awful good to get back to civilization! I certainly been seeing some hick towns! I mean—Course the folks there are the best on earth, but, gee whiz, those Main Street burgs are slow, and you fellows can't hardly appreciate what it means to be here with a bunch of live ones!"

To which one of his listeners responds with equal fervor—and more of Lewis's satire directed to the middling qualities of Zenith which only replicate those of the small towns:

> "You bet!" exulted Orville Jones. "They're the best folks on earth, those small-town folks, but, oh, mama! what conversation! Why, say, they can't talk about anything but the weather and the ne-oo Ford, by heckalorum!" (117)

What is lacking about Zenith in comparison with Gopher Prairie is a strong flavor of the Midwest. In the high-satiric preface Lewis tacked on to *Main Street*, Gopher Prairie is placed in a distinctly Midwestern landscape of "wheat and corn and dairies and little groves," yet the point is made that the story the novel tells would be the same in Montana or Kentucky, New York state or the Carolinas. Zenith, located in the state of Winnemac, a typical locale of the Old Northwest (a region Eastern in its villages and industries, Lewis would point out in *Arrowsmith*, Midwestern in its fields and farms), is a far more generalized landscape. When Babbitt motors to work in Zenith's business center he cannot tell whether he is "in a city of Oregon or Georgia, Ohio or Maine, Oklahoma or Manitoba" (52). In Gopher Prairie the rural countryside of farms and hunting fields is close at hand; in Zenith it is a distant memory associated with Babbitt's upstate village childhood in Catawba or the straggly remains in vacant lots of the old orchard that had made way twenty years earlier for his neighborhood of Floral Heights. *Babbitt* is simply not a Midwestern novel in the sense that *Main Street* is, though Lewis's further exploration of the foibles of the middle class would once again seem to its audience to especially define middling existence in the region of the country that now appeared to be its natural home.

6

Through the novel's first seven chapters Lewis adheres to his original conception, following Babbitt with a minutely detailed eye through a single day. We see him in the bedroom with his wife, at work in the office, at leisure in the Zenith Athletic Club, at home with the newspaper and his squabbling children, finally in bed again and fading into the oblivion of sleep. The satire is already complete—the narrowness, ignorance, materialism, and moral relativism of the middle-level commercial class laid bare. Babbitt's world, as Lewis summarizes it, is that of the Elk, the Booster, and the Chamber of Commerce; what it lacks, as he directly specifies, is "joy and passion and wisdom" (95). Nonetheless, the satire goes on and on through another twenty-seven chapters, Lewis relentless in his documentation. As Babbitt goes to sleep at the end of chapter 7, Lewis widens the novel out with a half-dozen pages on what others are doing in Zenith at the same moment, providing a bridge of sorts to the wider display of his research effort.

With the diligence of a cultural anthropologist he dissects the mores of American life with set pieces on leisure, marriage and the family, sport, religion, economics, politics, and such subsidiary areas as professional conventions, barbershops, and the speakeasy. In terms of the satire, the book's chapters could be reordered at will in that they only add weight to the long-evident point. What holds them together in Lewis's arrangement is the story of Babbitt's rebellion woven through them, providing the novel with its slender plot line. During lunch at the Zenith Athletic Club with Paul Riesling, his one close friend and former college roommate who has denied himself a life in the arts and gone into the family roofing business, Babbitt reveals the sole redeeming quality that makes him a figure of some sympathy—a dim sense of dissatisfaction with his life:

> "Kind of comes over me: here I've pretty much done all the things I ought to; supported my family, and got a good house and a six-cylinder car, and built up a nice little business, and I haven't any vices 'specially, except smoking—and I'm practically cutting that out, by the way. And I belong to the church, and play enough golf to keep in trim, and I only associate with good decent fellows. And yet, even so, I don't know that I'm entirely satisfied!" (60–61)

Through the cheery regularity of his life the unease continues to surface at odd intervals. When he spends two days in bed after eating a "questionable clam," he descends into self pity, and there his life suddenly appears to him as "incredibly mechanical":

> Mechanical business—a brisk selling of badly built houses. Mechanical religion— a dry, hard church, shut off from the real life of the streets, inhumanly respectable as a top-hat. Mechanical golf and dinner-parties and bridge and conversation. Save with Paul Riesling, mechanical friendships—back-slapping and jocular, never daring to essay the test of quietness.

Yet nothing can be done to escape his life since Babbitt is incapable of imagining an alternative. He can only yearn for—something: "I don't hardly want to go back to work," he realizes. "I'd like to—I don't know" (234).

Dissatisfaction at length becomes rebellion when Paul, years of frustration behind him, shoots his wife, Zila, and is sentenced to three years in prison. Separated from Paul, Babbitt feels his life is meaningless. When his wife goes East to stay with relatives, he uses his freedom in bewildered forays into romance in hopes of finding something different. Eventually he falls into a love affair with the attractive widow Tanis Judique, and through her becomes involved in the sybaritic activities of her friends. When the affair cools, and Tanis drops from the story, Lewis shifts the rebellion to Babbitt's involvement with the Good Citizens' League, a group of the best people banded together to enforce decent standards through social pressure. Babbitt stoutly refuses to join, even when called upon by three leading citizens "with the air of a Vigilante committee in frontier days" (371). The price of his intransigence is the loss of friends and business, bringing fear for his future.

Resolution comes in the form of a fortunate accident. When his wife undergoes an operation for acute appendicitis, Babbitt's love for her is rekindled and his friends close ranks and rally around. Moved now by affection for the world he had renounced, he joins the League and is soon lending a vigorous voice to "the crimes of labor unions, the perils of immigration, and the delights of golf, morality, and bank-accounts" (390). In the book's final chapter Babbitt is reinserted into his mechanical life, and happily so. He is "secure again and popular," and he knows that he will never again "endanger his security and popularity by straying from the Clan of Good Fellows" (397). Although he is given a brave edge of resistance—as is Carol at the end of *Main Street* when she insists she has kept the faith if not fought the good fight—it is clear, as it is with Carol, that the middling life of Zenith finally triumphs as fully as the village virus of Gopher Prairie.

Thoughts come over Babbitt now that "had never weakened him in his days of belligerent conformity" (397). In a final scene he sides with his son Ted in a dispute over Ted's plans, after a sudden marriage, to quit college and take a factory job. To his son Babbitt confesses the devastating truth about his life:

> " . . . practically, I've never done a single thing I've wanted to in my whole life! I don't know's I've accomplished anything except just get along. I figure out I've made about a quarter of an inch out of a possible hundred rods."

Yet out of his sense of personal failure comes a bold assertion of independence for Ted:

> "Take your factory job, if you want to. Don't be scared of the family. No, nor all of Zenith. Nor of yourself, the way I've been. Go ahead, old man! The world is yours!" (401)

The scene duplicates the ending of *Main Street* when Carol directs Kennicott's attention to their sleeping daughter and tells him the child is a "bomb to blow up smugness" who will carry Carol's anarchist hopes into the better world of the future (450). But as with the ending of the earlier novel, it does nothing to change the fact of ultimate defeat. Babbitt understands now the depths of his entrapment as he did not when the novel opened, and to this degree he is a changed and sympathetic figure. Yet the hard truth remains; as he clearly understands, he is "through with all adventuring" (397). That realization had come to him well before the end of the novel during a second trip to the Maine woods. An initial trip had been made with Paul Riesling, but now Babbitt conducts the flight alone, hoping to free himself in nature and in the company of rough woodsmen. What he finds in Maine is only greater loneliness—and a realization that Zenith is not an external skin to shed but a condition of the mind and spirit. It is burned deeply within him, beyond removal. He realizes at this point the truth the novel tells about him: Babbitt is condemned to be Babbitt.

> Thus it came to him merely to run away was folly, because he could never run away from himself.
> That moment he started for Zenith. In his journey there was no appearance of flight, but he was fleeing, and four days afterward he was on the Zenith train. He knew that he was slinking back not because it was what he longed to do but because it was all he could do. He scanned again his discovery that he could never run away from Zenith and family and office, because in his own brain he bore the office and family and every street and disquiet and illusion of Zenith. (300–301)

Like Carol, Babbitt is allowed over the course of the novel to swing between the values of accommodation to his environment and flight from it. Like Carol, he is allowed to have a fling with freedom, the affair with Tanis Judique and the resistance to the Good Citizens' League duplicating her Washington adventure. And like Carol, he is a figure who draws the reader's sympathy while remaining throughout the novel an object of Lewis's satire. His final capitulation to Zenith seems, however, more crushing than Carol's defeat at the hands of Gopher Prairie. There is about the ending of *Babbitt* a particularly airless quality. Indeed, the novel as a whole offers nothing by way of an alternative to the conformity and essential mindlessness of middle-class life—nothing that resembles the sturdy adherence to duty of Will Kennicott or the invigorating prairie landscape beyond Gopher Prairie. What Lewis wishes for Babbitt—the ideal that generates the satire—is a true individuality, but the novel offers no signposts indicating that route or any other out of his wasteland. His great good friend Paul Riesling cannot control his own life let alone aid Babbitt. When Babbitt visits Paul in prison he finds his friend's spirit shattered and comes away feeling that "his own self seemed to have died" (280). He ventures alone then to Maine, "seeking Paul's spirit in the wilderness," but there he discovers that the rustic guide, Joe Paradise—a vigorous outdoor replacement, or so Babbitt hopes, for the artistically-inclined Paul—thinks only of going to town and opening a swell shoe store (295). It is when he learns of Joe's humble ambition that Babbitt understands the futility of trying to escape Zenith since he bears Zenith within.

The no-exit quality of the book's assault on middle-class American life troubled some readers at the time of publication, leaving them with the sense, as George Santayana said, of "no suggestion of the direction . . . in which salvation may come."[52] Another complaint was offered by Edith Wharton, to whom Lewis had dedicated the book. She praised his verbal energy but did not think the novel as good as *Main Street* because Carol's life before she arrived in Gopher Prairie gives her some means of comparison while Babbitt is "up to his chin & over" with Zenith and comparisons must be suggested by Lewis through the indirect means of his satire. A second and more telling point made by Wharton was the suggestion that Lewis use slang more sparingly in his dialogue— enough only to give it *"colour."*[53] Present-day readers are likely to agree. Lewis's delight in his ability to mimic American talk always seems on the verge of overwhelming the thin line of his story, and in fact does so in the ten pages devoted to reproducing Babbitt's windy oratory before the Zenith Real Estate Board.

But while Wharton's advice was sensible, it was advice Lewis could not heed. His approach to fiction was never to suggest but to document, not to imply but to insist; in his indictment of the middle class everything was grist for his mill. Lack of restraint in his prose was as apparent in *Babbitt* as it had been in *Main Street*, causing him to shift abruptly from quick-moving serviceable language ("a trout leaped, and fell back in a silver circle") to passages that blur into a purple haze. Babbitt's erotic reveries about his "fairy child," meant to suggest his dim dissatisfaction with his life, are replete with "mysterious groves" and "perilous moors," his Maine adventures garnished with "lavender-misted mountains" and "ample-bosomed" maple trees. Yet while it is easy enough to point out the lack of conventional artistic control in Lewis's prose, and in very nearly every other aspect of his work, his literary sins hardly seem to matter. With *Babbitt* he did not create a realistic character but an authentic type; he did not explore the truth of individual existence but provided the rollicking cartoon truth of a typical existence. The on-rushing language of cliché and inflation seems wholly fitting for a novel that captured so superbly the surfaces of a certain level of American life while careening past all that was nuanced and individual in that life.

7

The novels that followed—*Arrowsmith* (1925), *Elmer Gantry* (1927), *Dodsworth* (1929)—had even less of a specific Midwestern character even though they continued to treat figures with Midwestern backgrounds and to dissect values associated with the middle class and hence with the Middle West. The story of Martin Arrowsmith released the strain of idealism that had coexisted with the dominant satire in *Main Street* and *Babbitt*, Lewis again creating a figure whom he understood as rebellious but at the same time, and more importantly, possessed of genuinely heroic qualities. In following Arrowsmith's rise from medical practice to the frontiers of medical research, the novel returned to the attack on the prairie town and the small city of the earlier novels, and it pilloried once again the commercial spirit and comfortable mediocrity of American life. Nonetheless, it was Arrowsmith's noble dedication to pure science that dominated the story and gave it a powerfully affirmative quality. The examination of Elmer Gantry's shady career led Lewis back to satire with a vengeance in a gleefully dark portrayal of the hypocrisy at the heart of evangelical religion. For his research effort this time he journeyed to Kansas City where he set up another temporary residence and engaged in such well-publicized endeavors as pulpit appearances and teaching Sunday school classes. Sam Dodsworth is a figure drawn from the throngs of Zenith, one of the manufacturing aristocrats Babbitt admires from afar. The novel about him, however, was essentially a travelogue that pursued the international theme of contrast between Europe and America together with the contrast between Sam's inherent good sense and his wife's mad search for culture and position.

When the Nobel Prize sealed Lewis's decade of success in 1930, his commercial stock was still riding high. In the critical estimates of his work, however, including those of the Swedish Academy, there was already the tendency to look back to *Main Street* and *Babbitt* for what was of major value in the work. To many observers it seemed evident by the decade's end that a writer who had once seemed so vividly attuned to a national mood had been left behind. In *Dodsworth*, Lewis had come out foursquare in favor of his businessman-hero's middle-brow world—exactly the world he had previously and notoriously, if always ambivalently, renounced. The Midwestern virtues that had been the other side of the coin of satire in *Main Street* and in *Babbitt* were now affirmed as providing integrity and solidity in the face of pretension and snobbery. Sam Dodsworth was simply a reverse Babbitt, as Lewis took pains to point out within the novel in listing the things Sam was not:

> He was not a Babbitt, not a Rotarian, not an Elk, not a deacon. He rarely shouted, never slapped people on the back, and he had attended only six baseball games since 1900. He knew, and thoroughly, the Babbitts and baseball fans, but only in business.

Even Zenith was transformed for the purposes of the novel. Sam sees it as a place of "Midwestern saneness" rather than sameness—a place "where the factories and skyscrapers were not too far from the healing winds across the cornfields."[54]

"Something very like a groan went up" from most parts of the American literary community, the critic Ludwig Lewisohn said about the annoucement of Lewis's Nobel Prize.[55] It had long been understood in Sweden that an American would be honored, with the two Midwesterners, Lewis and Dreiser, considered the front runners. In the final voting Lewis had won out over Dreiser by a two-to-one vote. Some of the displeasure that greeted the award came from a feeling that Dreiser was the more deserving as the ground-breaking American realist, a feeling Lewis took into account in his acceptance speech with a tribute to Dreiser while making his biting point about America's moralizing treatment of its writers. Others felt that the Swedish prize stemmed not from literary merit so much as the fact that Lewis's novels only confirmed European prejudices about American life. Anderson complained in a letter to a friend that "Dreiser has had real tenderness in him. Lewis never. It seems to me that Lewis must have got it [the Nobel Prize] out of European dislike of America rather than liking."[56] Mencken had welcomed the announcement of the prize because it "was very bad news for all the professors," but he thought that Lewis, for his own good, should have declined it as he had earlier declined the Pulitzer Prize for *Arrowsmith*.[57] It was sure to make him more cautious as a writer in the sense of overlooking all that he would produce thereafter and weighing heavily upon his sense of responsibility.

The year before the prize, 1929, saw the publication of *A Farewell to Arms*, *The Sound and the Fury*, and *Look Homeward, Angel* as well as *Dodsworth*. Lewis's book was in many ways the most controlled and surely the least gaudy of his major novels, the latter quality perhaps due to his autobiographical use in depicting the unhappy union of Sam and Fran Dodsworth of his own failed first marriage. Yet in the company of the novels of that year Lewis's book and Lewis himself seemed old-fashioned and out of fashion, a radical turnabout from his fire-breathing position at the beginning of the decade when he had seemed, in T. K. Whipple's wonderful image, a Red Indian in an enemy's country in the alertness with which he probed the foibles of his countrymen. It was a critical view that, despite the steady production of another ten novels after the prize, held firm up to his death in 1951.

In that year Joseph Wood Krutch, in a judicious article in the *Nation*, raised the question of Lewis's ultimate importance. Krutch paid appropriate tribute to Lewis's energy and his staying power; to his credit he did not "give up, as many another writer has done, when it became evident that he could never again enjoy such a furor as he had once created." But the hard work that had produced twenty-two novels aside, Krutch wondered if Lewis had "won some enduring fame or was it all mere notoriety?" Were his novels in any way works of art or simply journalistic polemics? Would his popularity come around again, the beneficiary "of a revival like that which has affected the works of Melville and James, or to a lesser extent those of Hawthorne and Stephen Crane? Would Lewis ever be 'rediscovered'?"

If revival there ever was, Krutch thought it would be based on *Main Street* and *Babbitt*, and of the two he believed *Babbitt* the better book because the more mythical. But what struck him most about the two novels was Lewis's mastery of the methods of best-seller fiction which produced books that were really pseudo-fiction documentaries—books "in which everything is recognizable as true but with the fidelity of a waxwork and no suggestion of any sort of autonomous life." Placed against this competition, best-sellerdom, Lewis's work would continue to stand out because of his far greater sincerity as a novelist and his astonishing gift of mimicry. Measured against loftier standards for the novel, however, his work would continue to fall short. Together with admiration for what Lewis had achieved, there would remain in the critical estimate a clear awareness of his limitations. The latter seemed summed up for Krutch in the recollection of a remark Arnold Bennett had once directed to his piano-playing daughter: "You have entertained us enough for one evening."[58]

Mark Schorer's massive biography in 1961 only strengthened the assessment of Lewis as an energetic and gifted entertainer more than a novelist of the first rank. Schorer concluded that it was beside the point to approach any Lewis novel as a work of art. *Main Street* and *Babbitt* endure for primarily nonliterary, cultural reasons—for Lewis's capacity both to define a level of national life that had been brought into existence after World War I and to reveal a self-lacerating (if mildly so) national denunciation of what had been so wrought. Today Lewis's literary attributes, principally his strenuous reporting and the surface authenticity of his novels, are now and then raised up against the thin interiority of recent American fiction,[59] but the praise is too hesitant and qualified to stir the beginnings of a revival. Lewis soon slips back into the honorable position Schorer assigned him in literary and cultural history. To read a Lewis novel for anything more still seems impossible.

But as Schorer and such critics before him as T. K. Whipple also made clear, to achieve what Lewis achieved was to accomplish a great deal. Through the brilliant spotlight of his satire he brought readers to see for the first time what others had not brought them to see—Gopher Prairie and Zenith, Carol Kennicott and George F. Babbitt, provincial America as it was rather than as it was presumed to be. Could we have afforded, Whipple asked, "to give up so effective a critic for a better writer?"[60] The distance between Lewis himself and the world he caricatured finally may have been too slight, his satire finally too comfortable, his razor-sharp eye finally too eager to merely reproduce. The truth may be, as Alfred Kazin maintained, that only a writer essentially uncritical of American life could render its surfaces with so much zest, that only a writer who did not want to surmount the national scene could give it back in such vivid images.[61] All the same, in the act of recasting his world in language— in first seeing it as it had not seen itself, then in giving it imaginative form— Lewis, paradoxically and forever, distinguished himself from it. The novelist John O'Hara saw this as a crucial point in any final estimate of the work in a remark directed to George Babbitt and Zenith but applicable to all that Lewis created:

> All the commonplaces about the similarities between Babbitt and Lewis himself ignore the factor that made Lewis and Babbitt totally dissimilar: Lewis, the only Lewis, saw Babbitt. All the other novelists and journalists and Babbitt himself were equally blind to Babbitt and Zenith and the United States of America until 1922.[62]

EIGHT

The Savor of the Soil

Poverty-stricken, unspeakably forlorn, the caravan
creaked along, advancing at a snail's pace, deeper and
deeper into a bluish-green infinity—on and on, and
always farther on. . . . It steered for Sunset Land! . . .

—*Giants in the Earth*

1

The saga of Martin Arrowsmith's rise to medical fame begins with a vignette
of his great-grandmother, a girl of fourteen, journeying through the Ohio wilderness. The situation could hardly be more dismal: the girl's mother has just
been buried near the Monongahela River; her father is sick with fever; on the
wagon floor play (in a characteristic Sinclair Lewis turn of phrase) "her brothers
and sisters, dirty brats, tattered brats, hilarious brats." But when at a fork in
the road her father suggests they turn south to relations in Cincinnati, she
staunchly refuses.

> "Nobody ain't going to take us in," she said. "We're going on jus' long as we
> can. Going West! They's a whole lot of new thing I aim to be seeing!"[1]

The reader is to understand that the driving idealism that will send Arrowsmith
west from the state of Winnemac to Wheatsylvania, North Dakota, and Nau-
tilus, Iowa, then east to Chicago and New York, was born in the determined
spirit of the pioneer stock that settled the Midwest. As Lewis envisions him, for
Arrowsmith there persists a dim but meaningful link to a past that for Carol
Kennicott is as removed as Camelot. In both cases, connection and disconnec-
tion, Lewis was paying tribute to the pioneering period and to a rural heartland
that still conjured up images of that time—to the breeze, as we learn on the
opening page of *Main Street*, "which had crossed a thousands miles of wheat-
lands" to belly Carol's taffeta skirt.

Lewis himself made sporadic returns to his Midwestern past throughout his
career with some intention of reestablishing himself in the region. To young

writers he regularly preached the doctrine of remaining where their roots were. He settled in for a time in the early 1940s as a creative writing instructor at the University of Wisconsin in Madison, while there cultivating the acquaintance of John Steuart Curry, a painter who had drawn national attention as one of the trio of Midwestern regionalists that included Grant Wood and Thomas Hart Benton. Another teaching stint shortly thereafter was at the University of Minnesota in Minneapolis. But Lewis was not cut out for the routine of the classroom nor residence in the Midwest, neither of which ever quite measured up to his expectations. It was in New England, the region of his forebears as he came to think of it, that he made the most diligent effort to sink roots with homes and farms at various times in Vermont, Massachusetts, and Connecticut. In his mock obituary in 1941 he would note that he had been born in a Minnesota hamlet but designate himself as the Last Surviving Connecticut Yankee.

Lewis had become involved in that year with the Readers Club, a book selection club that reprinted each month a book that had not received the attention it merited in its original publication. In his two years as one of its judges he was deeply involved in its choices. For an anthology published by the club in 1943, *The Three Readers* (Lewis along with Clifton Fadiman and Carl Van Doren), his particular choices were short novels by Eleanor Green and Ruth Suckow, Midwesterners both. Lewis announced in introductory remarks to the volume that while the two writers had ventured to the East and West coasts (in the case of Suckow, "aberrations into heathen California and Greenwich Village"), they had had the good sense to return to their native states of Wisconsin and Iowa. Both novelettes were rooted in the history "of that bright, hardy country which stands at the head of the Great Valley," and both revealed "how varied the prairie civilization became in less than three generations." Lewis added that while young writers of the region had flocked to European coffee houses in the 1920s in response to a "beauty that their pioneer ancestors never conceived," there was nonetheless a continuity between the older generation and the present one in their responsiveness to life.

> . . . the older generation once had, in the first sight of the young wheat, in sleep after toil, in visits to the neighbors, in reading aloud from the Old Testament's poetry and tricky ethics, in annual pilgrimages to some vasty city of five hundred population, a course of pleasures that were not essentially different from the ecstasies of these young people over a dive bomber or over the Shostakovich *Seventh* conducted by Mitropoulos.[2]

In his choices for the anthology Lewis was exhibiting his usual enthusiasm for fellow writers, especially those from out of the Midwest. In championing the particular causes of Green and Suckow he was also revealing an awareness of, and in some measure fondness for, a movement of literary regionalism that had sprung up in the Midwest at the same time that writers were carrying the banner of liberation from the genteel and the sentimental to 57th Street and Greenwich Village and the Left Bank. The regionalist writers stayed home or returned home. Although they were often equally in rebellion against the quaint effects of local-color writing or Victorian restriction, they defined themselves in opposition to the modern as it was most vividly revealed in the disorienting qualities of the urban exodus. If one noted only that Lewis was the most peripatetic of the peripatetic band of major writers to emerge from the Midwest, there was considerable irony in his favorable attention to those who remained in place—as there was in his expressions of affection for the Midwest if *Main Street* and *Babbitt* are viewed only as concentrated attacks upon the region. In his embrace of the regionalists Lewis was, in fact, drawing on the complex of attitudes that led to his warmth of feeling for Will Kennicott, for the golden prairie landscape close by Gopher Prairie and far removed from Zenith, for the pioneer inheritance of Martin Arrowsmith—on that side of him that looked back upon his own life in Sauk Centre, as he would describe it, as both a good time and a good place.

2

Little magazines like *Poetry* and the *Little Review* played a critical role in providing a voice for the Chicago renaissance, as to a lesser extent did opinion journals such as the *Friday Literary Review* and *Reedy's Mirror*. For Midwestern literary regionalism in roughly the same period the *Midland* held a similar place. In many ways it *was* Middle Western regionalism—defining its aims, giving encouragement, providing a publishing outlet for writers from the region while promoting their careers beyond it. At the same time, the magazine inspired publishing ventures in other areas of the country, little magazines devoted, as was the *Midland*, to expressing a regional spirit. In the Midwest the agrarian realists of the 1880s and 1890s had formed something of a regionalist group with Garland as the leading promoter, as had to a considerable extent the turn-of-the-century Indiana romancers. But with the appearance of *The Midland: A Magazine of the Middle West* in 1915 literary regionalism in the Midwest became self-conscious and prophetic, preaching a doctrine of regional identification as the healthy core of all American writing.

The magazine was conceived by John T. Frederick, a farm boy with a passion for contemporary writing, during his undergraduate years at the University of Iowa. An important influence on the young Frederick was a professor and administrator at the University, C. F. Ansley, who would also play a role in Iowa's eventual prominence as a center of creative writing. Ansley had heard and been deeply influenced by the Harvard philosopher Josiah Royce's lecture at the University in 1902 on the "higher provincialism" as a way of resisting the forces of industrialism that were promoting dull sameness in the country. "Let your province then be your first social idea," Royce had declared. "Cultivate its young men, and keep them near you. Foster provincial independence."[3] Such views, conveyed to Frederick through a student and faculty writing group organized by Ansley, combined with his reading of John Macy's *The Spirit of*

American Literature, published in 1913, with its proclamation that "American literature is too globe-trotting, it has too little savour [*sic*] of the soil," and calling for a fresh concentration on the native reality. "The truth is," Macy argued, "the whole country is crying out for those who will record it, satirize it, chant it. As literary material, it is a virgin land, ancient as life and fresh as a wilderness."[4] Among the few writers who had made some headway in this direction, he named a band of Midwesterners: Eggleston, Howe, Riley, and Dreiser.

When Frederick began actively planning his magazine in the spring of 1914 he had already formulated an editorial policy of literary regionalism. The magazine made its appearance in January 1915, three years after the advent of *Poetry*, as a monthly (later to become a bi-monthly and remain so for most of its existence), carefully designed and printed, with thirty-two pages devoted to short fiction, poetry, and essays. (When stories soon came pouring in, the mixture changed to mostly fiction with some poetry and brief reviews.) In an editorial statement Frederick provided a simple rationale for the magazine: although the region possessed a distinct regional consciousness, "the spirit of the Middle West does not at present find adequate expression. . . . It is waiting for self-expression."[5] Behind that brief statement was a more complex editorial vision built around the conviction that the regional diversity of American life was not sufficiently recognized because of the literary centralization of Eastern publishing houses. The East also exercised a harmful commercial influence on writers, causing them to angle their work to the standardized interests of high-paying magazines and major publishers. In an editorial after five years of publication Frederick explained that when he began publishing there was not, and still was not, a general literary magazine between the Alleghenies and the Rockies, with the result that writers had to seek publication far from home. What followed upon this was a "tendency to false emphasis, distortion, in literary interpretations." The editors of the *Midland*, on the other hand, were familiar with the life of the region and so in a position to be "helpful to good writers whose interpretations are true."[6] The magazine urged writers to stay in their home regions and allow their work to develop naturally out of a genuine response to place rather than from preconceived and artificial notions of character, plot, or taste. Historically, the magazine saw itself as part of a new movement of Midwestern literature that had begun in the second decade of the century following the pioneering work of the agrarian realists (or critical realists, as Frederick called them) and then the "period of stagnation"[7] dominated by the Indiana romancers that had set in at the turn of the century.

The Midwest the *Midland* had in mind was a region within a region—the Midwest of farms and small towns, not the urban Midwest of industry and cities. It wished, moreover, to balance the drab rural portraits of the agrarian realists that had found reinforcement in the work of Masters and Anderson and Lewis with more positive images of the Great Valley—images drawn by writers who were loyal friends of the region. All the same, the magazine was uneasy with local-color writing that fastened on regional peculiarities, and it was in stern opposition to the remnants of the genteel tradition and the work of commercial romancers. What the magazine sought, essentially, was freedom from stereotypical treatments of the Midwest, whether seen as a region of grim farms and restrictive towns or a region of folksy perfection.

If a work seemed to arise from an authentic response to the region, as did Masters's *Spoon River Anthology* and Sandburg's *Chicago Poems*, it drew the *Midland's* praise. Dreiser was treated sympathetically in its pages, and Anderson was warmly greeted for his deep attachment to the Midwest and refusal to bend to popular tastes. About Lewis the magazine was divided. It was aware that he dealt in types, and that his work had fostered stock portraits of the Midwest from post-*Main Street* writers; yet it was equally understood that he worked on a higher level than other popular writers of the time. After Lewis's Nobel Prize the magazine responded with an article rare in its page, a mildly satirical essay, unsigned, called "What Babbitt Thinks of Sinclair Lewis." Presumably written by Frederick or Frank Luther Mott, the magazine's associate editor in its later years, the buisnessman-author recognizes himself in Lewis's novel at the same time that he points out things Lewis left out. He does not believe that *Babbitt* was deserving of the Nobel Prize yet allows that he would "rather see an American get a prize for writing about American business men than for writing about old South American ruins and old Greek women like another fellow did."[8]

Of the major Midwestern figures, Willa Cather came closest to meeting the magazine's ideal of a writer who steered clear of stereotyped treatments while picturing the region in basically hopeful, positive tones. Her strongest quality in the magazine's eyes was an ability to assimilate character and setting. About "Neighbour Rosicky" in *Obscure Destinies*, a work that seemed to Frederick "reminiscent of *My Ántonia*, and on a par with its greatness," the editor was unusually personal in his praise: "I am almost afraid to say how much I like this story. It expresses for me, as definitely as anything I have read and as beautifully, the subtle and profound relation between certain men and the earth which is one of the most significant facts of my experience."[9]

Since the *Midland* did not pay contributors, none of the established names of Midwestern writing appeared in its pages. It was an outlet for writers just beginning to find their voice and their material—writers of promise. Over the years few of its writers sustained their promise, with the result that most are now long forgotten. An exception is Ruth Suckow, the magazine's most important discovery. In 1921 Frederick carried "Uprooted" in the *Midland*, Suckow's first published story, then persuaded the Iowa-born writer to come to Iowa City as his editorial assistant for a six-month period. Suckow was exactly the sort of writer the magazine envisioned: one who had returned to the Midwest after education at the University of Denver; one whose stories were in the technical mode favored by the magazine, realistic and plotless; most important of all, one who could could be critical of the region but whose strongest impulses were quietly celebratory. In a later evaluation Frederick would describe her work as devoid of the hostility and resentment toward the Midwest that had led to the satires of Masters and Lewis. It was, as such, "true regionalism."

> The work of Ruth Suckow is free from both of these prevailing limitations of regional writing. She is not hostile toward the Middle West—not a resentful critic. This does not mean that there is nothing of the ugliness of middle western life in her books. There is plenty. But it is always balanced by something else, always tempered, always presented with essential fairness. I think it is altogether accurate to say that Miss Suckow loves the Middle West. I am sure it is accurate to say that she understands it.[10]

"Uprooted" treats a family conference called to decide where the old folks, father and mother, will be moved since they are too feeble to continue living on their own. The middle-aged children are portrayed with satire, oblivious to the principal value asserted in the story, "how people seemed to take root in a place,"[11] and thus unaware of the sadness involved in removing them from it. Yet the satire remains mild, devoid of any cutting edge. "Retired," also carried in the *Midland* in 1921, makes the same point about the importance of place and roots, though with somewhat darker tones than is usual in a Suckow story. The brief account follows Seth Patterson, a retired farmer, through a day of enforced idleness in the country town to which he and his wife have moved. While she continues with the housework she knew on the farm, he occupies himself only with errands, talk with other retired farmers, and hours spent in a rocking chair, aware of the irony that such emptiness is what he had worked for: " . . . to sit in a rocking-chair, with enough in the bank, not to have to work like a horse all day in any weather—take some ease. To live in town, having things a little nicer than on the farm." The sense of being uprooted from the only life he cares for causes him, in the story's conclusion, to anticipate the coming of death. "When a man's work was over," he muses, "what was there left to live for, anyway?"[12] A story that appeared in the *Century* in 1923, "Renters," captures the sense of dislocation felt by a farm family when the owners come on an inspection tour of the farm, in so doing underscoring the rights of ownership. After they leave, Beth, the farm wife, is overwhelmed by a sense of hopelessness: "The farm belonged to others. They could send her off if they chose. She had nothing, was nothing."[13] In "A Start in Life" a young girl from a poor family is sent to work in the home of a prosperous family and knows the loneliness of being in a place "where she didn't belong" and where "no one would try to comfort her."[14] An especially fine story, "The Resurrection," tells of a family's surprise when they enter the parlor to view the prepared body of the dead mother. To all of them, her children and grandchildren, she looks different—surprisingly young, the signs of the years and her labors replaced with beauty. Only her husband realizes that it is the look of her girlhood that has been returned to her—"her virgin untouched self." He is awed by this "artistry of death," feeling it must be a sign, but in his age and bewilderment he cannot pursue its meaning. In the story's last line he can only murmur a commonplace remark to a granddaughter: "Your Grandma looks—real nice—don't she, Nellie?"[15]

Suckow's most ambitious venture for the *Midland* was "A Rural Community," published in 1922, a story that draws on Garland's theme of rural return in "Up the Coule" but wholly reverses its tone of hopeless gloom. Ralph Chapin, a globe-trotting journalist, visits the Iowa town of Walnut to see again Luke Hockaday and his wife, a retired farm couple who had raised him as an orphan among their own children. He views himself as wholly changed from a plain farm boy; now he is "easily sure of the superiority of his life" as a writer and man of the world. But with his return and the old folks' pleasure in seeing him, his "boyhood self" comes over him and he feels strangely unsettled, conscious of a void at the center of his being. He wishes there were something in life that he could feel as attached to as the old people are to the rolling hills within which they live. The Hockaday children and grandchildren gather in the evening to see Ralph, a scene that parallels the party for Howard McLane in Garland's story in its initial awkwardness. When the talk shifts to the flow of rural matters, Ralph becomes a listener and feels an odd pleasure in the country atmosphere that is evoked. There is none of Garland's sense of the bitterness of farm people, of the feeling of suppressed life. Ralph is aware only of

> the deep stabilities of country life—the slow inevitable progression of the seasons, the nearness to earth and sky and weather, the unchanging processes of birth and death, the going of the birds in the fall and their sure return in the spring, the coming, night after night, of the familiar stars to the wide country sky.

In the deeply-rooted quality of the country lives displayed during the party, a narrow but serene sense of belonging, he realizes that he himself has "something to tie to," a past that remains present. When he leaves Walnut on the night train he feels "steadied, deeply satisfied." Although once settled on the train he is transformed into someone who is "alert, modern, a traveller again," he remains conscious of the "silent spreading country outside" that produces a fulfilling "quietude" within him.[16]

3

During the 1920s Mencken played an important role in promoting the *Midland*, just as he had earlier in securing the reputations of Dreiser, Cather, and Anderson. The relationship began when Frederick sent him some of his own stories for publication in *Smart Set*. Mencken printed Frederick's work and also recommended that the new publishing house of Knopf publish his first novel, *Druida*. When the novel appeared, Mencken reviewed it favorably in *Smart Set*, but some of his warmest words were directed to Frederick's magazine, extravagantly praised as "probably the most influential literary periodical ever set up in America though its actual circulation has always been small."[17] In turn,

Frederick generously steered some of his best writers to Mencken and the larger audience provided by New York publication.

Suckow's work appeared in Mencken's magazines and the editor privately brought her to the attention of such luminaries as Lewis. "I lately unearthed a girl in Iowa," he told the novelist in a letter, "who seems to me to be superb. She follows after Dreiser and Anderson, but she is also a genuine original."[18] Eventually, Suckow published more stories in *Smart Set* (and later in Mencken and George Jean Nathan's *American Mercury*) than in the *Midland*, and through the connection with Mencken she found a publisher in Knopf for a collection of her early stories, *Iowa Interiors* (1926), as well as later works. Her first book with the publishing house—Mencken urging the wisdom of publishing a novel before a volume of stories—was *Country People* in 1924, a work that he had apparently first directed to the *Century* due to its length and the need for magazine serialization.

In his comments on the work as it reappeared in *The Three Readers*, Lewis found it homely and direct as against thunderous or fanciful—and it is surely that. Through a curiously distant and flat-toned narrative voice, the story follows the life of August Kaetterhenry, an Iowa farmer of German descent, from childhood through retirement and death. We see his marriage to Emma Stille, the coming of children, the furious work of building up a prosperous farm and a comfortable bank balance, the onset of age and illness, the retirement to the country town and construction of a new home, idleness for August and continued activity for Emma, August's eventual stroke and death, Emma finding a new life on her own in the company of the town's widows. Although there is little that is dramatic in the account—Suckow seems intent on flattening out what little there is that might be dramatically rendered (for example, anti-German feeling in the rural district during the First War)—there is a clear and moving authority in her handling of the lives of hard-working country people. She knows deeply the minutiae of their lives, knows their baffled yet stoic response to the mystery of their own existence. It is the very rural ordinariness of the Kaetterhenrys that is the story's subject—exactly the quality, as Suckow saw it, that distinguishes the work from typical treatments of farm life. In a comment quoted by Lewis in his introduction to the work in *The Three Readers*, she defined *Country People* in terms of several conventions of farm fiction from which it is happily free:

> There is no writer or artist concealed among its characters who is destined to come back . . . to write a book about, or paint a picture of, the farm of August Kaetterhenry. August himself never offers a soliloquy upon The Soil; he never seduces a hired girl; and he dies in bed, not overlooking his broad acres, nor clutching a handful of his own good earth.[19]

Although Suckow had success as a novelist, especially with her lengthy 1934 novel *The Folks*, her quiet effects are best displayed in short fiction. Mencken was acting as a publicist when he declared her "the most remarkable woman now writing short stories in the Republic" after the appearance of *Iowa Interiors*; what is true is that her stories, honestly felt and ably crafted, were the best work to come out of the self-conscious Midwestern regionalism that centered about the *Midland* in the 1920s and early 1930s. To the occasional charge that her stories were unassuming to the point of dullness, Frederick replied that her fictional realm was the everyday world in which most people actually lived. It was the significance of the familiar that she sought to reveal, and some of her stories seemed to him simply "unparalleled in the whole field of American realism." At the same time, he wished for more range in her choice of material ("After all, life *is* occasionally violent, occasionally fantastic")[20] and somewhat brighter colors in her use of language.

4

In such mild criticism of Suckow, Frederick may have had in mind the contrasting fictional world of her Minnesota contemporary, O. E. Rölvaag. In introducing *Country People* in *The Three Readers* Lewis had distinguished Suckow's quiet virtues from the "thunderous pietists as Rölvaag, whose Norske God rides every blizzard."[21] Suckow herself surely had Rölvaag in mind when she maintained that her novelette was not a heightened " 'saga of the pioneers' nor yet 'an epic of the soil.' "[22]

In the milieu of Midwestern regionalist writing in the 1920s *Giants in the Earth* was impossible to overlook. The epic account of Norwegian immigrant life on the Dakota prairie was an immediate success when it appeared the year following *Iowa Interiors*, lifting its hitherto obscure fifty-one-year-old author to literary attention. Frederick thought the book and its successor in Rölvaag's trilogy of pioneer life, *Peder Victorious*, major contributions to the regional movement. They possessed the feel of the prairies; they were "rooted in real earth." He also thought them part of an equally important movement to give literary expression to silent immigrant groups within the country. "To thoughtful readers," Frederick concluded, "Rölvaag's novels must seem among the most valuable books of our day."[23]

In approaching Rölvaag's work it is useful to keep Frederick's second point in mind. Although no one wrote more vividly or in more detail about the experience of land-taking on the Midwestern frontier—experience alluded to rather then recreated in Cather's *O Pioneers!*—Rölvaag's deepest fictional concerns were directed to the fate of Norwegian immigrants within the American melting pot. His fundamental subject was the spiritual cost of Americanization—a subject forged in the private experience of a man divided between two cultures. In 1896 Rölvaag had emigrated from a Norwegian fishing village just beneath the Arctic Circle, a world of mountains and sea, of medieval legend and dogmatic Lutheran piety. At age twenty he was old enough to have established abiding roots yet young enough to respond to the lure of greater opportunity in the New World. When an uncle living in South Dakota sent money for the passage, Rölvaag exchanged a seaman's life for farm chores in a flattened landscape that, as he noted in a diary, was "very monotonous . . . almost nothing except prairie."[24]

Restlessness with country labor and the stirring of ambition to, as he put it, "accomplish *something*," turned him toward education.[25] Three years at a Lutheran preparatory school in South Dakota were followed by St. Olaf's College in Northfield, Minnesota, where he systematically pursued Norwegian literature and particularly the work of Ibsen and Björnson. A college graduate at the advanced age of twenty-nine and after nearly a decade in America, he returned to Norway for graduate work, then in 1906 began teaching Norwegian at St. Olaf in the preparatory school and the college. Subsequently, he married Jennie Berdahl of Garretson, South Dakota, whose father and uncles had been early pioneers in the valley of the Sioux River north of Sioux Falls. He was settled now into what would be an academic career of teaching Norwegian literature, compiling textbooks, and promoting Norwegian-American cultural causes.

His first imaginative work, *Letters from America* (*The Third Life of Per Smevik* in a later English translation), written in Norwegian and published under a pseudonym in 1912, was an autobiographical fiction in the form of letters from an immigrant newcomer in South Dakota back to his father and brother in Norway. The book sold little but it established Rölvaag as a novelist and the cross-cultural experience of Norwegian-Americans as his subject. The three novels that followed were similarly written in Norwegian and published in Minneapolis for the small Norwegian-American audience. An announcement in 1923 that the eminent Norwegian novelist Johan Bojer was coming to America for material for a major novel about Norwegian pioneers fired Rölvaag's ambition for a larger literary impact. The subject seemed properly his. He immediately took a leave of absence from St. Olaf, retired to a cabin he had built in the Minnesota north woods, and plunged in. For material he drew on his own early experience in South Dakota together with those of his wife's family. His father-in-law was bombarded with letters seeking details that would give the book a documentary quality, and Rölvaag later acknowledged about the finished work that "some of the incidents—many of them, in fact—have actually happened; they are taken from stories told me."[26] He was also considerably influenced by a knowledge of Norwegian literary traditions, and especially his sense of such sweeping historical epics as Knut Hamsun's *Growth of the Soil* and Bojer's *The Last of the Vikings*.

The book was published in Norway to considerable acclaim in two volumes in 1924 and 1925 under the titles *In Those Days*— and *The Founding of the Kingdom*. (Bojer's novel of pioneering appeared in Norway just weeks after Rölvaag's first volume; in 1925 it was published in an English translation as *The Emigrants*.) Rölvaag's alertness to the spiritual tragedy of emigration made the book seem sharply new, and in his use in dialogue of a free-flowing idiomatic Norwegian laced with Americanisms he also seemed to be breaking fresh ground in technique. Hoping to repeat the American success of such major Norwegian figures as Hamsun and Sigrid Undset, he had a literal English translation of the book prepared with the help of a number of literary friends. Then Lincoln Colcord, an American writer and editor who had become friendly with Rölvaag while visiting in Minneapolis, reworked the text in collaboration with the author. In a foreword to the American edition Rölvaag would acknowledge that Colcord "unified and literally rewrote the English text."[27] Through Colcord's agency the book was accepted for publication by Harper's in a single volume with a title drawn, as was the title of the Norwegian edition, from the book of Genesis, *Giants in the Earth: A Saga of the Prairie*. Book-of-the-Month Club selection together with serious critical treatment sent the work into repeated printings. Despite the fact that it was a translation from the Norwegian and its author an unknown Norwegian-American professor, it seemed to most reviewers an authentically American book stamped with the experience of the Midwest. It was praised both as a revealing account of pioneer days and a skillful literary work in which characters came vividly to life against a background of riveting action. Carl Sandburg, writing in the *Chicago Daily News*, immediately elevated the book to the top rank of American fiction:

> If we should be asked to name six most important and fascinating American novels past and present, *Giants in the Earth* would be one of them. It is so tender and simple. It is so terrible and panoramic, piling up its facts with incessantly subtle intimations, that it belongs among the books to be kept and cherished.[28]

5

In particularly lucid comment in the *Saturday Review* at the time of publication, Allen Nevins found *Giants in the Earth* "half an adventure story, a realistic description of the physical facts of the homesteader's life fifty miles from anywhere on the Dakota plains, and half a penetrating study of pioneer psychology."[29] Commentary on the book ever since has taken note of the two-sidedness of Rölvaag's work: a rousing story of taming the virgin prairie and establishing the agrarian garden through concentration on the expansive figure of Per Hansa, and a painful story of the inner costs of pioneering through concentration on the brooding figure of Beret. "If in one sense the conquest of the continent is the great American epic," Parrington declared about the Per Hansa-Beret division, "in another sense it is the great American tragedy."[30] Better than anyone before him or since, Rölvaag managed to capture that division at the heart of the pioneer enterprise—the complex mixture of attainment and defeat, of epic adventure and tragic failure. There is irony in the fact that the classic account of prairie pioneering comes so late within Midwestern writing—after the agrarian realists, after Chicago and the revolt from the village, nearly at the end of the regionalist movement—and that it comes in a work written in Norwegian and first directed to a Norwegian audience. But Rölvaag's American experience was still closely tied to pioneer times through his memory of his own early years on a South Dakota farm and the recollections of his wife's family. His professional commitment to preserving Norwegian culture also provided an obvious concern with the past as well as an inevitably ambiguous response to all things American. Cather's concentration on immigrant figures in her Nebraska fiction—Alexandra, Ántonia, Rosicky, Frank Shabata, Mr. Shimerda, Anton Cuzak—produced an imaginative detachment from her material that allowed the portrayal of both gain and loss on the land. For Rölvaag, an immigrant turned professor-writer with a foot in two cultures, both responses were deeply a part of his imagination and naturally expressed in the far more sharply opposed emotional centers of his fiction. The divisions in Cather that seem created through formal aesthetic distancing, seem in Rölvaag the inescapable effect of background.

The heroic qualities of Western pioneering that Cather places in Alexandra and Ántonia, Rölvaag gives to Per Hansa: shrewdness, determination, optimism, an innate sense of connection to the land. The vast prairie with its extreme conditions and potential richness unlocks within him grand dreams of possibility. After an arduous wagon journey from Minnesota his first sight of the area of Norwegian settlement near Sioux Falls inspires the ecstasy of possession:

> This vast stretch of beautiful land was to be his—yes, *his*—and no ghost of a dead Indian would drive him away! . . . His heart began to expand with a mighty exaltation. An emotion he had never felt before filled him and made him walk erect. . . . "Good God!" he panted. "This kingdom is going to be *mine!*"[31]

The ghost of the Indian refers to a grave that Per Hansa had detected on the land he will claim—a discovery meant to give the reader pause, as it does Per Hansa's friends in the Spring Creek settlement, Tönseten and Hans Olsa. But for Per Hansa any thought of spirits inhabiting the land is overridden by the vast excitement of the moment. He has no qualms, no second thoughts, and herein Rölvaag locates his hubris. Per Hansa is "like the child who constantly cries: 'More—more!' " (110). While deeply appealing, his fierce will is also powerfully presumptive; it lacks a mature awareness of human frailty that mocks finally all hope. From the beginning of the story it is certain that Per Hansa is destined to fail. He is a giant on the earth fatally unaware of giants in the earth.

What Per Hansa lacks Beret possesses in abundance. Her first view of the land of the new settlement radically opposes his:

> . . . Was this the place? . . . *Here!* . . . Could it be possible? . . . She stole a glance at the others, at the half-completed hut, then turned to look more closely at the group standing around her; and suddenly it struck her that *here something was about to go wrong.* . . . For several days she had sensed this same feeling; she could not seem to tear herself loose from the grip of it. . . . A great lump kept coming up in her throat; she swallowed hard to keep it back, and forced herself to look calm. Surely, surely, she mustn't give way to tears now, in the midst of all this joy . . . (28–29)

For Beret the West—America itself—is seductive, a Sunset Land that loosens the hold of tradition and belief, tempting men into the sinful belief that all is possible. The prairie in particular is a Puritan wilderness alive with evil spirits in the form of the trolls of Norwegian folk belief, filling her with dread, overpowering all human effort. One of the members of the Spring Creek settlement confidently announces that "we're through now with all that troll business over in Norway!" (207). But Beret is not deceived; the old belief in a supernatural world remains alive for her. When she watches a wagon of settlers moving farther west into the distance it seems as if "the prairie were swallowing up the people, the wagon, the cows and all" (329). The sense of impending doom again comes over her:

> To people this desert would be as impossible as to empty the sea. For how could folk establish homes in an endless wilderness? Was it not the Evil One that had struck them with blindness? . . . (330)

In their different ways both Per Hansa and Beret are creations of the Old World. In Norway the established lines of his life had spurred the restless Per Hansa to leave, certain that only in America was there a "country where a poor devil can get ahead!" (226). Beret, on the other hand, a timid soul, had felt secure and protected within the traditions of home, family, and religious belief. Transported to the unknown prairie of the New World, Per Hansa's exuberant life thrives while Beret's inwardness gives way to fear, melancholy, and finally madness. America magnifies what is already present in the two temperaments, producing sharp and at last incompatible extremes. When Per Hansa is away from the settlement seeking supplies or wood, Beret covers the windows of the sod hut to keep out the night and pushes an immigrant chest against the door. She is delighted by his ingenuity when he paints the walls a dazzling white, but then comes to feel blinded by snow outside and white walls inside and keeps her eyes lowered to the dark earthen floor. When Per Hansa reveals how he removed property stakes of Irish settlers, an act that saved land claimed by his neighbors Tönseten and Hans Olsa, Beret is aware only of a sinful deed: "Where I come from, it was always considered a shameful sin to destroy another man's landmarks. . . . But here, I see, people are proud of such doings!" (154).

The division between the two reaches a climax with the locust plague. A rich harvest causes Tönseten to speak expansively to Hans Olsa and Per Hansa about the accomplishment of the settlement:

> "Well, boys, in my opinion the Land of Canaan didn't have much on this country—no I'm damned if it had! Do you suppose the children of Israel ever smelt a westerly breeze like this? Why, folks it's blowing honey!" (340)

What in fact the wind is blowing is a black cloud of locusts that soon descend upon the fields. Tönseten and Hans Olsa interpret the infestation as divine wrath, but Per Hansa rejects such "silly gabble": "Do you really suppose *He* needs to take the bread out of your mouth?" (343). He fires his gun into the fields, temporarily scattering the locusts, and is able to save his harvest. When he returns home he is apprehensive since Beret had not appeared during the effort to preserve the fields. He finds the door blocked by the immigrant chest; when he manages to force the door open he finds her huddled inside the chest with two of their children. He is nearly himself reduced to madness, listening helplessly as Beret whispers to him:

> "Hasn't the devil got you yet? He has been all around here to-day. . . . Put the chest back in front of the door right away! He doesn't dare to take the chest, you see. . . . We must hide in it—all of us!" (348)

The scene closes with one of the mystical personifications of the prairie which Rölvaag drops into the narrative to underscore both Beret's sense of demonic power and the futility of human endeavor in the great wilderness:

> . . . That night the Great Prairie stretched herself voluptuously; giantlike and full of cunning, she laughed softly into the reddish moon. "Now we will see what human might may avail against us! . . . Now we'll see! . . . " (349)

From the low point of the Per Hansa-Beret conflict Rölvaag turns the novel toward an apparently happy resolution. The arrival of the locusts becomes a plague that ravages the prairie through four summers, Rölvaag sharply compressing both the time and the Spring Creek community's feeble hold on survival. With the fifth summer the locusts miraculously depart and an itinerant minister arrives—an equal miracle in the eyes of the pious Norwegians. A church service is held and children baptized, including the American-born son of Per Hansa and Beret bearing a triumphant name that Beret considers a sacrilege, Peder Victorious. When the minister says the name aloud during the christening, Beret shouts out her objection: "This sin shall not happen! How can a man be *victorious* out here, where the evil one gets us all! . . . Are you all stark mad?" (378). Later the minister speaks with Per Hansa and learns the story of Beret's growing derangement brought on by her sense of the sinfulness of the pioneer venture and of Per Hansa's anguished resistance. When the minister tells him the child's name is handsome (" . . . why, it sings like a beautiful melody!"), Per Hansa finds comfort (386). To Beret the minister proposes a communion service to be held in her house and with the immigrant chest as an altar. During the service the minister, though conscious only of his own inadequacy, speaks to the people with great power; when he places his hand on Beret, she feels released from all sin, all burden instantly lifted from her soul. With the healing of her spirit comes a new stability and an eagerness for life. She feels she has been absent from her home for a long time but has now returned, once again and for good a wife and mother. Per Hansa, witnessing the transformation, is overjoyed.

At this point in the story he is the most successful farmer in the community, respected and envied for his ingenuity and ambition. He also has offspring to succeed him and has come to some accommodation with his wife. The kingdom he envisioned is at hand. Appropriately, Rölvaag begins the book's final section with a sweeping tribute to stalwart pioneers:

> And it was as if nothing affected people in those days. They threw themselves blindly into the Impossible, and accomplished the Unbelievable. If anyone succumbed in the struggle—and that happened often—another would come and take his place. Youth was in the race; the unknown, the untried, the unheard-of, was in the air; people caught it, were intoxicated by it, threw themselves away, and laughed at the cost. Of course it was possible—everything was possible out here. There was no such thing as the Impossible any more. (425)

But in the blind ambition that lends pioneering an epic quality is its inner flaw—the absence of a sense of limitation, an indifference to cultural loss that accompanies economic gain. The final chapter, with its heavily ominous title "The Great Plain Drinks the Blood of Christian Men and Is Satisfied," brings Per Hansa to his inevitable tragic end. When Hans Olsa becomes deathly ill while tending his cattle during a blizzard, Beret, steeped in piety since being freed of sin, persuades him that a minister must come to bring him communion. Hans Olsa's longing for the minister and Beret's pleading cause Per Hansa to set off on skis across the prairie buried in snow. He understands the mission as a fool's errand; the winter conditions make it treacherous, and he believes Hans Olsa a good man who requires no absolution from a minister. While he bitterly accuses Beret of driving him into the jaws of death, he can resist neither her desire nor Hans Olsa's need. On the day Per Hansa leaves the settlement he says nothing to his wife. The following spring his body is found propped against a haystack as if he had been waiting for the weather to clear. "His face was ashen and drawn," the book's final lines report. "His eyes were set toward the west" (465).

The ending can be read in an affirmative light in the sense that although Per Hansa has fallen the settlement has been established. His eyes remain set on the West, the Sunset Land of pioneer hope; his sons will follow his example, carrying on the dream of founding a kingdom. Indeed, Per Hansa's last thoughts are of Peder Victorious: "Something great must come of you—you who are so tenderly watched over!" (464). Rölvaag had provided a text for this reading of the ending with the recognition, in the passage just noted, that "If anyone succumbed in the struggle—and that happened often—another would come and take his place" (425). But a darker reading of the ending seems more persuasive. In this view Per Hansa's death only underscores Rölvaag's awareness of the high cost, cultural and spiritual as well as physical, that accompanied the unleashing of material ambition on the virgin prairie. Beret's response to pioneering—her dread of the barren land, her longing for the familiar world left behind in Norway, her superstition and Lutheran piety—is not held out as correct. In the latter part of the novel Per Hansa says of her, with what appears to be Rölvaag's agreement: "There are some people, I know now, who never should emigrate, because, you see, they can't take pleasure in that which is to come—they simply can't see it!" (385). Nonethless, Beret's view, despite the excesses Rölvaag attaches to it, represents an admirable human caution and a sensitivity to the past and traditional values. If the novel is understood as a continuing argument between Per Hansa and Beret, Beret does not emerge as right but she seems, in Rölvaag's final balancing of the two figures, more right than Per Hansa. Such a view of the novel is strengthened, of course, when *Giants in the Earth* is placed as the first volume of a trilogy examining Norwegian-American experience, with Beret as the continuing character bearing Rölvaag's essential message.

6

Rölvaag was in failing health when *Giants in the Earth* appeared in English, yet in the four years left to him he completed *Peder Victorious* (1929) and *Their Fathers' God* (1931), both appearing first in Norwegian and then in English translations. Inevitably, the latter novels seemed pale in comparison with *Giants*. The vital figure of Per Hansa is gone and the heroic period of first settlement is over; the struggle with nature that had given dramatic intensity to the first novel gives way to the inward struggle with cultural heritage. Rölvaag was aware of the difference, writing to Lincoln Colcord while working on *Peder Victorious* that the novel would not have "the sweep, the vastness, and the lift" of *Giants*. In another letter at the time he explained that in *Giants* he had drawn on two great American stories, the Westward movement and immigration, and had tried to show both "the plus and minus in terms of the human equation" in a way that would be true to the general experience of all immigrant groups in the Midwest.[32] *Peder Victorious*, on the other hand, was directed more to "the inner side of the problem," and so he had set himself the task of "building up a soul, using for material the innumerable impressions of the environment in which it grew."[33]

The soul is that of Peder, the first born of the Spring Creek settlement, and the inner side of the problem is the spiritual desolation that follows upon his abandonment of his Norwegian cultural heritage.[34] Rölvaag examines Peder's adolescence in *Peder Victorious* and his marriage and adult life in *Their Fathers' God*, both stories set against a background of the settlement's development into a bustling Midwestern village. Struggling with the contradictory demands of home and community, Peder, more sensitive and questioning than his brothers and sister, becomes a figure of revolt against all his mother values, his dreams turned, as had been his father's, to the future. After Per Hansa's death Beret is overwhelmed with guilt, then takes over direction of the farm and makes it the finest in the area, ironically fulfilling Per Hansa's ambition to found a kingdom. But her deepest concern is to preserve the past despite the indifference of the community and the seductive attractions of the American melting pot, a single-minded and ultimately futile desire that brings her into repeated conflicts with her son.

At length, Peder marries an Irish-Catholic, Susie Doheny, and in the final book of the trilogy Rölvaag traces a union doomed by unbridgeable differences of background and personality. In responding unwittingly to their cultural heritages both characters defeat any notion of American homogeneity. Following a fall and a broken hip Beret, worn of heart as much as body, dies and is buried beside Per Hansa. Subsequently, Peder loses his wife and his son following an act of rage in which, after learning that Susie has had their son secretly baptized, he destroys the symbols of her belief, her crucifix, holy water vessel, and rosary. The following morning he finds a note, left by his wife before her flight, that reads in part: "Now I've lived the Blessed Day, I've been to the End of the World and have found out what it looks like. I'll never go near there again, because it is an accursed place."[35] The sardonic reference is to the secular vision Peder had earlier held out to her of going together to the "end of the world" with their "blessed day" lasting forever. The reader is to understand that Peder is now adrift alone on the pluralistic American sea, all saving cultural links to the past severed. Beret and Per Hansa die in body, Peder Victorious in spirit—the ultimate loss in Rölvaag's tragedy of immigration and the fulfillment of Beret's dire prophecy in *Giants in the Earth*: "How can a man be *victorious* out here, where the evil one gets us all!"[36]

7

The year before Rölvaag's death in November 1931, and just as the English translation of *Their Fathers' God* appeared, John Frederick moved the editorial offices of the *Midland* from Iowa City to Chicago and changed the magazine's subtitle to "A National Literary Magazine." For some time contributions had been arriving from throughout the country, and the new subtitle was belated recognition of the magazine's national stature. Beyond this, Frederick implied in an editorial that the regionalist movement had accomplished its aims—or at least, as he put it, "the modern regional movement in American literature has matured in a great body of good writing."[37] The standardization of American writing continued, however, as did its commercial centralization in New York, and the *Midland* meant to carry on its resistance to both tendencies by remaining in the Midwest but in its central city. Frederick pointed out that "Chicago seems among American cities most likely to make a challenge to New York's domination immediately effective"; it possessed a rich literary tradition, and from it emanated influential journals such as *Poetry*, now in its eighteenth year. He could not entirely avoid the irony that the *Midland* had come to Chicago long after its literary renaissance was over, nor that nearly all the major names once associated with Chicago writing had left for New York and points beyond. He could only offer the mild rejoinder that "it is not clear that New York has improved their work"—and the hope that there were new Chicago writers ready to take their place and "to remain here if any effective answer to the call of New York is to be found."[38] For a brief time the magazine prospered in its new surroundings, with contributions increasing and subscriptions topping a thousand. But with Chicago and the nation soon sunk in the Depression, Frederick and his wife, Esther, who had long overseen the magazine's business side, were no longer able to sustain publication with personal funds, and the end was in sight. With an issue in the late spring of 1933 the *Midland* concluded its surprisingly long eighteen-year run. Frederick remained in Chicago as a professor at Northwestern, book reviewer, producer of a nationwide radio program called "Of Men and Books," and as Illinois director of the Federal Writers' Project, a position from which he exercised a good deal of influence on young writers.[39] Later, after a distinguished career in the English Department at Notre Dame, Frederick would return to teaching at the University of Iowa.

The death of the *Midland* is as appropriate a date as any for marking the end of the regionalist movement as a significant current within Midwestern literature. Regionalist writing continued on after the *Midland* but it increasingly lacked the complexity at the heart of the best work, the contrary impulses to celebrate and resist, return and leave, love and hate. Instead, it turned back to unrelieved melodramas of rural blight or, far more frequently, to the folksy and saccharine mood of turn-of-the-century popular Indiana writing. Work in the latter vein found fresh philosophical underpinning in a new agrarian romanticism identified with the regionalist painters of the thirties and a general back-to-the-land mentality of a Depression-battered and suspicious rural America. Against the general confusion and insecurity of the present, the countryside offered—or could be made to seem to offer—a world of clarity and order. Grant Wood's 1935 essay "Revolt against the City," together with the mannered simplicity of his popular agrarian paintings of the period, summed up in Midwestern dress the argument behind the new mood. America of the Depression, Wood held, had turned introspective. In so doing it had rediscovered the old frontier virtues, chief among them being self-reliance, that had been obscured by a false prosperity in the land. Together with the culture at large, writers and artists had now come home, there to reestablish their connection with the good earth. The movement of rural return was national in scope but it had particular strength in the Midwest because, as Wood put it, "the region has always stood as the great conservative section of the country," a quality to be ridiculed in boom times but prized as a virtue in unsettled conditions.[40]

Phil Strong's successful 1932 novel *State Fair* offers an illustration of the retreat of regionalist writing into the comfortable light entertainment of agrarian romanticism—as, indeed, might any of Laura Ingalls Wilder's *Little House* books for young people that began appearing in the same year. The settled satisfactions of rural life are taken for granted in Strong's story. There are no struggles with economic woes or recalcitrant nature, no suggestions of buried lives or hungers for urban lights. The only turmoil in the lives of Strong's Iowa farm family comes with the annual trek to the state fair. Will Abel Frake win a prize for his hog, Blue Boy, or Melissa Frake for her pickles? Will their son and daughter, late adolescents, find sexual adventure? The answer in each case is yes. Nothing cuts deep in the story; the affairs of the children with more worldly figures are treated with a breezy amorality that suggests they are simple life adjustments—or another of the rewards of the state fair. Some ten years earlier Strong had published a story in the *Midland* that Frederick had thought marked by honest characterization and an accurate sense of the atmosphere of a small Iowa town. About *State Fair* the editor registered mostly disappoint-ment. Although it had some moments of true feeling for the country landscape, the work was essentially a trivial and tawdry concoction in which "farm people and the farm festival are treated with a brisk smartness verging constantly on caricature."[41]

Robert Cantwell in the *New Republic* took note of the difference between Strong's Midwest and the dominant literary conception of the region that had been built up over the previous two decades:

> Now, in "State Fair," the emphasis is neatly reversed. The Middle West is no longer the villain, but the hero. There are no frustrated farmers' wives, no baffled philosophers, no unhappy young people longing to get to Chicago or New York or Paris. The state fair is only a brief idyll in the idyllic lives of the Frakes, and the Frakes are prosperous people, intelligent, tolerant and not too whimsical.[42]

Josephine Johnson's successful 1934 novel *Now in November* was a more rec-ognizable Midwestern work, if a no more satisfying one in literary terms, in which the region provides the setting for total failure. The figurative style of the twenty-four-year-old author—like Strong a former contributor to the *Mid-land*—only partially frees the account of farm misery in Missouri from a simple Depression melodrama of ill-fated love, death, and suicide. One passage sug-gests the unbroken grimness of the rural scene during a summer drought, the land meant to provide a mirror for the broken lives of the Haldmarne family as narrated by one of the daughters, Marget:

> By July half of the corn was dead and flapped in the fields like brittle paper. The pastures burned to a cinder. I stumbled once in the woods and the ash of dry leaves flew up like a dust. Milk shriveled up in the cows. Prices went up, we heard again, but Dad got no more for his milk and got less for the cows he sold, since nearly all other farmers were selling off. The creeks were dry rock-beds then, hot stones that sent up a quiver in the air. The ponds were holes cracked open and glazed with a drying mud. I kept hearing the calves bawl all the time, hot and thirsty in the pastures, but could only water them in the evenings. We had to haul from a pond three miles away, and the horses got sores, even with rest when we borrowed Ramsey's mules. The heat was like a hand on the face all day and night. When everything was finally dead, I thought that relief from hope would come, but hope's an obsession that never dies.—Perhaps the ponds will fill up

again . . . the fall pastures might come back with rain . . . the cistern get deep
again. . . . . There was still the awful torture of hope that would die only with life.[43]

In comparison with such pathos, Garland's dreary farms and Howe's blighted
country town seem almost appealing.

The new romantic opposition to urban-industrial life can be read in another
popular Midwestern novel of the early thirties, Louis Bromfield's *The Farm*. A
loose and plotless account, more family chronicle than fiction, the work traces
the historical forces that shaped the lives of varied figures associated with a
northern Ohio farm. From its origins with the arrival of the founding figure in
the Western Reserve in 1815, the farm is developed into a Jeffersonian world
of ideal and essentially aristocratic rural life. Then begins a long decline in the
face of town growth and a commercial spirit originally brought into the agrarian garden by Yankee shopkeepers. Against the new American money power
that Bromfield associates with the legacy of Alexander Hamilton, the pure
Jeffersonian existence on the land can offer no resistance. Through the figure
of Johnny Willingdon, a fourth-generation member of the family who provides
a thin center of consciousness in the novel, Bromfield can only lament its passing in the recollections of the lives of those who cannot escape the wreckage of
rural life about them yet stubbornly persist in seeing in abandoned farms "a
series of small paradises," in their souls believing "the land to be the finest and
most honorable of all that which might occupy the energies of man."[44] At
length, the farm is sold and Johnny Willingdon is off to Europe and the First
War, the family's dream of agrarian perfection—and with it, as Bromfield directly remarks in a preface, a lost world of integrity and idealism—a casualty
of demon progress.

State Fair was a first novel and a major success—a Literary Guild selection
followed by a Hollywood film version with Will Rogers as Abel Frake. (In later
years the work would have ongoing life as, oddly enough, a film musical.) For
the next twenty years Strong, his native Iowa left behind for Connecticut, produced a steady stream of briskly-written popular entertainments about rural
life, all of them as free of complication as his first success.[45] *Now in November*
was likewise a first novel and won a Pulitzer Prize for its young author. Bromfield, on the other hand, was an established literary figure when he produced
The Farm. In 1926 he had won a Pulitzer Prize for his novel, *Early Autumn*,
and Sinclair Lewis had mentioned him in his Nobel Prize address in a roll call
of worthy American writers that included Cather, Anderson, and Hemingway.[46] He had fought in the war, worked as a newspaperman, and with the
immediate success of his novels had become a long-time expatriate in France.
From a distance, he maintained, he found himself all the more a creation of his
native land:

I feel more American than I have ever felt before, even in those days when I dwelt
in the sacred Middle West—that spot chosen by God with the promptings of
certain critical Joseph Smiths for the American literary millennium. Far from the

madding [*sic*] crowd, I find that all my senses, my perceptions, have become with regard to America sharpened and more highly sensitive.[47]

Publication of *The Farm* coincided, however, with nostalgic talk about joining the expatriate exodus of the thirties back to America and there buying a farm. The deed was accomplished in 1939 with the establishment of Malabar Farm in Ohio and Bromfield's recreation of himself as a rural squire and, in a series of nonfiction books, agricultural sage. Although in the twenties Bromfield had been ranked among the rising young literary stars, from the beginning critics had complained of a false note of romanticism in his work. Hemingway, who had become acquainted with him in France, informed Fitzgerald in a letter in 1927 that Bromfield's next book was going to be about a "preacher," then gleefully dismissed the writer's claim to serious attention:

> . . . Bloomfield [Bromfield] will probably make him a decayed old new england preacher named Cabot Cabot Cabot and naturally he talks only with God—to rhyme with Cod. But sooner or later I can see that the decayed French aristocracy will come into the book and they will all be named the Marquis Deidre de Chanel and will be people whom Louis Bromfield the most brilliant and utterly master of his craft of all the younger generation of decayed french aristocracy novelists will have studied first hand himself at the Ritz and Ciros.[48]

In a review of *The Farm* in the *New Republic*, T. S. Matthews was less colorful but equally alert to Bromfield's penchant for noble lineage. He found the work a "diffuse attempt to read aristocratic meaning into Mr. Bromfield's Ohio background," and added: "Effusive with facts, facile with conventional ideas and opinions, Mr. Bromfield also has the gift of revelation: he shows us that what he is writing about is fake."[49]

Fake is probably too strong a word, but it is clear that in *The Farm* there is a vast thinning out of Midwestern life as literary material. Gone is the complex texture of the twisted apples Sherwood Anderson had located in his Ohio experience, replaced with a disillusioned salute to a sentimentalized rural Ohio set in simple opposition to the debased modern age—argument more than art. *Now in November* and *State Fair* lack even a sense of opposition; in one, farm life has sunk into utter futility, in the other, it exists in a dreamy haze beyond tension or threat or even much historical memory. In the latter work the pioneer past is vaguely rekindled during a drive through the darkened countryside on the way to the fair grounds, yet it possesses no real existence in the story.[50] It is merely part of the dim background of idealized rural life, having no more bearing on the characters' lives than its opposite, the urban present. After his return to the farm from the state fair, Abel Frake's son can casually dismiss Des Moines, and whatever threat to rural bliss it might represent, with the remark, "It's all right—too big."[51]

In the stories in *Obscure Destinies*, the collection published in the same year as *State Fair* and the year before *The Farm*, Cather composed her last moving hymn to the vanished pioneer era. The title came from Gray's elegy for "the humble joys and destiny obscure" of the poor, but it seemed fitting in another sense in the suggestion of a kind of Midwestern writing become rare amid the reawakened rural romanticism of the thirties. Cather's stories richly celebrated country life yet at the same time revealed her particular blending of elements that are both pastoral and anti-pastoral, romantic and realistic, affirmative and skeptical. John Frederick had thought her the ideal Midwestern writer, and it was exactly her kind of serenely managed complexity in treatments of the region that the *Midland* sought to foster. But for the less able or less serious such two-sidedness as Cather's was always hard to emulate. In the popular Midwestern regionalism of the thirties it seemed nearly impossible; the work tended to break apart, offering fictional worlds of simple rural defeat or equally simple rural perfection. Robert Cantwell finally dismissed *State Fair's* "dreamy Iowa" on the grounds that readers had too much prior literary evidence "indicating quite clearly that it does not exist."[52] Cather's capacity in *Obscure Destinies* to hold two visions together, regional dreams commingled with regional realities, in a satisfying artistic whole had indeed become obscure in Midwestern writing.

NINE

We Are All
Middle Westerners

One would think of Wisconsin as the ideal state to live
in, a paragon of civic success, but for the fact that the
young people dream only of getting away. And there
are already a fair number of Middle-Westerners about
the world; a sort of vagrant chosen race like the Jews.

—*Good-Bye Wisconsin*

1

A year after the *Midland*'s move to Chicago, Ruth Suckow returned to the
University of Iowa to give a talk about Midwestern literature. Aware that she
was speaking against a background of secured literary identity in the region,
she confidently listed among the central accomplishments of Midwestern writing *Main-Travelled Roads, Spoon River Anthology, Chicago Poems, Winesburg,
Ohio, My Ántonia,* and *Main Street.*[1] She was hardly unaware, all the same, of
the massive cultural resistance to the region that had been stimulated by just
some of the books she had mentioned. The Midwest as it had emerged from
such works was meager, small-minded, provincial—a region subsumed into a
state of mind that Ford Madox Ford, as Suckow noted, had defined from the
vantage point of Europe as Middle Westishness. The desire of a regional magazine such as the *Midland* for a more balanced and hopeful picture had done
little to counteract this dominant conception.

Suckow's strategy in her remarks was not to contest Ford's term but revise
it to refer to the attractive aspects of the region as they appeared, for example,
in Cather's work—"to a certain downright quality, a plainness, a simple freshness." It referred to authenticity and the lack of pretense, to the "solid center,
the genuine *interior*, of the United States." She urged writers not to resist Middle Westishness but to recognize it as the "one best, inalienable quality of the
Middle West." It was the only real source of a genuinely regional literature that
is confidently "what it is—not a false front, a cheap dye color, a pale copy or
a flash-in-the-pan spurious brilliance, a diluted or pretentious imitation of
something else."[2]

As the term was used in Ford's preface to a collection of stories from the *Transatlantic Review* published in 1926, it had very different meaning. It pointed to a mentality rather than a place—specifically, to the modern mind as it was experienced everywhere in the postwar world. "We are all Middle Westerners," Ford announced, in the sense that we are all now aware of an "enormous disillusionment . . . and an enormous awakening." The particular American version of this world-wide phenomenon was the sense of great things done; the pioneering moment was over (the "Far, Wild or Pioneer Wests," as Ford said, crowded out) and nothing could be seen looming ahead but dun-colored, humdrum life. We had no choice but to turn inward upon ourselves, away from the shores of expansion and toward the flattened, middling, uninspiring quality of our lives. For evidence of the spread of Middle Westishness Ford pointed to the manuscripts that poured into his journal, all insistently rendering lives of sheer boredom, lives of people who had given up hope. "There was in fact no generic difference," he noted, "between manuscripts from England and manuscripts from the North American Middle West. The life depicted was the same—exactly the same—the points of view were astonishingly similar."[3] In an article in the *Bookman* in 1929 about the state of American poetry, Allen Tate echoed Ford's view of the extended cultural meaning that now attached to the Middle West. The term applied not only to a region but to "any community where the population is restless and its activities industrialized," Tate said, and added that "New York absorbs and intensifies the motives of all our Middle Wests."[4]

In the wake of the popular success of *Main Street* and *Babbitt* at the beginning of the decade, the geographic Midwest became a convenient whipping boy throughout the twenties for all that was wrong with American life. It offered what Frederick J. Hoffman has called a metaphor of abuse that pictured, on the one hand, a featureless rural world of farms and small towns, and, on the other, an interior landscape of conventional values, commercial greed, and spiritual aridity.[5] At the deepest level it embodied a sweeping critique of middle-class life as thoroughly identified with the American Midwest. For the regionalists associated with John Frederick's magazine the country's interior was the Great Valley of authentic American life—middling, as Ruth Suckow maintained, in the appealing sense of being the source of ordinary virtue and common feeling. But in the dominant imagination of the time the reverse was true. Middling meant lack of fulfillment; it meant cramped lives, compromised lives, defeated lives. Middle Westishness simply summed up all that was wrong with America in the twenties, and the American Midwest—despite Ford's insistence on the international applicability of his term—was its rightful home.

2

Frederick reported in the *Midland* that he was able to penetrate only a brief way through the "thickets of Local Color" in Carl Van Vechten's *The Tattooed Countess*, finding nothing of the whimsical lightness that had graced *Peter*

Whiffle, a popular earlier work.[6] Sinclair Lewis, less protective about the Midwest, was more perceptive. He announced in the *Saturday Review* that with the novel Van Vechten had ventured upon Midwestern material and made it "real and amusing." He had captured the complacency of a "Ioway" town—its "Covered Wagon plus Elbert Hubbard plus lawn-mower innocence"—while retaining the trademark quality of his fiction, a gay and civilized charm.[7] The difference in the two responses to Van Vechten's highly successful 1924 novel illustrates something of the distance throughout the decade between, on the one hand, the regionalist search for a Midwestern literature exuding positive qualities and, on the other, more typical portraits in which the region, in tones of bemusement or active disdain, comes to represent all that is narrow, backward, and repressed. It suggests as well something of the widespread acceptance of the latter view of the region in that Van Vechten's novel is, at least to some degree, a lightly humorous parody of conventional attacks on Midwestern culture in the vein of the two major manifestos of the twenties, *Main Street* and *Babbitt*. It assumes an audience both familiar with and in agreement with the broad indictment of the region following from Lewis's work—an audience, as mentioned earlier, that could be depended upon to understand exactly John Riddell's 1929 parody of "The Gloomy Mid-West Story."

Van Vechten had left Cedar Rapids, Iowa, in 1899 for the University of Chicago, a moon-calf figure like Floyd Dell's Felix Fay who had found a fairly rich life in an energetic provincial city yet yearned for more complete immersion in the arts. At the University he came under the influence of Robert Herrick, among others, and turned to writing; after graduation a journalism career was launched with the *Chicago American*. In 1906, before the first rumblings of the Chicago renaissance, he was off to New York, living for a time in the same building as Lewis and writing a commissioned article for a magazine edited by Dreiser. Music and the theater now claimed his attention and he soon became a staff critic for the *New York Times*. In 1908 the newspaper sent him to Paris where he was again, as he had been in his Chicago days, a generation in advance of a literary flowering. It was not until 1922 that Van Vechten turned from criticism to fiction with *Peter Whiffle: His Life and Work*, the first of seven novels that gained him a reputation as a witty and mannered stylist and one of the most fashionable writers of the decade.

In mood, *The Tattooed Countess*, his sole use of his Midwestern background in fiction, swings between whimsical romantic comedy (as suggested in the subtitle, "A romantic novel with a happy ending") and a serious, if lightly sketched, revolt-from-the-village satire directed to the narrow gauge of Midwestern life. In both its moods the novel always seems on the verge of self-parody, the sophisticated author overtaken by his mocking use of well-worn materials. Seen in the best light, the novel could be described in terms used by Louis Bromfield in a review of a later work of Van Vechten's: "Mr. Van Vechten is not ponderous in his books, but he comes much nearer to depicting the American scene than many a laborious corn-fed realist."[8] Somerset Maugham equally stressed Van Vechten's light touch when he told him (the remark used on the dust jacket of later printings of the book) that he had succeeded in a difficult genre.

> I am always looking for light books and in England, at all events, seldom find them, for most writers think that a light book is the same as a frivolous one, and do not realize that it requires really much more thought, knowledge, culture, and experience than a book dealing with elemental emotions.
>
> I think *The Tattooed Countess* is a triumph in this difficult genre. I admire exceedingly the way in which you have avoided every temptation to force the note, and the discretion with which you have let your exquisite humour get its own laughter with never so much as a nudge in the reader's ribs to bring to his notice that here is something to laugh at.[9]

What there is to laugh at is Van Vechten's playful variation on the familiar theme of Midwestern return. Countess Ella Nattatorrini comes back to visit her strait-laced sister in Maple Valley, the Cedar Rapids-like city of her youth, following the failure of a love affair with a younger man. The year is 1897 and the Countess is now a worldly European, rich, pampered, and well proportioned at age fifty. (In a film version called *A Woman of the World* she was played by the sultry Pola Negri.) At once she comes up against provincial taboos: she wears make-up, smokes cigarettes, is used to dining in the evening rather than at noon. Most offensive of all is the tattoo on her wrist where, as her sister points out, "it *shows*!" She adds: "It wouldn't have been so bad if it had been on the back or the . . . thigh, where it could be covered."[10] Along with its Midwestern hypocrisy Van Vechten gently pillories Maple Valley's Main Street boosterism—its pride in its new high school and water works and depot. "There ain't a city of its size in the state," the Countess is told repeatedly, "that's so enterprising" (54).

Van Vechten piles on the staples of Midwestern fiction with the introduction into the story of a romantic youth hungering for a larger life and a sympathetic teacher secretly in love with her star pupil. Gareth Johns wants, naturally, to be a writer ("I want to know everything, *everything*. . . . When I do, then, perhaps, I can write about Iowa") but is held back by inexperience, the dull routine of the city, and a father who is preoccupied with business (77). When the Countess and Gareth are brought together, a process of mutual seduction begins. He stirs her need for passion while for him she is "the way out, the prospective fulfiller of his visions" (228). She treads cautiously in the affair for fear of frightening the young man away, not knowing that he is as amoral as she—a boy who is "almost entirely free from inhibitions, prejudices, who was intolerant only of superstitions, conventions, and village moral idiocies" (229).

At length, the two declare their love in a scene in which parody turns delightfully ludicrous:

> Mon petit chou! she cried. Ma soisoif! Ma faifaim! Adorable! . . . I will be everything to you: mother, mistress, wife. Tu es mon bebe!
> Countess, he began . . .

Call me Ella, call me your fafemme!
Ella!
She interrupted him with another kiss. (260)[11]

Using the subterfuge that Gareth is off as a student to the University of Chicago, they meet in the city and embark for Europe, there to live as free spirits. Maple Valley, the inquisitorial Midwestern city, does not remain in the dark. In the closing chapter two neighbor women savor a report that Gareth and the Countess have been seen boarding a New York train together. One of them says, giving a final stamp to the novel's satiric intent, "Good riddance to bad rubbidge. There's an undesirable element in this town and it's gettin' out, thank goodness," thereby leaving Iowa as once again a "pure one hundred per cent American state, an' it's lookin' up!" (285–86).

3

While working on his next novel, *Firecrackers* (1925), Van Vechten said his aim in fiction was to "create moods, to awaken unconscious echoes of the past, to render to shadows their real importance."[12] In its sober tone the declaration of intent seems more fittingly directed to the work of Glenway Wescott, another of the well-regarded Midwestern writers of the twenties for whom the escape from the suffocating embrace of Middle Westishness provided both a pattern for living and subject matter for fiction. Wescott's use of his regional background was more extensive than Van Vechten's and more complex, with the result that his work still holds some claim on literary attention. He shared deeply in the flight of the gifted out of the Midwest—becoming, in fact, one of the quintessential expatriates of the period—that had been vigorously predicted by the Countess Nattatorrini in *The Tattooed Countess*:

> "You'd better look out! You don't know what you're doing to the next generation. They won't stand it; no one with any brains would stand it! They'll revolt! They'll break loose! You'll see. Mark my words, you'll see!" (130)

At the same time, his fictional reconstruction of the regional past is marked by melancholy affection for the heirs of the pioneers who have fallen from earlier simplicity and grace—by lyric feeling, as Ruth Suckow perceptively noted about Wescott's work, for "the withering and going to seed (along with the blossoms!) of New England in the West."[13]

After a boyhood in rural Wisconsin, Wescott, twenty years younger than Van Vechten, followed the same path as the Iowa writer but at an accelerated pace—to the University of Chicago, to New York, to Paris all by age twenty-four. *The Apple of the Eye*, his first novel, published in the same year as *The Tattooed Countess*, was the work of a precocious young man of twenty-three (who by his own reckoning had been working on the novel since age seventeen) that seemed to John Frederick in the *Midland* notable for a "frankly archaic" style yet one that captured Midwestern life "beautifully and truly."[14] Primarily an account of a country boy's struggle with Puritan and anti-Puritan attitudes toward sex, the novel ends in familiar Midwestern fashion with the hero off to a new life at the university in Madison, freed from his past but with his thoughts turned back to his mother and her restrictive religion:

> He found a seat, put up his suitcases; and the train started slowly. He stared out the window, his eyes wide but extremely dim, thinking of his mother as she drove back over the autumn roads, clinging to her faith in him, praying for the perfection of his life.[15]

With the novel Wescott opened up the vein of regional material that he would exploit in his first four works. By far the most important of these is *The Grandmothers*, a family chronicle which appeared as a Harper's Prize Novel in 1927 and briefly established him as one of the major talents of the postwar generation of young American writers.

Frederick's emphasis on Wescott's prose manner was taken up in most contemporary comments on the novel. Suckow found it a lyric work that was "delicate, faintly ornate like the big old houses of the 1880s on aging Wisconsin streets, touched with an oversweet breath of autumnal decay, of an autumn that comes too soon."[16] As a stylist Wescott seems deeply indebted to Sherwood Anderson. His surfaces are unlike Anderson in that they are highly mannered and baroque, but there is the same abstract, elusive, expository manner with only sparing use of dramatic scenes. And there is the same creation of moments of poetic feeling that grow out of accounts of Midwestern lives treated with respect yet marked by a distinct sense of loss. Wescott's characters are not Anderson's grotesques but they are viewed from a postpioneer attitude of distinct regret. Where a wilderness had once been conquered, the narrator of *The Grandmothers* remarks of them, a wilderness remains—a "wilderness of history and hearsay, that distorted landscape of a dream which had come true before it had been dreamed."[17] As the narrator understands them, both the outer worlds and the inner landscapes of the characters are darkened with economic gloom, archaic virtues, failed dreams, and a gnawing sense of grievance.

A third-generation descendant of Wisconsin pioneers, Alwyn Tower, a young writer and obviously Wescott's persona, sets down what he remembers and imagines of his family history in a series of linked portraits, following an admonition from one of his grandmothers used as the book's epigraph: "You do not see me as I once was. Children, get out the photographs." Although the time frame of his pictures of his family and of himself shifts within the book, the decision to recreate what he calls "one family's intimate history" comes to him as a mature writer living as an expatriate in a hotel on the French Riviera when he rereads with dissatisfaction an essay he had written at age nineteen on the development of America. The feeling comes over him that "he had no native land—he had a family instead," and he decides to tell the stories of that family in the hope they will stand for the larger whole. His stories, he says in Anderson-like tones, will be

> like a series of question marks; questions which did not require an answer, questions at peace. He was content with their ambiguities, so he knew that they were the end of understanding, or at any rate, the end of trying to understand.
>
> Trying to understand, for his own sake, shadowy men, women, and children. . . . (33)

The boyish essay that he rereads is written in an inflated style yet reflects the mature Alwyn's sense of the disappointment that followed the extravagant hope brought to America by immigrant groups.

> *Meanwhile the colonists had moved and moved again, from east to west, into every corner of the continent; and each migration repeated, with a little less religion and a little more weariness, the pilgrimage which had brought them there: disappointed men going further, hoping still . . .*
>
> *At last there was no corner where wealth and joy might be thought to dwell, no riverbed without a city, no empty valley, no more coasts. At last those pilgrims who had failed to discover their hearts' desire had to look for it in heaven, as it had been in Europe, as it has always been. Disillusioned but imaginative, these went through the motions of hope, still pioneers.* (28–29)[18]

He realizes that the phrase "disillusioned but imaginative" accurately describes the men in the Tower branch of his family, and on the back pages of the essay he revises it into a comment on one family and a failure to achieve in each generation the American dream. It was a perennial failure that had stoked perennial resentment.

> *They said little, but this conviction took possession of all their minds: they were not born to be beasts of burden; they should not have to work as these others worked; they were not menials, but deserved a sweeter fate; life was unjust. This conviction was inherited by every Tower, from father to son; and in that inheritance younger son shared equally with elder. A grievance was their birthright. . . .* (32)

As Alwyn relates the stories of his family—mother and father, aunts and uncles, both sets of grandparents—his tone is warm and sympathetic. He wants to love and praise them all. Yet an awareness of twisted lives and failed hopes is woven throughout his affectionate memories. Through the lives of his elders he glimpses in the countryside the wilderness of the Mississippi Valley as it existed sixty years before where "the pioneers had crept, with chests and sickles, axes, flails, and oxen in docile pairs." But the heroic past is long "buried under the plowed land, the feet of modern men, and the ripening crops" (8). Now there is only a uniformity and flatness to experience and above all a sense of unrealized ambition. In his own life Alwyn is keenly aware of decline:

He had not handled a rifle, an axe, a hammer, or a plow, on its [Wisconsin's] great and tedious body. Nor had he eaten in a sort of habitual starvation the turnips which according to his grandfather had tasted like "Paradise apples." He had not feared God, nor begotten children, nor lived by the sweat of his brow. And perhaps he never would. . . . (366)

Even for his grandfather Tower, a pioneer figure who died when Alwyn was twelve, the West to which he had given his life ("that point of the compass which had glittered with hope like a star") had come to resemble the East. The light had gone out of it and his every dream had turned into a "rendezvous with disappointment" (53).

Late in the novel Alwyn, writing now from the perspective of a young man who has left Wisconsin for school in Chicago, contrasts the city and the country and finds the latter the more wanting. If in the city there is greed and complaint, country life is no more than "self-supporting"; in the words of Alwyn's mother, "no worthy gifts to the world" have come from it. The herculean labor of the pioneers and their descendents has accomplished very little. In an inventory of present-day country life Alwyn concludes that there are only

Shabby and gloomy farms, unserviceable virtues, broken hearts, large family re- unions, grievances of those (like Alwyn himself) with ideas above their station, other grievances and old-time religion. . . . Where literal wilderness had been con- quered, a wilderness still, overrun by peasant immigrants, but still ineffectually governed by the early settlers' wistful young, by their habits of poverty-stricken conquerors. There was this difference between Chicago and Wisconsin: in the country the avidity had never been assuaged. There were blank spaces between the badly cultivated fields; there were areas of craving and brute force which poverty had been too God-fearing, prosperity not eager enough, to lay hands upon. Across the Mississippi Valley the barbed-wire fences lay like the staves of music paper on which as yet there were scarcely any notes. . . . It had not kept its promise, so it was still the promised land. (372)

In the concluding chapter he tells of the death of his grandmother Duff and the long, slow dying of his grandmother Tower, events which signal the beginning of his separation from his Wisconsin past. Throughout the book—hence its title—mothers and grandmothers are seen as the figures who direct and main- tain, dominant presences holding together the life that had originally been won by restless men who now live with faded expectations. In a final image Alwyn sees his grandmother Tower's small house from a distance as he walks to town to send a message about her death, and in the dusk he whispers good-bye to the family dead, freeing himself from them. Yet he is aware of their continuing presence in memory and uncertain whether he can discover real freedom in his own life or must repeat the narrow circles of their lives (387).

Wescott's next book, a collection of stories published in 1928 as *Good-Bye Wisconsin*, returns to the theme of separation in its title story. More a rambling personal essay in the form of an introduction to the collection than a work of short fiction ("this diary, this stock-taking," Wescott calls it),[19] it tells of an expatriate writer's return to his parents' home in a Wisconsin town, self-consciously aware of himself as a liberated figure back in an alien country. A tour of the town the morning after his arrival, like Carol Kennicott's first tour of Gopher Prairie, provides a catalogue of its insufficiency beneath a placid and prosperous surface: tedium, churches that have become no more than clubs, sexual fear, above all a "sluggish emotional atmosphere" (39). The countryside beyond the town offers no alternative but is merely "the source of the sunrises, the bad weather, and the food, and of certain books already a little out of date" (15). Because of progress in the form of radios, telephones, and automobiles, the countryside now exists only as spacious suburbs beyond the towns. Although the writer notes that one might possibly imagine Wisconsin an ideal place, in fact the young dream only of escape; already there are a "fair number of Middle-Westerners about the world; a sort of vagrant chosen race like the Jews" (26). Among those who have taken flight or simply long to, there is a wish, among many other wishes, for an altered literature of country life:

> No more weather-bound farmers, they beg; no more of the inarticulate, no more love limited to unfortunate stables and desperation growing faint between rows of spoiled corn, no more poverty-stricken purity, no more jeering or complaining about lamentable small towns. . . . They or their fathers have had enough of all this. Who can blame them? (30–31)

The narrator decides that in his own work he will avoid problems specific to Wisconsin in favor of human appetites experienced everywhere. Middle Westishness thus put behind him as subject matter, he leaves Wisconsin as a place, returning with a sense of relief to New York on his way back to France. Yet the poverty of Wisconsin as literary material remains on his mind, leading to a considered abandonment of the Midwest as so lacking finally in definition as to be beyond the literary pale:

> The Middle West is nowhere; an abstract nowhere. However earnestly writers proud of being natives of it may endeavor to give it form and character, it remains out of focus, amorphous, and a mystery. . . . There is no Middle West. It is a certain climate, a certain landscape; and beyond that, a state of mind of people born where they do not like to live. (38–39)[20]

At the end of the story the narrator mentions two non-Midwestern books he would like to write. One would be an "indoor book" dealing solely with human emotions and devoid of parts played by the "weather or swamps or the beasts of the fields" (43). Another would be a book written for the eye rather than the ear, a work of such purity of style that he himself as the writer, "with my origins and my prejudices and my Wisconsin, will seem to have disappeared" (45).

"Good-Bye Wisconsin" is mannered and fragmented, a set of attitudes rather than a developed argument. The generally undistinguished stories that follow use Wisconsin settings, and Wescott would once again treat Wisconsin in *The Babe's Bed* in 1930; yet in the opening essay-story he effectively conveys a sense of the exhaustion of the Midwest as serious literary material by an expatriate postwar generation of writers in flight from American life. To turn away from the region as material was to resist Middle Westishness. It was to resist what the narrator of "Good-Bye Wisconsin," characterizing the inner world of the stories that follow in the collection, calls "a strangely limited moral order" (31). When this constricted world of small houses and small towns and small lives is "set beside a complicatedly unfolding reality" that is modern life, it seems to the narrator "little or not enough." He must lift his sights away, beyond (32).

To fail to do so—to return to Wisconsin and then remain—would be creative death, the theme of the final story in the collection. A composer, Hubert Redd, returns in "The Whistling Swan" to his northern Wisconsin home from Europe after his Chicago patron withdraws support. Here he is confronted with the prospect of marriage to an old girlfriend and a teaching job in a small college. The possibility still exists of another patron and a return to Europe, and during a walk in the woods with his father's gun he reflects on the shallow soil of Wisconsin for the artist:

> He said to himself that he did not like this country because it was merely in the process of becoming what other countries were perfectly. Would not staying there, for any such craftsman or inventor as a musician, be perversely going back to the beginning instead of starting where others had left off? (357–58)

The native sounds he hears in the woods suggest music but he rejects them as overly familiar. They are "of a style which was passing—too closely related to too many sounds, too far removed from easy speech and tragic outcry both" (359). When a swan springs up in front of him he shoots it out of fright, a moment heavily freighted with symbolism in that, dying, the swan whistles and releases a "heavy stream of music" that is husky and crude, signaling the death of Hubert's music as well (361). He immediately returns home, ready to accept wife and teaching job, knowing that he will be held in Wisconsin by some magnetism that will make him "almost content with his apparent loss." His fate as a composer is surely one in which he will "hold his peace—a dumb, wholesome, personal peace." At the end of the story he thinks bravely about his decision ("Talk about Paris, who cared, who cared?"), but the result of his inability to say goodbye to Wisconsin is clearly the death of whatever genuine creative impulse he possessed (362).

4

In a letter in 1925 to Maxwell Perkins, his editor at Scribner's, Fitzgerald mocked writers who were still telling stories about simple, inarticulate farmers and turning out books full of the "Feel of the Soil." He spun out a capsule history of rural writing for Perkins that placed Garland as the discoverer of the farmer in the American Midwest. Anderson had then rediscovered the farmer in Ohio, Cather had turned him into a Swede, and Suckow had gotten in (Fitzgerald put the date as 1922) just as the door was closing and the rural literary ground exhausted. The present facts were that the farmer represented only a miniscule part of the population, he had never been bound to the soil in the manner of European peasants, and "if [he] has any sensitivity whatsoever . . . he is in the towns before he's twenty." Fitzgerald went on:

> Either Lewis, Lardner and myself have been badly fooled, or else using [the farmer] as typical American material is simply *a stubborn seeking for the static in a world that for almost a hundred years had simply not been static*. Isn't it a fourth rate imagination that can find only that old property farmer in all this amazing time and land?[21]

Fitzgerald's mention of Ring Lardner in the company of himself and Lewis as Midwestern writers who had turned their backs on rural life as material recalls Lardner's status as yet another writer from the region who experienced sudden critical acclaim in the twenties. When Lardner left behind the prestigious "In the Wake of the News" column in the *Chicago Tribune* in the summer of 1919 and departed for the East, he already had carved out a reputation as a popular humorist. Among those who had come under his spell was a young high-school journalist in suburban Oak Park, Ernest Hemingway. Lardner's *Saturday Evening Post* stories about the braggart baseball "busher" Jack Keefe had been drawn together in *You Know Me Al* in 1916, with stories about the adventures of a resolute low-brow and his snobbish wife appearing in *Gullible's Travels, Etc.* the following year. But despite his local renown, Lardner had had no connection with Chicago's literary renaissance, and it was not until he was taken up in New York by Mencken, Carl Van Doren, and Edmund Wilson with the publication of *How to Write Short Stories* (1924), *The Love Nest* (1926), and his collected stories in *Round Up* (1929) that he passed from the role of well-paid journalist and popular entertainer to serious writer and major satirist of American life. Another factor in his rise to literary fame was his friendship with Fitzgerald, his neighbor in Great Neck on Long Island, who took upon himself the task of promoting Lardner's career with Max Perkins and generally trumpeting the fellow Midwesterner's significance. In Fitzgerald's novel *Tender Is the Night*, Lardner would sit for the portrait of Abe North.

Lardner's chief virtue as a writer was an uncanny ear for semiliterate speech and the racy American vernacular, both of which he employed in probing with dead-pan humor and wicked satire the shortcomings of modern life. In this he bore resemblance to Lewis (the two were born within weeks of each other in 1885) and to some extent Anderson, as Edmund Wilson saw in a review when he noted that Lardner's stories were "a series of studies of American types almost equal in importance to those of Sherwood Anderson and Sinclair Lewis." But Wilson also went on to notice the quality that seemed to decisively separate Lardner from Lewis: Lardner was "less likely than Lewis to caricature, and hence to falsify, because he is primarily interested in studying a kind of person rather than in drawing up an indictment."[22] Anderson made a roughly similar point in a *New Republic* article in 1922 treating Gertrude Stein, Paul Rosenfeld, Lewis, and Lardner. Anderson acknowledged Lewis's skill at reporting outer surfaces but pointed to his neglect of inner forces, among them light-hearted qualities of ordinary life that he thought the more rounded work of Lardner revealed through humor. He added:

> Life in American towns and cities is barren enough and there are enough people saying that with the growth of industrialism it has become continually more and more ugly, but Mr. Paul Rosenfeld and Mr. Ring Lardner apparently do not find it altogether barren and ugly. For them and for a growing number of men and women in America there is something like a dawn that Mr. Lewis has apparently sensed but little.[23]

Lardner's stories, a good many of them at least, now seem far darker in implication than Anderson suggests, hardly pointing to anything like a dawn in American life. There are repeated accounts of discord in marriages and mean-spirited bridge players and soulless suburban existence, and such celebrated stories as "Haircut" and "Champion" treat cruel figures who heap suffering upon others. Beneath the humor and zany word play of Lardner's fiction often runs a sober undercurrent or biting edge, as, for example, in "Anniversary," a story whose perfectly-controlled ending brings to mind the closing domestic scene of *Main Street*. When a husband forgets his wedding anniversary, his wife reminds him of it at the end of a boring evening during which he reads the newspaper and delivers a rambling monologue while she plays solitaire. When he offers to remember the anniversary the following day with flowers, the wife replies:

> "I don't want any flowers. But there is something I would like you to give me. And you don't have to wait until tomorrow."
> "What is it?"
> "A punch in the eye," said Mrs. Taylor.
> "You're feeling kind of funny, aren't you? Did Florence have a shot of their home-made gin in her bag?"
> "No. And I'm not feeling funny. I'm just sleepy. I think I'll go to bed."
> Louis was reading again.
> "It says: 'Experiments in the raising of sisal are being made in Haiti.' I don't suppose you happen to know what sisal is."
> But Mrs. Taylor was on her way up-stairs.[24]

Mencken saw Lardner as a natural ally in the effort to reveal the truth about the "Low Down American." "Lardner sees into him, and clear through him," Mencken wrote. "He is not sentimentalized. One recognizes, at the start, mainly his racy and preposterous speech, but soon recognizes, too, the shrunken and grotesque soul within him."[25] The comment is just yet it neglects the playfulness, amusement, and even sympathy that is also apparent in Lardner's handling of his characters and their narrow lives. Such qualities remove the stories from Mencken's harsh scorn and from Lewis's caricatures— qualities that draw Lardner's satire back, as Anderson rightly sensed, from depicting a world that is altogether barren and ugly. Lardner always remembered his early years in the turn-of-the-century small-town Midwest with pleasure, and perhaps his memories of that life, less ambivalent than those of either Anderson or Lewis, kept his work from drifting into a bitter indictment of the world around him. Jonathan Yardley, Lardner's biographer, stresses the writer's Midwestern roots and the foundation of his work in the region. Lardner's move from Chicago to the East had the effect, Yardley holds, of "cutting himself off from the land and people that nourished his work."[26]

Like the other critically-acclaimed Midwestern writers of the twenties, however, Lardner had no doubt about the need to leave the region behind. "Small towns are fine to grow up in," he once said, "and a writer finds out a lot of things in small towns he can't learn anywhere else. But it wouldn't be the same as you got older in a small town."[27] In *The Big Town*, linked stories in the loose form of a novel that Lardner published in 1921, a wife declares from the vantage point of South Bend, Indiana, "They's only one place . . . New York City," and her husband replies in a typical throw-away Lardner line, "I've heard of it."[28] Despite the unflattering nature of his portraits of life in the big city and its environs, Lardner seldom chose to look back at the provincial scene. When he did (in, for example, stories such as "Haircut" and "The Maysville Minstrel") his view was equally unflattering. Midwestern experience may have lent an element of sympathy and understanding to his work, but it provided no center that could be returned to or built upon. For Lardner there remained a blankness at the core of modern life that could be revealed with comedy and word play and hilarious nonsense but that did not yield, as it did eventually for Anderson and Lewis, to a need to affirm. In this he seems far closer in spirit, finally, to the early work of his younger admirers, Fitzgerald and Hemingway, than to such contemporaries as Lewis and Anderson, and far closer to the literary temper of his time.

5

Regional experience also had little direct bearing on the work of Hart Crane, the most important poetic voice among the young writers of the twenties from out of the Midwest. In 1916 the seventeen-year-old Crane, an exact contemporary of Hemingway, left Cleveland and the long-settled Western Reserve towns of his Ohio youth behind, bypassing the Chicago renaissance in favor of New York and Greenwich Village. Here he became acquainted with the new writers of the day, Anderson among them, through such literary journals as the *Pagan* and Margaret Anderson's *Little Review* after its removal from Chicago. But he was also aware of an older tradition stemming from the Midwestern poetry of Masters, Lindsay, and Sandburg. He could refer sympathetically to Anderson's "love for rows of corn on flat lands, fields bending over rolling Ohio hills, and the smell of barns under the warm hours of noon,"[29] and could say that he understood *Winesburg* because he had lived himself in a such a place. To a journalist he could warmly proclaim the significance of Midwestern writing: "Have you read Carl Sandburg's 'Cornhuskers,' Dreiser's novels, Edgar Lee Masters' poems . . . ? These men have recognized realities that are close to us and our present day life, and we cannot afford to ignore them."[30]

Crane's enthusiasm for the older Midwestern writers was to some extent the result of his friendship with Harriet Moody, the widow of the University of Chicago poet-professor William Vaughn Moody. Crane's father, the owner of a chocolate factory and concerned about his son's fondness for poetry rather than business, had discussed the boy with Mrs. Moody, who ran a successful catering business in Chicago to which the elder Crane supplied chocolates. Closely acquainted with the writers of the Chicago renaissance and other leading literary figures of the day, she advised giving free rein to Crane's interest in poetry and asked to see his work. A correspondence soon developed in which the young poet sent off his work and the older woman responded with sympathetic and encouraging notes together with exciting news about the literary world.

In 1919, soon after his twentieth birthday, Crane returned to Ohio to work in one of his enterprising father's businesses in Akron, there beginning a correspondence with Anderson that touched upon the older writer's unhappy business days in Cleveland and Elyria as well as providing criticism of poems Crane sent along. At the time Crane was reading the demanding work of the new poets, among them Wallace Stevens and William Carlos Williams, yet he was also drawn to the more direct and vigorously colloquial work of his Midwestern predecessors. "Porphyro in Akron," a poem that appeared in the *Double Dealer* in 1921, shows the evident influence of Sandburg's Chicago poems:

> Greeting the dawn,
> A shift of rubber workers presses down
> South Main.
> With the stubbornness of muddy water
> It dwindles at each cross-line
> Until you feel the weight of many cars
> North-bound, and East and West,
> Absorbing and conveying weariness,—
> Rumbling over the hills.[31]

Almost immediately, however, Crane would turn away from the impressionistic social content of such a poem to more emotional and technically complex expression suggested by the example of the French Symbolists and the new modernist poets, and his interest in Anderson as a literary craftsman would begin to wane.

Allen Tate, who greeted Crane's first book, *White Buildings*, published in 1926 after the poet's permanent return to New York, as "probably the most distinguished first book ever issued in the country," perceptively placed Crane's subsequent work against a background of Midwestern writing. The Midwestern poets had begun with an interest in local speech and the local scene, but in Tate's view their work had rapidly given way, especially in the case of Sandburg, to an aggressive Americanism that invariably sought to speak for the country as a whole. By Crane's time the Midwestern movement in poetry was in collapse, leaving successors no localized traditions or values that could be built upon. Although regions were still the genuine resources for a native literature, Crane with his Midwestern background was drawn to a larger, national vision, and so in his central and most ambitious work, *The Bridge*, he tried to create an American epic. Tate acknowledged that the appearance of the poem would be a major event in contemporary letters, far more important than anything attempted by earlier Midwestern poets, but he added that "of its success in creating a national myth it is our privilege to be sceptical in advance."[32]

After the poem's publication in book form in 1930 Tate repeated his view that its vast theme, the myth of America, was a dead abstraction that could not be redeemed by Crane's immense verbal skill. Often brilliant in its parts, the work was structurally flawed and lacked overall coherence. In the strongest section, "The River," Crane—as he himself described his intention—tried to transport the reader to the Midwest, there to follow the wanderings of three tramps who stand as leftover figures of the rootless pioneers:

> Under a world of whistles, wires and steam
> Caboose-like they go ruminating through
> Ohio, Indiana—blind baggage—
> To Cheyenne tagging . . . Maybe Kalamazoo.[33]

Surface attention to the Midwest also provided the subject of what Tate thought the most mistaken section of the long poem, "Indiana," a monologue of a woman of the 1850s whose son is leaving an Indiana farm for the sea. Tate called the section a "nightmare of sentimentality,"[34] a judgment he might have reinforced by noting the similarity between some of the lines ("Come back to Indiana—not too late! / [Or will you be a ranger to the end?]")[35] and the saccharine nature of popular end-of-the-century Indiana writing. Tate, himself influenced by the views of T. S. Eliot and others that great poetry depended upon tradition, held that the overall problem with the work, and with Crane's poetry in general, was that his world lacked a firm center. His Midwestern past had simply provided him with no philosophical background that might have given his work an effective inner framework. What the poet deeply required was a return to the local culture from which he had sprung. "Only a return to the provinces," Tate declared, "to the small, self-contained centres of life, will put the all-destroying abstraction, America, safely to rest." But for Crane there was no such past to return to, no "fixed points in the firmament" or "settled ideas of conscience."[36] As a Midwesterner, he was left with the tendency to look beyond the region for meaning—and with his own particularly fractured experience of the turmoil of modern life. The result was a romantic poetry of pure sensation that could not sustain the linked lyrics and sweeping intention of *The Bridge*. It was work that was at its best in isolated and glittering fragments, yet work that—as Tate nonetheless concluded—"remains the great poetic achievement of his [Crane's] generation."[37]

6

In "Good-Bye Wisconsin" Glenway Wescott expressed his and a generation's response to Middle Westishness in a tidy epigram: "How much sweeter to come and go than to stay; that by way of judgment upon Wisconsin"(32). However, his best work, *The Grandmothers*, testifies to something of richer literary substance than the literal experience of coming and going—the return in memory and imagination to what has been left behind. The need for escape remains; the judgment upon Wisconsin holds firm. But within the roomy spaces of memory the claims of the past, the claims of people and place and event, are intermingled with the grounds for flight, past and present linked in a complex texture of sympathy and resistance. With the deaths of his grandmothers at the end of the novel Alywn Tower realizes he is ready to leave Wisconsin and his family; he is "glad to go and leave them behind." At the same time, he realizes, as suggested before, that the past is not so easily set aside. His family will stay with him, lodged in memory that is experienced both as pain and comfort, for the rest of his days.

> But he felt that he would have need of them all, gods or pioneers or whatever they were, to lead an entire life; and if there were any he had not called upon, those would probably take him by surprise; certain of them, those of the passions and disasters, would spring on him when he was lonely, have their way with him, and leave him hurt for a while by the side of the road—the last one would leave him dead. Out of pride he wanted to be able to love and praise them all, even the last one. . . . (387–88)

Returns to a region of memory, accompanied or not by actual returns, have provided the inner substance of some of the best works of Midwestern writing—Jim Burden's sustained account of "what I remember about Ántonia," Nick Carraway's less central but still crucial "vivid memories" of the sensible homeland to which he flees after Gatsby's death. No Midwestern writer drew more deeply upon memory than Hemingway, together with Fitzgerald and Crane the most important and enduring of the young literary figures from the region to find critical success in the twenties. Yet to speak of Hemingway or of Fitzgerald or Crane in this context is to be made aware of the fading of regional identity as a meaningful way of approaching the writers who came of age in the period and who swiftly and irrevocably left the Midwest behind.

With the early work of Hemingway, Fitzgerald, and Crane, together with that of such lesser figures as Van Vechten, Wescott, and Lardner, the Midwestern ascendancy in American writing came to an end, lost in the experimentation, the preoccupation with language and form, and the concentration on private experience of the modernist spirit in literature. Writers now had their eye on other and more distant terrain—beyond region, beyond America, often beyond society itself. Beyond the ostensible settings, their work was most deeply located in an interior landscape suggested in the resonant titles of some of Hemingway's stories: "In Another Country," "The Capital of the World," "A Clean, Well-Lighted Place." It was work whose deepest impulses no longer arose from lingering regional awareness but from the dislocations of modern life and especially from psychological experience. With the generation of Hemingway, Fitzgerald, and Crane the sense of alikeness that had briefly nourished Midwestern writing, whether directed to country life or town and city life, gave way before what Ford called the enormous disillusionment and enormous awakening of modern times.

This said, it remains that throughout their careers both Hemingway and Fitzgerald looked back upon their early Midwestern years with considerable, if never unambiguous, nostalgia. Through memory they could return to the local cultures from which they had sprung—the very act that Tate called for in his criticism of Crane. Through Nick Carraway in *The Great Gatsby*, Fitzgerald expressed his deep if idealized feeling for the St. Paul of his youth, and in later life he put the same emotion into his letters. Nearly a decade after the novel he told an old friend from the city that he would prefer that his daughter, Scottie, have her debut in St. Paul rather than Baltimore, where the Fitzgeralds were then living.

> This in spite of the fact that having rambled so much I no longer regard St. Paul as my home any more than the eastern seaboard or the Riviera. This is said with no disloyalty but simply because after all my father was an easterner and I went East to college and I never did quite adjust myself to those damn Minnesota winters. It was always freezing my cheeks, being a rotten skater, etc.—though many events there will always fill me with a tremendous nostalgia.

Fitzgerald added that he was desperate for news of old St. Paul aquaintances. "Who runs things now?" he asked. "So many of us have emigrated . . . and so many new names keep popping up when I get hold of a St. Paul paper that I cling in spirit to the few friends I still have there."[38] Hemingway similarly looked back upon the northern Michigan of his youthful summers as one of his beloved literary landscapes. He evoked it in such nonfiction works as *Death in the Afternoon* and *Green Hills of Africa*, and in his imaginative writing it provided both background and refuge for the first of his fictional heroes, Nick Adams.

"As soon as it was safe for the boy to travel," Carlos Baker began his pioneering biography of Hemingway, "they bore him away to the northern woods."[39] Windemere, the summer cottage on Walloon Lake near Petoskey, Michigan, was a welcome alternative to the Chicago suburb of Oak Park and a life of Victorian propriety in the large family of a local doctor and an artistic and ambitious mother. It was a place for hunting and fishing in a still pristine world of pine forests, trout streams, and clear lakes. It provided a different kind of education than Oak Park, one that drew Hemingway closer to the father than the mother and toward the vigorous, self-reliant, outdoor life of his early hero, Theodore Roosevelt.

In the summer of 1919 Hemingway, a wounded veteran of the ambulance service in Italy in the days before American entry into the Great War, was back in northern Michigan after several difficult months of living within family restrictions in Oak Park. He was writing stories now as well as rediscovering the pleasures of the lake. A camping trip that summer with two companions to the Fox River in the Upper Peninsula of Michigan near the shores of Lake Superior would give him material he would use eventually in "Big Two-Hearted River." Through the fall he stayed on in Michigan, living in a rented room in Petoskey and writing stories. After a few months as a space-rate writer for the *Toronto Star Weekly*, a return to his career as a journalist begun before the war on the *Kansas City Star*, he was back in Michigan the following summer, living apart from his family and among a circle of summer people.

In the fall of 1920 he began a brief but significant interlude in Chicago, working as a writer and editor for a house organ called *The Co-Operative Commonwealth* and through friends meeting Anderson. Although still in the harness of his advertising job, Anderson at age forty-four was a celebrated author, a mythical figure of rebellion, and along with Sandburg one of the last remaining ties to the glory days of the Chicago renaissance. Between Anderson and the young man he recognized as possessed of "extraordinary talent"[40] something of a father-son, mentor-pupil relationship quickly developed. Anderson introduced Hemingway to Sandburg, instructed him in his reading and about the fresh currents of the modernist movement, and read his manuscripts. Perhaps his most important contribution to Hemingway's development was simply allowing him to observe close-up the way the literary life was conducted. From Anderson, Hemingway learned among other things that a writer rigorously guarded his privacy, even setting up writing quarters apart from his wife; that he avoided the many traps of hack writing; that it was necessary to cultivate editors and publishers; that as a professional he was paid for his work. Under Anderson's guidance Hemingway's interest shifted from the popular fiction that had preoccupied him to serious literature, and for the first time he became aware of a native tradition in writing as against his Oak Park education that had emphasized British literature. Anderson spoke of Whitman and Twain, of Dreiser and Mencken and Van Wyck Brooks, of contemporary novels like Dell's *Moon-Calf* and *The Briary Bush*, of periodicals like *Poetry*, the *Little Review*, and the *Dial*.

During the period, if not before, Hemingway read with admiration

Anderson's stories in *Winesburg, Ohio*. At the end of his life in *A Moveable Feast* he would remember that he

> liked some of [Anderson's] short stories very much. They were simply written and sometimes beautifully written and he knew the people he was writing about and cared deeply for them.[41]

When he came to write his own first important book he would be influenced by Anderson's use of interconnected stories to create something of a novel's effect and his treatment of the development of a young man in the figure of George Willard. From the beginning of their association, however, Hemingway was put off by Anderson's mystical tendencies and the repetitive manner of his prose, qualities he would parody in *The Torrents of Spring*. But it had probably never been literary instruction he had sought from the older author so much as instruction in how to go about being a writer,[42] and here Anderson proved invaluable. Anderson's final gift to Hemingway was his enthusiasm for Paris as a place where a writer could live well and cheaply and as a vantage point for gaining perspective on America in his stories. Just back from the city himself (where he had happily found *Winesburg* displayed prominently in the window of Shakespeare and Company, Sylvia Beach's lending library and bookstore), Anderson was willing to provide letters of introduction that would open the way to the expatriate literary community that included Gertrude Stein, Pound, and Joyce. When the Toronto newspaper followed with the offer of a position as a roving feature correspondent based in Paris, Hemingway took Anderson's advice and left Chicago for the City of Lights with his new wife, Hadley. It was the beginning of his career as a serious writer.

In those days young writers from everywhere were descending upon Paris, but to Ford Madox Ford most of them seemed to have come from the American Midwest. "Young America from the limitless prairies leapt, released, on Paris," he would note. "They stampeded with the madness of colts when you let down the sliprails between dried pasture and green."[43] Among the Midwestern writers soon included in Hemingway's circle of expatriate acquaintances were Louis Bromfield, Josephine Herbst, and Robert McAlmon together with Fitzgerald and Wescott. Even before his sudden rise to fame Hemingway's literary dislikes were vivid and absolute; for Fitzgerald he had strong, if wary, admiration, but for the Wisconsin writer he had nothing but scorn. In a scene in *The Sun Also Rises* his satiric fire was directed to Wescott's affected British accent and his homosexuality. "He was from New York by way of Chicago," Jake Barnes explains about Roger Prentiss (the surname changed from Prescott at the insistence of Maxwell Perkins, Hemingway's editor at Scribner's, because of the resemblance to Wescott), "and was a rising new novelist. He had some sort of an English accent. I asked him to have a drink."

> "Thanks so much," he said, "I've just had one."
> "Have another."

"Thanks, I will then."

We got the daughter of the house over and each had a *fine à l'eau.*

"You're from Kansas City, they tell me," he said.

"Yes."

"Do you find Paris amusing?"

"Yes."

"Really?"

I was a little drunk. Not drunk in any positive sense but just enough to be careless.

"For God's sake," I said, "yes. Don't you?"

"Oh, how charmingly you get angry," he said. "I wish I had that faculty."[44]

Beneath the personal disdain was a literary argument. In a letter Hemingway informed Bromfield that Wescott's "stuff was fundamentally unsound" and a "literary fake."[45] As against Wescott's lyric and literary manner, a prose style that sought rhetorical effect, Hemingway was discovering in Paris a fresh language of deceptive simplicity, one that created poetry without poetic language. And there was a difference in material. Hemingway was writing about Europe and the experience of the war and its aftermath while Wescott was turned back upon Wisconsin and family history. (In a letter to Perkins, Fitzgerald found Wescott's *The Apple of the Eye* "pretty much the old stuff" previously treated by Cather, Anderson, and Suckow, and he added his doubt about the actual existence of an American "peasantry": "I suspect tragedy in the American countryside because all the people capable of it move to the big towns at twenty. All the rest is pathos.")[46] After the appearance of *The Sun Also Rises* and the story collection that followed, *Men Without Women*, Hemingway would remark that in Oak Park where he was considered an embittered realist his mother probably wished he were Wescott or some highly respectable Fairy Prince with an English accent and a taste for grandmothers.[47] Nonetheless, Hemingway's first book, *Three Stories & Ten Poems*, published in Paris in 1923 by McAlmon, a writer born in Kansas and brought up in South Dakota and Minnesota and possessed of a well-to-do wife, contained a story with a Midwestern locale, "Up in Michigan."[48] And his first important book, *In Our Time* in 1925, contained several stories, eventually among his most celebrated, in which he went back in memory to the wounds of family experience and the first of his beloved landscapes. "I've written a number of stories," he would write his father in an attempt to describe the book, "about the Michigan country—the country is always true—what happens in the stories is fiction."[49]

7

"Give us peace in our time, O Lord," the Book of Common Prayer asks, but Hemingway's use of its language in the title of the collection is only ironic. Nick Adams, the central figure in most of the stories, encounters a world in which only violence reigns. In "Indian Camp," Doctor Adams takes his young son with him on a mission across the lake to deliver a baby at an Indian shanty, using the occasion to jauntily instruct the boy on the hard ways of the world. It turns out that the delivery is a Caesarean section performed with a jack-knife and without anaesthetic, the incision sewn with fishing leader. Nick pleads with his father to give the woman something to stop her screaming, but the father's awareness of the effect on the boy comes only with the discovery that the woman's husband, unable to bear the screams, has slit his throat with a razor in an upper bunk of the shanty. What follows is a scene in which father and son row back across the lake, all the father's exhilaration now gone, and a dialogue on the mysteries of self-inflicted death made all the more haunting by the present-day reader's awareness of the suicides of both of the real-life counterparts:

"Why did he kill himself, Daddy?"
"I don't know, Nick. He couldn't stand things, I guess."
"Do many men kill themselves, Daddy?"
"Not very many, Nick."
"Do many women?"
"Hardly ever."
"Don't they ever?"
"Oh, yes. They do sometimes."

The story ends with images of natural serenity—the sun rising over the hills, a bass jumping, Nick trailing his hand in the water and finding it warm—and a resulting sense of security that, with his father in the stern of the boat rowing, causes Nick to feel "quite sure that he would never die."[50] A masterpiece of compression and suggestion, the story introduces Nick to the certain violence of life and the sobering inability of the father—by implication, anyone—to shield him from it. The calm of the ending only heightens the realization that Nick *will* die, and perhaps die in the agony of violence.

The subsequent stories in *In Our Time* add to Nick's education in less dramatic ways. In "The Doctor and the Doctor's Wife"—among the flood of stories (along with "Indian Camp" and "Cross-Country Snow") coming from Midwesterners that Ford chose to print in the *Transatlantic Review*—the violence is emotional but no less devastating. Once again Doctor Adams fails in his son's estimation. When an Indian half-breed comes to the family cottage to cut up logs and accuses him of stealing them, Doctor Adams threatens him only to back down in humiliating defeat. When he tells his wife what has happened, explaining that the Indian has picked a quarrel because he owes money for medical service, she insists he must be wrong. Again he backs down, all the while ritualistically cleaning a shotgun in an effort to gain control of himself. In a final scene that parallels the ending of "Indian Camp" the Doctor and young Nick go off into the woods in search of black squirrels, nature again providing a serene setting but the implied estrangement between father and son only deepened.

In "The End of Something" an older Nick abruptly breaks up with his sweetheart, and in "The Three-Day Blow" the parting is discussed with a friend over whiskey during the first storm of the fall, Nick reserving for his own thoughts the ambiguous pain the girl's loss causes. In "The Battler" Nick is riding the rails near Mancelona, presumably intending to leave Michigan behind, when a brakeman slams him off the freight and he falls in with a punchdrunk former fighter and his black companion, the two bumming around the country since their release from prison. When the fighter turns violently upon Nick without explanation, the companion coolly saps him with a blackjack and advises Nick that it would be wise to leave before the fighter awakens. When Nick reappears in the north country in "Big Two-Hearted River," the final story in the collection, the physical violence of "The Battler" has been experienced in actual warfare as seen in two of the prose miniatures that Hemingway alternated with the stories, a device that served to reinforce the ironic meaning of the book's title and knit together the stories into something of the feeling of a novel. But the story itself, as Hemingway told Gertrude Stein when he finished writing it, is one in which "nothing happens."[51] There is only a minutely detailed account of camping and fishing, the story ending with Nick's decision not to fish in a swampy part of the river where big fish could be hooked but not landed and where fishing consequently was a "tragic adventure." "There were," he concludes, "plenty of days coming when he could fish the swamp."[52]

Beneath the story's bland surface a good deal is happening in the reader's sense of the inner drama of a troubled young man. Nick brings to the solitary camping trip the experience of the Great War—in the context of the stories of *In Our Time*, the battlefield experience and resulting mental and spiritual fallout attributed to Krebs in "Soldier's Home," or his own war experience as revealed in such later Nick Adams stories as "Now I Lay Me" and "A Way You'll Never Be." In *A Moveable Feast* Hemingway gave weight to the view of Nick as a casualty of war with the remark that the story was about "coming back from the war but there was no mention of the war in it."[53] One can equally attribute Nick's unease to the family experience related in "Indian Camp" and "The Doctor and the Doctor's Wife." The actual camping trip upon which the story was based had followed not only Hemingway's return from the war in Italy but his flight from family life in Oak Park and at Walloon Lake. Nonetheless, in "Big Two-Hearted River" there are no references to battlefield trauma nor domestic stress; all the reader knows with certainty about Nick's inner state is that when he arrives on the river he feels a vast sense of release: "He felt he had left everything behind, the need for thinking, the need to write, other needs. It was all back of him" (179). The first sight of trout in the stream transports him to an earlier and happier time, causing him to feel "all the old feeling" (178). When, suddenly, his "mind was starting to work" he is able to "choke it" because he is tired and concentrate wholly on the camping experience (191). What exactly Nick has put behind him and why he resists thinking and what his other needs might be is left unexplained. The reader senses acutely Nick's inner tension as revealed in the methodical attention to the details of camping and fishing, but Nick himself as he is seen within the boundaries of the story remains a mystery.[54]

In the first story in *In Our Time* Nick trails his hand in a lake and experiences a momentary return to earlier innocence; in the last he wades a stream and is momentarily reconnected to his old feelings. In both stories tension remains—the aftermath of Nick's first confrontation with violence in one, his unexplored inner unease in the other. Nothing is permanently altered. Still, the Michigan landscape offers shelter and stability, a realm of deep and satisfying comfort, however fleeting. Just as Nick Carraway responds to Gatsby's death by retreating to a conception of the Midwest as the warm center of the world, so too Nick Adams in "Big Two-Hearted River" returns to it as the "good place" where inside his tent he has the feeling of "home." In the good place "nothing could touch him":

> Inside the tent the light came through the brown canvas. It smelled pleasantly of canvas. Already there was something mysterious and homelike. Nick was happy as he crawled inside the tent. He had not been unhappy all day. This was different though. Now things were done. There had been this to do. Now it was done. . . . He had made his camp. He was settled. Nothing could touch him. It was a good place to camp. He was there, in the good place. He was in his home where he had made it. Now he was hungry. (186–87)

8

After he left Chicago for Paris in 1921 Hemingway made only two brief return journeys to northern Michigan. His mother eventually gave him Windemere Cottage as his inheritance, hoping he and his sons would use it in summers, but even though he dutifully paid taxes on the property he had nothing more to do with it. In 1946, in one of her last letters to him, his mother told him of the cottage's sad condition:

> I walked over to Windemere, and thought of all the happy days we spent there. I grieved to realize that you cared nothing for the place and had never been even to see it in the past eleven years. . . . For some time it was broken into almost every winter by marauders. . . . the mice have gnawed holes into the house . . . the front porch floor and roof are fast disappearing. The steps . . . have rotted away. The neighbors call it the haunted house. . . . The yard is littered with broken down trees. . . . The woodshed and boathouse have lost their roofs.[55]

But if the cottage could be put behind him so completely, the life it had once contained could not. Shortly after his mother's death in 1951 Hemingway began writing a long work about Nick Adams based on an incident that had happened in northern Michigan at about the time of his sixteenth birthday in the summer of 1915. After Hemingway illegally shot a blue heron he went into hiding from the local game wardens at an uncle's house, following his mother's instructions, before eventually pleading guilty and paying a fine. In "The Last Good Country," the title of the lengthy work published in an edited version as an unfinished story after his death, the game violation is transformed into the killing of a deer out of season, his mother cooperates with the authorities, and the flight in the company of his tomboyish sister, Littless, is to a last remaining area of virgin timber—the setting of the story's title. Here they set up camp near a spring where Nick has camped before, using the very firestones he has used before.

> "It's a very old place," Nick said. "The firestones are Indian."
> "How did you come to it straight through the woods with no trail and no blazes?"
> "Didn't you see the direction sticks on the three ridges?"
> "No."
> "I'll show them to you sometime."
> "Are they yours?"
> "No. They're from the old days."
> "Why didn't you show them to me?"
> "I don't know," Nick said. "I was showing off I guess."
> "Nickie, they'll never find us here."
> "I hope not," Nick said."[56]

The old place in the woods provides the same magic setting as Big Two-Hearted River. Here Nick's woodland skills offer self-sufficiency, and here there is shelter from external pursuit just as on the river he can quell internal demons. It has been suggested that Hemingway meant the work as a north woods *Huckleberry Finn*, with Nick the picaresque hero, Littless the ever-faithful companion, and the journey in nature a flight from the constraints both of law and family life.[57] The story, however, opens up another concern, that of sexual crosscurrents between Nick and his little sister, and perhaps this contributed to Hemingway's inability to bring it to a conclusion. He worked on the manuscript, at any event, over the course of a decade, but the published story is left with no resolution in sight. In the context of Midwestern writing, the work's unfinished state seems fitting. For Hemingway in middle age a northern Michigan of memory could still function as the warm center of the world—a place of refuge, the last good country. But the competing impulse since his departure for Paris at the beginning of the twenties had been to leave the Midwest behind as the ragged edge of the universe. It was part of a world—with a hypocritical, Victorian Oak Park as its true center—that had vanished as completely as certain high-flown words for the disillusioned hollow man of *A Farewell to Arms*, Frederick Henry, who "had seen nothing sacred, and the things that were glorious had no glory and the sacrifices were like the stockyards at Chicago if nothing was done with the meat except to bury it."[58] The Midwest as a place and a way of life could not hold Hemingway's imagination in the central way it did those of his older Midwestern contemporaries, Anderson and Cather and Lewis. Their fictional territory simply could never to the same extent be his—or his generation's. When the older writers had the temerity to venture into his preserve, the personal wasteland of the modern world, Hemingway was quick to point out their shortcomings—as he did, for example, when he told Edmund Wilson that Cather's war scenes in *One of Ours* had been lifted from *Birth of a Nation*: "I identified episode after episode, Catherized. Poor woman she had to get her war experience somewhere."[59]

To the end of his life Hemingway retained his deep responsiveness to the physical landscape, that of the Midwest included. Three years before his death he took a long and happy automobile trip from Key West to Ketchum, Idaho, during which he made a point of driving west from Chicago so his wife, Mary, as he wrote in a letter, could see "the beautiful part of Northern Illinois which I hadn't seen since used to go prairie chicken hunting with my father with a wagon and two pair of dogs."[60] And in a letter written less than a month before his death from Rochester, Minnesota, where he was hospitalized during treatment at the Mayo Clinic, he told a young boy about the attractive landscape of the upper reaches of the Mississippi Valley:

> The country is beautiful around here and I've had a chance to see some wonderful country along the Mississippi where they used to drive the logs in the old lumbering days and the trails where the pioneers came north. Saw some good bass jump in the river. I never knew anything about the upper Mississippi before and it is really a very beautiful country and there are plenty of pheasants and ducks in the fall.[61]

All the same, his literary country at the end of his life was still located elsewhere. His last efforts were devoted to an old enthusiasm for Spain and bullfighting in *The Dangerous Summer* and to his highly selective memories of starting out as a writer in Paris in the twenties in *A Moveable Feast*. In the latter work he recalled writing "The Three-Day Blow" in a café on the Place St.-Michel and making it a "wild, cold, blowing day" in the story since it was that sort of day in Paris. He said he had made the discovery that away from Michigan he could write about it better ("That was called transplanting yourself, I thought, and it could be as necessary with people as with other sorts of growing things"),[62] but the detachment he had in mind was not only a matter of physical separation. In Paris he found the psychic distance that allowed him to free himself from his Midwestern background. He was never entirely free; in Paris he wrote memorably about that background, and a Midwestern boyhood would remain with him forever. But in Paris in the twenties other places and other experiences claimed an imagination turned to the enormous disillusionment and awakening of the time.

In "Fathers and Sons," a Nick Adams story that appeared in a 1933 collection, *Winner Take Nothing*, a mature Nick of thirty-eight who is now a father himself recalls the Midwestern woodland life he had once shared with his father. Always in the early spring of the year or in the fall the memory of his father comes back to him. The memory is powerful, and Hemingway captures it in marvelously evocative images. Yet the story reveals as well the unbridgeable distance between Nick and his father—the fact that they had lived not only in different places but in different psychological and moral terrain. "The towns he lived in," Nick reflects, "were not towns his father knew. After he was fifteen he had shared nothing with him."[63] The lines provide an epitaph of sorts for the Midwestern literary ascendancy. With the end of the twenties and the early work of Hemingway, perhaps the most gifted and influential writer of all from out of the Midwest, the fragile sense of alikeness that had sustained serious Midwestern writing was gone. For the time being at least the territory ahead was in another country.

Postscript

In his Nobel Prize address Sinclair Lewis had praise for the new young American writers who were "most of them living now in Paris" and there forging a literature that "refused to be genteel and traditional and dull."[1] But with the decade of the thirties the exiles would begin the return journey from Paris, and for many of them the period would be marked by the literary rediscovery of America. The poet from St. Louis, T. S. Eliot, who had indelibly charted the wasteland of the postwar world would also provide a text in "Little Gidding" for the journey back: "And the end of our exploring / Will be to arrive where we started / And know the place for the first time."[2] Eventually, despite the erosion of regional distinctions in every part of the country, a body of work would accumulate that could again be identified under at least a subheading as Midwestern literature. Chicago reappeared as a compelling subject in work by Richard Wright, Willard Motley, James T. Farrell, Nelson Algren, and Saul Bellow. The Midwest of farms and towns was reimagined by, among others, Wright Morris, Robert Bly, J. F. Powers, William Maxwell, R. V. Cassill, James Purdy, Jim Harrison, Curtis Harnack, Louise Erdrich, Larry Woiwode, Douglas Unger, Will Weaver, Ron Hansen, Jon Hassler, Patricia Hampl, Jonis Agee. Writers from outside the region offered work solidly rooted in Midwestern experience—Philip Roth's novel *When She Was Good* (1967), for example, and works of literary nonfiction such as Truman Capote's *In Cold Blood* (1965) and C. D. B. Bryan's *Friendly Fire* (1976).

The old ambivalence at the heart of literary treatments of the Midwest seemed as evident as ever. There was the same swinging back and forth, as Lewis remarked in his address about American writing as a whole, "from optimism to pessimism and back" that is the "fate of any one who writes or speaks of anything in America—the most contradictory, the most depressing, the most stirring, of any land in the world today."[3] The Midwest still offered itself as the warm center of the world and the ragged edge of the universe. William Gass's story "In the Heart of the Heart of the Country" ends with the poet-narrator, in exile from love in a "small town fastened to a field in Indiana," watching the snow fall on main street on an evening in Christmas week. The scene is as bleak and touched with as haunting a sense of loss as any of Anderson's tales of the Midwestern grotesque:

The windows of the stores have been bedizened. Shamelessly they beckon. But I am alone, leaning against a pole—no . . . there is no one in sight. They're all at home, perhaps by their instruments, tuning in on their evenings, and like Ramona, tirelessly playing and replaying themselves. There's a speaker perched in the [water] tower, and through the boughs of falling snow and over the vacant streets, it drapes the twisted and metallic strains of a tune that can barely be distinguished—yes, I believe it's one of the jolly ones, it's "Joy to the World." There's no one to hear the music but myself, and though I'm listening, I'm no longer certain. Perhaps the record's playing something else.

In the country fastness life is "vacant and barren and loveless"—a world in which "everything is gray, and everyone is out of luck who lives here." The poet-narrator is merciless in his litany of denunciation. Still, his mood shifts, perceptions change. The "vital data" he offers about the town allows an autumn glimpse of an alternative world in the heart of the heart of the country:

> The shade is ample, the grass is good, the sky a glorious fall violet; the apple trees are heavy and red, the roads are calm and empty; corn has sifted from the chains of tractored wagons to speckle the streets with gold and with the russet fragments of the cob, and a man would be a fool who wanted, blessed with this, to live anywhere else in the world.[4]

In *We Have All Gone Away* (1973), Curtis Harnack's bittersweet memoir of growing up on an Iowa farm, rural life is evoked in Cather-like tones as a haven of sanity and rich nourishment:

> The sickly, pale natural color of butter would change in spring when the Holsteins found new, succulent grass. They gave thanks to the season's advent in their deep-gold butter. We were never far from the pleasure a plant took in growing, an animal in living. At night I'd stare heavenward at the curds of stars called the Milky Way. In a galaxy of such infinite milkiness, we were alive and attentive here at the nourishing breast of the world.

Yet for all its deep comforts, the farm is never sufficient. Like Jim Burden and Lena Lingard and Tiny Soderball, Harnack and his brothers and sisters are meant to leave it behind for different lives in a larger and more complicated world. Farm life is a stepping-stone on an outward journey, one they will never retrace. The memoir ends with the author's recollection of yet another Midwestern leave-taking:

> The land here might nourish our bodies, build stamina and spirit, but in our progress through the years, it too would have to be left behind for what it could never do for us. The mindlessness of Nature would erode our ambitions to hurl ourselves into life and make our marks. Only in a man-made environment—the city—could one forget the humdrum futility of the years in passage. The illusion that there was a lot to *do* in life besides merely *being* in life could only be sustained in an urban setting. In this way our generation, using the mulched dead matter of

agrarian life like projectile fuel for our thrust into the future, became part of that enormous vitality springing out of rural America.[5]

Whether works such as these—and no doubt many more that might be mentioned—have brought renewed life, if not a renewed ascendancy, to Midwestern literature in a postmodernist era I leave as a question. Is it no longer true, as Allen Tate maintained in reference to stories and novels in a 1959 essay, that "with the exception of Fitzgerald and Hemingway, the region north of the Potomac and Ohio Rivers has become the stepsister of American fiction?"[6] What seems evident, at any event, is that the Midwest as a place is more than ever in danger of vanishing completely, erased as a fact by more pragmatic ways of thinking about regional alignment within the country or absorbed into a featureless mass-media culture national in scope. Yet at the same time the idea of the Midwest seems stubbornly with us. Earnest nonfiction books devoted to the region still appear, their titles suggesting the pursuit of an elusive but still absorbing concept—Richard Rhodes's *The Inland Ground: An Evocation of the American Middle West* (1970), for example, or a collection of personal responses to the region edited by Michael Martone called *A Place of Sense: Essays in Search of the Midwest* (1988). State anthologies of prose and poetry abound—*New Territory* (1990), for one, a collection of short fiction by Indiana writers. An angry populist film like *Country* (1984) dramatizes the enduring plight of farmers caught between commercial necessity and the garden myth of agrarian perfection. A sensitive recollection of Michigan farm life, Howard Kohn's *The Last Farmer: An American Memoir* (1988), captures the tangle of feelings associated with leaving the land, as does Harnack's book and Richard Critchfield's portrait of his rural North Dakota family in *Those Days: An American Album* (1986). Richard Rhodes's *Farm: A Year in the Life of an American Farmer* (1989), on the other hand, reveals the continuing vitality of country life for those who remain behind on the land. In a collection of essays, *Letters from the Country* (1981), Carol Bly probes the inner and outer lives of those who remain behind in a Minnesota town more than a half-century after Gopher Prairie has passed into the national imagination. From the restless road journey recounted in *Blue Highways* William Least Heat-Moon turns in *Prairy Erth* (1991) to a sympathetic "deep map" investigation of a single Kansas county located near the geographic center of the contiguous states.

At the end of *The Great Gatsby*, the East now distorted for him following Gatsby's murder, Nick Carraway decides that the survivors—he and Jordan Baker and Tom and Daisy Buchanan—are all Westerners and for that reason possessed of "some deficiency in common which made us subtly unadaptable to Eastern life." How the label of Westerner—which for Nick means Midwesterner—fits each member of this uneasy grouping he does not explain, nor does it matter. For Nick it is wholly clear. The Midwest exists, and at this moment in the story it holds out to him an inviting vision as the warm center of the world, a place of order to set against his disillusioned experience of the East. The power of that inviting vision is irresistible, so overwhelming as to bear Nick back to it despite his recognition that it exists only in the past, "already behind him."

"I see now," he says, "that this has been a story of the West, after all. . . . " It really has not been, at least not in any central sense. But as Nick says later on, "that's no matter"[7]: it *seems* to be a story in which place, the West in its Midwestern dress, has a significant bearing on character and event, on ongoing life. That sort of story continues to exercise a hold on the mind and the imagination, and there seems no reason—whatever the fate of the Midwest of fact—to expect anything less in the future. The story of the West goes on.

Notes

1. Warm Center, Ragged Edge

1. Flannery O'Connor, *Mystery and Manners* (New York: Noonday Press, 1970), 58.

2. Allen Tate, "The New Provincialism," *Essays of Four Decades* (Chicago: Swallow, 1968), 536, 545.

3. John T. Frederick, Introduction to *Out of the Midwest*, ed. John T. Frederick (New York: McGraw-Hill, 1944), xv.

4. Saul Bellow, "Chicago and American Culture," *Chicago Guide*, 22 (May 1973), 87.

5. Ibid., 84.

6. Alfred Kazin, *On Native Grounds* (New York: Harcourt, Brace and World, 1942), 314.

7. F. O. Matthiessen, *American Renaissance* (New York: Oxford University Press, 1941), vii.

8. Allen Tate, "A Southern Mode of the Imagination," *Essays of Four Decades*, 591.

9. Mark Twain, *Life on the Mississippi, Mississippi Writings* (New York: Library of America, 1982), 565.

10. For modest efforts in this direction see Thomas T. McAvoy, "What Is the Midwestern Mind?", *The Midwest: Myth or Reality?*, ed. Thomas T. McAvoy (Notre Dame, IN: University of Notre Dame Press, 1961), 53–72, and David D. Anderson, "Notes toward a Definition of the Mind of the Midwest," *MidAmerica 3* (East Lansing, MI: Center for the Study of Midwestern Literature and Culture, 1976), 7–16.

11. Max Lerner, *America as a Civilization* (New York: Simon and Schuster, 1957), 189.

12. This view is developed in Andrew R. L. Cayton and Peter S. Onuf, *The Midwest and the Nation* (Bloomington: Indiana University Press, 1990).

13. Sherwood Anderson, *Sherwood Anderson's Memoirs: A Critical Edition*, ed. Ray Lewis White (Chapel Hill: University of North Carolina Press, 1969), 241–42.

14. Richard Ford, *The Sportswriter* (New York: Vintage Books, 1986), 7.

15. Jonathan Raban, *Old Glory: An American Voyage* (New York: Simon and Schuster, 1981), 194.

16. Diane Johnson, "The Heart of the Heart of the Country," *New York Review of Books*, November 19, 1981, 12.

17. Glenway Wescott, "Good-Bye Wisconsin," *Good-Bye Wisconsin* (New York: Harper and Brothers, 1928), 39.

18. For a discussion of the boundaries of the Midwest from a geographer's point of view and an account of the evolution of the name "Middle West" see James R. Shortridge, *The Middle West, Its Meaning in American Culture* (Lawrence: University Press of Kansas, 1989), especially chapters 1 and 2.

19. William H. Gass, "In the Heart of the Heart of the Country," *In the Heart of the Heart of the Country and Other Stories* (New York: Perennial Library, 1969), 186.

20. Richard Gray, *Writing the South: Ideas of an American Region* (New York: Cambridge University Press, 1986), xi.

21. Sherwood Anderson, *Sherwood Anderson's Memoirs*, 337. In the original edition of Anderson's memoirs, put together and considerably revised by Paul Rosenfeld and

published by Harcourt, Brace in 1942, the line appears (page 241) as "It was the time in which something blossomed in Chicago and the Middle West."

22. F. Scott Fitzgerald, *The Great Gatsby* (New York: Scribner's, 1925), 177.

23. Ford Madox Ford, *It Was the Nightingale* (New York: Octagon Books, 1975), 338.

24. H. L. Mencken, "The Literary Capital of the United States," *Nation* [London], 27 (April 17, 1920), 92. Abraham Cahan and James Branch Cabell were the two exceptions.

25. Ruth Suckow, "Middle Western Literature," *English Journal*, 21 (March 1932), 176.

26. I follow here Henry Nash Smith's discussion of the development of Western literature in *Virgin Land: The American West as Symbol and Myth* (Cambridge, MA: Harvard University Press, 1970), 211–49.

27. Frank Norris, "The Literature of the West," *Novels and Essays* (New York: Library of America, 1986), 1178, 1176.

28. William T. Coggeshall, ed., *The Poets and Poetry of the West* (Columbus, OH: Follett, Foster and Company, 1860), v.

29. John Finley, "To Indiana," *The Poets and Poetry of the West*, 84.

30. Bernard Duffey, for example, makes this point in *The Chicago Renaissance in American Letters* (East Lansing: Michigan State College Press, 1954), 91–92.

31. See, for example, John T. Frederick's Introduction to *Out of the Midwest*, xv–xviii, and John T. Flanagan, "A Soil for the Seeds of Literature," in *The Heritage of the Middle West*, ed. John J. Murray (Norman: University of Oklahoma Press, 1958), 198–233.

32. Warner Berthoff, *The Ferment of Realism* (New York: Cambridge University Press, 1981), x.

33. That sensibility is neatly captured in Patricia Hampl's *Spillville* (Minneapolis: Milkweed Editions, 1987), 40: "Saying a place is flat is another way of pretending it's simpler than it is. Nebraska is flat, we say. And Kansas is flat. North and South Dakota, and Iowa—flat, flat, flat. Yet here we are, Iowa . . . outside of Spillville, and it's all up and down, dips and curves."

34. James Bryce, *The American Commonwealth*, vol. 2, 2nd rev. ed. (London: Macmillan, 1890), 684–85.

35. William Faulkner, "Sherwood Anderson: An Appreciation," *Atlantic*, 191 (June 1953), 27.

36. The tour is described in Harrison T. Meserole, "The Dean in Person: Howells' Lecture Tour," *Western Humanities Review*, 10 (Autumn 1956), 337–47.

37. The lecture was published for the first time in William M. Gibson, ed., *Howells and James: A Double Billing* (New York: New York Public Library, 1958), 15, 21.

38. Quoted in Donald Pizer, *Hamlin Garland's Early Work and Career* (Berkeley: University of California Press, 1960), 28.

39. Frank Norris, "A Plea for Romantic Fiction," *Novels and Essays*, 1166.

40. John Updike, "Howells as Anti-Novelist," *New Yorker*, July 13, 1987, 78–88.

41. Theodore Dreiser, "Indiana: Her Soil and Light," *Nation*, 117 (October 3, 1923), 348–49.

42. Ford Madox Ford, *It Was the Nightingale*, 339.

43. John Riddell, "J. Riddell Memorial Award Short Best Stories," *Vanity Fair*, 32 (April 1929), 95.

44. Theodore Dreiser, *A Hoosier Holiday* (New York: John Lane, 1916), 18.

45. Glenway Wescott, *Good-Bye Wisconsin*, 39.

46. Flannery O'Connor, *Mystery and Manners*, 59.

47. Jay Martin makes this point about American regional writing in the period 1880–1900 in *Harvests of Change: American Literature, 1865–1914* (Englewood Cliffs, NJ: Prentice-Hall, 1967), 87–88.

48. Quoted in Hermione Lee, *Willa Cather: Double Lives* (New York: Pantheon, 1989), 13.

49. Willa Cather, *A Lost Lady, Later Novels* (New York: Library of America, 1990), 58–59.

50. F. Scott Fitzgerald, *The Great Gatsby*, 182.

51. Irving Howe makes this point about what he calls the regionalism of urban American Jewish writers in *World of Our Fathers* (New York: Simon and Schuster, 1976), 586.

52. The central account of the garden myth is in Book 3, "The Garden of the World," of *Virgin Land*. See also the carefully phrased examination of the myth in Richard Hofstadter's chapter on "The Agrarian Myth and Commercial Realities" in *The Age of Reform* (New York: Knopf, 1959), 23–59. Alan Trachtenberg provides a concise summary of Smith's views in *The Incorporation of America* (New York: Hill and Wang, 1982), 20–22.

53. Herbert Quick, *Vandemark's Folly* (Indianapolis: Bobbs-Merrill, 1922), 112–13.

54. I follow here the discussion of agricultural history in the opening chapter of Richard Hofstadter, *The Age of Reform*. For similar views drawn from the experience of Iowa see Ray Allen Billington, "The Garden of the World: Fact and Fiction," in *The Heritage of the Middle West*, 27–53. A full account of agricultural development in the nineteenth century in the central Midwest is in Allan G. Bogue, *From Prairie to Corn Belt* (Chicago: University of Chicago Press, 1963).

55. The remark appears in a brief discussion of Midwestern literature in the *Columbia Literary History of the United States*, ed. Emory Elliott and others (New York: Columbia University Press, 1988), 772–77. Cox maintains (p. 774) that "what characterizes the dominant literature from the Midwest in this century [the twentieth] is its essential noninterest in the land, as if writers fully comprehended how much the land had become a means of production rather than a realm of freedom." As I try to show, writers of the Midwestern ascendancy had a more complex response to the cultivated landscape than the passage indicates, passionate awareness combined with indifference, affirmation with denial.

56. Alexis de Tocqueville, *Democracy in America*, ed. Phillips Bradley, vol. 2 (New York: Knopf, 1953), 157.

57. John Mack Faragher, *Sugar Creek: Life on the Illinois Prairie* (New Haven: Yale University Press, 1986), 237.

58. Mark Twain, *Life on the Mississippi*, 561.

59. Edgar Lee Masters, *The Sangamon* (New York: Farrar and Rinehart, 1942), 87.

60. Henry Nash Smith, *Virgin Land*, 193.

61. F. Scott Fitzgerald, "The Ice Palace," *The Short Stories of F. Scott Fitzgerald*, ed. Matthew J. Bruccoli (New York: Scribner's, 1989), 55.

62. F. Scott Fitzgerald, *The Great Gatsby*, 3 (subsequent page references given in the text).

63. Gore Vidal, "Dawn Powell, the American Writer," *New York Review of Books*, November 5, 1987, 53.

2. Rude Despair

1. The remark is quoted in Donald Pizer, *Hamlin Garland's Early Work and Career*, 29.

2. Hamlin Garland, *Roadside Meetings* (New York: Macmillan, 1930), 113. Although they are not mentioned here, Garland had already made some fledgling attempts at short fiction.

3. The letter, dated July 13, 1886, is quoted in Donald Pizer, *Hamlin Garland's Early Work and Career*, 26.

4. Edward Eggleston, *The Hoosier School-Master* (Bloomington: Indiana University Press, 1984), 122, 5. The edition is a reprint of the original 1871 edition published by Orange, Judd, and Co. Subsequent page references are given in the text.

5. Frank Norris, "The Great American Novelist," *Novels and Essays*, 1181.

6. Daniel H. Borus, *Writing Realism: Howells, James, and Norris and the Mass Market* (Chapel Hill: University of North Carolina Press, 1989), 15.

7. For details of Eggleston's life I follow William Peirce Randel, *Edward Eggleston* (New York: King's Crown Press, 1946).

8. Quoted in William Peirce Randel, *Edward Eggleston*, 127.

9. Alice Cary's work is examined in Annette Kolodny, *The Land before Her: Fantasy and Experience of the American Frontiers, 1630–1860* (Chapel Hill: University of North Carolina Press, 1984), 178–99.

10. Bernard Duffey, *The Chicago Renaissance in American Letters*, 93.

11. Hamlin Garland, *My Friendly Contemporaries* (New York: Macmillan, 1923), 131.

12. Joseph Kirkland, *Zury: The Meanest Man in Spring County* (Urbana: University of Illinois Press, 1956), 1. The edition is a reprint of the original 1887 edition published by Houghton, Mifflin. Subsequent page references are given in the text.

13. Caroline Kirkland's work is examined in Annette Kolodny, *The Land before Her*, 131–58.

14. Quoted in Clyde E. Henson, *Joseph Kirkland* (New York: Twayne, 1962), 87. I follow this work for details of Kirkland's life.

15. Quoted in Clyde E. Henson, *Joseph Kirkland*, 97.

16. Richard Hofstadter, *The Age of Reform*, 40, 43.

17. Joseph Kirkland, *The McVeys: An Episode* (Boston: Houghton, Mifflin, 1888), 1.

18. Quoted in Hamlin Garland, *Roadside Meetings*, 111.

19. John William Ward makes this point in a perceptive afterword to a paperback edition of the novel (Signet, 1964). For details of Howe's life I draw on this work and on introductions to paperback editions by Sylvia E. Bowman (College and University Press, 1962) and Brom Weber (Holt, Rinehart, and Winston, 1964) and on S. J. Sackett, *E. W. Howe* (New York: Twayne, 1972).

20. Twain's letter and Howells's review are reprinted in the Signet edition of the novel, pages 310–15.

21. E. W. Howe, *The Story of a Country Town* (Boston: James R. Osgood and Company, 1884), 1 (subsequent page references given in the text).

22. William Dean Howells, "Open Letter," Signet edition of *The Story of a Country Town*, 314.

23. Garland, *Roadside Meetings*, 94.

24. Hamlin Garland, "Up the Coule," *Main-Travelled Roads* (Boston: Arena Publishing Company, 1891), 130.

25. Hamlin Garland, *A Son of the Middle Border* (New York: Macmillan, 1917), 365, 367–68.

26. Quoted in Donald Pizer, *Hamlin Garland's Early Work and Career*, 68. For details of Garland's life I follow this work and Jean Holloway, *Hamlin Garland: A Biography* (Austin: University of Texas Press, 1956), as well as Garland's autobiographical works.

27. Hamlin Garland, *A Son of the Middle Border*, 419.

28. William Dean Howells, "Editor's Study," *Critical Essays on Hamlin Garland*, ed. James Nagel (Boston: G. K. Hall, 1982), 35. Published originally in *Harper's Weekly*, 83 (September 1891), 639–40.

29. Hamlin Garland, *A Son of the Middle Border*, 418.

30. Hamlin Garland, *A Daughter of the Middle Border* (New York: Macmillan, 1921), 28.

31. The remark appears in Thomas A. Bledsoe's introduction to a paperback edition of *Main-Travelled Roads* (New York: Holt, Rinehart and Winston, 1965), ix.

32. Larzer Ziff develops this view of the Midwestern imagination and Garland's embodiment of it in *The American 1890s* (New York: Viking, 1966), 73–92, 93–108.

33. Quoted in Warner Berthoff, *The Ferment of Realism*, 136.

34. William Dean Howells, "Editor's Study," 35.

35. Hamlin Garland, "Under the Lion's Paw," *Main-Travelled Roads*, 217 (subsequent page references given in the text). The six stories in the original edition of the book are "A Branch Road," "Up the Coule," "Among the Corn Rows," "The Return of a Private," "Under the Lion's Paw," and "Mrs. Ripley's Trip."

36. The point is elaborated in Donald Pizer, *Hamlin Garland's Early Work and Career*, 54–58.

37. Hamlin Garland, "A Day's Pleasure," *Main-Travelled Roads* (New York: Harper and Brothers, 1899), 257–58, 259.

38. Hamlin Garland, "God's Ravens," *Main-Travelled Roads* (1899 edition), 318, 322.

39. Hamlin Garland, *A Son of the Middle Border*, 463.

40. William Dean Howells, "Editor's Study," 35.

41. Donald Pizer, Introduction to *Main-Travelled Roads* (Columbus, OH: Merrill Publishing Company, 1970), xv. This essay, drawing on Pizer's *Hamlin Garland's Early Work and Career*, is an acute short discussion of Garland's strengths and weaknesses as a writer.

42. Quoted in Jean Holloway, *Hamlin Garland*, 207–208.

3. The Voice of Want

1. Quoted in James Woodress, *Booth Tarkington: Gentleman from Indiana* (New York: Lippincott, 1954), 74.

2. Hamlin Garland, *Roadside Meetings*, 237, 238.

3. Ibid., 282, 283.

4. Ibid., 283.

5. Anonymous review of *Prairie Folks, Critical Essays on Hamlin Garland*, 53. The review appeared originally in *Nation*, 56 (June 1, 1893), 408.

6. Allan G. Bogue gives an account of agricultural history during the period in *From Prairie to Corn Belt*, 280–87.

7. Hamlin Garland, *Roadside Meetings*, 283.

8. Quoted in Larzer Ziff, *The American 1890s*, 88.

9. Quoted in Richard Lingeman, *Theodore Dreiser: At the Gates of the City, 1871–1907* (New York: Putnam's, 1986), 233.

10. Quoted in James Woodress, *Booth Tarkington*, 17.

11. Hamlin Garland, *Crumbling Idols*, ed. Jane Johnson (Cambridge, MA: Harvard University Press, 1960), 24.

12. Quoted in Kenneth S. Lynn, *Mark Twain and Southwestern Humor* (Boston: Little, Brown, 1959), 187. Twain's remark appears in the context of a discussion of childhood in post-Civil War literature.

13. James T. Farrell, "The Frontier and James Whitcomb Riley," in *Poet of the People: An Evaluation of James Whitcomb Riley* (Bloomington: Indiana University Press, 1951), 102. The lines from the Riley poem mentioned above are quoted by Farrell (p. 64). For Riley as a children's poet I draw on Jeannette Covert Nolan's essay in this volume, "Riley as a Children's Poet." She notes as well (p. 18) that there is "little to indicate that Riley wrote of the people around him exactly as he saw them, actually as they were, or ever had been."

14. James Whitcomb Riley, "A Country Pathway," *Riley Farm-Rhymes* (Indianapolis: Bobbs-Merrill, 1901), 117–26.

15. This view is suggested in James Woodress, *Booth Tarkington*, 82.

16. Booth Tarkington, *The Gentleman from Indiana* (New York: Doubleday and McClure, 1899), 1, 384.

17. Booth Tarkington, "The Middle West," *Harper's Monthly*, 106 (December 1902), 76, 78, 81.

18. Vernon L. Parrington, *The Beginnings of Critical Realism in America: 1860–1920* (New York: Harcourt, Brace, 1930), 375.

19. Quoted in W. A. Swanberg, *Dreiser* (New York: Scribner's, 1965), 296. For details of Dreiser's life I follow this work, Ellen Moers's *Two Dreisers* (New York: Viking, 1969), and especially the two volumes of Richard Lingeman's life of Dreiser, *Theodore Dreiser: At the Gates of the City* and *Theodore Dreiser: An American Journey, 1908–1945* (New York: Putnam's, 1990).

20. Ernest Hemingway, *The Torrents of Spring* (New York: Scribner's, 1926), 82.

21. Dreiser's contribution to the song is discussed in Richard Lingeman, *Theodore Dreiser: At the Gates of the City*, 178–79.

22. Theodore Dreiser, "Indiana: Her Soil and Light," 348, 349.

23. Meredith Nicholson, *The Hoosiers* (New York: Macmillan, 1915), 1, 217. This edition is a reprint with postscript of the original 1900 edition.

24. Theodore Dreiser, *A Hoosier Holiday*, 390.

25. Quoted in the historical commentary appended to the Pennsylvania Edition of *Sister Carrie* (Philadelphia: University of Pennsylvania Press, 1981), 523. For full details about the revision and publication of the book see this volume.

26. Theodore Dreiser, *Sister Carrie* (New York: Library of America, 1987), 11 (subsequent page references given in the text).

27. Willa Cather, *My Ántonia, Early Novels and Stories* (New York: Library of America, 1987), 711.

28. F. Scott Fitzgerald, *The Great Gatsby*, 177.

29. Larzer Ziff gives strong emphasis to the shattering effects of Dreiser's early experience in the final chapter of *The American 1890s*, 334–48.

30. Richard Lingeman amplifies this point in *Theodore Dreiser: At the Gates of the City*, 242–44.

31. When H. L. Mencken asked for information about the background of *Sister Carrie*, Dreiser included Roe among the authors he had read. See Ellen Moers, *Two Dreisers*, 73.

32. Quoted in Richard Lingeman, *Theodore Dreiser: At the Gates of the City*, 419.

33. Ibid., 413.

34. Ellen Moers, *Two Dreisers*, 101.

35. Donald Pizer uses the term in reference to Drouet, Hurstwood, and Ames in a strong analysis of the novel in *The Novels of Theodore Dreiser* (Minneapolis: University of Minnesota Press, 1976), 66.

36. Ellen Moers suggests that the novel is moving at this point from its nineteenth-century beginning to a twentieth-century conclusion. *Two Dreisers*, 158.

37. Randolph Bourne, "Theodore Dreiser," *New Republic*, 2 (April 17, 1915), 8.

38. For a discussion of Jennie as a figure of pathos rather than tragedy see Warwick Wadlington, "Pathos and Dreiser," *Critical Essays on Theodore Dreiser*, ed. Donald Pizer (Boston: G. K. Hall, 1981), 213–27.

39. Theodore Dreiser, *Jennie Gerhardt* (New York: Library of America, 1987), 815 (subsequent page references given in the text).

40. F. O. Matthiessen, *Theodore Dreiser* (New York: William Sloane, 1951), 113.

41. H. L. Mencken, "A Novel of the First Rank," *Critical Essays on Theodore Dreiser*, 209. The review appeared originally in *Smart Set*, 35 (November 1911), 153–55.

42. F. Scott Fitzgerald, *This Side of Paradise* (London: Penguin, 1963), 189.

43. Randolph Bourne, "Theodore Dreiser," 8.

44. T. K. Whipple, *Spokesmen* (Berkeley: University of California Press, 1963), 82.

45. Theodore Dreiser, *Dawn* (New York: Horace Liveright, 1931), 159.

46. Theodore Dreiser, *A Book about Myself* (New York: Boni and Liveright, 1922), 451–52.

4. Beacon across the Prairies

1. Floyd Dell, "Theodore Dreiser's Chicago," *Friday Literary Review*, February 23, 1912, I. The passage is also quoted in Bernard Duffey, *The Chicago Renaissance in American Letters*, 178. In addition to this work, Chicago's literary role in the period is examined in Dale Kramer, *Chicago Renaissance* (New York: Appleton-Century, 1966), and in Carl S. Smith, *Chicago and the American Literary Imagination, 1880–1920* (Chicago: University of Chicago Press, 1984).

2. Sinclair Lewis, "The American Fear of Literature," *The Man from Main Street*, eds. Harry E. Maule and Melville H. Cane (New York: Random House, 1953), 8.

3. Henry F. May, *The End of American Innocence* (New York: Knopf, 1959), 101–102.

4. Floyd Dell, *Moon-Calf* (New York: Knopf, 1920), 394. Ellipses in the passage are Dell's.

5. Hamlin Garland, *Crumbling Idols*, 119.

6. William Morton Payne, Review of *Rose of Dutcher's Coolly*, *Critical Essays on Hamlin Garland*, 61. Published originally in *Dial*, 20 (February 1, 1896), 80.

7. W. P. Trent, "Mr. Hamlin Garland's New Novel," *Critical Essays on Hamlin Garland*, 63. Published originally in *Bookman*, 2 (February 1896), 512–14.

8. Hamlin Garland, *A Daughter of the Middle Border*, 28.

9. Quoted in Donald Pizer, Introduction to Hamlin Garland, *Rose of Dutcher's Coolly* (Lincoln: University of Nebraska Press, 1969), xxiii.

10. Details of Fuller's life are drawn from Bernard R. Bowron, Jr., *Henry B. Fuller of Chicago* (Westport, CT: Greenwood Press, 1974).

11. Henry B. Fuller, *The Cliff-Dwellers* (New York: Harper and Brothers, 1893), 50–51.

12. Henry B. Fuller, *With the Procession* (New York: Harper and Brothers, 1895), 248.

13. The term is used in Fuller's article, "The Upward Movement in Chicago," *Atlantic*, 80 (October 1897), 534–47.

14. Hamlin Garland, *Roadside Meetings*, 284.

15. Quoted in Bernard Bowron, *Henry B. Fuller of Chicago*, 172.

16. Bernard Bowron, *Henry B. Fuller of Chicago*, 9.

17. Quoted in Blake Nevius, *Robert Herrick: The Development of a Novelist* (Berkeley: University of California Press, 1962), 53. I follow this work for details of Herrick's life.

18. Quoted in Blake Nevius, *Robert Herrick*, 85.

19. Robert Herrick, *The Web of Life* (New York: Garrett Press, 1970), 56. The edition is a photographic reprint of the original edition published by Macmillan in 1900.

20. Ibid., 135.

21. Fuller's letter and Herrick's explanation are quoted in Blake Nevius, *Robert Herrick*, 87.

22. Floyd Dell, "Robert Herrick's Chicago," *Friday Literary Review*, January 26, 1912, 1.

23. Theodore Dreiser, *Sister Carrie*, 4.

24. Hamlin Garland, *Crumbling Idols*, 91.

25. Hamlin Garland, *Rose of Dutcher's Coolly* (Lincoln: University of Nebraska Press, 1969), 16, 22. The edition follows the original 1895 edition published in Chicago by Stone and Kimball. Subsequent page references are given in the text.

26. For an 1899 edition of the novel published in New York by Macmillan, Garland added a brief final scene in which Rose and Mason arrive at his Chicago apartment following their marriage. Garland seems to have meant to blunt criticism that Rose and Mason had not intended a properly legal marriage—and to soften Mason's views of the hazards of marriage with a glimpse of domestic bliss.

27. Donald Pizer, Introduction to *Rose of Dutcher's Coolly*, xvii–xviii.

28. Details of Dell's life are drawn from a critical biography by George Thomas Tanselle, *Faun at the Barricades: The Life and Work of Floyd Dell* (Ph.D. diss., Northwestern University, 1959). I am also grateful to this work for many insights into Dell's fiction. Dell's autobiography, *Homecoming* (Port Washington, NY: Kennikat Press, 1969), treats his life through his first thirty-five years. The work was published originally by Holt, Rinehart, and Winston in 1933.

29. Sherwood Anderson, *Sherwood Anderson's Memoirs*, 23.

30. Quoted in George Thomas Tanselle, *Faun at the Barricades*, 92.

31. Quoted in Bernard Duffey, *The Chicago Renaissance in American Letters*, 175.

32. Floyd Dell, *Homecoming*, 244.

33. Ibid., 361.

34. Floyd Dell, *Moon-Calf*, 60 (subsequent page references given in the text).

35. The critical reaction is quoted in George Thomas Tanselle, *Faun at the Barricades*, 266, 267, 269.

36. F. Scott Fitzgerald to James Branch Cabell, dated Christmas, 1920, *The Letters of F. Scott Fitzgerald*, ed. Andrew Turnbull (New York: Scribner's, 1963), 464–65.

37. Carl Van Doren, "Contemporary American Novelists," *Nation*, 113 (October 12, 1921), 407, 411–12.

38. Floyd Dell, *Homecoming*, 343.

39. Floyd Dell, *The Briary-Bush* (New York: Knopf, 1921), 425 (subsequent page references given in the text).

40. Floyd Dell, *Homecoming*, 345.

41. The best critical treatment of the novel is found in Donald Pizer's chapter devoted to it in *The Novels of Theodore Dreiser*, 183–200.

42. Theodore Dreiser, *The Titan* (New York: John Lane, 1914), 347 (subsequent page references given in the text).

43. H. L. Mencken, "A Novel of the First Rank," *Critical Essays on Theodore Dreiser*, 209. Published originally in *Smart Set*, 35 (November 1911), 153–55.

44. H. L. Mencken, "The Titan," *Critical Essays on Theodore Dreiser*, 239, 240, 241. Published originally in *Smart Set*, 43 (August 1914), 153–57.

45. Sherwood Anderson, "Dreiser," *Critical Essays on Theodore Dreiser*, 13. Published originally in *Little Review*, 3 (April 1916), 5.

5. The Sweetness of Twisted Apples

1. H. L. Mencken, "A Literary Behemoth," *Critical Essays on Theodore Dreiser*, 252. Published originally in *Smart Set*, 47 (December 1915), 150–54.

2. Sherwood Anderson, *Sherwood Anderson's Memoirs*, 401.

3. Carl Van Doren, "Contemporary American Novelists," 408.

4. Quoted in Daryl Hine, Introduction to *The Poetry Anthology, 1912–1977* (Boston: Houghton Mifflin, 1978), xxxix.

5. Margaret Anderson, "What We Are Fighting For," *Little Review*, 2 (May 1915), 4.

6. Quoted in Kim Townsend, *Sherwood Anderson* (Boston: Houghton Mifflin, 1987), 99.

7. Margaret Anderson, "Our First Year," *Little Review*, 1 (February 1915), 6.

8. Quoted in Eleanor Ruggles, *The West-Going Heart: A Life of Vachel Lindsay* (New York: Norton, 1959), 156.

9. I follow the revised edition of Lindsay's work in *The Poetry of Vachel Lindsay*, ed. Dennis Camp, vol. 1 (Peoria, IL: Spoon River Poetry Press, 1984). "The Illinois Village" appears on pages 167–68.

10. Quoted in Eleanor Ruggles, *The West-Going Heart*, 172.

11. Vachel Lindsay, "General William Booth Enters into Heaven," *The Poetry of Vachel Lindsay*, 148–49.

12. Vachel Lindsay, "The Kallyope Yell," *The Poetry of Vachel Lindsay*, 247–50.

13. Vachel Lindsay, "The Congo," *The Poetry of Vachel Lindsay*, 174–78.

14. Vachel Lindsay, "Adventures While Singing These Songs," *The Poetry of Vachel Lindsay*, vol. 3, 942.

15. Vachel Lindsay, "Adventures While Preaching Hieroglyphic Sermons," *The Poetry of Vachel Lindsay*, vol. 3, 961. For a revisionist view of Lindsay's importance see Ann Massa, *Vachel Lindsay: Fieldworker for the American Dream* (Bloomington: Indiana University Press, 1970). Elizabeth Hardwick discusses Lindsay's "foolhardy career" in "Wind from the Prairie," *New York Review of Books* (September 26, 1991), 9–16.

16. T. K. Whipple, *Spokesmen*, 185–86.

17. Quoted in North Callahan, *Carl Sandburg: His Life and Works* (University Park: Pennsylvania State University Press, 1987), 57. Penolope Niven's biography, *Carl Sandburg* (New York: Scribner's, 1991), appeared too late for my use.

18. Ibid., 81.

19. Carl Sandburg, *Chicago Poems* (New York: Henry Holt, 1916), 21, 15, 10, 35. T. K. Whipple, whose critical views of the authors of this period I find otherwise so perceptive, thought "Mamie" "an example of Sandburg at his worst; he is not trying to see or to describe Mamie as she really is, but is engaged in exploiting and reveling in his own pity." *Spokesmen*, 175.

20. Quoted in North Callahan, *Carl Sandburg*, 85.

21. Carl Sandburg, "Prairie," *The Complete Poems of Carl Sandburg* (New York: Harcourt Brace Jovanovich, 1970), 79–85.

22. Edgar Lee Masters, *Across Spoon River* (New York: Farrar and Rinehart, 1936), 335. For a critical study of Masters's work see Ronald Primeau, *Beyond 'Spoon River': The Legacy of Edgar Lee Masters* (Austin: University of Texas Press, 1981).

23. Ibid., 337.

24. Ibid., 339.

25. Quoted in Richard Lingeman, *Theodore Dreiser: An American Journey*, 105.

26. Edgar Lee Masters, *Across Spoon River*, 340.

27. Quoted in Richard Lingeman, *Theodore Dreiser: At the Gates of the City*, 296.

28. Quoted in Max Putzel, *The Man in the Mirror: William Marion Reedy and His Magazine* (Cambridge, MA: Harvard University Press, 1963), 7.

29. In the book version "Webster Ford" also appears as the final epitaph. Edgar Lee Masters, *Spoon River Anthology* (New York: Macmillan, 1935), 270 (subsequent page references given in the text).

30. Harriet Monroe, *A Poet's Life* (New York: Macmillan, 1938), 378.

31. Max Putzel, *The Man in the Mirror*, 198.

32. Edgar Lee Masters, *Across Spoon River*, 330.

33. Floyd Dell, "Spoon River People," *New Republic*, 2 (April 17, 1915), 14–15.

34. Ezra Pound, "Webster Ford," *Egoist*, 2 (January 1, 1915), 11–12.

35. Quoted in Noel Stock, *The Life of Ezra Pound* (New York: Random House, 1970), 169.

36. Harriet Monroe, *A Poet's Life*, 378–79.

37. Ibid., 378.

38. Bernard Duffey offers a case, unconvincing to my mind, for "The Spoonaid" as

a useful, if clumsy, addition to the work in *The Chicago Renaissance in American Letters*, 162–66.

39. Mae Swenson, Introduction to Edgar Lee Masters, *Spoon River Anthology* (New York: Collier Books, 1962), 10.

40. Sherwood Anderson to Van Wyck Brooks, May 31, 1918, *Letters of Sherwood Anderson*, ed. Howard Mumford Jones and Walter B. Rideout (Boston: Little, Brown, 1953), 39.

41. Sherwood Anderson, *Sherwood Anderson's Memoirs*, 551.

42. Sherwood Anderson, *Winesburg, Ohio* (New York: B. W. Huebsch, 1919), 303 (subsequent page references given in the text).

43. Brom Weber, *Sherwood Anderson* (Minneapolis: University of Minnesota Press, 1964), 26.

44. Sherwood Anderson to Van Wyck Brooks, May 31, 1918, *Letters of Sherwood Anderson*.

45. William Faulkner, "Sherwood Anderson: An Appreciation," 28.

46. F. Scott Fitzgerald to Maxwell Perkins, June 1, 1925, *The Letters of F. Scott Fitzgerald*, 187.

47. Hart Crane, "Sherwood Anderson," *The Complete Poems and Selected Letters and Prose of Hart Crane*, ed. Brom Weber (New York: Liveright, 1966), 208, 209.

48. For details of Anderson's life I follow the most recent biographical study, Kim Townsend's *Sherwood Anderson*.

49. Carl Van Doren, "Contemporary American Novelists," 408.

50. Hart Crane, Review of *Winesburg, Ohio*, *The Complete Poems and Selected Letters and Prose of Hart Crane*, 205.

51. Sherwood Anderson, *Sherwood Anderson's Memoirs*, 352–53.

52. Mencken and Roscoe are quoted in Kim Townsend, *Sherwood Anderson*, 157.

53. Kim Townsend describes the breakdown as a "fugue state," meaning a state of flight from the complications of a previous existence. See *Sherwood Anderson*, 81–82.

54. Sherwood Anderson, *Sherwood Anderson's Memoirs*, 336.

55. Quoted in Kim Townsend, *Sherwood Anderson*, 92.

56. Sherwood Anderson, *Sherwood Anderson's Memoirs*, 211.

57. Sherwood Anderson, *Windy McPherson's Son* (New York: B. W. Huebsch, 1922), 348.

58. Sherwood Anderson, *Marching Men* (New York: John Lane, 1917), 156, 150 (subsequent page references given in the text).

59. Sherwood Anderson, *Mid-American Chants* (New York: John Lane, 1918), 7, 13.

60. Sherwood Anderson to Paul Rosenfeld, October 24, 1921, *Letters of Sherwood Anderson*, 78–79.

61. Malcolm Cowley, Introduction to *Winesburg, Ohio* (New York: Penguin Books, 1976), 11.

62. Sherwood Anderson to Paul Rosenfeld, October 24, 1921, *Letters of Sherwood Anderson*, 76–81.

63. Sherwood Anderson, *Poor White* (New York: B. W. Huebsch, 1920), 369.

64. Ibid., 371.

65. Quoted in Kim Townsend, *Sherwood Anderson*, 227. The emphases are Fitzgerald's.

66. William Faulkner, "Sherwood Anderson: An Appreciation," 28, 29.

6. Home Pasture

1. Sherwood Anderson, *Sherwood Anderson's Memoirs*, 317.

2. Saul Bellow, "Chicago and American Culture," 88.

3. Ford Madox Ford, *It Was the Nightingale*, 17.

4. For details of Cather's life I follow James Woodress, *Willa Cather, A Literary Life* (Lincoln: University of Nebraska Press, 1987).

5. Harold Bloom makes this point in a brief but insightful discussion of Cather in the introduction to *Willa Cather's My Ántonia*, ed. Harold Bloom (New York: Chelsea House, 1987), 2. Cather's romantic imagination is explored at book length in Susan J. Rosowski, *The Voyage Perilous: Willa Cather's Romanticism* (Lincoln: University of Nebraska Press, 1986).

6. Floyd Dell, "A Good Novel," reprinted in *Dictionary of Literary Biography, Documentary Series*, vol. 1 (Detroit: Gale Research Co., 1982), 67. The review appeared originally in *Friday Literary Review*, July 25, 1913.

7. Willa Cather, *The Kingdom of Art: Willa Cather's First Principles and Critical Statements, 1893–1896*, ed. Bernice Slote (Lincoln: University of Nebraska Press, 1966), 223–24.

8. Ibid., 331.

9. Willa Cather, *My Ántonia* (New York: Library of America, 1987), 718.

10. Willa Cather, "Peter," *Willa Cather's Collected Short Fiction, 1892–1912* (Lincoln: University of Nebraska Press, 1965), 543.

11. Willa Cather, "On the Divide," *Collected Short Fiction*, 494.

12. Late in life Cather said the story was written in an English course and that the detail about Canute's carving had been added by her professor before he sent the story to the *Overland Monthly*. See James Woodress, *Willa Cather*, 106–107.

13. See James Woodress, *Willa Cather*, 78.

14. Willa Cather, "On the Divide," 495–96.

15. William Allen White, "A Story of the Highlands," *The Real Issue* (New York: Doubleday, Page and Company, 1909), 287. Published originally in 1896.

16. Quoted in James Woodress, *Willa Cather*, 92.

17. This is the view of Woodress, Cather's most thorough biographer. For his sensible discussion of her views of sex and marriage see especially *Willa Cather*, 124–27 and 141–42.

18. Quoted in James Woodress, *Willa Cather*, 126.

19. Willa Cather, "Eric Hermannson's Soul," *Collected Short Fiction*, 360, 369, 378.

20. Ibid., 363, 377, 376.

21. Willa Cather, "A Wagner Matinee," *Collected Short Fiction*, 240, 236, 239, 242.

22. Quoted in Sharon O'Brien, *Willa Cather: The Emerging Voice* (New York: Oxford University Press, 1987), 286.

23. Willa Cather, "The Sculptor's Funeral," *Collected Short Fiction*, 182.

24. Ibid., 179.

25. Quoted in James Woodress, *Willa Cather*, 203.

26. Ibid., 202.

27. Willa Cather, *The Kingdom of Art*, 332.

28. Willa Cather, "The Bohemian Girl," *Collected Short Fiction*, 29.

29. Cather's reactions to the Southwest are examined in considerable detail in Sharon O'Brien, *Willa Cather*, 403–418.

30. Quoted in Sharon O'Brien, *Willa Cather*, 421.

31. Willa Cather, *O Pioneers!* (New York: Library of America, 1987), 139 (subsequent page references given in the text).

32. Quoted in James Woodress, *Willa Cather*, 240.

33. For example, see David Daiches's reservations about the book's structure in *Willa Cather* (Ithaca, NY: Cornell University Press, 1951).

34. Quoted in James Woodress, *Willa Cather*, 239.

35. Willa Cather, *My Ántonia*, 713–14 (subsequent page references to the novel given in the text). The introduction was extensively revised by Cather for a 1926 edition of the novel. The Library of America edition follows the original 1918 introduction; the revised introduction is printed in the notes, pages 1332–34.

36. Quoted in James Woodress, *Willa Cather*, 301.

37. Susan J. Rosowski locates the novel's essential distinction in its capacity to "mean so many things to so many people." *The Voyage Perilous*, 75.

38. In an essay to which I am indebted for its reading of the novel in light of a vision of national potential, James E. Miller, Jr., remarks that "no one with the name of Jim Burden could be a totally *un*allegorical figure." Miller treats Jim's "burden" as one of possible guilt, both in an individual and in a social sense, for failure to attain and hold the vision. Here I use the term to suggest his lack of conscious awareness of what he records in the diminishment of the symbolic plough, a gap between dream and reality (*"My Ántonia* and the American Dream," *Prairie Schooner*, 48 [Summer 1974], 112–23).

39. The remark appears in a prefatory note to *Not under Forty*, a collection of essays published in 1936. It is quoted by James Woodress, *Willa Cather*, 335.

40. Willa Cather, *One of Ours* (New York: Library of America, 1987), 1025 (subsequent page references given in the text).

41. Quoted in Hermoine Lee, *Willa Cather*, 183.

42. Willa Cather, "Neighbour Rosicky," *Obscure Destinies* (New York: Knopf, 1932), 40 (subsequent page references given in the text).

43. Willa Cather, *My Ántonia*, 724.

44. Willa Cather, *O Pioneers!*, 290.

45. T. K. Whipple, *Spokesmen*, 155.

46. Harold Bloom, Introduction to *Willa Cather's My Ántonia*, 1.

7. Bewildered Empire

1. Sinclair Lewis, "The American Fear of Literature," 8.

2. Sinclair Lewis, "A Hamlet of the Plains," *The Man from Main Street*, 172. The article is a review of Cather's *One of Ours*.

3. T. K. Whipple, *Spokesmen*, 219.

4. Quoted in Mark Schorer, *Sinclair Lewis: An American Life* (New York: McGraw-Hill, 1961), 680. For details of Lewis's life and my general understanding of his fiction I am indebted to this central work. In his review of Cather's *One of Ours*, Lewis remarked: "In the world of the artist it is the little, immediate, comprehensible things—jackknives or kisses, bath sponges or children's wails—which illuminate and fix the human spectacle; and for the would-be painter of our Western world a Sears-Roebuck catalogue is (to one who knows how to choose and who has his imagination from living life) a more valuable reference book than a library of economics, poetry, and the lives of the saints. This axiom Miss Cather knows." The remark well applies to Lewis's detailed art but hardly to Cather's ("A Hamlet of the Plains," 173).

5. John Hersey, "Sinclair Lewis," *Life Sketches* (New York: Knopf, 1989), 24.

6. Willa Cather, *My Ántonia*, 840.

7. Sinclair Lewis, "The Long Arm of the Small Town," *The Man from Main Street*, 272.

8. Sinclair Lewis, *Babbitt* (New York: Harcourt, Brace, 1922), 301.

9. Mark Schorer suggests that the style of excess in Lewis's work might have been influenced by the broad Midwestern humor of writers like George Ade and Finley Peter Dunne (*Sinclair Lewis*, 289).

10. Frederick J. Hoffman, *The Twenties: American Writing in the Postwar Decade* (New York: Viking, 1955), 364.

11. Sinclair Lewis, "A Hamlet of the Plains," 172.

12. T. K. Whipple, *Spokesmen*, 208, 209.

13. Sherwood Anderson, "Four American Impressions," *New Republic*, 32 (October 11, 1922), 172.

14. Sinclair Lewis, "The Death of Arrowsmith," *The Man from Main Street*, 106, 105.

15. Quoted in Mark Schorer, *Sinclair Lewis*, 102.

16. Sinclair Lewis, "The American Fear of Literature," 15.

17. Sinclair Lewis, *Dodsworth* (New York: Harcourt, Brace, 1929), 3.

18. Sinclair Lewis, "The American Fear of Literature," 16.

19. Quoted in Mark Schorer, *Sinclair Lewis*, 171.

20. For details of this curious service, see Mark Schorer, *Sinclair Lewis*, 164–65.

21. Henry F. May, *The End of American Innocence*, 216–17.

22. Quoted in Mark Schorer, *Sinclair Lewis*, 334–35.

23. Sinclair Lewis, *Main Street* (New York: Harcourt, Brace and Howe, 1920), 9–10 (subsequent page references given in the text).

24. Quoted in Mark Schorer, *Sinclair Lewis*, 230.

25. Sinclair Lewis, "I'm a Stranger Here Myself," *I'm a Stranger Here Myself and Other Stories* (New York: Dell, 1962), 19, 21, 31. Schorer calls the story the "first sustained work recognizably written by the author of *Main Street*" (*Sinclair Lewis*, 230).

26. Sinclair Lewis, *The Job: An American Novel* (New York: Harper and Brothers, 1917), 104–105.

27. Sinclair Lewis, *Free Air* (New York: Harcourt, Brace and Howe, 1919), 36.

28. Sinclair Lewis to Alfred Harcourt, May 19, 1920, in *From Main Street to Stockholm: Letters of Sinclair Lewis, 1919–1930*, ed. Harrison Smith (New York: Harcourt, Brace, 1952), 29.

29. Donald Brace to Sinclair Lewis, May 21, 1920, *From Main Street to Stockholm*, 29.

30. Sinclair Lewis to Alfred Harcourt, November 27, 1920, *From Main Street to Stockholm*, 48.

31. Mark Schorer cites this passage as evidence of Lewis's self-caricature, revealing the romantic yearnings of a Minnesota youth for a more inspiring historical soil (*Sinclair Lewis*, 293).

32. T. K. Whipple, *Spokesmen*, 224.

33. Floyd Dell, *Homecoming*, 344.

34. The Lewis-Dell exchange over interpretations of Carol and Felix is examined in G. Thomas Tanselle, "Sinclair Lewis and Floyd Dell: Two Views of the Midwest," *Twentieth Century Literature*, 9 (January 1964), 175–84. The quoted passages appear on page 177 of the article.

35. Sherwood Anderson to Hart Crane, March 4, 1921, *Letters of Sherwood Anderson*, 70.

36. Sherwood Anderson, "Four American Impressions," 172.

37. T. K. Whipple, *Spokesman*, 227.

38. Sinclair Lewis, "The American Fear of Literature," 8.

39. Sinclair Lewis to Alfred Harcourt, December 21, 1920, *From Main Street to Stockholm*, 58.

40. Quoted in Carlos Baker, *Ernest Hemingway: A Life Story* (New York: Scribner's, 1969), 161.

41. Ernest Hemingway, "On Writing," *The Nick Adams Stories* (New York: Scribner's, 1972), 248.

42. Carl Van Doren, "Contemporary American Novelists," 410.

43. Ibid.

44. Quoted in Mark Schorer, *Sinclair Lewis*, 274.

45. Ibid., 300.

46. Sinclair Lewis, "Two Letters to Carl Van Doren," *The Man from Main Street*, 137, 141.

47. Ibid., 135.

48. Sinclair Lewis to Alfred Harcourt, December 28, 1920, *From Main Street to Stockholm*, 59.

49. Sinclair Lewis, *Main Street*, 262.

50. Sinclair Lewis to Alfred Harcourt, December 17, 1920, *From Main Street to Stockholm*, 57.

51. Sinclair Lewis to Alfred Harcourt, December 28, 1920, *From Main Street to Stockholm*, 59.

52. Quoted in Mark Schorer, *Sinclair Lewis*, 354.

53. Wharton's letter is reproduced in Mark Schorer, *Sinclair Lewis*, 346. The British edition of *Babbitt* had a glossary at the end explaining some 125 American slang expressions.

54. Sinclair Lewis, *Dodsworth*, 11, 55.

55. Quoted in Mark Schorer, *Sinclair Lewis*, 546.

56. Quoted in Richard Lingeman, *Theodore Dreiser: An American Journey*, 343.

57. H. L. Mencken, *The Diary of H. L. Mencken*, ed. Charles A. Fecher (New York: Knopf, 1989), 5.

58. Joseph Wood Krutch, "Sinclair Lewis," *Nation*, 172 (February 24, 1951), 179–80.

59. For a recent use of *Elmer Gantry* in this fashion see Tom Wolfe's defense of the reportorial role in realistic fiction, "Stalking the Billion-Footed Beast," *Harper's*, 279 (November 1989), 45–56.

60. T. K. Whipple, *Spokesmen*, 228.

61. Alfred Kazin, *On Native Grounds*, 221.

62. Quoted in Mark Schorer, *Sinclair Lewis*, 351.

8. The Savor of the Soil

1. Sinclair Lewis, *Arrowsmith* (New York: Harcourt, Brace, 1925), 1.

2. Sinclair Lewis, "Introductory Remarks," *The Three Readers* (New York: The Press of the Readers Club, 1943), 173–77.

3. Quoted in Milton M. Reigelman, *The Midland: A Venture in Literary Regionalism* (Iowa City: University of Iowa Press, 1975), 3. I follow this study for details about Frederick and his magazine. The magazine is also given significant treatment in Frederick J. Hoffman, Charles Allen, and Carolyn F. Ulrich, *The Little Magazine: A History and a Bibliography* (Princeton, NJ: Princeton University Press, 1947), 128–47.

4. John Macy, *The Spirit of American Literature* (New York: Modern Library [no date]), 9, 15. Originally published by Doubleday, Page in 1913. Frederick took note of the influence of Macy's book in a 1931 essay, "Ruth Suckow and the Middle Western Literary Movement," *English Journal*, 20 (January 1931), 3, 8.

5. [Untitled editorial statement], *The Midland, A Magazine of the Middle West*, 1 (January 1915), 36.

6. "After Five Years," *Midland*, 6 (January-February-March, 1920), 1.

7. Frederick used the expression in the introduction to his anthology of Midwestern writing, *Out of the Midwest*, xvi.

8. "What Babbitt Thinks of Sinclair Lewis," *Midland*, 17 (January-February 1931), 5.

9. John T. Frederick, "I've Been Reading—", *Midland*, 19 (September-October 1932), 139.

10. John T. Frederick, "Ruth Suckow and the Middle Western Literary Movement," 1, 5.

11. Ruth Suckow, "Uprooted," *Iowa Interiors* (New York: Knopf, 1926), 106.

12. Ruth Suckow, "Retired," *Iowa Interiors*, 138.

13. Ruth Suckow, "Renters," *Iowa Interiors*, 131.
14. Ruth Suckow, "A Start in Life," *Iowa Interiors*, 17.
15. Ruth Suckow, "The Resurrection," *Iowa Interiors*, 198–99, 199.
16. Ruth Suckow, "A Rural Community," *Iowa Interiors*, 171, 173, 181, 183, 184. Reigelman finds this a representative *Midland* story—and also typical of the fiction Suckow published in the magazine. Of her four stories, however, it is the most directly affirmative, lacking any critical sense of Midwestern life or any satire or irony balancing its affirmation.
17. Quoted in Milton M. Reigelman, *The Midland*, 20.
18. Mencken is quoted in a letter Lewis sent to his publisher, Harcourt, Brace, praising Suckow's work as "lucid, remarkably real, firm, jammed with promise." Lewis urged the publishing house to claim her before Knopf. Sinclair Lewis to Alfred Harcourt and Donald Brace, January 20, 1922, *From Main Street to Stockholm*, 95.
19. Quoted in Sinclair Lewis, *The Three Readers*, 176.
20. John T. Frederick, "Ruth Suckow and the Middle Western Literary Movement," 5, 7.
21. Sinclair Lewis, *The Three Readers*, 176.
22. Quoted in Sinclair Lewis, *The Three Readers*, 176.
23. John T. Frederick, "I've Been Reading—," *Midland*, 15 (March-April 1929), 93.
24. Quoted in Paul Reigstad, *Rölvaag: His Life and Art* (Lincoln: University of Nebraska Press, 1972), 28. For details of Rölvaag's life I follow this work and Einar Haugen, *Ole Edvart Rölvaag* (Boston: Twayne, 1983).
25. Quoted in Paul Reigstad, *Rölvaag*, 30.
26. Quoted in Einar Haugen, *Ole Edvart Rölvaag*, 83.
27. For an account of the Rölvaag-Colcord collaboration see Einar Haugen, *Ole Edvart Rölvaag*, 93–94.
28. Quoted in Paul Reigstag, *Rölvaag*, 116.
29. Quoted in Einar Haugen, *Ole Edvart Rölvaag*, 95.
30. V. L. Parrington, *The Beginnings of Critical Realism in America, 1860–1920*, 388.
31. O. E. Rölvaag, *Giants in the Earth: A Saga of the Prairie* (New York: Harper and Brothers, 1927), 36. The ellipses are Rölvaag's—a mannerism of the English translation. In the Norwegian edition dashes are used. Subsequent page references are given in the text.
32. Both letters are quoted in Einar Haugen, *Ole Edvart Rölvaag*, 102.
33. Quoted in Paul Reigstad, *Rölvaag*, 129.
34. For a reading in which Beret rather than Peder is seen as the central figure in Rölvaag's trilogy see Harold P. Simonson, *Prairies Within: The Tragic Trilogy of Ole Rölvaag* (Seattle: University of Washington Press, 1987).
35. O. E. Rölvaag, *Their Fathers' God* (New York: Harper and Brothers, 1931), 338.
36. O. E. Rölvaag, *Giants in the Earth*, 378. Rölvaag apparently intended a fourth novel in the series in which Peder would reclaim his Norwegian heritage while pursuing his American dreams. See Paul Reigstad, *Rölvaag*, 147–48, and Kristoffer F. Paulson, "Rölvaag as Prophet: The Tragedy of Americanization," in *Ole Rölvaag: Artist and Cultural Leader*, ed. Gerald Thorson (Northfield, MN: St. Olaf College Press, 1975), 63 n6.
37. John T. Frederick, "Editorial," *Midland*, 16 (January-February 1930), 59.
38. John T. Frederick, "Editorial," *Midland*, 16 (November-December 1930), 370.
39. Frederick was described by one of his writers as "a lean, warm-faced Iowan, slow and deliberate, thoughtful and sensitive, who would do anything for a writer." Quoted in Jerre Mangione, *The Dream and the Deal: The Federal Writers' Project, 1935–1943* (Boston: Little, Brown, 1972), 84. Mangione calls Frederick (page 119) "easily the most effective" of the Project directors operating in major American cities.

40. Grant Wood, "The Revolt against the City," reprinted in James M. Dennis, *Grant Wood: A Study in American Art and Culture* (New York: Viking, 1975), 232. The essay was published originally as a pamphlet in Iowa City, Iowa, in 1935.

41. John T. Frederick, "I've Been Reading," *Midland*, 19 (September-October 1932), 139.

42. Robert Cantwell, "This Side of Paradise," *New Republic*, 71 (July 6, 1932), 215.

43. Josephine Johnson, *Now in November* (New York: Simon and Schuster, 1934), 143–44. Ellipses are the author's. The novel was reissued in 1985 by Carol and Graf as a rediscovered classic of both feminist and Depression writing.

44. Louis Bromfield, *The Farm* (New York: Harper and Brothers, 1933), 295.

45. For biographical information on Strong see Clarence A. Andrews, *A Literary History of Iowa* (Iowa City: University of Iowa Press, 1972), 103–113.

46. For biographical information on Bromfield see Morrison Brown, *Louis Bromfield and His Books* (Fair Lawn, NJ: Essential Books, 1957), and David D. Anderson, *Louis Bromfield* (New York: Twayne, 1964).

47. Louis Bromfield, "Expatriate—Vintage 1927," *Saturday Review*, 3 (March 19, 1927), 657.

48. Ernest Hemingway to F. Scott Fitzgerald, March 31, 1927, in *Ernest Hemingway: Selected Letters, 1917–1961*, ed. Carlos Baker (New York: Scribner's, 1981), 249. Three years later Fitzgerald brought up the case of Bromfield in a letter to his agent, Harold Ober, defending his own slow pace of production: "I could have published four lousy, half-baked books in the last five years and people would have thought I was at least a worthy young man not drinking myself to pieces in the south seas—but I'd be dead as Michael Arlen, Bromfield, Tom Boyd, Callaghan and the others who think they can trick the world with the hurried and the second-rate" (F. Scott Fitzgerald to Harold Ober [received May 13, 1930], *The Letters of F. Scott Fitzgerald*, 395).

49. T. S. Matthews, "Fiction vs. Blurbs," *New Republic*, 76 (September 20, 1933), 162. Edmund Wilson was even less charitable. In a 1944 review he traced Bromfield's decline from "one of the younger writers of promise" to the "fourth rank": " . . . by unremitting industry and a kind of stubborn integrity that seems to make it impossible for him to turn out his tripe without thoroughly believing in it, he has gradually made his way into the fourth rank, where his place is now secure" (Edmund Wilson, "What Became of Louis Bromfield," *New Yorker*, 20 [April 8, 1944], 75).

50. John Frederick would reprint this scene from the novel under the title "Night Journey" in *Out of the Midwest*. It illustrated, he noted, Strong's feeling for the Iowa landscape.

51. Phil Strong, *State Fair* (New York: Century, 1932), 261.

52. Robert Cantwell, "This Side of Paradise," 216.

9. We Are All Middle Westerners

1. Suckow's remarks were printed as an article, "Middle Western Literature," 176.

2. Ruth Suckow, "Middle Western Literature," 180, 181.

3. Ford Madox Ford, Preface to *Transatlantic Stories* (New York: Dial, 1926), x, ix-x, xxi, xxiii.

4. Allen Tate, "American Poetry since 1920," *The Bookman*, 68 (January 1929), 508.

5. Frederick J. Hoffman, *The Twenties: American Writing in the Postwar Decade* (New York: Viking, 1955), 327–35.

6. John T. Frederick, "Brief Reviews," *Midland*, 11 (February 15, 1925), 100.

7. Sinclair Lewis, " 'Ioway' and the Countess," *Saturday Review of Literature*, 1 (August 30, 1924), 75.

8. Quoted in Bruce Kellner, *Carl Van Vechten and the Irreverent Decades* (Norman: University of Oklahoma Press, 1968), 168. I follow this work for details of Van Vechten's life. For Van Vechten's life and work see also Donald Pizer, "The Novels of Carl Van Vechten and the Spirit of the Age," *Toward a New American Literary History*, eds. Louis J. Budd, Edwin H. Cady, and Carl L. Anderson (Durham, NC: Duke University Press, 1980), 211–29.

9. Ibid., 156.

10. Carl Van Vechten, *The Tattooed Countess* (New York: Knopf, 1924), 43. Ellipses are part of Van Vechten's style. Subsequent page references are given in the text.

11. Van Vechten—perhaps influenced by Gertrude Stein, with whom he conducted a long friendship—eschews quotation marks for dialogue.

12. Quoted in Bruce Kellner, *Carl Van Vechten and the Irreverent Decades*, 166.

13. Ruth Suckow, "Middle Western Literature," 177.

14. John T. Frederick, "Brief Reviews," *Midland*, 11 (February 15, 1925), 99.

15. Glenway Wescott, *The Apple of the Eye* (New York: Dial, 1924), 292. For brief biographical material on Wescott see "A Chronology: Glenway Wescott, 1901–1987," *Continual Lessons: The Journals of Glenway Wescott*, ed. Robert Phelps (New York: Farrar Straus Giroux, 1990), ix-xix.

16. Ruth Suckow, "Middle Western Literature," 176–77.

17. Glenway Wescott, *The Grandmothers: A Family Portrait* (New York: Harper and Brothers, 1927), 8, 372–73 (subsequent page references given in the text).

18. Ellipses Wescott's, as is the use of italics.

19. Glenway Wescott, *Good-Bye Wisconsin*, 31 (subsequent page references given in the text).

20. Ellipses mine.

21. F. Scott Fitzgerald to Maxwell Perkins, June 1, 1925, *The Letters of F. Scott Fitzgerald*, 187. Fitzgerald was agitated in the letter by a particular farm novel, Thomas Boyd's *Through the Wheat*, which had been published by Scribner's in 1923. Boyd had been the literary editor of a St. Paul newspaper.

22. Quoted in Jonathan Yardley, *Ring* (New York: Random House, 1977), 276. I follow this work for details of Lardner's career.

23. Sherwood Anderson, "Four American Impressions," 172.

24. Ring Lardner, "Anniversary," *The Ring Lardner Reader*, ed. Maxwell Geismar (New York: Scribner's, 1963), 132. The story appeared originally in *The Love Nest and Other Stories* in 1926.

25. Quoted in Jonathan Yardley, *Ring*, 287.

26. Jonathan Yardley, *Ring*, 209.

27. Quoted in Jonathan Yardley, *Ring*, 45.

28. Ring Lardner, *The Big Town* (New York: Scribner's, 1925), 13. The book was published originally by Bobbs-Merrill in 1921.

29. Hart Crane, "Sherwood Anderson," *The Complete Poems and Selected Letters and Prose of Hart Crane*, ed. Brom Weber (New York: Liveright, 1966), 209–210.

30. Quoted in John Unterecker, *Voyager: A Life of Hart Crane* (New York: Farrar, Straus and Giroux, 1969), 156. I follow this work for details of Crane's life.

31. Hart Crane, "Porphyro in Akron," *The Complete Poems and Selected Letters and Prose of Hart Crane*, 144.

32. Allen Tate, "American Poetry since 1920," 507, 508.

33. Hart Crane, "The River," *The Complete Poems and Selected Letters and Prose of Hart Crane*, 64.

34. Allen Tate, "Hart Crane," *Essays of Four Decades*, 318.

35. Hart Crane, "Indiana," *The Complete Poems and Selected Letters and Prose of Hart Crane*, 79.

36. Allen Tate, "American Poetry since 1920," 508.

37. Allen Tate, "Crane: The Poet as Hero," *Essays of Four Decades*, 328.

38. F. Scott Fitzgerald to Mrs. William Hamm, October 24, 1934, *The Letters of F. Scott Fitzgerald*, 516–17.

39. Carlos Baker, *Ernest Hemingway: A Life Story* (New York: Scribner's, 1969), 1.

40. Sherwood Anderson to Lewis Galantiere, November 28, 1921, *Letters of Sherwood Anderson*, 82.

41. Ernest Hemingway, *A Moveable Feast* (New York: Scribner's, 1964), 27–28.

42. Michael Reynolds develops this view in a discussion of the Anderson-Hemingway relationship in *The Young Hemingway* (New York: Basil Blackwell, 1986), 188. For details of Hemingway's life I follow this work, Baker's biography, and Kenneth S. Lynn, *Hemingway* (New York: Simon and Schuster, 1987).

43. Ford is quoted in Carlos Baker, *Hemingway, The Writer as Artist*, 4th ed. (Princeton, NJ: Princeton University Press, 1972), 19.

44. Ernest Hemingway, *The Sun Also Rises* (New York: Scribner's, 1926), 21.

45. Ernest Hemingway to Louis and Mary Bromfield, March 8, 1927, *Selected Letters*, 195.

46. F. Scott Fitzgerald to Maxwell Perkins, April 22, 1925, *The Letters of F. Scott Fitzgerald*, 179.

47. The remark is paraphrased in Carlos Baker, *Ernest Hemingway*, 189.

48. The following year McAlmon's Paris press (Contact Publishing Company) published his own novel, *Village: As It Happened through a Fifteen Year Period*, an account of resolutely unhappy rural life in the prairie town of Wentworth, North Dakota.

49. Ernest Hemingway to Dr. C. E. Hemingway, March 20, 1925, *Selected Letters*, 153.

50. Ernest Hemingway, "Indian Camp," *In Our Time* (New York: Scribner's, 1930), 21.

51. Ernest Hemingway to Gertrude Stein and Alice B. Toklas, August 15, 1924, *Selected Letters*, 122.

52. Ernest Hemingway, "Big Two-Hearted River," *In Our Time*, 211, 212 (subsequent page references given in the text).

53. Ernest Hemingway, *A Moveable Feast*, 76.

54. "First and last," Kenneth S. Lynn says about the story, "Nick remains an enigma." Lynn persuasively resists earlier readings that attribute Nick's inner state solely to his war experience. See pages 104–108 in Lynn's *Hemingway*.

55. Quoted in Michael Reynolds, *The Young Hemingway*, 141.

56. Ernest Hemingway, "The Last Good Country," *The Nick Adams Stories* (New York: Scribner's, 1972), 88.

57. See Kenneth S. Lynn, *Hemingway*, 56. Lynn also relates in detail the real-life background of the story and places it within an overall emphasis on sexual uncertainty in Hemingway's work.

58. Ernest Hemingway, *A Farewell to Arms* (New York: Scribner's, 1929), 185.

59. Ernest Hemingway to Edmund Wilson, November 25, 1923, *Selected Letters*, 105.

60. Ernest Hemingway to Patrick Hemingway, November 24, 1958, *Selected Letters*, 888.

61. Ernest Hemingway to Frederick G. Saviers, June 15, 1961, *Selected Letters*, 921.

62. Ernest Hemingway, *A Moveable Feast*, 5.

63. Ernest Hemingway, "Fathers and Sons," *The Nick Adams Stories*, 265.

Postscript

1. Sinclair Lewis, "The American Fear of Literature," 17.

2. T. S. Eliot, *Collected Poems, 1909–1962* (New York: Harcourt, Brace and World, 1963), 288.

3. Sinclair Lewis, "The American Fear of Literature," 9.

4. William Gass, "In the Heart of the Heart of the Country," 172, 206, 180, 187.

5. Curtis Harnack, *We Have All Gone Away* (Garden City, NY: Doubleday, 1973), 76, 188.

6. Allen Tate, "A Southern Mode of the Imagination," 578.

7. F. Scott Fitzgerald, *The Great Gatsby*, 177, 182.

Index

Ade, George, 56
Agee, Jonis, 222
Agricultural Advertising (periodical), 107
Alger, Horatio, 152
Algren, Nelson, 222
American Mercury (periodical), 181
Anderson, Irwin, 106–107
Anderson, Margaret, 92–93, 208
Anderson, Sherwood, 2, 3, 4, 6, 9, 13, 15, 67, 81, 82, 85, 88, 90, 91, 92–93, 95, 102, 103–117, 118, 119, 120, 149, 152, 160–161, 162, 164, 172, 177, 178, 180, 181, 193, 194, 201, 206, 207, 208, 213–214, 215, 219, 222
  "Adventure," 111–112
  "An Awakening," 112
  "Book of the Grotesque, The," 104, 106
  Dark Laughter, 116–117
  "Death," 113
  Death in the Woods, 116
  "Departure," 114
  "Drink," 111
  "Hands," 104–106
  Horses and Men, 116, 117
  "Loneliness," 110
  Many Marriages, 116
  Marching Men, 107, 109
  Mid-American Chants, 109–110, 115, 116
  "Mother," 113
  "New Note," 92–93
  "Paper Pills," 114–115
  Poor White, 81, 106, 115–116, 161
  "Queer," 111
  "Respectability," 112
  "Sophistication," 111, 113–114
  Story Teller's Story, A, 117
  "Strength of God, The," 106, 112
  Tar: A Midwest Childhood, 117
  "Teacher, The," 113
  Triumph of the Egg, The, 116, 117
  "Untold Lie, The," 111
  Windy McPherson's Son, 107, 108–109, 110, 116, 162
  Winesburg, Ohio, 4, 9, 13, 91, 103, 104–106, 110–115, 116, 117, 160, 161, 162, 196, 209, 214
Ansley, C. F., 176
Arena Publishing Company, 39
Arena (periodical), 39, 40
Armour, Philip, 58
Atlantic, 5, 14, 28, 117

Baker, Carlos, 212–213
Baker, Ray Stannard, 127
Bartok, Bela, 151
Beach, Sylvia, 214
Bellow, Saul, 2, 3, 15, 118, 222
Benda, W. T., 133
Bennett, Arnold, 163, 173
Benton, Thomas Hart, 175
Bercovitch, Sacvan, 12
Berdahl, Jennie, 183
Bergson, Henri, 151
Berthoff, Warner, 12
Birth of a Nation, 220
Björnson, Björnstjerne, 183
Bloom, Harold, 145
Bly, Carol, 224
  Letters from the Country, 224
Bly, Robert, 222
Bojer, Johan, 183
  Emigrants, The, 183
  Last of the Vikings, The, 183
Bookman (periodical), 197
Boston Transcript, 25
Bourne, Randolph, 63, 67, 133
Brace, Donald, 154
Bromfield, Louis, 193–194, 198, 214, 215
  Early Autumn, 193
  Farm, The, 193, 194
Brooks, Van Wyck, 103, 106, 115, 213
Broun, Heywood, 84
Browne, Maurice, 82, 88
Bryan, C. D. B., 222
  Friendly Fire, 222
Bryan, William Jennings, 140
Bryce, James, 12–13
  American Commonwealth, The, 12–13
Butcher, Fanny, 84

Cantwell, Robert, 192, 195
Capote, Truman
  In Cold Blood, 222
Carleton, Will, 29
Carlyle, Thomas, 122
Cary, Alice, 29
Cash, W. J., 4
Cassill, R. V., 222
Cather, Willa, 2, 3, 4, 17, 67, 119–145, 146–149, 150, 152, 156, 178, 180, 182, 185, 193, 194, 196, 206, 215, 219, 220
  Alexander's Bridge, 128, 129

April Twilights, 125
"Bohemian Girl, The," 128–129
Death Comes for the Archbishop, 142, 145
"Eric Hermannson's Soul," 124–125
Lost Lady, A, 18, 142, 145
"Lou, the Prophet," 122
Lucy Gayheart, 119, 142
My Ántonia, 9, 13, 59, 121, 122, 124, 133–139, 142, 143, 144, 145, 146, 147, 178, 196
"Neighbour Rosicky," 142–144, 145, 178
O Pioneers!, 9, 13, 119, 120, 129–132, 133, 139, 143, 144, 145, 146, 182
Obscure Destinies, 142–144, 145, 178, 194–195
"On the Divide," 122–123
One of Ours, 139–142, 148, 152, 220
"Paul's Case," 125, 142
"Peter," 122
Professor's House, The, 142
"Sculptor's Funeral, The," 126–127, 142
Shadows on the Rock, 142
Song of the Lark, The, 119, 132
Troll Garden, The, 125–127
"Wagner Matinee, A," 125–126, 129
Century (periodical), 14, 40, 179, 181
Chap-Book (periodical), 70
Chicago, University of, 74, 108, 200, 209
Chicago American, 198
Chicago Daily News, 56, 85, 96, 184
Chicago Evening Post, 82, 91
Chicago Globe, 56, 57
Chicago Tribune, 56, 84, 106, 206
Coggeshall, William T., 10
  Poets and Poetry of the West, The, 10
Colcord, Lincoln, 184, 189
Cook, George Cram, 81, 84, 151
Cooper, James Fenimore, 10, 29
Co-Operative Commonwealth, The (periodical), 213
Cosmopolitan, 120, 124
Country (film), 224
Cowley, Malcolm, 110
Cox, James M., 20
Crane, Hart, 2, 3, 4, 103–104, 117, 161, 208–211, 212
  Bridge, The, 210–211
  "Porphyro in Akron," 209
  White Buildings, 210
Crane, Stephen, 51, 52, 60, 172
Crevecoeur, J. Hector St. John, 19
Critchfield, Richard, 224
  Those Days, 224
Currey, Margery, 82, 108
Curry, John Steuart, 175

Daly, Augustin, 62
  Under the Gaslight, 62
Darrow, Clarence, 98

Darwin, Charles, 3
Dell, Floyd, 2, 69–70, 71, 76, 81–87, 88, 91, 92, 93, 100, 108, 109, 118, 119, 120, 151, 160, 213
  Briary-Bush, The, 81, 83, 86–87, 213
  Homecoming, 83
  Moon-Calf, 81, 83–87, 91, 160, 213
Denver, University of, 178
Dial (periodical), 71, 106, 116, 213
Dodge, B. W. Company, 69
Dondore, Dorothy A., 10
Doran, George H. Company, 153
Dorion, Charles, 149
Dostoyevsky, Fyodor, 151
Doubleday and McClure, 49
Doubleday, Frank, 58
Doubleday, Page (company), 58
Double Dealer (periodical), 209
Dreiser, Theodore, 2, 3, 13, 16, 52, 54, 55–68, 69–70, 71, 73, 76, 79, 85, 87–90, 91, 92, 95, 97, 98, 99–100, 103, 108, 109, 149, 161, 164, 165, 171–172, 177, 178, 180, 181, 198, 209, 213
  Financier, The, 87, 88
  Hoosier Holiday, A, 16, 67
  "Indiana: Her Soil and Light," 15–16, 55
  Jennie Gerhardt, 13, 64–67, 87, 88, 89
  Newspaper Days, 67
  Sister Carrie, 9, 57–64, 65, 67, 69, 71, 73, 79, 83, 88, 89, 90, 98, 99
  Titan, The, 88–90, 98, 165
Duffey, Bernard, 29, 86, 102, 118
Dunne, Finley Peter, 56

E. W. Howe's Monthly, 35
Eddy, Mary Baker, 127
Eggleston, Edward, 2, 11, 15, 25, 26–30, 31, 34, 40, 50, 162, 177
  Circuit Rider, The, 28
  Hoosier School-Master, The, 9, 27–30, 31, 34, 38, 162
  Roxy, 28
Eggleston, George Cary, 28
Eliot, T. S., 92, 116, 210, 222
  "Little Gidding," 222
Emerson, Ralph Waldo, 3, 4, 5
English Journal, 9
Erdrich, Louise, 222
Everybody's Magazine, 126

Fadiman, Clifton, 175
Faragher, John Mack, 21
Farrell, James T., 52, 222
Faulkner, William, 3, 4, 6, 13, 103, 117, 145
  Absalom, Absalom!, 3
  Sherwood Anderson and Other Famous Creoles, 117
  Sound and the Fury, The, 3, 13, 172

Federal Writers' Project, 191
Ficke, Arthur Davison, 104
Field, Eugene, 56
Field, Marshall, 58
Finley, John, 11
Fitzgerald, F. Scott, 2, 3, 4, 22–24, 66, 81, 85, 103, 115, 117, 161, 194, 205–206, 208, 211, 212, 214, 215, 224
  Great Gatsby, The, 9, 22–24, 59, 212, 218, 224–225
  "Ice Palace, The," 22
  Tender Is the Night, 206
  This Side of Paradise, 24, 66, 81
Flanagan, John T., 10
Flower, B. O., 39
Ford, Ford Madox, 9, 16, 119, 196, 197, 214, 216
Ford, Richard, 6
  Sportswriter, The, 6
Forster, E. M., 162
Frank, Waldo, 106, 109, 115
Franklin, Benjamin, 19
Frederick, Esther, 191
Frederick, John T., 2, 176–181, 182, 190–191, 192, 195, 197, 201
  Druida, 180
Freud, Sigmund, 151
Friday Literary Review, 82–83, 88, 92, 108, 119, 176
Frost, Robert, 92, 106
Fuller, Henry B., 2, 72–73, 75, 88, 92, 98, 107
  Chatelaine of La Trinité, The, 72
  Chevalier of Pensieri-Vani, The, 72
  Cliff-Dwellers, The, 72, 73
  Last Refuge, The, 73
  With the Procession, 72–73

Gale, Zona, 2, 85, 160, 162
  Miss Lulu Bett, 160
Gallagher, William D., 10
  Poetical Literature of the West, The, 10
Galsworthy, John, 163
Garland, Hamlin, 2, 11, 14, 15, 25–26, 30, 34, 38–48, 49, 50, 51, 52, 53, 60, 67, 70–71, 73, 76–81, 88, 92, 93–94, 98, 99, 107, 118, 120, 146, 147, 148, 150, 152–153, 156, 161, 176, 180, 193, 206
  "Among the Corn-Rows," 44, 45, 47
  Boy Life on the Prairie, 26
  "Branch-Road, A," 43–44, 45, 47, 77
  Crumbling Idols, 40, 52, 70, 76, 80
  "Day's Pleasure, A," 45–46, 77
  "God's Ravens," 46
  Jason Edwards, 40
  Main-Travelled Roads, 9, 26, 38–48, 47, 49, 70, 71, 120, 147, 149, 150, 196
  Member of the Third House, A, 40
  "Mrs. Ripley's Trip," 26, 45
  Prairie Folks, 40
  Prairie Songs, 70

"Return of a Private, The," 44–45, 47
Rose of Dutcher's Coolly, 40, 60, 71, 76–81, 150
Son of the Middle Border, A, 47
Spoil of Office, A, 40
"Under the Lion's Paw," 41–42, 43, 44, 46, 47
"Up the Coule," 42–43, 44, 45, 47, 48, 77, 180
Gass, William, 7, 222–223
  "In the Heart of the Heart of the Country," 7–8, 222–223
George, Henry, 39, 41
Gilder, Richard Watson, 40
Glaspell, Susan, 81, 151
Gray, Richard, 8
Gray, Thomas, 195
Greek Anthology, The, 99
Green, Eleanor, 175
Gregory, Lady Augusta, 82

Hackett, Francis, 82, 110
Hamilton, Alexander, 193
Hampl, Patricia, 222
Hamsun, Knut, 183
  Growth of the Soil, 183
Hansen, Harry, 85, 118
Hansen, Ron, 222
Harcourt, Alfred, 154, 164, 165
Harcourt, Brace (company), 154
Harnack, Curtis, 222, 223–224
  We Have All Gone Away, 223–224
Harper and Brothers, 65, 184
Harper's Monthly, 14, 31, 54, 107
Harper's Weekly, 26, 40
Harrison, Jim, 222
Harvard University, 73, 134
Hassler, Jon, 222
Hawthorne, Nathaniel, 3, 13, 172
  Scarlet Letter, The, 13
Hearth and Home (periodical), 28, 38
Hecht, Ben, 118
Hegger, Grace Livingstone, 152
Hemingway, Ernest, 2, 4, 13, 54, 93, 116–117, 141, 149, 161–162, 193, 194, 206, 208, 211, 212, 212–221, 224
  "Battler, The," 217
  "Big Two-Hearted River," 213, 217–218
  "Capital of the World, The," 212
  "Clean, Well-Lighted Place, A," 212
  "Cross-Country Snow," 216
  Dangerous Summer, The, 220
  Death in the Afternoon, 212
  "Doctor and the Doctor's Wife, The," 216
  "End of Something, The," 217
  Farewell to Arms, A, 172, 219
  "Fathers and Sons," 220–221
  Green Hills of Africa, 161–162, 212
  "In Another Country," 212
  In Our Time, 215–218

"Indian Camp," 215–216, 217
"Last Good Country, The," 219
Men Without Women, 215
Moveable Feast, A, 214, 217, 220
"Now I Lay Me," 217
"Soldier's Home," 217
Sun Also Rises, The, 214–215
"Three-Day Blow, The," 217, 220
Three Stories & Ten Poems, 215
Torrents of Spring, The, 116–117, 214
"Up in Michigan," 215
"Way You'll Never Be, A," 217
"Winner Take Nothing," 220
Hemingway, Hadley, 214
Hemingway, Mary, 220
Henry, Arthur, 57
Herbst, Josephine, 214
Herrick, Robert, 73–75, 76, 92, 107, 118, 165, 198
Gospel of Freedom, The, 74
Memoirs of an American Citizen, The, 75, 165
Web of Life, The, 74–75
Hersey, John, 147
Hoffman, Frederick J., 148, 197
Hofstadter, Richard, 32
Home Monthly, 124
Houghton Mifflin (company), 133
Howe, E. W., 11, 25, 26, 30, 34–38, 40, 50, 102, 150, 177, 193
Man Story, A, 35
Moonlight Boy, A, 35
Mystery of the Locks, The, 35
Story of a Country Town, The, 25, 34–38, 102
Howells, William Dean, 5, 11, 13, 14, 15, 25, 28, 31, 35, 37, 39, 41, 46, 47, 51, 52, 60, 72, 99, 150
Leatherwood God, The, 5
New Leaf Mills, 5
"Novel-Writing and Novel-Reading," 14, 51
Huebsch, B. W. (company), 110
Huxley, T. H., 98

Ibsen, Henrik, 76, 183
Indiana University, 56
Iowa, University of, 176, 191, 196

James, Henry, 3, 41, 120, 131, 172
Jefferson, Thomas, 19
Jewett, Sarah Orne, 127–128, 129
Country of the Pointed Firs, The, 127
Johnson, Diane, 6
Johnson, Josephine, 192–193
Now in November, 192–193, 194
Joyce, James, 92, 110, 163, 214
Ulysses, 93

Kansas City Star, 213
Kazin, Alfred, 3, 173

Keats, John, 95
Kirkland, Caroline, 25
Forest Life, 31
New Home—Who'll Follow?, A, 31
Western Clearings, 31
Kirkland, Joseph, 11, 25–26, 30–34, 35, 39, 40, 50, 150
McVeys: An Episode, The, 34
Zury, 25, 30–34, 39
Knopf, Alred A. (company), 133, 180, 181
Knox College, 98
Kohn, Howard, 224
Last Farmer, The, 224
Krutch, Joseph Wood, 172–173

Lane, Cornelia, 107
Lane, John Company, 108
Lardner, Ring, 2, 56, 118, 206–208, 212
"Anniversary," 207
Big Town, The, 208
"Champion," 207
Gullible's Travels, Etc., 206
"Haircut," 207, 208
How to Write Short Stories, 206
Love Nest, The, 206
"Maysville Minstrel, The," 208
Round Up, 206
You Know Me Al, 206
Lawrence, D. H., 92, 110, 163
Least Heat-Moon, William, 224
Blue Highways, 224
PrairyErth, 224
Lerner, Max, 6
Lewis, John L., 109
Lewis, Sinclair, 2, 3, 4, 15, 16, 69–70, 81, 84, 85, 146–173, 174–176, 177, 178, 179, 181, 193, 198, 206–207, 208, 219, 222
Arrowsmith, 148, 166, 170–171, 172, 174
Babbitt, 13, 16, 148, 149, 161, 164–170, 171, 172, 176, 178, 197, 198
Dodsworth, 148, 150, 170–171, 172
Elmer Gantry, 148, 170–171
Free Air, 154
Hike and the Aeroplane, 152
"I'm a Stranger Here Myself," 153
Job, The, 152, 153–154, 155
Main Street, 9, 13, 16, 81, 84, 147, 148, 149–150, 154–164, 165, 166, 168, 170, 171, 172, 174, 176, 178, 196, 197, 198, 207
"Nature, Inc.," 153
Our Mr. Wrenn, 152
"Pioneer Myth, The," 164
Trail of the Hawk, The, 152
Lewisohn, Ludwig, 171
Lincoln, Abraham, 5, 97, 109
Lindbergh, Charles, 152
Lindsay, Vachel, 2, 82, 92, 93–95, 97, 100, 102, 118, 140, 161, 209
"Abraham Lincoln Walks at Midnight," 95
"Bryan, Bryan, Bryan, Bryan," 95

Lindsay, (*Continued*)
  "Chinese Nightingale, The," 95
  Collected Poems, 95
  "Congo, The," 95
  "General William Booth Enters into Heaven," 93, 94
  "Illinois Village, The," 93
  "Kallyope Yell, The," 94
  "Proud Farmer, The," 93
  Tramp's Excuse, The, 93
Little Review, 90, 92–93, 103, 104, 151, 176, 208
Lombard College, 95
London, Jack, 83, 151
Look Homeward, Angel (Wolfe), 3, 172
Lowell, Amy, 96
Lowell, James Russell, 29
  Biglow Papers, The, 29
Lyceumite, The (periodical), 95
Lynn, Kenneth S., 4

MacKenzie, Compton, 163
Macy, John, 176–177
  Spirit of American Literature, The, 176–177
Mahogany Tree (periodical), 122
Major, Charles, 15, 50
  When Knighthood Was in Flower, 50
Martone, Michael, 224
  Place of Sense, A, 224
Marx, Karl, 151
Masses (periodical), 81, 106, 108, 109, 151
Masters, Edgar Lee, 2, 3, 21, 60–61, 85, 88, 91, 92, 97–103, 104, 106, 109, 118, 161, 164, 177, 178, 179, 209
  Great Valley, The, 100
  New Spoon River, The, 100
  Songs and Satires, 100
  Spoon River Anthology, 4, 9, 13, 85, 91, 97–103, 104, 106, 161, 162, 164, 178, 196
Matthews, T. S., 194
Matthiessen, F. O., 3, 4, 12, 66
  American Renaissance, 12
Maugham, Somerset, 198–199
Maxwell, William, 222
May, Henry F., 60, 70, 151–152
McAlmon, Robert, 214, 215
McClure's, 119, 125, 127, 128
McClure, Phillips, and Company, 125
McClure, S. S., 49, 125, 127, 128, 132, 133
McCutcheon, George Barr, 15, 50
  Graustark, 50
Melville, Herman, 13, 172
  Moby-Dick, 3
Mencken, H. L., 9, 66, 89–90, 91, 106, 132, 152, 165, 172, 180–182, 206, 207–208, 213
Midland (periodical), 176–180, 182, 190–191, 192, 195, 196, 197, 201
Miller, Perry, 3
Minnesota, University of, 175
Mitchell, Tennessee, 109

Moers, Ellen, 61
Monroe, Harriet, 82, 92, 93, 95, 96, 97, 98, 99, 100–101
Moody, Harriet, 209
Moody, William Vaughn, 74, 209
Morris, Wright, 222
Motley, Willard, 222
Mott, Frank Luther, 28, 178
  Golden Multitudes, 28

Nashville Agrarians, 4
Nathan, George Jean, 181
Nation, 85, 109, 161, 164, 172
Nebraska, University of, 119, 122, 123, 124, 133
Nebraska State Journal, 123–124
Negri, Pola, 199
Nevins, Allen, 184
New Republic, 109, 110, 161, 192, 194, 207
New Territory, 224
New York Evening Post, 164
New York Review of Books, 6
New York Times, 96, 198
New York World, 57, 63
Newberry Library, 88
Nicholson, Meredith, 55, 161, 162
  Hoosiers, The, 55
Nietzsche, Friedrich, 151
Norris, Frank, 10, 27, 58, 60, 70, 83
  McTeague, 15, 58
  Octopus, The, 15
  Pit, The, 15, 70, 83
Northwestern University, 191
Notre Dame, University of, 191

Oberlin Academy, 150
O'Connor, Flannery, 1, 3, 4, 7, 13, 17
  Violent Bear It Away, The, 13
O'Hara, John, 173
Ohio State Journal, 7
Orange, Judd, and Company, 28
Osgood, James R. (company), 35
Overland Monthly, 122

Pagan (periodical), 208
Parrington, V. L., 54, 184
Percy, Walker, 17
Perkins, Maxwell, 205–206, 214, 215
Phillips Exeter, 53
Picasso, Pablo, 3
Pittsburgh Leader, 124
Pizer, Donald, 47, 79
Poetry (periodical), 82, 91, 92, 94, 95, 96, 97, 99, 103, 110, 151, 176, 177, 190, 213
Pound, Ezra, 82, 92, 100, 116, 214
Powers, J. F., 222
Princeton University, 53
Publisher's Weekly, 35
Purdy, James, 222

Quick, Herbert, 19
  Vandemark's Folly, 19

Raban, Jonathan, 6, 7
  Old Glory, 6
Ransom, John Crowe, 3
Rascoe, Burton, 106, 118
Red Book, 151
Reedy's Mirror (periodical), 99, 100, 176
Reedy, William Marion, 99
Rhodes, Richard, 224
  Farm, 224
  Inland Ground, The, 224
Riddell, John, 16, 198
  "Gloomy Mid-West Story, The," 16, 198
Riley, James Whitcomb, 2, 15, 29, 49, 50, 51,
  52–53, 55, 67, 68, 162, 177
  "Airly Days, The," 52
  "Country Pathway, A," 52–53
  "Good, Old-Fashioned People, The," 52
  "Old-Swimmin'-Hole, The," 49
  "Watermelon Time," 49
  "When the Frost Is on the Punkin," 49
Rockefeller, John D., 73–74
Roe, E. P., 60
  Barriers Burned Away, 60
Rogers, Will, 193
Rölvaag, O. E., 2, 182–190
  Giants in the Earth, 9, 13, 182, 183–189,
  190
  Letters from America, 183
  Peder Victorious, 182, 189–190
  Their Fathers' God, 189–190
Roosevelt, Theodore, 213
Rosenfeld, Paul, 106, 115, 207
Roth, Philip, 222
  When She Was Good, 222
Rourke, Constance, 148
Royce, Josiah, 176
Rusk, Ralph L., 10

St. Olaf's College, 183
Sandburg, Carl, 2, 92, 95–97, 98, 99, 103, 109,
  118, 178, 184, 209, 210, 213
  "Chicago," 96
  Chicago Poems, 9, 13, 96–97, 98, 178, 196
  Cornhuskers, 97, 109, 209
  "Mamie," 96
  "Mill-Doors," 96
  "Muckers," 96
  People, Yes, The, 96
  "Prairie," 97
  "Subway," 96
  "Working Girls," 96
Santayana, George, 169–170
Saturday Evening Post, 153, 206
Saturday Review, 184, 198
Schnitzler, Arthur, 82
Schoenberg, Arnold, 151
Schorer, Mark, 4, 148, 151, 154, 173

Scribner's, Charles (company), 205, 214
Seven Arts (periodical), 106, 109, 110, 151
Shaw, George Bernard, 82
Sheldon, Charles M., 50
  In His Steps, 50
Sinclair, Upton, 70, 151
  Jungle, The, 70
Smart Set (periodical), 89, 153, 180, 181
Smith, Henry Nash, 18, 21, 23
  Virgin Land, 18, 23
South Bend Times, 56
Spencer, Herbert, 39, 60, 98
Steffens, Lincoln, 127
Stein, Gertrude, 3, 110, 207, 214, 217
  Tender Buttons, 110
Stevens, Wallace, 92, 209
Stieglitz, Alfred, 108
Stokes, Frederick A. Company, 152
Stone and Kimball (company), 70
Stratton-Porter, Gene, 15, 29, 55, 67, 162
  Freckles, 55
  Girl of the Limberlost, 55
Strindberg, August, 82
Strong, Phil, 191–192
  State Fair, 191–192, 193, 194, 195
Suckow, Ruth, 2, 9, 175, 178–182, 196, 197,
  201, 206, 215
  Country People, 181
  Folks, The, 181
  Iowa Interiors, 13, 181, 182
  "Renters," 179
  "Resurrection, The," 179–180
  "Retired," 179
  "Rural Community, A," 180
  "Start in Life, A," 179
  "Uprooted, The," 179
Swenson, May, 101
Synge, J. M., 82

Taine, Hippolyte, 29
  Philosophy of Art in the Netherlands, 29
Tarbell, Ida, 127
Tarkington, Booth, 2, 15, 29, 30, 49, 50, 51,
  52, 53–55, 67, 68, 107, 162, 165
  Alice Adams, 54
  Gentleman from Indiana, The, 49, 51, 53–54
  Magnificent Ambersons, The, 54, 165
  Midlander, The, 54
  "Middle West, The," 54, 107
Tate, Allen, 1, 2, 5, 7, 197, 210–211, 212, 224
  "Ode to the Confederate Dead," 3
  "Southern Mode of the Imagination, A," 5–6
Taylor, J. F. Company, 65
Thompson, Maurice, 50, 52
  Alice of Old Vincennes, 50
  Hoosier Mosaics, 51
Three Readers, The, 175, 181
Tocqueville, Alexis de, 21
Toronto Star Weekly, 213, 214
Transatlantic Review, 9, 197, 216

Turner, Frederick Jackson, 7, 18–19, 23
Twain, Mark, 4, 5, 15, 21, 25, 28, 35, 52, 70,
    109, 116, 213
    Adventures of Huckleberry Finn, The, 4, 66,
        219
    Life on the Mississippi, 4, 21
    Tragedy of Pudd'nhead Wilson, The, 4

Undset, Sigrid, 183
Unger, Douglas, 222
Updike, John, 15

Van Doren, Carl, 85, 92, 104, 161, 162, 163,
    164, 175, 206
Van Vechten, Carl, 2, 197–200, 212
    Firecrackers, 200
    Peter Whiffle, 197–198
    Tattooed Countess, The, 197–200
Vanity Fair (periodical), 16
Vidal, Gore, 22
Village Magazine, 93
Vogue, 152

Walden (Thoreau), 3
Wallace, Lew, 50, 51
    Ben-Hur, 50
Walpole, Hugh, 163
Warren, Robert Penn, 3
Weaver, Will, 222
Weber, Brom, 103
Wells, H. G., 163
    History of Mr. Polly, The, 152
Wescott Glenway, 2, 7, 16, 22, 200–205, 212,
    214–215
    Apple of the Eye, The, 200–201, 215
    Babe's Bed, The, 205
    "Good-Bye Wisconsin," 203–204, 205, 211
    Good-Bye Wisconsin, 203
    Grandmothers, The, 9, 201–203, 211
    "Whistling Swan, The," 205
West, Nathanael, 13
    Miss Lonelyhearts, 13
Wharton, Edith, 170
Whipple, T. K., 67, 95, 144, 146–147, 148,
    160, 161, 172, 173
White, William Allen, 123, 159
    Real Issue, The, 123
Whitman, Walt, 3, 4, 39, 70, 129, 213
Wilder, Laura Ingalls, 191
Williams, William Carlos, 92, 116, 209
Wilson, Edmund, 206–207, 220
Wisconsin, University of, 77, 175, 201
Wittenberg Academy, 107
Woiwode, Larry, 222
Wood, Grant, 175, 191
    "Revolt against the City," 191
Woodress, James, 123
Woolf, Virginia, 163
Wright, Richard, 222

Yale University, 150–151
Yardley, Jonathan, 208
Yeats, William Butler, 82, 92, 95
Yerkes, Charles, 87–88, 98

Ziff, Larzer, 60

Ronald Weber, Professor of American Studies at Notre Dame, is the author of *The Literature of Fact; Seeing Earth: Literary Responses to Space Exploration*; and *Hemingway's Art of Nonfiction*. He has also published novels and short fiction.